Roots of Strategy
Book 2

Roots of Strategy

Book 2

3 Military Classics

du Picq's BATTLE STUDIES
Clausewitz's PRINCIPLES OF WAR
Jomini's ART OF WAR

Stackpole Books

Published by
STACKPOLE BOOKS
Cameron and Kelker Streets
P.O. Box 1831
Harrisburg PA 17105

Printed in the United States of America

10 9 8 7 6

Library of Congress Cataloging-in-Publication Data
Roots of Strategy. Book 2.

Includes index.
Contents: Battle studies / by Ardant du Picq —
Principles of war / by Carl von Clausewitz —
Jomini's Art of war.
1. Military art and science. 2. Strategy.
I. Ardant du Picq, Charles Jean Jacques Joseph,
1821–1870. Etudes sur le combat. English. 1987.
II. Clausewitz, Carl von, 1780–1831. Wichtigsten
Grundsätze des Kriegführens. English. 1987.
III. Jomini, Henri, baron, 1779–1869. Précis de
l'art de la guerre. English. 1987.
U102R736   1987   355'.02   86-23195
ISBN 0-8117-2260-0

CONTENTS

Publisher's Foreword

This volume contains three of the most influential military classics written in the nineteenth century.

Accompanying the texts are the introductions that appeared with them when they were published in separate editions over a quarter of a century ago. The student of modern warfare will find especially valuable Brig. Gen. J. D. Hittle's introduction to Jomini's *Art of War*, which compares and contrasts Jomini's writings with those in Clausewitz's *Principles of War*.

Like those in the first volume of *Roots of Strategy*, these works have stood the test of time. They are presented here with the hope that the reader will find them to be useful guides to understanding modern military thought.

Stackpole Books
1987

COLONEL ARDANT DU PICQ

BATTLE STUDIES

Ancient and Modern Battle

Colonel Ardant du Picq

French Army

Translated from the Eighth Edition in the French

by

Colonel John N. Greely

Field Artillery, U.S. Army

and

Major Robert C. Cotton

General Staff (Infantry), U.S. Army

TRANSLATION OF A LETTER FROM
MARSHAL FOCH TO MAJOR GENERAL A. W. GREELY,
DATED MALSHERBE, OCTOBER 23, 1920

MY DEAR GENERAL:

Colonel Ardant du Picq was the exponent of *moral force,* the most powerful element in the strength of armies. He has shown it to be the preponderating influence in the outcome of battles.

Your son has accomplished a very valuable work in translating his writings. One finds his conclusions amply verified in the experience of the American Army during the last war, notably in the campaign of 1918.

Accept, my dear General, my best regards.

F. FOCH.

LE MARÉCHAL FOCH

Mon cher Général,

Le Colonel Ardant du Picq a été l'avocat de la force morale, de l'élément le plus puissant de la valeur des armées. Il en a montré l'influence prépondérante dans le sort des batailles. C'est une œuvre des plus utiles qu'a faite M. votre fils en traduisant ses écrits. Il en trouverait d'ailleurs une large justification dans l'attitude de l'armée américaine au cours de la dernière guerre notamment dans la campagne de 1918.

Croyez, mon cher Général, à mes meilleurs sentiments

F. Foch.

Letter from Marshal Foch to Major General A. W. Greely
Dated Malsherbe, October 23, 1920

CONTENTS

13

Appendices

PREFACE

By Frank H. Simonds

Author of "History of the World War,"
"'They Shall Not Pass'—Verdun," Etc.

In presenting to the American reading public a translation of a volume written by an obscure French colonel, belonging to a defeated army, who fell on the eve of a battle which not alone gave France over to the enemy but disclosed a leadership so inapt as to awaken the suspicion of treason, one is faced by the inevitable interrogation —" Why? "

Yet the answer is simple. The value of the book of Ardant du Picq lies precisely in the fact that it contains not alone the unmistakable forecast of the defeat, itself, but a luminous statement of those fundamental principles, the neglect of which led to Gravelotte and Sedan.

Napoleon has said that in war the moral element is to all others as three is to one. Moreover, as du Picq impressively demonstrates, while all other circumstances change with time, the human element remains the same, capable of just so much endurance, sacrifice, effort, and no more. Thus, from Caesar to Foch, the essential factor in war endures unmodified.

And it is not the value of du Picq's book, as an explanation of the disasters of 1870, but of the triumphs of 1914–18, which gives it present and permanent interest. It is not as the forecast of why Bazaine, a type of all French commanders of the Franco-Prussian

War, will fail, but why Foch, Joffre, Pétain will succeed, that the volume invites reading to-day.

Beyond all else, the arresting circumstances in the
fragmentary pages, perfect in themselves but incomplete in the conception of their author, is the intellectual
and the moral kinship they reveal between the soldier
who fell just before the crowning humiliation of Gravelotte and the victor of Fère Champenoise, the Yser and
the colossal conflict of 1918 to which historians have
already applied the name of the Battle of France,
rightly to suggest its magnitude.

Read the hastily compiled lectures of Foch, the
teacher of the École de Guerre, recall the fugitive but
impressive words of Foch, the soldier, uttered on the
spur of the moment, filled with homely phrase, and
piquant figure and underlying all, one encounters the
same integral conception of war and of the relation of
the moral to the physical, which fills the all too scanty
pages of du Picq.

" For me as a soldier," writes du Picq, " the smallest
detail caught on the spot and in the heat of action is
more instructive than all the Thiers and the Jominis in
the world." Compare this with Foch explaining to
his friend André de Mariecourt, his own emotions at
the critical hour at Fère Champenoise, when he had to
invent something new to beguile soldiers who had retreated for weeks and been beaten for days. His tactical problem remained unchanged, but he must give his
soldiers, tired with being beaten to the " old tune " a
new air, which would appeal to them as new, something
to which they had not been beaten, and the same philosophy appears.

Du Picq's contemporaries neglected his warning, they
saw only the outward circumstances of the Napoleonic

and Frederican successes. In vain du Picq warned them that the victories of Frederick were not the logical outgrowth of the minutiae of the Potsdam parades. But du Picq dead, the Third Empire fallen, France prostrated but not annihilated by the defeats of 1870, a new generation emerged, of which Foch was but the last and most shining example. And this generation went back, powerfully aided by the words of du Picq, to that older tradition, to the immutable principles of war.

With surprising exactness du Picq, speaking in the abstract, foretold an engagement in which the mistakes of the enemy would be counterbalanced by their energy in the face of French passivity, lack of any control conception. Forty years later in the École de Guerre, Foch explained the reasons why the strategy of Moltke, mistaken in all respects, failed to meet the ruin it deserved, only because at Gravelotte Bazaine could not make up his mind, solely because of the absence in French High Command of precisely that " Creed of Combat " the lack of which du Picq deplored.

Of the value of du Picq's work to the professional soldier, I naturally cannot speak, but even for the civilian, the student of military events, of war and of the larger as well as the smaller circumstances of battle, its usefulness can hardly be exaggerated. Reading it one understands something, at least of the soul as well as the science of combat, the great defeats and the great victories of history seem more intelligible in simple terms of human beings. Beyond this lies the contemporaneous value due to the fact that nowhere can one better understand Foch than through the reading of du Picq.

By translating this volume of du Picq and thus

making it available for an American audience whose
interest has been inevitably stirred by recent events,
the translators have done a public as well as a professional service. Both officers enjoyed exceptional opportunities and experiences on the Western front.
Col. Greely from Cantigny to the close of the battle of
the Meuse-Argonne was not only frequently associated
with the French army, but as Chief of Staff of our own
First Division, gained a direct knowledge of the facts
of battle, equal to that of du Picq, himself.

On the professional side the service is obvious, since
before the last war the weakness of the American like
the British Army, a weakness inevitable, given our iso-
lation, lay in the absence of adequate study of the
higher branches of military science and thus the absence of such a body of highly skilled professional
soldiers, as constituted the French or German General
Staff. The present volume is a clear evidence that
American officers themselves have voluntarily undertaken to make good this lack.

On the non-professional side and for the general
reader, the service is hardly less considerable, since it
supplies the least technically informed with a simply
comprehensible explanation of things which almost
every one has struggled to grasp and visualize during
the last six years extending from the battle of Marne in
1914 to that of the Vistula in 1920.

Of the truth of this latter assertion, a single example
will perhaps suffice. Every forthcoming military study
of the campaign of 1914 emphasizes with renewed
energy the fact that underlying all the German conceptions of the opening operations was the purpose to repeat the achievement of Hannibal at Cannae, by bringing the French to battle under conditions which should,

on a colossal scale, reproduce those of Hannibal's greatest victory. But nowhere better than in du Picq's volume, are set forth the essential circumstances of the combat which, after two thousand years gave to Field Marshal von Schlieffen the root ideas for the strategy expressed in the first six weeks of 1914. And, as a final observation, nowhere better than in du Picq's account, can one find the explanation of why the younger Moltke failed in executing those plans which gave Hannibal one of the most shining triumphs in all antiquity.

Thus, although he died in 1870, du Picq lives, through his book, as one of the most useful guides to a proper understanding of a war fought nearly half a century later.

Frank H. Simonds.

Snowville, New Hampshire,
  October 15, 1920.

TRANSLATORS' NOTE

COLONEL ARDANT DU PICQ's " Battle Studies " is a French military classic. It is known to every French army officer; it is referred to as an established authority in such works as Marshal Foch's " The Principles of War." It has been eagerly read in the original by such American army officers as have chanced upon it; probably only the scarcity of thinking men with military training has precluded the earlier appearance of an American edition.

The translators feel that the war with Germany which brought with it some military training for all the best brains of the country has prepared the field for an American edition of this book. They are sure that every American reader who has had actual battle experience in any capacity will at some point say to himself, " That is absolutely true . . . " or, " That reminds me of the day . . . "

Appendices II, III, IV, and V, appearing in the edition from which this translation is made, deal with issues and military questions entirely French and not of general application. They are therefore not considered as being of sufficient interest to be reproduced herein. Appendix VI of the original appears herein as Appendix II.

The translation is unpretentious. The translators are content to exhibit such a work to the American military public without changing its poignancy and originality. They hope that readers will enjoy it as much as they have themselves.

J. N. G.
R. C. C.

INTRODUCTION

WE present to the public the complete works of Colonel Ardant du Picq, arranged according to the plan of the author, enlarged by unpublished fragments and documents.

These unpublished documents are partially known by those who have read " Studies on Combat " (Hachette & Dumaine, 1880). A second edition was called for after a considerable time. It has left ineffaceable traces in the minds of thinking men with experience. By its beauty and the vigor of its teachings, it has created in a faithful school of disciples a tradition of correct ideas.

For those familiar with the work, there is no need for emphasizing the importance and usefulness of this rejuvenated publication. In it they will find new sources of interest, which will confirm their admiration for the author.

They will also rejoice in the popularity of their teacher, already highly regarded in the eyes of his profession on account of his presentation of conclusions, the truth of which grows with years. His work merits widespread attention. It would be an error to leave it in the exclusive possession of special writers and military technicians. In language which is equal in power and pathetic beauty, it should carry its light much further and address itself to all readers who enjoy solid thought. Their ideas broadened, they will, without fail, join those already initiated.

No one can glance over these pages with indifference. No one can fail to be moved by the strong and substantial intellect they reveal. No one can fail to feel their profound depths. To facilitate treatment of a subject which presents certain difficulties, we shall confine ourselves to a succinct explanation of its essential elements, the general conception that unites them, and the purpose of the author. But we must not forget the dramatic mutilation of the work unfortunately never completed because of the glorious death of Ardant du Picq.

When Colonel Ardant du Picq was killed near Metz in 1870 by a Prussian shell, he left works that divide themselves into two well-defined categories:

(1) Completed works:

Pamphlet (printed in 1868 but not intended for sale), which forms the first part of the present edition: Ancient Battle.

A series of memoirs and studies written in 1865. These are partly reproduced in Appendices I and II herein.

(2) Notes jotted down on paper, sometimes developed into complete chapters not requiring additions or revision, but sometimes abridged and drawn up in haste. They reveal a brain completely filled with its subject, perpetually working, noting a trait in a rapid phrase, in a vibrating paragraph, in observations and recollections that a future revision was to compile, unite and complete.

The collection of these notes forms the second part: Modern Battle.

These notes were inspired by certain studies or memoirs which are presented in Appendices I–V, and a Study on Combat, with which the Colonel was occupied, and of which we gave a sketch at the end of the pamphlet of 1868. He himself started research among the officers of his acquaintance, superiors, equals or subordinates, who had served in war. This occupied a great part of his life.

In order to collect from these officers, without change or misrepresentation, statements of their experiences while leading their men in battle or in their divers contacts with the enemy, he sent to each one a questionnaire, in the form of a circular. The reproduction herein is from the copy which was intended for General Lafont de Villiers, commanding the 21st Division at Limoges. It is impossible to over-emphasize the great value of this document which gives the key to the constant meditations of Ardant du Picq, the key to the reforms which his methodical and logical mind foresaw. It expounds a principle founded upon exact facts faithfully stated. His entire work, in embryo, can be seen between the lines of the questionnaire. This was his first attempt at reaction against the universal routine surrounding him,

From among the replies which he received and which his family carefully preserved, we have extracted the most conclusive. They will be found in Appendix II — Historical Documents. Brought to light, at the urgent request of the author, they complete the book, corroborating statements by examples. They illuminate his doctrines by authentic historical depositions.

In arranging this edition we are guided solely by the absolute respect which we have for the genius of Ardant du Picq. We have endeavored to reproduce his papers in their entirety, without removing or adding anything. Certain disconnected portions have an inspired and fiery touch which would be lessened by the superfluous finish of an attempt at editing. Some repetitions are to be found; they show that the appendices were the basis for the second part of the volume, Modern Battle. It may be stated that the work, suddenly halted in 1870, contains criticisms, on the staff for instance, which aim at radical reforms.

ERNEST JUDET.

BATTLE STUDIES

A MILITARY THINKER

NEAR Longeville-les-Metz on the morning of August 15, 1870, a stray projectile from a Prussian gun mortally wounded the Colonel of the 10th Regiment of the Line. The obscure gunner never knew that he had done away with one of the most intelligent officers of our army, one of the most forceful writers, one of the most clear-sighted philosophers whom sovereign genius had ever created.

Ardant du Picq, according to the Annual Register, commanded but a regiment. He was fitted for the first rank of the most exalted. He fell at the hour when France was thrown into frightful chaos, when all that he had foreseen, predicted and dreaded, was being terribly fulfilled. New ideas, of which he was the unknown trustee and unacknowledged prophet, triumphed then at our expense. The disaster that carried with it his sincere and revivifying spirit, left in the tomb of our decimated divisions an evidence of the necessity for reform. When our warlike institutions were perishing from the lack of thought, he represented in all its greatness the true type of military thinker. The virile thought of a military thinker alone brings forth successes and maintains victorious nations. Fatal indolence brought about the invasion, the loss of two provinces, the bog of moral miseries and social evils which beset vanquished States.

The heart and brain of Ardant du Picq guarded faithfully a worthy but discredited cult. Too frequently in the course of our history virtues are forsaken during long periods, when it seems that the entire race is hopelessly abased. The mass perceives too late in rare individuals certain wasted talents — treasures of sagacity, spiritual vigor, heroic and almost supernatural comprehension. Such men are prodigious exceptions in times of material decadence and mental laxness. They inherit all the qualities that have long since ceased to be current. They serve as examples and rallying points for other generations, more clearsighted and less degenerate. On reading over the extraordinary work of Ardant du Picq, that brilliant star in the eclipse of our military faculties, I think of the fatal shot that carried him off before full use had been found for him, and I am struck by melancholy. Our fall appears more poignant. His premature end seems a punishment for his contemporaries, a bitter but just reproach.

Fortunately, more honored and believed in by his successors, his once unappreciated teaching contributes largely to the uplift and to the education of our officers. They will be inspired by his original views and the permanent virtue contained therein. They will learn therefrom the art of leading and training our young soldiers and can hope to retrieve the cruel losses of their predecessors.

Ardant du Picq amazes one by his tenacity and will power which, without the least support from the outside, animate him under the trying conditions of his period of isolated effort.

In an army in which most of the seniors disdained the future and neglected their responsibilities, rested satisfied on the laurels of former campaigns and relied on superannuated theories and the exercises of a poor parade, scorned foreign organizations and believed in an acquired and constant superiority that dispenses with all work, and did not suspect even the radical transformations which the development of rifles and rapid-fire artillery entail; Ardant du Picq worked for the common good. In his modest retreat, far from the pinnacles of glory, he tended a solitary shrine of unceasing activity and noble effort. He burned with the passions which ought to have moved the staff and higher commanders. He watched while his contemporaries slept.

Toward the existing system of instruction and preparation which the first blow shattered, his incorruptible honesty prevented him from being indulgent. While terrified leaders passed from arrogance or thoughtlessness to dejection and confusion, the blow was being struck. Served by his marvelous historical gifts, he studied the laws of ancient combat in the poorly interpreted but innumerable documents of the past. Then, guided by the immortal light which never failed, the feverish curiosity of this soldier's mind turned towards the research of the laws of modern combat, the subject of his preference. In this study he developed to perfection his psychological attainments. By the use of these attainments he simplified the theory of the conduct of war. By dissecting the motor nerves of the human heart, he released basic data on the essential principles of combat. He discovered the secret of combat, the way to victory.

Never for a second did Ardant du Picq forget that combat is the object, the cause of being, the supreme manifestation of armies. Every measure which de-

parts therefrom, which relegates it to the middle ground
is deceitful, chimerical, fatal. All the resources accumulated in time of peace, all the tactical evolutions,
all the strategical calculations are but conveniences,
drills, reference marks to lead up to it. His obsession
was so overpowering that his presentation of it will
last as long as history. This obsession is the rôle of
man in combat. Man is the incomparable instrument
whose elements, character, energies, sentiments, fears,
desires, and instincts are stronger than all abstract rules,
than all bookish theories. War is still more of an art
than a science. The inspirations which reveal and
mark the great strategists, the leaders of men, form the
unforeseen element, the divine part. Generals of genius draw from the human heart ability to execute a
surprising variety of movements which vary the routine; the mediocre ones, who have no eyes to read
readily therein, are doomed to the worst errors.

Ardant du Picq, haunted by the need of a doctrine
which would correct existing evils and disorders, was
continually returning to the fountain-head. Anxious
to instruct promising officers, to temper them by irrefutable lessons, to mature them more rapidly, to inspire
them with his zeal for historical incidents, he resolved
to carry on and add to his personal studies while aiding
them. Daring to take a courageous offensive against
the general inertia of the period, he translated the
problem of his whole life into a series of basic questions. He presented in their most diverse aspects, the
basic questions which perplex all military men, those
of which knowledge in a varying degree of perfection
distinguish and classify military men. The nervous
grasp of an incomparable style models each of them,
carves them with a certain harshness, communicates to

them a fascinating yet unknown authority which crystallizes them in the mind, at the same time giving to them a positive form that remains true for all armies, for all past, present and future centuries. Herewith is the text of the concise and pressing questions which have not ceased to be as important to-day (1902) as they were in 1870:

" *General,*

" In the last century, after the improvements of the rifle and field artillery by Frederick, and the Prussian successes in war — to-day, after the improvement of the new rifle and cannon to which in part the recent victories are due — we find all thinking men in the army asking themselves the question: ' How shall we fight to-morrow? ' We have no creed on the subject of combat. And the most opposing methods confuse the intelligence of military men.

" Why? A common error at the starting point. One might say that no one is willing to acknowledge that it is necessary to understand yesterday in order to know to-morrow, for the things of yesterday are nowhere plainly written. The lessons of yesterday exist solely in the memory of those who know how to remember because they have known how to see, and those individuals have never spoken. I make an appeal to one of those.

" The smallest detail, taken from an actual incident in war, is more instructive for me, a soldier, than all the Thiers and Jominis in the world. They speak, no doubt, for the heads of states and armies but they. never show me what I wish to know — a battalion, a company, a squad, in action.

" Concerning a regiment, a battalion, a company, a

squad, it is interesting to know: The disposition taken
to meet the enemy or the order for the march toward
them. What becomes of this disposition or this march
order under the isolated or combined influences of accidents of the terrain and the approach of danger?

" Is this order changed or is it continued in force
when approaching the enemy?

" What becomes of it upon arriving within the range
of the guns, within the range of bullets?

" At what distance is a voluntary or an ordered
disposition taken before starting operations for commencing fire, for charging, or both?

" How did the fight start?   How about the firing?
How did the men adapt themselves?   (This may be
learned from the results: So many bullets fired, so
many men shot down — when such data are available.)
How was the charge made?   At what distance did the
enemy flee before it?   At what distance did the charge
fall back before the fire or the good order and good dispositions of the enemy, or before such and such a movement of the enemy?   What did it cost?   What can
be said about all these with reference to the enemy?

" The behavior, i. e., the order, the disorder, the
shouts, the silence, the confusion, the calmness of the
officers and men whether with us or with the enemy,
before, during, and after the combat?

" How has the soldier been controlled and directed
during the action?   At what instant has he had a tendency to quit the line in order to remain behind or to
rush ahead?

" At what moment, if the control were escaping from
the leader's hands, has it no longer been possible to
exercise it?

" At what instant has this control escaped from the

battalion commander? When from the captain, the
section leader, the squad leader? At what time, in
short, if such a thing did take place, was there but a
disordered impulse, whether to the front or to the rear
carrying along pell-mell with it both the leaders and
men?

" Where and when did the halt take place?

" Where and when were the leaders able to resume
control of the men?

" At what moments before, during, or after the day,
was the battalion roll-call, the company roll-call made?
The results of these roll-calls?

" How many dead, how many wounded on the one
side and on the other; the kind of wounds of the officers, non-commissioned officers, corporals, privates,
etc., etc.?

" All these details, in a word, enlighten either the
material or the moral side of the action, or enable it
to be visualized. Possibly, a closer examination
might show that they are matters infinitely more instructive to us as soldiers than all the discussions im-
aginable on the plans and general conduct of the campaigns of the greatest captain in the great movements
of the battle field. From colonel to private we are
soldiers, not generals, and it is therefore our trade that
we desire to know.

" Certainly one cannot obtain all the details of the
same incident. But from a series of true accounts
there should emanate an ensemble of characteristic details which in themselves are very apt to show in a
striking, irrefutable way what was necessarily and forcibly taking place at such and such a moment of an action in war. Take the estimate of the soldier obtained
in this manner to serve as a base for what might pos-

sibly be a rational method of fighting. It will put us on guard against *a priori* and pedantic school methods.

" Whoever has seen, turns to a method based on his knowledge, his personal experience as a soldier. But experience is long and life is short. The experiences of each cannot therefore be completed except by those of others.

" And that is why, General, I venture to address myself to you for your experiences.

" Proofs have weight.

" As for the rest, whether it please you to aid or not, General, kindly accept the assurance of most respectful devotion from your obedient servant."

" The reading of this unique document is sufficient to explain the glory that Ardant du Picq deserved. In no other career has a professional ever reflected more clearly the means of pushing his profession to perfection; in no profession has a deeper penetration of the resources been made.

" It pleases me particularly to associate the two words ' penseur ' and ' militaire,' which, at the present time, the ignorance of preconceived opinion too frequently separates. Because such opinion is on the verge of believing them to be incompatible and contradictory.

Yet no calling other than the true military profession is so fitted to excite brain activity. It is preëminently the calling of action, at the same time diverse in its combinations and changing according to the time and locality wherein it is put to practice. No other profession is more complex nor more difficult, since it has for its aim and reason the instruction of men to overcome by training and endurance the fatigue and perils against which the voice of self-preservation is raised in fear; in other words, to draw from nature what is most opposed and most antipathic to this nature.

There is, however, much of routine in the customs of military life, and, abuse of it may bring about gross satires which in turn bring it into derision. To be sure, the career has two phases because it must fulfill simultaneously two exigencies. From this persons of moderate capacity draw back and are horrified. They solve the question by the sacrifice of the one or the other. If one considers only the lower and somewhat vulgar aspect of military life it is found to be composed of monotonous obligations clothed in a mechanical procedure of indispensable repetition. If one learns to grasp it in its ensemble and large perspective, it will be found that the days of extreme trial demand prodigies of vigor, spirit, intelligence, and decision! Regarded from this angle and supported in this light, the commonplace things of wearisome garrison life have as counterweights certain sublime compensations. These compensations preclude the false and contemptible results which come from intellectual idleness and the habit of absolute submission. If it yields to their narcotic charms, the best brain grows rusty and atrophies in the long run. Incapable of virile labor, it rebels at a renewal of its processes in sane initiative. An army in which vigilance is not perpetual is sick until the enemy demonstrates it to be dead.

Far, then, from attaching routine as an indispensable companion to military discipline it must be shown continually that in it lies destruction and loss. Military discipline does not degenerate except when it has not known the cult of its vitality and the secret of its grandeur. The teachers of war have all placed this truth as a preface to their triumphs and we find the most illustrious teachers to be the most severe. Listen to this critique of Frederick the Great on the maneuvers which he conducted in Silesia:

" The great mistake in inspections is that you officers amuse yourselves with God knows what buffooneries and never dream in the least of serious service. This is a source of stupidity which would become most dangerous in case of a serious conflict. Take shoemakers and tailors and make generals of them and they will not commit worse follies! These blunders are made on a small as well as on a large scale. Consequently, in the greatest number of regiments, the private is not well trained; in Zaramba's regiment he is the worst; in Thadden's he amounts to nothing; and to no more in Keller's, Erlach's, and Haager's. Why? Because the officers are lazy and try to get out of a difficulty by giving themselves the least trouble possible."

In default of exceptional generals who remold in some campaigns, with a superb stroke, the damaged or untempered military metal, it is of importance to supply it with the ideals of Ardant du Picq. Those who are formed by his image, by his book, will never fall into error. His book has not been written to please æsthetic preciseness, but with a sincerity which knows no limit. It therefore contains irrefutable facts and theories.

The solidity of these fragmentary pages defies time; the work interrupted by the German shell is none the less erected for eternity. The work has muscles, nerves and a soul. It has the transparent concentration of reality. A thought may be expressed by a single word. The terseness of the calcined phrase explains the interior fire of it all, the magnificent conviction of the author. The distinctness of outline, the most astounding brevity of touch, is such that the vision of the future bursts forth from the resurrection of the past. The work contains, indeed, substance and marrow of a prophetic experience.

Amidst the praise rendered to the scintillating beauties of this book, there is perhaps, none more impressive than that of Barbey d'Aurevilly, an illustrious literary man of a long and generous patrician lineage. His comment, kindled with lyric enthusiasm, is illuminating. It far surpasses the usual narrow conception of technical subjects. Confessing his professional ignorance in matters of war, his sincere eulogy of the eloquent amateur is therefore only the more irresistible.

" Never," writes Barbey d'Aurevilly, " has a man of action — of brutal action in the eyes of universal prejudice — more magnificently glorified the spirituality of war. Mechanics — abominable mechanics — takes possession of the world, crushing it under its stupid and irresistible wheels. By the action of newly discovered and improved appliances the science of war assumes vast proportions as a means of destruction. Yet here, amid the din of this upset modern world we find a brain sufficiently master of its own thoughts as not to permit itself to be dominated by these horrible discoveries which, we are told, would make impossible Fredericks of Prussia and Napoleons and lower them to the level of the private soldier! Colonel Ardant du Picq tells us somewhere that he has never had entire faith in the huge battalions which these two great men, themselves alone worth more than the largest battalions, believed in. Well, to-day, this vigorous brain believes no more in the mechanical or mathematical force which is going to abolish these great battalions. A calculator without the least emotion, who considers the mind of man the essential in war — because it is this mind that makes war — he surely sees better than anybody else a profound change in the exterior conditions of war which he must consider. But the spiritual conditions which are produced in war have not changed. Such, is the eternal mind of man raised to its highest power by discipline. Such, is the Roman cement of this discipline that makes of men indestructible walls. Such, is the cohesion, the solidarity between men and their leaders. Such, is the moral influence of the impulse which gives the certainty of victory.

" ' To conquer is to advance,' de Maistre said one day, puzzled at this phenomenon of victory. The author of " Etudes sur le Combat " says more simply : ' To conquer is to be sure to overcome.' In fine, it is the mind that wins battles, that will always win them, that always has won them throughout the world's history. The spirituality, the moral quality of war, has not changed since those times. Mechanics, modern arms, all the artillery invented by man and his science, will not make an end to this thing, so lightly considered at the moment and called the human soul. Books like that of Ardant du Picq prevent it from being disdained. If no other effect should be produced by this sublime book, this one thing would justify it. But there will be others — do not doubt it — I wish merely to point out the sublimity of this didactic book which, for me, has wings like celestial poetry and which has

carried me above and far away from the materialistic
abjectness of my time. The technique of tactics and
the science of war are beyond my province. I am not,
like the author, erudite on maneuvers and the battle
field. But despite my ignorance of things exclusively
military, I have felt the truth of the imperious demonstrations with which it is replete, as one feels the presence of the sun behind a cloud. His book has over
the reader that moral ascendancy which is everything
in war and which determines success, according to the
author. This ascendancy, like truth itself, is the sort
which cannot be questioned. Coming from the superior mind of a leader who inspires faith it imposes obedience by its very strength. Colonel Ardant du Picq
was a military writer only, with a style of his own.
He has the Latin brevity and concentration. He re-
tains his thought, assembles it and always puts it out in
a compact phrase like a cartridge. His style has the
rapidity and precision of the long-range arms which
have dethroned the bayonet. He would have been a
writer anywhere. He was a writer by nature. He
was of that sacred phalanx of those who have a style
all to themselves."

Barbey d'Aurevilly rebels against tedious techni-
calities. Carried away by the author's historical and
philosophical faculties, he soars without difficulty to
the plane of Ardant du Picq. In like manner, du Picq
ranges easily from the most mediocre military operations to the analysis of the great functions of policy of
government and the evolution of nations.

Who could have unraveled with greater finesse the
causes of the insatiable desires of conquest by the new
power which was so desirous of occupying the leading
rôle on the world's stage? If our diplomats, our min-

isters and our generals had seized the warning of 1866, the date of the defeat of Austria, it is possible that we might have been spared our own defeats.

" Has an aristocracy any excuse for existing if it is not military? No. The Prussian aristocracy is essentially military. In its ranks it does accept officers of plebeian extraction, but only under condition that they permit themselves to be absorbed therein.

" Is not an aristocracy essentially proud? If it were not proud it would lack confidence. The Prussian aristocracy is, therefore, haughty; it desires domination by force and its desire to rule, to dominate more and more, is the essence of its existence. It rules by war; it wishes war; it must have war at the proper time. Its leaders have the good judgment to choose the right moment. This love of war is in the very fiber, the very makeup of its life as an aristocracy.

" Every nation that has an aristocracy, a military nobility, is organized in a military way. The Prussian officer is an accomplished gentleman and nobleman; by instruction or examination he is most capable; by education, most worthy. He is an officer and commands from two motives, the French officer from one alone.

" Prussia, in spite of all the veils concealing reality, is a military organization conducted by a military corporation. A nation, democratically constituted, is not organized from a military point of view. It is, therefore, as against the other, in a state of unpreparedness for war.

" A military nation and a warlike nation are not necessarily the same. The French are warlike from organization and instinct. They are every day becoming less and less military.

" In being the neighbor of a military nation, there

is no security for a democratic nation; the two are born
enemies; the one continually menaces the good influences, if not the very existence of the other. As long
as Prussia is not democratic she is a menace to us.

" The future seems to belong to democracy, but, before this future is attained by Europe, who will say
that victory and domination will not belong for a time
to military organization? It will presently perish for
the lack of sustenance of life, when having no more
foreign enemies to vanquish, to watch, to fight for control, it will have no reason for existence."

In tracing a portrait so much resembling bellicose
and conquering Prussia, the sharp eye of Ardant du
Picq had recognized clearly the danger which immediately threatened us and which his deluded and trifling
fellow citizens did not even suspect. The morning
after Sadowa, not a single statesman or publicist had
yet divined what the Colonel of the 10th Regiment of
the Line had, at first sight, understood. Written before the catastrophes of Frœschwiller, Metz and Sedan,
the fragment seems, in a retrospective way, an implac-
able accusation against those who deceived themselves
about the Hohenzollern country by false liberalism or
a softening of the brain.

Unswerved by popular ideas, by the artificial, by
the trifles of treaties, by the chimera of theories, by
the charlatanism of bulletins, by the nonsense of romantic fiction, by the sentimentalities of vain chivalry,
Ardant du Picq, triumphant in history, is even more
the incomparable master in the field of his laborious
days and nights, the field of war itself. Never has a
clearer vision fathomed the bloody mysteries of the
formidable test of war. Here man appears as his
naked self. He is a poor thing when he succumbs to

unworthy deeds and panics.   He is great under the impulse of voluntary sacrifice which transforms him under fire and for honor or the salvation of others makes
him face death.

The sound and complete discussions of Ardant du
Picq take up, in a poignant way, the setting of every
military drama.   They envelop in a circle of invariable
phenomena the apparent irregularity of combat, determining the critical point in the outcome of the battle.
Whatever be the conditions, time or people, he gives
a code of rules which will not perish.   With the enthusiasm of Pascal, who should have been a soldier, Ardant
du Picq has the preëminent gift of expressing the infinite in magic words.   He unceasingly opens an abyss
under the feet of the reader.   The whole metaphysics
of war is contained therein and is grasped at a single
glance.

He shows, weighed in the scales of an amazing exact-
itude, the normal efficiency of an army; a multitude
of beings shaken by the most contradictory passions,
first desiring to save their own skins and yet resigned
to any risk for the sake of a principle.   He shows the
quantity and quality of possible efforts, the aggregate
of losses, the effects of training and impulse, the intrinsic value of the troops engaged.   This value is the
sum of all that the leader can extract from any and
every combination of physical preparation, confidence,
fear of punishment, emulation, enthusiasm, inclination,
the promise of success, administration of camps, fire
discipline, the influence of ability and superiority, etc.
He shows the tragic depths, so somber below, so luminous above, which appear in the heart of the combatant
torn between fear and duty.   In the private soldier the
sense of duty may spring from blind obedience; in the

non-commissioned officer, responsible for his detachment, from devotion to his trade; in the commanding officer, from supreme responsibility! It is in battle that a military organization justifies its existence. Money spent by the billions, men trained by the millions, are gambled on one irrevocable moment. Organization decides the terrible contest which means the triumph or the downfall of the nation! The harsh rays of glory beam above the field of carnage, destroying the vanquished without scorching the victor.

Such are the basic elements of strategy and tactics!

There is danger in theoretical speculation of battle, in prejudice, in false reasoning, in pride, in braggadocio. There is one safe resource, the return to nature.

The strategy that moves in elevated spheres is in danger of being lost in the clouds. It becomes ridiculous as soon as it ceases to conform to actual working tactics. In his classical work on the decisive battle of August 18, 1870, Captain Fritz Hœnig has reached a sound conclusion. After his biting criticism of the many gross errors of Steinmetz and Zastrow, after his description of the triple panic of the German troops opposite the French left in the valley and the ravine of the Mance, he ends by a reflection which serves as a striking ending to the book. He says, " The grandest illustration of Moltke's strategy was the battle of Gravelotte-Saint Privat; but the battle of Gravelotte has taught us one thing, and that is, the best strategy cannot produce good results if tactics is at fault."

The right kind of tactics is not improvised. It asserts itself in the presence of the enemy but it is learned before meeting the enemy.

" There are men," says Ardant du Picq, " such as Marshal Bugeaud, who are born military in character,

mind, intelligence and temperament.   Not all leaders
are of this stamp.   There is, then, need for standard
or regulation tactics appropriate to the national character which should be the guide for the ordinary commander and which do not exact of him the exceptional
qualities of a Bugeaud."

" Tactics is an art based on the knowledge of how to
make men fight with their maximum energy against
fear, a maximum which organization alone can give."

" And here confidence appears.   It is not the enthusiastic and thoughtless confidence of tumultuous or improvised armies that gives way on the approach of
danger to a contrary sentiment which sees treason
everywhere; but the intimate, firm, conscious confidence which alone makes true soldiers and does not disappear at the moment of action."

" We now have an army.   It is not difficult for us to
see that people animated by passions, even people who
know how to die without flinching, strong in the face
of death, but without discipline and solid organization, are conquered by others who are individually less
valiant but firmly organized, all together and one for
all."

" Solidarity and confidence cannot be improvised.
They can be born only of mutual acquaintanceship
which establishes pride and makes unity.   And, from
unity comes in turn the feeling of force, that force
which gives to the attack the courage and confidence of
victory.   Courage, that is to say, the domination of the
will over instinct even in the greatest danger, leads
finally to victory or defeat."

In asking for a doctrine in combat and in seeking to
base it on the moral element, Ardant du Picq, was

ahead of his generation. He has had a very great influence. But, the doctrine is not yet established.

How to approach the adversary? How to pass from the defensive to the offensive? How to regulate the shock? How to give orders that can be executed? How to transmit them surely? How to execute them by economizing precious lives? Such are the distressing problems that beset generals and others in authority. The result is that presidents, kings and emperors hesitate, tremble, interrogate, pile reports upon reports, maneuvers upon maneuvers, retard the improvement of their military material, their organization, their equipment.

The only leaders who are equal to the difficulties of future war, come to conclusions expressed in almost the same terms. Recently General de Negrier, after having insisted that physical exhaustion determined by the nervous tension of the soldier, increased in surprising proportions according to the invisibility of the adversary, expressed himself as follows:

" The tide of battle is in the hands of each fighter, and never, at any time, has the individual bravery of the soldier had more importance.

" Whatever the science of the superior commander, the genius of his strategic combinations, the precision of his concentrations, whatever numerical superiority he may have, victory will escape him if the soldier does not conduct himself without being watched, and if he is not personally animated by the resolution to conquer or to perish. He needs much greater energy that formerly.

" He no longer has the intoxication of ancient attacks in mass to sustain him. Formerly, the terrible anxiety of waiting made him wish for the violent blow, dangerous, but soon passed. Now, all his normal and physical powers are tried for long hours and, in such a test, he will have but the resoluteness of his own heart to sustain him.

" Armies of to-day gain decisions by action in open order, where each soldier must act individually with will and initiative to attack the enemy and destroy him.

" The Frenchman has always been an excellent rifleman, intelligent, adroit and bold. He is naturally brave. The metal is good; the problem is to temper it. It must be recognized that to-day this task is not easy. The desire for physical comfort, the international theories which come therefrom, preferring economic slavery and work for the profit of the stranger to the struggle, do not incite the Frenchman to give his life in order to save that of his brother.

" The new arms are almost valueless in the hands of weakhearted soidiers, no matter what their number may be. On the ontrary, the demoralizing power of rapid and smokeless firing, which certain armies still persist in not acknowledging, manifests itself with so much the more force as each soldier possesses greater valor and cool energy.

" It is then essential to work for the development of the moral forces of the nation. They alone will sustain the soldier in the distressing test of battle where death comes unseen.

" That is the most important of the lessons of the South African war. Small nations will find therein the proof that, in preparing their youth for their duties as soldiers and creating in the hearts of all the wish for sacrifice, they are certain to live free; but only at this price."

This profession of faith contradicts the imbecile sophisms foolishly put into circulation by high authority and a thoughtless press, on the efficiency of the mass, which is nothing but numbers, on the fantastic value of new arms, which are declared sufficient for gaining a victory by simple mechanical perfection, on the suppression of individual courage. It is almost as though courage had become a superfluous and embarrassing factor. Nothing is more likely to poison the army. Ardant du Picq is the best specific against the heresies and the follies of ignorance or of pedantry. Here are some phrases of unerring truth. They ought to be impressed upon all memories, inscribed upon the walls of our military schools. They ought to be learned as lessons by our officers and they ought to rule them as regulations and pass into their blood:

" Man is capable of but a given quantity of fear. To-day one must swallow in five minutes the dose that one took in an hour in Turenne's day."

" To-day there is greater need than ever for rigid formation."

" Who can say that he never felt fear in battle? And with modern appliances, with their terrible effect on the nervous system, discipline is all the more necessary because one fights only in open formation."

" Combat exacts a moral cohesion, a solidarity more compact that ever before."

" Since the invention of fire arms, the musket, rifle, cannon, the distances of mutual aid and support are increased between the various arms. The more men think themselves isolated, the more need they have of high morale."

" We are brought by dispersion to the need of a cohesion greater than ever before."

" It is a truth, so clear as to be almost naïve, that if one does not wish bonds broken, he should make them elastic and thereby strengthen them."

" It is not wise to lead eighty thousand men upon the battle field, of whom but fifty thousand will fight. It would be better to have fifty thousand all of whom would fight. These fifty thousand would have their hearts in the work more than the others, who should have confidence in their comrades but cannot when one-third of them shirk their work."

" The rôle of the skirmisher becomes more and more predominant. It is more necessary to watch over and direct him as he is used against deadlier weapons and as he is consequently more prone to try to escape from them at all costs in any direction."

" The thing is then to find a method that partially regulates the action of our soldiers who advance by fleeing or escape by advancing, as you like, and if something unexpected surprises them, escape as quickly by falling back."

" Esprit de corps improves with experience in wars. War becomes shorter and shorter, and more and more violent; therefore, create in advance an esprit de corps."

These truths are eternal. This whole volume is but their masterful development. They prove that together with audacious sincerity in the coördination of facts and an infallible judgment, Ardant du Picq possessed prescience in the highest degree. His prophetic eye distinguished sixty years ago the constituent principles of a good army. These are the principles which lead to victory. They are radically opposed to those which enchant our parliamentarians or military politicians, which are based on a fatal favoritism and which precipitate wars.

Ardant du Picq is not alone a superior doctrinaire. He will be consulted with profit in practical warlike organization. No one has better depicted the character of modern armies. No one knew better the value of what Clausewitz called, "The product of armed force and the country's force . . . the heart and soul of a nation."

No more let us forget that he launched, before the famous prediction of von der Goltz, this optimistic view well calculated to rekindle the zeal of generals who struggle under the weight of enormous tasks incident to obligatory service.

"Extremes meet in many things. In the ancient times of conflict with pike and sword, armies were seen to conquer other solid armies even though one against two. Who knows if the perfection of long-range arms might not bring back these heroic victories? Who knows whether a smaller number by some combination of good sense or genius, or morale, and of appliances will not overcome a greater number equally well armed?"

After the abandonment of the law of 1872, and the repeal of the law of 1889, and before the introduction of numerous and disquieting reforms in recruitment and consequently, in the education of our regiments, would it not be opportune to study Ardant du Picq and look for the secret of force in his ideas rather than in the deceptive illusions of military automatism and materialism?

The martial mission of France is no more ended than war itself. The severities of war may be deplored, but the precarious justice of arbitration tribunals, still weak and divested of sanction, has not done away with its intervention in earthly quarrels. I do not suppose that

my country is willing to submit to the mean estate,
scourged with superb contempt by Donoso Cortes, who
says :—

" When a nation shows a civilized horror of war, it
receives directly the punishment of its mistake. God
changes its sex, despoils it of its common mark of viril-
ity, changes it into a feminine nation and sends conquerors to ravish it of its honor."

France submits sometimes to the yoke of subtle dia-
lecticians who preach total disarmament, who spread
insanely disastrous doctrine of capitulation, glorify
disgrace and humiliation, and stupidly drive us on to
suicide. The manly counsels of Ardant du Picq are
admirable lessons for a nation awakening. Since she
must, sooner or later, take up her idle sword again, may
France learn from him to fight well, for herself and for
humanity!

ERNEST JUDET.

PARIS, October 10, 1902.

Ardant du Picq has said little about himself in his
writings. He veils with care his personality. His
life and career, little known, are the more worthy of
the reader's interest, because the man is as original
as the writer. To satisfy a natural curiosity, I asked
the Colonel's family for the details of his life, enshrined
in their memory. His brother has kindly furnished
them in a letter to me. It contains many unpublished
details and shows traits of character which confirm
our estimate of the man, Ardant du Picq. It completes
very happily the impression made by his book.

"PARIS, October 12, 1903.

" *Sir,*

" Herewith are some random biographical notes on the author of 'Etudes sur le Combat' which you requested of me.

" My brother entered Saint-Cyr quite late, at twenty-one years, which was I believe the age limit at that time. This was not his initial preference. He had a marked preference for a naval career, in which adventure seemed to offer an opportunity for his activity, and which he would have entered if the circumstances had so permitted. His childhood was turbulent and somewhat intractable; but, attaining adolescence, he retained from his former violence a very pronounced taste for physical exercise, especially for gymnastics, little practiced then, to which he was naturally inclined by his agility and muscular strength.

" He was successful in his classes, very much so in studies which were to his taste, principally French composition. In this he rose above the usual level of schoolboy exercises when the subject interested him. Certain other branches that were uninteresting or distasteful to him, as for instance Latin Grammar, he neglected. I do not remember ever having seen him attend a distribution of prizes, although he was highly interested, perhaps because he was too interested. On these occasions, he would disappear generally after breakfast and not be seen until evening. His bent was toward mechanical notions and handiwork. He was not uninterested in mathematics but his interest in this was ordinary. He was nearly refused entrance to Saint-Cyr. He became confused before the examiners and the results of the first part of the tests were almost negligible. He consoled himself with his favorite maxim as a young man: 'Onward philosophy.' Considering the first test as over and done with, he faced the second test with perfect indifference. This attitude gave him another opportunity and he came out with honors. As he had done well with the written test on ' Hannibal's Campaigns,' he was given a passing grade.

" At school he was liked by all his comrades for his good humor and frank and sympathetic character. Later, in the regiment, he gained naturally and without effort the affection of his equals and the respect of his subordinates. The latter were grateful to him for the real, cordial and inspiring interest he showed in their welfare, for he was familiar with the details of the service and with the soldier's equipment. He would not compromise on such matters and prevaricators who had to do with him did not emerge creditably.

" It can be said that after reaching manhood he never lied. The absolute frankness from which he never departed under any circumstances gave him prestige superior to his rank. A mere Lieutenant, he voted ' No ' to the Coup d'Etat of December 2, and was admonished by his colonel who was sorry to see him compromise thus his future. He replied with his usual rectitude: ' Colonel, since my opinion was asked for, I must suppose that it was wanted.'

" On the eve of the Crimean war, his regiment, (67th) not seeming destined to take the field, he asked for and obtained a transfer to the light infantry (9th Battalion). It was with this battalion that he served in the campaign. When it commenced, he made his first appearance in the fatal Dobrutscha expedition. This was undertaken in a most unhealthy region, on the chance of finding there Cossacks who would have fur-

nished matter for a communiqué. No Cossacks were
found, but the cholera was. It cut down in a few
hours, so as to speak, a large portion of the total
strength. My brother, left with the rear guard to
bury the dead, burn their effects and bring up the sick,
was in his turn infected. The attack was very violent
and he recovered only because he would not give in to
the illness. Evacuated to the Varna hospital, he was
driven out the first night by the burning of the town
and was obliged to take refuge in the surrounding fields
where the healthfulness of the air gave him unexpected
relief. Returned to France as a convalescent, he remained there until the month of December (1854).
He then rejoined his regiment and withstood to the
end the rigors of the winter and the slowness of the
siege.

" Salle's division to which the Trochu brigade belonged, and in which my brother served, was charged
with the attack on the central bastion. This operation
was considered a simple diversion without a chance of
success. My brother, commanding the storming column of his battalion, had the good fortune to come
out safe and sound from the deadly fire to which he
was exposed and which deprived the battalion of several good officers. He entered the bastion with a
dozen men. All were naturally made prisoners after
a resistance which would have cost my brother his life
if the bugler at his side had not warded off a saber
blow at his head. Upon his return from captivity,
in the first months of 1856, he was immediately made
major in the 100th Regiment of the Line, at the instance of General Trochu who regarded him highly.
He was called the following year to the command of

the 16th Battalion of Foot Chasseurs. He served
with this battalion during the Syrian campaign where
there was but little serious action.

" Back again in France, his promotion to the grade
of lieutenant-colonel, notwithstanding his excellent rat-
ings and his place on the promotion list, was long re-
tarded by the ill-will of Marshal Randon, the Minister
of War. Marshal Randon complained of his independent character and bore him malice from an incident
relative to the furnishing of shoes intended for his battalion. My brother, questioned by Marshal Niel about
the quality of the lot of shoes, had frankly declared
it bad.

" Promoted finally to lieutenant-colonel in the 55th
in Algeria, he took the field there in two campaigns,
I believe. Appointed colonel of the 10th of the Line
in February, 1869, he was stationed at Lorient and
at Limoges during the eighteen months before the
war with Germany. He busied himself during this
period with the preparation of his work, soliciting
from all sides first-hand information. It was slow in
coming in, due certainly to indifference rather than
ill-will. He made several trips to Paris for the purpose of opening the eyes of those in authority to the
defective state of the army and the perils of the situation. Vain attempts! 'They take all that philoso-
phically,' he used to say.

"Please accept, Sir, with renewed acknowledgements
of gratitude, the expression of my most distinguished
sentiments.

                          " C. ARDANT DU PICQ.

"P. S. As to the question of atavism in which you
showed some interest in our first conversation, I may
say that our paternal line does not in my knowledge

include any military man.   The oldest ancestor I know of, according to an album of engravings by Albert Dürer, recovered in a garret, was a gold and silver-smith at Limoges towards the end of the sixteenth century.   His descendants have always been traders down to my grandfather who, from what I have heard said, did not in the least attend to his trade.   The case is different with my mother's family which came from Lorraine.   Our great-grandfather was a soldier, our grandfather also, and two, at least, of my mother's brothers gave their lives on the battlefields of the First Empire.   At present, the family has two representatives in the army, the one a son of my brother's, the other a first cousin, once removed, both bearing our name.

" C. A. DU P."

RECORD OF MILITARY SERVICE OF
COLONEL ARDANT DU PICQ

Ardant du Picq (Charles-Jean-Jacques-Joseph), was born October 19, 1821 at Périgueux (Dordogne). Entered the service as a student of the Special Military School, November 15, 1842.

Sub-Lieutenant in the 67th Regiment of the Line, October 1, 1844.

Lieutenant, May 15, 1848.

Captain, August 15, 1852.

Transferred to the 9th Battalion of Foot Chasseurs, December 25, 1853.

Major of the 100th Regiment of the Line, February 15, 1856.

Transferred to the 16th Battalion of Chasseurs, March 17, 1856.

Transferred to the 37th Regiment of the Line, January 23, 1863.

Lieutenant Colonel of the 55th Regiment of the Line, January 16, 1864.

Colonel of the 10th Regiment of Infantry of the Line, February 27, 1869.

Died from wounds at the military hospital in Metz, August 18, 1870.

CAMPAIGNS AND WOUNDS

Orient, March 29, 1854 to May 27, 1856. Was taken prisoner of war at the storming of the central bastion (Sebastopol) September 8, 1855; returned from enemy's prisons December 13, 1855.

Served in the Syrian campaign from August 6, 1860 to June 18, 1861; in Africa from February 24, 1864 to April 14, 1866; in Franco-German war, from July 15, 1870 to August 18, 1870.

Wounded — a comminute fracture of the right thigh, a torn gash in the left thigh, contusion of the abdomen — by the bursting of a projectile, August 15, 1870, Longeville-les-Metz (Moselle).

DECORATIONS

Chevalier of the Imperial Order of the Legion of Honor, Dec. 29, 1860.

Officer of the Imperial Order of the Legion of Honor, September 10, 1868.

Received the medal of H. M. the Queen of England.

Received the medal for bravery in Sardinia.

Authorized to wear the decoration of the fourth class of the Ottoman Medjidie order.

EXTRACT FROM THE HISTORY OF THE 10TH INFANTRY REGIMENT

CAMPAIGN OF 1870

On the 22nd of July, the three active battalions of the 10th Regiment of Infantry of the Line left Limoges and Angoulême by rail arriving on the 23rd at the camp at Châlons, where the 6th Corps of the Rhine Army was concentrating and organizing, under the command of Marshal Canrobert. The regiment, within this army corps, belonged to the 1st Brigade (Pechot) of the 1st Division (Tixier).

The organization on a war footing of the 10th Regiment of Infantry of the Line, begun at Limoges, was completed at the Châlons camp.

The battalions were brought up to seven hundred and twenty men, and the regiment counted twenty-two hundred and ten present, not including the band, the sappers and the headquarters section, which raised the effectives to twenty-three hundred men.

The troops of the 6th Corps were soon organized and Marshal Canrobert reviewed them on the 31st of July.

On August 5th, the division received orders to move to Nancy. It was placed on nine trains, of which the first left at 6 A. M. Arriving in the evening at its destination, the 1st brigade camped on the Leopold Racetrack, and the 10th Regiment established itself on the Place de la Grève.

The defeats of Forbach and Reichshofen soon caused these first plans to be modified. The 6th Corps was ordered to return to the Châlons camp. The last troops of the 2d Brigade, held up at Toul and Commercy, were returned on the same trains.

The 1st Brigade entrained at Nancy, on the night of August 8th, arriving at the Châlons camp on the afternoon of August 8th.

The 6th Corps, however, was to remain but a few days in camp. On the 10th it received orders to go to Metz. On the morning of the 11th the regiment was again placed on three successive trains. The first train carrying the staff and the 1st Battalion, arrived at Metz without incident. The second train, transporting the 2d Battalion and four companies of the 3d was stopped at about 11 P. M. near the Frouard branch.

The telegraph line was cut by a Prussian party near Dieulouard, for a length of two kilometers, and it was feared the road was damaged.

In order not to delay his arrival at Metz, nor the progress of the trains following, Major Morin at the head of the column, directed his commands to detrain and continue to Metz.

He caused the company at the head of the train to alight (6th Company, 2d Battalion, commanded by Captain Valpajola) and sent it reconnoitering on the road, about three hundred meters in advance of the train. All precautions were taken to assure the security of the train, which regulated its progress on that of the scouts.

After a run of about eight kilometers in this way, at Marbache station, all danger having disappeared and communication with Metz having been established, the

train resumed its regulation speed. In consequence of
the slowing up of the second column, the third followed at a short distance until it also arrived. On
the afternoon of the 12th, the regiment was entirely
united.

The division of which it was a part was sent beyond
Montigny and it camped there as follows:

The 9th Chasseurs and 4th Regiment of the Line,
ahead of the Thionville railroad, the right on the Moselle, the left on the Pont-à-Mousson highway; the
10th Regiment of the Line, the right supported at the
branch of the Thionville and Nancy lines, the left in
the direction of Saint-Privat, in front of the Montigny
repair shops of the Eastern Railroad lines.

The regiment was thus placed in the rear of a redoubt under construction. The company of engineers
was placed at the left of the 10th near the earth-works
on which it was to work.

Along the ridge of the plateau, toward the Seille, was
the 2d Brigade, which rested its left on the river and
its right perpendicular to the Saint-Privat road, in rear
of the field-work of this name. The divisional batteries were behind it.

The division kept this position August 13th and
during the morning of the 14th. In the afternoon, an
alarm made the division take arms, during the engagement that took place on the side of Vallières and
Saint-Julien (battle of Borny). The regiment immediately occupied positions on the left of the village
of Montigny.

At nightfall, the division retired to the rear of the
railroad cut, and received orders to hold itself in readiness to leave during the night.

The regiment remained thus under arms, the 3d Battalion (Major Deschesnes), passing the night on grand guard in front of the Montigny redoubt.

Before daybreak, the division marched over the bank of the Thionville railroad, crossed the Moselle, and, marching towards Gravelotte, descended into the plain south of Longeville-les-Metz, where the principal halt was made and coffee prepared.

Scarcely had stacks been made, and the men set to making fires, about 7 A. M., when shells exploded in the midst of the troops. The shots came from the Bradin farm, situated on the heights of Montigny, which the division had just left the same morning, and which a German cavalry reconnaissance patrol supported by two pieces had suddenly occupied.

The Colonel had arms taken at once and disposed the regiment north of the road which, being elevated, provided sufficient cover for defilading the men.

He himself, stood in the road to put heart into his troops by his attitude, they having been a little startled by this surprise and the baptism of fire which they received under such disadvantageous circumstances.

Suddenly, a shell burst over the road, a few feet from the Colonel, and mutilated his legs in a frightful manner.

The same shell caused other ravages in the ranks of the 10th. The commander of the 3d Battalion, Major Deschesnes, was mortally wounded, Captain Reboulet was killed, Lieutenant Pone (3d Battalion, 1st Company), and eight men of the regiment were wounded. The Colonel was immediately taken to the other side of the highway into the midst of his soldiers and a surgeon called, those of the regiment being already engaged in caring for the other victims of the terrible shot.

In the meantime, Colonel Ardant du Picq asked for Lieut.-Colonel Doleac, delivered to him his saddle-bags containing important papers concerning the regiment and gave him his field glasses. Then, without uttering the least sound of pain, notwithstanding the frightful injury from which he must have suffered horribly, he said with calmness: " My regret is to be struck in this way, without having been able to lead my regiment on the enemy."

They wanted him to take a little brandy, he refused and accepted some water which a soldier offered him.

A surgeon arrived finally. The Colonel, showing him his right leg open in two places, made with his hand the sign of amputating at the thigh, saying: " Doctor, it is necessary to amputate my leg here."

At this moment, a soldier wounded in the shoulder, and placed near the Colonel, groaned aloud. Forgetting his own condition, the Colonel said immediately to the surgeon: " See first, doctor, what is the matter with this brave man; I can wait."

Because of the lack of instruments it was not possible to perform the amputation on the ground, as the Colonel desired, so this much deplored commander was transported to the Metz hospital.

Four days later (19th of August), Coloned Ardant du Picq died like a hero of old, without uttering the least complaint. Far from his regiment, far from his family, he uttered several times the words which summed up his affections: " My wife, my children, my regiment, adieu! "

PART I

ANCIENT BATTLE

INTRODUCTION

BATTLE is the final objective of armies and man is the fundamental instrument in battle. Nothing can wisely be prescribed in an army — its personnel, organization, discipline and tactics, things which are connected like the fingers of a hand — without exact knowledge of the fundamental instrument, man, and his state of mind, his morale, at the instant of combat.

It often happens that those who discuss war, taking the weapon for the starting point, assume unhesitatingly that the man called to serve it will always use it as contemplated and ordered by the regulations. But such a being, throwing off his variable nature to become an impassive pawn, an abstract unit in the combinations of battle, is a creature born of the musings of the library, and not a real man. Man is flesh and blood; he is body and soul. And, strong as the soul often is, it can not dominate the body to the point where there will not be a revolt of the flesh and mental perturbation in the face of destruction.

The human heart, to quote Marshal de Saxe, is then the starting point in all matters pertaining to war.

Let us study the heart, not in modern battle, complicated and not readily grasped, but in ancient battle. For, although nowhere explained in detail, ancient battle was simple and clear.

Centuries have not changed human nature. Passions, instincts, among them the most powerful one of

65

self-preservation, may be manifested in various ways according to the time, the place, the character and temperament of the race. Thus in our times we can admire, under the same conditions of danger, emotion and anguish, the calmness of the English, the dash of the French, and that inertia of the Russians which is called tenacity. But at bottom there is always found the same man. It is this man that we see disposed of by the experts, by the masters, when they organize and discipline, when they order detailed combat methods and take general dispositions for action. The best masters are those who know man best, the man of to-day and the man of history. This knowledge naturally comes from a study of formations and achievements in ancient war.

The development of this work leads us to make such an analysis, and from a study of combat we may learn to know man.

Let us go even back of ancient battle, to primeval struggle. In progressing from the savage to our times we shall get a better grasp of life.

And shall we then know as much as the masters? No more than one is a painter by having seen the methods of painting. But we shall better understand these able men and the great examples they have left behind them.

We shall learn from them to distrust mathematics and material dynamics as applied to battle principles. We shall learn to beware of the illusions drawn from the range and the maneuver field.

There, experience is with the calm, settled, unfatigued, attentive, obedient soldier, with an intelligent and tractable man-instrument in short, and not with the nervous, easily swayed, moved, troubled, distrait, excited, restless being, not even under self-control, who is the fighting man from general to private. There are strong men, exceptions, but they are rare.

These illusions, nevertheless, stubborn and persistent, always repair the very next day the most damaging injuries inflicted on them by experience. Their least dangerous effect is to lead to prescribing the impractical, as if ordering the impractical were not really an attack on discipline, and did not result in disconcerting officers and men by the unexpected and by surprise at the contrast between battle and the theories of peacetime training.

Battle, of course, always furnishes surprises. But it furnishes less in proportion as good sense and the recognition of truth have had their effect on the training of the fighting man, and are disseminated in the ranks. Let us then study man in battle, for it is he who really fights.

CHAPTER I

MAN IN PRIMITIVE AND ANCIENT COMBAT

MAN does not enter battle to fight, but for victory. He does everything that he can to avoid the first and obtain the second.

War between savage tribes, between Arabs, even today,[1] is a war of ambush by small groups of men of which each one, at the moment of surprise, chooses, not his adversary, but his victim, and is an assassin. Because the arms are similar on both sides, the only way of giving the advantage to one side is by surprise. A man surprised, needs an instant to collect his thoughts and defend himself; during this instant he is killed if he does not run away.

The surprised adversary does not defend himself, he tries to flee. Face to face or body to body combat with primitive arms, ax or dagger, so terrible among enemies without defensive arms, is very rare. It can take place only between enemies mutually surprised and without a chance of safety for any one except in victory. And still . . . in case of mutual surprise, there is another chance of safety; that of falling back, of flight on the part of one or the other; and that chance is often seized. Here is an example, and if it does not concern savages at all, but soldiers of our days, the fact is none the less significant. It was observed by a man of warlike temperament who has related what he saw

[1] General Daumas (Manners and Customs of Algeria). Nocturnal Surprise and Extermination of a Camp.

69

with his own eyes, although he was a forced spectator, held to the spot by a wound.

During the Crimean War, on a day of heavy fighting, two detachments of soldiers, A and B, coming around one of the mounds of earth that covered the country and meeting unexpectedly face to face, at ten paces, stopped thunderstruck. Then, forgetting their rifles, they threw stones and withdrew. Neither of the two groups had a decided leader to lead it to the front, and neither of the two dared to shoot first for fear that the other would at the same time bring his own arm to his shoulder. They were too near to hope to escape, or so they thought at least, although in reality, reciprocal firing, at such short ranges, is almost always too high. The man who would fire sees himself already killed by the return fire. He throws stones, and not with great force, to avoid using his rifle, to distract the enemy, to occupy the time, until flight offers him some chance of escaping at point-blank range.

This agreeable state of affairs did not last long, a minute perhaps. The appearance of a troop B on one flank determined the flight of A, and then the opposing group fired.

Surely, the affair is ridiculous and laughable.

Let us see, however. In a thick forest, a lion and a tiger meet face to face at a turn in the trail. They stop at once, rearing and ready to spring. They measure each other with their eyes, there is a rumbling in their throats. The claws move convulsively, the hair stands up. With tails lashing the ground, and necks stretched, ears flattened, lips turned up, they show their formidable fangs in that terrible threatening grimace of fear characteristic of felines.

Unseen, I shudder.

The situation is disagreeable for both: movement ahead means the death of a beast. Of which? Of both perhaps.

Slowly, quite slowly, one leg, bent for the leap, bending still, moves a few inches to the rear. Gently, quite gently, a fore paw follows the movement. After a stop, slowly, quite slowly, the other legs do the same, and both beasts, insensibly, little by little, and always facing, withdraw, up to the moment where their mutual withdrawal has created between them an interval greater than can be traversed in a bound. Lion and tiger turn their backs slowly and, without ceasing to observe, walk freely. They resume without haste their natural gaits, with that sovereign dignity characteristic of great seigneurs. I have ceased to shudder, but I do not laugh.

There is no more to laugh at in man in battle, because he has in his hands a weapon more terrible than the fangs and claws of lion or tiger, the rifle, which instantly, without possible defense, sends one from life into death. It is evident that no one close to his enemy is in a hurry to arm himself, to put into action a force which may kill him. He is not anxious to light the fuse that is to blow up the enemy, and himself at the same time.

Who has not observed like instances between dogs, between dog and cat, cat and cat?

In the Polish War of 1831, two Russian and two Polish regiments of cavalry charged each other. They went with the same dash to meet one another. When close enough to recognize faces, these cavalrymen slackened their gait and both turned their backs. The Russians and Poles, at this terrible moment, recognized each other as brothers, and rather than spill fraternal

blood, they extricated themselves from a combat as if
it were a crime.   That is the version of an eyewitness
and narrator, a Polish officer.

What do you think of cavalry troops so moved by
brotherly love?

But let us resume:

When people become more numerous, and when the
surprise of an entire population occupying a vast space
is no longer possible, when a sort of public conscience
has been cultivated within society, one is warned beforehand.   War is formally declared.   Surprise is no
longer the whole of war, but it remains one of the
means in war, the best means, even to-day.   Man can
no longer kill his enemy without defense.   He has
forewarned him.   He must expect to find him standing and in numbers.   He must fight; but he wishes to
conquer with as little risk as possible.   He employs
the iron shod mace against the staff, arrows against
the mace, the shield against arrows, the shield and
cuirass against the shield alone, the long lance against
the short lance, the tempered sword against the iron
sword, the armed chariot against man on foot, and
so on.

Man taxes his ingenuity to be able to kill without
running the risk of being killed.   His bravery is born
of his strength and it is not absolute.   Before a stronger
he flees without shame.   The instinct of self-preservation is so powerful that he does not feel disgraced in
obeying it, although, thanks to the defensive power of
arms and armor he can fight at close quarters.   Can
you expect him to act in any other way?   Man must
test himself before acknowledging a stronger.   But
once the stronger is recognized, no one will face him.

Individual strength and valor were supreme in primitive combats, so much so that when its heroes were killed, the nation was conquered. As a result of a mutual and tacit understanding, combatants often stopped fighting to watch with awe and anxiety two champions struggling. Whole peoples often placed their fate in the hands of the champions who took up the task and who alone fought. This was perfectly natural. They counted their champion a superman and no man can stand against the superman.

But intelligence rebels against the dominance of force. No one can stand against an Achilles, but no Achilles can withstand ten enemies who, uniting their efforts, act in concert. This is the reason for tactics, which prescribe beforehand proper means of organization and action to give unanimity to effort, and for discipline which insures united efforts in spite of the innate weakness of combatants.

In the beginning man battled against man, each one for himself, like a beast that hunts to kill, yet flees from that which would kill him. But now prescriptions of discipline and tactics insure unity between leader and soldier, between the men themselves. Besides the intellectual progress, is there a moral progress? To secure unity in combat, to make tactical dispositions in order to render it practically possible, we must be able to count on the devotion of all. This elevates all combatants to the level of the champions of primitive combat. Esprit appears, flight is a disgrace, for one is no longer alone in combat. There is a legion, and he who gives way quits his commanders and his companions. In all respects the combatant is worth more.

So reason shows us the strength of wisely united effort; discipline makes it possible.

Will the result be terrible fights, conflicts of extermination? No! Collective man, a disciplined body
of troops formed in tactical battle order, is invincible
against an undisciplined body of troops. But against
a similarly disciplined body, he becomes again primitive man. He flees before a greater force of destruction when he recognizes it or when he foresees it.
Nothing is changed in the heart of man. Discipline
keeps enemies face to face a little longer, but cannot
supplant the instinct of self-preservation, and the sense
of fear that goes with it.

Fear! . . .

There are officers and soldiers who do not know it,
but they are people of rare grit. The mass shudders;
because you cannot suppress the flesh. This trembling
must be taken into account in all organization, discipline, arrangements, movements, maneuvers, mode of
action. All these are affected by the human weakness
of the soldier which causes him to magnify the strength
of the enemy.

This faltering is studied in ancient combat. It is
seen that of nations apt in war, the strongest have been
those who, not only best have understood the general
conduct of war, but who have taken human weakness
into greatest account and taken the best guarantees
against it. It is notable that the most warlike peoples
are not always those in which military institutions and
combat methods are the best or the most rational.

And indeed, in warlike nations there is a good dose
of vanity. They only take into account courage in
their tactics. One might say that they do not desire to
acknowledge weakness.

The Gaul, a fool in war, used barbarian tactics.

After the first surprise, he was always beaten by the Greeks and Romans.

The Greek, a warrior, but also a politician, had tactics far superior to those of the Gauls and the Asiatics.

The Roman, a politician above all, with whom war was only a means, wanted perfect means. He had no illusions. He took into account human weakness and he discovered the legion.

But this is merely affirming what should be demonstrated.

CHAPTER II

GREEK tactics developed the phalanx; Roman tactics, the legion; the tactics of the barbarians employed the square phalanx, wedge or lozenge.

The mechanism of these various formations is explained in all elementary books. Polybius enters into a mechanical discussion when he contrasts the phalanx and the legion. (Book 18.)

The Greeks were, in intellectual civilization, superior to the Romans, consequently their tactics ought to have been far more rational. But such was not the case. Greek tactics proceeded from mathematical reasoning; Roman tactics from a profound knowledge of man's heart. Naturally the Greeks did not neglect morale nor the Romans mechanics,[1] but their primary considerations were diverse.

What formation obtained the maximum effort from the Greek army?

What methods caused the soldiers of a Roman army to fight most effectively?

The first question admits of discussion. The Roman solved the second.

The Roman was not essentially brave. He did not

[1] Among the Romans, mechanics and morale are so admirably united, that the one always comes to the aid of the other and never injures it.

produce any warrior of the type of Alexander. It is acknowledged that the valorous impetuosity of the barbarians, Gauls, Cimbri, Teutons, made him tremble. But to the glorious courage of the Greeks, to the natural bravery of the Gauls he opposed a strict sense of duty, secured by a terrible discipline in the masses. It was inspired in the officers by a sentiment of the strongest patriotism.

The discipline of the Greeks was secured by exercises and rewards; the discipline of the Romans was secured also by the fear of death. They put to death with the club; they decimated their cowardly or traitorous units.

In order to conquer enemies that terrified his men, a Roman general heightened their morale, not by enthusiasm but by anger. He made the life of his soldiers miserable by excessive work and privations. He stretched the force of discipline to the point where, at a critical instant, it must break or expend itself on the enemy. Under similar circumstances, a Greek general caused Tyrtæus to sing.[1] It would have been curious to see two such forces opposed.

But discipline alone does not constitute superior tactics. Man in battle, I repeat, is a being in whom the instinct of self-preservation dominates, at certain moments, all other sentiments. Discipline has for its aim the domination of that instinct by a greater terror. But it cannot dominate it completely. I do not deny the glorious examples where discipline and devotion have elevated man above himself. But if these examples are glorious, it is because they are rare; if they are

[1] The Romans did not make light of the influence of a poet like Tyrtæus. They did not despise any effective means. But they knew the value of each.

admired, it is because they are considered exceptions, and the exception proves the rule.

The determination of that instant where man loses his reasoning power and becomes instinctive is the crowning achievement in the science of combat. In general, here was the strength of the Roman tactics. In particular cases such successful determination makes Hannibals and Cæsars.

Combat took place between masses in more or less deep formation commanded and supervised by leaders with a definite mission. The combat between masses was a series of individual conflicts, juxtaposed, with the front rank man alone fighting. If he fell, if he was wounded or worn out, he was replaced by the man of the second rank who had watched and guarded his flanks. This procedure continued up to the last rank. Man is always physically and morally fatigued in a hand-to-hand tournament where he employs all his energy.

These contests generally lasted but a short time. With like morale, the least fatigued always won.

During this engagement of the first two ranks, the one fighting, the other watching close at hand, the men of the rear ranks waited inactive at two paces distance for their turn in the combat, which would come only when their predecessors were killed, wounded or exhausted. They were impressed by the violent fluctuations of the struggle of the first rank. They heard the clashes of the blows and distinguished, perhaps, those that sank into the flesh. They saw the wounded, the exhausted crawl through the intervals to go to the rear. Passive spectators of danger, they were forced to await its terrible approach. These men were subjected to the poignant emotions of combat without being supported by the animation of the struggle. They were thus placed under the moral pressure of the greatest of anxieties. Often they could not stand it until their turn came; they gave way.

The best tactics, the best dispositions were those that made easiest a succession of efforts by assuring the relief by ranks of units in action, actually engaging only the necessary units and keeping the rest as a support or reserve outside of the immediate sphere of moral tension. The superiority of the Romans lay in such tactics and in the terrible discipline which prepared and assured the execution. By their resistance against fatigue which rude and continual tasks gave them and by the renewal of combatants in combat, they secured greater continuity of effort than any others.[1]

The Gauls did not reason. Seeing only the inflexible line, they bound themselves together, thus rendering relief impracticable. They believed, as did the Greeks, in the power of the mass and impulse of deep files, and did not understand that deep files were powerless to push the first ranks forward as they recoiled in the face of death. It is a strange error to believe that the last ranks will go to meet that which made the first ones fall back. On the contrary, the contagion of recoil is so strong that the stopping of the head means the falling back of the rear!

The Greeks, also, certainly had reserves and supports in the second half of their dense ranks. But the idea of mass dominated. They placed these supports and reserves too near, forgetting the essential, man.

The Romans believed in the power of mass, but from the moral point of view only. They did not multiply

[1] Also their common sense led them to recognize immediately and appropriate arms better than their own.

the files in order to add to the mass, but to give to the combatants the confidence of being aided and relieved. The number of ranks was calculated according to the moral pressure that the last ranks could sustain.

There is a point beyond which man cannot bear the anxiety of combat in the front lines without being engaged. The Romans did not so increase the number of ranks as to bring about this condition. The Greeks did not observe and calculate so well. They sometimes brought the number of files up to thirty-two and their last files, which in their minds, were doubtless their reserves, found themselves forcibly dragged into the material disorder of the first ones.

In the order by maniples in the Roman legion, the best soldiers, those whose courage had been proved by experience in battle, waited stoically, kept in the second and third lines. They were far enough away not to suffer wounds and not to be drawn in by the front line retiring into their intervals. Yet they were near enough to give support when necessary or to finish the job by advancing.

When the three separate and successive maniples of the first cohort were united in order to form the united battle cohort of Marius and of Cæsar, the same brain placed the most reliable men in the last lines, i.e., the oldest. The youngest, the most impetuous, were in the first lines. The legion was not increased simply to make numbers or mass. Each had his turn in action, each man in his maniple, each maniple in its cohort, and, when the unit became a cohort, each cohort in the order of battle.

We have seen that the Roman theory dictated a depth of ranks to furnish successive lines of combatants. The genius of the general modified these established formations. If the men were inured to war, well-trained, reliable, tenacious, quick to relieve their file leaders, full of confidence in their general and their own comrades, the general diminished the depth of the files, did away with the lines even, in order to increase the number of immediate combatants by increasing the front. His men having a moral, and sometimes also a physical endurance superior to that of the adversary, the general knew that the last ranks of the latter would not, under pressure, hold sufficiently to relieve the first lines nor to forbid the relief of his own. Hannibal had a part of his infantry, the Africans, armed and drilled in the Roman way; his Spanish infantrymen had the long wind of the Spaniards of to-day; his Gallic soldiers, tried out by hardship, were in the same way fit for long efforts. Hannibal, strong with the confidence with which he inspired his people, drew up a line less deep by half than the Roman army and at Cannæ hemmed in an army which had twice his number and exterminated it. Cæsar at Pharsalus, for similar reasons, did not hesitate to decrease his depth. He faced double his strength in the army of Pompey, a Roman army like his own, and crushed it.

We have mentioned Cannæ and Pharsalus, we shall study in them the mechanism and the morale of ancient combat, two things which cannot be separated. We cannot find better examples of battle more clearly and more impartially exhibited. This is due in one case to the clear presentation of Polybius, who obtained his information from the fugitives from Cannæ, possibly even from some of the conquerors; in the other it is due to the impassive clearness of Cæsar in describing the art of war.

CHAPTER III

RECITAL of Polybius:

" Varro placed the cavalry on the right wing, and rested it on the river; the infantry was deployed near it and on the same line, the maniples drawn close to each other, with smaller intervals than usual, and the maniples presenting more depth than front.

" The cavalry of the allies, on the left wing, completed the line, in front of which were posted the light troops. There were in that army, including the allies, eighty thousand foot and a little more than six thousand horse.

" Meanwhile Hannibal had his slingers and light troops cross the Aufidus and posted them in front of his army. The rest crossed the river at two places. He placed the Iberian and Gallic cavalry on the left wing, next the river and facing the Roman cavalry. He placed on the same line, one half of the African infantry heavily armed, the Iberian and Gallic infantry, the other half of the African infantry, and finally the Numidian cavalry which formed the right wing.

" After he had thus arrayed all his troops upon a single line, he marched to meet the enemy with the Iberian and Gallic infantry moving independently of the main body. As it was joined in a straight line with the rest, on separating, it was formed like the convex face of a crescent. This formation reduced its depth in the center. The intention of the general was to

commence the battle with the Iberians and Gauls, and
have them supported by the Africans.

" The latter infantry was armed like the Roman infantry, having been equipped by Hannibal with arms
that had been taken from the Romans in preceding battle. Both Iberians and Gauls had shields; but their
swords were quite different. The sword of the former
was as fit for thrusting as for cutting while that of the
Gauls only cut with the edge, and at a limited distance.
These troops were drawn up as follows: the Iberians
were in two bodies of troops on the wings, near the Africans; the Gauls in the center. The Gauls were nude;
the Iberians in linen shirts of purple color, which to the
Romans was an extraordinary and frightening spectacle. The Carthaginian army consisted of ten thousand
horse and little more than forty thousand foot.

" Æmilius commanded the right of the Romans,
Varro the left; the two consuls of the past year, Servilius and Attilius, were in the center. On the Carthaginian side, Hasdrubal had the left under his orders,
Hanno the right, and Hannibal, who had his brother
Mago with him, reserved for himself the command of
the center. The two armies did not suffer from the
glare of the sun when it rose, the one being faced to
the South, as I remarked, and the other to the North.

" Action commenced with the light troops, which
were in front of both armies. The first engagement
gave advantage to neither the one nor the other. Just
as soon as the Iberian and Gallic cavalry on the left
approached, the conflict became hot. The Romans
fought with fury and rather more like barbarians than
Romans. This falling back and then returning to the
charge was not according to their tactics. Scarcely did
they become engaged when they leaped from their

horses and each seized his adversary. In the mean-while the Carthaginians gained the upper hand. The greater number of the Romans remained on the ground after having fought with the greatest valor. The others were pursued along the river and cut to pieces without being able to obtain quarter.

" The heavily armed infantry immediately took the place of the light troops and became engaged. The Iberians and Gauls held firm at first and sustained the shock with vigor; but they soon gave way to the weight of the legions, and, opening the crescent, turned their backs and retreated. The Romans followed them with impetuosity, and broke the Gallic line much more easily because the wings crowded toward the center where the thick of the fighting was. The whole line did not fight at the same time. The action commenced in the center because the Gauls, being drawn up in the form of a crescent, left the wings far behind them, and presented the convex face of the crescent to the Romans. The latter then followed the Gauls and Iberians closely, and crowded towards the center, to the place where the enemy gave way, pushing ahead so forcibly that on both flanks they engaged the heavily armed Africans. The Africans on the right, in swinging about from right to left, found themselves all along the enemy's flank, as well as those on the left which made the swing from left to right. The very circumstances of the action showed them what they had to do. This was what Hannibal had foreseen; that the Romans pursuing the Gauls must be enveloped by the Africans. The Romans then, no longer able to keep their formation [1] were forced to defend

[1] This is an excuse. The maniple was of perfect nobility and, without the least difficulty, could face in any direction.

themselves man to man and in small groups against those who attacked them on front and flank [1].

" Æmilius had escaped the carnage on the right wing at the commencement of the battle. Wishing, according to the orders he had given, to be everywhere, and seeing that it was the legionary infantry that would decide the fate of the battle, he pushed his horse through the fray, warded off or killed every one who opposed him, and sought at the same time to reanimate the ardor of the Roman soldiers. Hannibal, who during the entire battle remained in the conflict, did the same in his army.

" The Numidian cavalry on the right wing, without doing or suffering much, was useful on that occasion by its manner of fighting; for, pouncing upon the enemy on all sides, they gave him enough to do so that he might not have time to think of helping his own people. Indeed, when the left wing, where Hasdrubal commanded, had routed almost all the cavalry of the Roman right wing, and a junction had been effected with the Numidians, the auxiliary cavalry did not wait to be attacked but gave way.

" Hasdrubal is said to have done something which proved his prudence and his ability, and which contributed to the success of the battle. As the Numidians were in great number, and as these troops were never more useful than when one was in flight before them, he gave them the fugitives to pursue, and led the Iberian and Gallic cavalry in a charge to aid the African infantry. He pounced on the Romans from

[1] This was an enveloping attack of an army and not of men or groups. The Roman army formed a wedge and was attacked at the point and sides of the wedge; there was not a separate flank attack. That very day the maniple presented more depth than front.

the rear, and having bodies of cavalry charge into the melee at several places, he gave new strength to the Africans and made the arms drop from the hands of the adversaries. It was then that L. Æmilius, a citizen who during his whole life, as in this last conflict, had nobly fulfilled his duties to his country, finally succumbed, covered with mortal wounds.

" The Romans continued fighting, giving battle to those who were surrounding them. They resisted to the last. But as their numbers diminished more and more, they were finally forced into a smaller circle, and all put to the sword. Attilius and Servilius, two persons of great probity, who had distinguished themselves in the combat as true Romans, were also killed on that occasion.

" While this carnage was taking place in the center, the Numidians pursued the fugitives of the left wing Most of them were cut down, others were thrown under their horses; some of them escaped to Venusia. Among these was Varro, the Roman general, that abominable man whose administration cost his country so dearly. Thus ended the battle of Cannæ, a battle where prodigies of valor were seen on both sides.

" Of the six thousand horse of which the Roman cavalry was composed, only seventy Romans reached Venusia with Varro, and, of the auxiliary cavalry, only three hundred men found shelter in various towns. Ten thousand foot were taken prisoners, but they were not in the battle.[1] Of troops in battle only about three thousand saved themselves in the nearby town; the balance, numbering about twenty thousand, died on the field of honor." [2]

[1] They had been sent to attack Hannibal's camp; they were repulsed and taken prisoner in their own camp after the battle.
[2] This extract is taken from the translation of Dom Thuillier.

Hannibal lost in that action in the neighborhood of four thousand Gauls, fifteen hundred Iberians and Africans and two hundred horses.

Let us analyze:

The light infantry troops were scattered in front of the armies and skirmished without result. The real combat commenced with the attack on the legitimate cavalry of the Roman left wing by the cavalry of Hannibal.

There, says Polybius, the fight grew thickest, the Romans fought with fury and much more like barbarians than like Romans; because this falling back, then returning to the charge was not according to their tactics; scarcely did they become engaged when they leaped from their horses and each seized his adversary, etc., etc.

This means that the Roman cavalry did not habitually fight hand to hand like the infantry. It threw itself in a gallop on the enemy cavalry. When within javelin range, if the enemy's cavalry had not turned in the opposite direction on seeing the Roman cavalry coming, the latter prudently slackened its gait, threw some javelins, and, making an about by platoons, took to the rear for the purpose of repeating the charge. The hostile cavalry did the same, and such an operation might be renewed several times, until one of the two, persuaded that his enemy was going to attack him

Livy does not state the precise number of Roman combatants. He says nothing had been neglected in order to render the Roman army the strongest possible, and from what he was told by some it numbered eighty-seven thousand two hundred men. That is the figure of Polybius. His account has killed, forty-five thousand; taken or escaped after the action, nineteen thousand. Total sixty-four thousand. What can have become of the twenty-three thousand remaining?

with a dash, turned in flight and was pursued to the limit.

That day, the fight becoming hot, they became really engaged; the two cavalry bodies closed and man fought man. The fight was forced, however; as there was no giving way on one side or the other, it was necessary actually to attack. There was no space for skirmishing. Closed in by the Aufidus and the legions, the Roman cavalry could not operate (Livy). The Iberian and Gallic cavalry, likewise shut in and double the Roman cavalry, was forced into two lines; it could still less maneuver. This limited front served the Romans, inferior in number, who could thus be attacked only in front, that is by an equal number. It rendered, as we have said, contact inevitable. These two cavalry bodies placed chest to chest had to fight close, had to grapple man to man, and for riders mounted on simple saddle cloths and without stirrup, embarrassed with a shield, a lance, a saber or a sword, to grapple man to man is to grapple together, fall together and fight on foot. That is what happened, as the account of Titus Livius explains it in completing that of Polybius. The same thing happened every time that two ancient cavalry organizations really had to fight, as the battle of the Tecinus showed. This mode of action was all to the advantage of the Romans, who were well-armed and well-trained therein. Note the battle of Tecinus. The Roman light infantry was cut to pieces, but the elite of the Roman cavalry, although surprised and surrounded, fought a-foot and on horse back, inflicted more casualties on the cavalry of Hannibal than they suffered, and brought back from the field their wounded general. The Romans besides were well led by Consul Æmilius, a man of head and heart, who, instead of fleeing when his cavalry was defeated, went himself to die in the ranks of the infantry.

Meanwhile we see thirty to thirty-four hundred Roman cavalrymen nearly exterminated by six to seven thousand Gauls and Iberians who did not lose even two hundred men. Hannibal's entire cavalry lost but two hundred men on that day.

How can that be explained?

Because most of them died without dreaming of selling their lives and because they took to flight during the fight of the first line and were struck with impunity from behind. The words of Polybius: " Most of them remained on the spot after having defended themselves with the utmost valor," were consecrated words before Polybius. The conquered always console themselves with their bravery and conquerors never contradict. Unfortunately, the figures are there. The facts of the battle are found in the account, which sounds no note of desperation. The Gallic and Roman cavalry had each already made a brave effort by attacking each other from the front. This effort was followed by the terrible anxiety of close combat. The Roman cavalrymen, who from behind the combatants on foot were able to see the second Gallic line on horse back, gave ground. Fear very quickly made the disengaged ranks take to their horses, wheel about like a flock of sheep in a stampede, and abandon their comrades and themselves to the mercy of the conquerors.

Yet, these horsemen were brave men, the elite of the army, noble knights, guards of the consuls. volunteers of noble families.

The Roman cavalry defeated, Hasdrubal passed his Gallic and Iberian troopers behind Hannibal's army, to attack the allied cavalry till then engaged by the Numidians.[1] The cavalry of the allies did not await the enemy. It turned its back immediately; pursued to the utmost by the Numidians who were numerous (three thousand), and excellent in pursuit, it was reduced to some three hundred men, without a struggle.

After the skirmishing of the light infantry troops, the foot-soldiers of the line met. Polybius has explained to us how the Roman infantry let itself be enclosed by the two wings of the Carthaginian army and taken in rear by Hasdrubal's cavalry. It is also probable that the Gauls and Iberians, repulsed in the first part of the action and forced to turn their backs, returned, aided by a portion of the light infantry, to the charge upon the apex of the wedge formed by the Romans and completed their encirclement.

But we know, as will be seen further on in examples taken from Cæsar, that the ancient cavalryman was powerless against formed infantry, even against the isolated infantryman possessing coolness. The Iberian and Gallic cavalry ought to have found behind the Roman army the reliable triarians penned in, armed with pikes.[2] It might have held them in check,

[1] The Numidian horsemen were a light irregular cavalry, excellent for skirmishing, harassing, terrifying, by their extraordinary shouts and their unbridled gallop. They were not able to hold out against a regular disciplined cavalry provided with bits and substantial arms. They were but a swarm of flies that always harasses and kills at the least mistake; elusive and perfect for a long pursuit and the massacre of the vanquished to whom the Numidians gave neither rest nor truce. They were like Arab cavalry, badly armed for the combat, but sufficiently armed for butchering, as results show. The Arabian knife, the Kabyle knife, the Indian knife of our days, which is the favorite of the barbarian or savage, must play its part.

[2] They formed the third Roman line according to the order of battle of the Legion. The contraction of the first line into a point would naturally hem them in.

forced them to give battle, but done them little or no harm as long as the ranks were preserved.

We know that of Hannibal's infantry only twelve thousand at the most were equipped with Roman weapons. We know that his Gallic and Iberian infantry, protected by plain shields, had to fall back, turn, and probably lost in this part of the action very nearly the four thousand men, which the battle cost them.

Let us deduct the ten thousand men that had gone to the attack of Hannibal's camp and the five thousand which the latter must have left there. There remain:

A mass of seventy thousand men surrounded and slaughtered by twenty-eight thousand foot soldiers, or, counting Hasdrubal's cavalry, by thirty-six thousand men, by half their number.

It may be asked how seventy thousand men could have let themselves be slaughtered, without defense, by thirty-six thousand men less well-armed, when each combatant had but one man before him. For in close combat, and especially in so large an envelopment, the number of combatants immediately engaged was the same on each side. Then there were neither guns nor rifles able to pierce the mass by a converging fire and destroy it by the superiority of this fire over diverging fire. Arrows were exhausted in the first period of the action. It seems that, by their mass, the Romans must have presented an insurmountable resistance, and that while permitting the enemy to wear himself out against it, that mass had only to defend itself in order to repel assailants.

But it was wiped out.

In pursuit of the Gauls and Iberians, who certainly were not able, even with like morale, to stand against the superior arms of the legionaries, the center drove all vigorously before it. The wings, in order to support it and not to lose the intervals, followed its movement by a forward oblique march and formed the sides of the salient. The entire Roman army, in wedge order, marched to victory. Suddenly the wings were attacked by the African battalions; the Gauls, the Iberians,[1] who had been in retreat, returned to the fight. The horsemen of Hasdrubal, in the rear, attacked the reserves.[2] Everywhere there was combat, unexpected, unforseen. At the moment when they believed themselves conquerors, everywhere, in front, to the right, to the left, in the rear, the Roman soldiers heard the furious clamor of combat.[3]

The physical pressure was unimportant. The ranks that they were fighting had not half their own depth. The moral pressure was enormous. Uneasiness, then terror, took hold of them; the first ranks, fatigued or wounded, wanted to retreat; but the last ranks, frightened, withdrew, gave way and whirled into the interior of the wedge. Demoralized and not feeling themselves supported, the ranks engaged followed them, and the routed mass let itself be slaughtered. The weapons fell from their hands, says Polybius.

The analysis of Cannæ is ended. Before passing to the recital of Pharsalus, we cannot resist the temptation, though the matter be a little foreign to the subject, to say a few words about the battles of Hannibal.

These battles have a particular character of stubborn-

[1] Brought back by Hannibal who had reserved to himself the command of the center.

[2] The triarians, the third Roman line.

[3] What effect this might have, was shown in the battle of Alisia, where Cæsar's men, forewarned by him, were nevertheless troubled by war-whoops behind them. The din of battle in rear has always demoralized troops.

ness explained by the necessity for overcoming the Roman tenacity. It may be said that to Hannibal victory was not sufficient. He must destroy. Consequently he always tried to cut off all retreat for the enemy. He knew that with Rome, destruction was the only way of finishing the struggle.

He did not believe in the courage of despair in the masses; he believed in terror and he knew the value of surprise in inspiring it.

But it was not the losses of the Romans that was the most surprising thing in these engagements. It was the losses of Hannibal. Who, before Hannibal or after him, has lost as many as the Romans and yet been conqueror? To keep troops in action, until victory comes, with such losses, requires a most powerful hand.

He inspired his people with absolute confidence. Almost always his center, where he put his Gauls, his food for powder, was broken. But that did not seem to disquiet or trouble either him or his men.

It is true that his center was pierced by the Romans who were escaping the pressure of the two Carthaginian wings, that they were in disorder because they had fought and pushed back the Gauls, whom Hannibal knew how to make fight with singular tenacity. They probably felt as though they had escaped from a press, and, happy to be out of it, they thought only of getting further away from the battle and by no means of returning to the flanks or the rear of the enemy. In addition, although nothing is said about it, Hannibal had doubtless taken precautions against their ever returning to the conflict.

All that is probably true. The confidence of the Gallic troops, so broken through, is none the less surprising.

Hannibal, in order to inspire his people with such confidence, had to explain to them before the combat his plan of action, in such a way that treachery could not injure him. He must have warned his troops that the center would be pierced, but that he was not worried about it, because it was a foreseen and prepared affair. His troops, indeed, did not seem to be worried about it.

Let us leave aside his conception of campaigns, his greatest glory in the eyes of all. Hannibal was the greatest general of antiquity by reason of his admirable comprehension of the morale of combat, of the morale of the soldier, whether his own or the enemy's. He shows his greatness in this respect in all the different incidents of war, of campaign, of action. His men were not better than the Roman soldiers. They were not as well armed, one-half less in number. Yet he was always the conqueror. He understood the value of morale. He had the absolute confidence of his people. In addition he had the art, in commanding an army, of always securing the advantage of morale.

In Italy he had, it is true, cavalry superior to that of the Romans. But the Romans had a much superior infantry. Had conditions been reversed, he would have changed his methods. The instruments of battle are valuable only if one knows how to use them, and Pompey, we shall see, was beaten at Pharsalus precisely because he had a cavalry superior to that of Cæsar.

If Hannibal was vanquished at Zuma, it was because genius cannot accomplish the impossible. Zuma proved again the perfect knowledge of men that Hannibal possessed and his influence over the troops. His third line, the only one where he really had reliable soldiers, was the only one that fought. Beset on all sides, it slew two thousand Romans before it was conquered.

We shall see later what a high state of morale, what desperate fighting, this meant.

CHAPTER IV

ANALYSIS OF THE BATTLE OF PHARSALUS, AND SOME CHARACTERISTIC EXAMPLES

HERE is Cæsar's account of the battle of Pharsalus.

" As Cæsar approached Pompey's camp, he noted that Pompey's army was placed in the following order:

" On the left wing were the 2nd and 3rd Legions which Cæsar had sent to Pompey at the commencement of the operation, pursuant to a decree of the Senate, and which Pompey had kept. Scipio occupied the center with the legions from Syria. The legion from Cilicia was placed on the right wing together with the Spanish cohorts of Afranius. Pompey regarded the troops already mentioned as the most reliable of his army. Between them, that is, between the center and the wings, he had distributed the remainder, consisting of one hundred and ten complete cohorts in line. These were made up of forty-five thousand men, two thousand of whom were veterans, previously rewarded for their services, who had come to join him. He had scattered them throughout the whole line of battle. Seven cohorts had been left to guard his camp and the neighboring forts. His right wing rested on a stream with inaccessible banks; and, for that reason, he had placed all his seven thousand cavalry [1], his archers and

[1] His cavalry consisted of seven thousand horse, of which five hundred were Gauls or Germans, the best horsemen of that time, nine hundred Galicians, five hundred Thracians, and Thessalians, Macedonians and Italians in various numbers.

his slingers (forty-two hundred men) on the left wing.

"Cæsar, keeping his battle order [1], had placed the 10th Legion on the right wing, and on the left, the 9th, which was much weakened by the combats of Dyr-rachium. To the latter he added the 8th in order to form something like a full legion from the two, and ordered them to support one another. He had eighty very completely organized cohorts in line, approximately twenty-two thousand men. Two cohorts had been left to guard the camp. Cæsar had entrusted the command of the left wing to Anthony, that of the right to P. Sylla, and of the center to C. Domitius. He placed himself in front of Pompey. But when he saw the disposition of the opposing army, he feared that his right wing was going to be enveloped by Pompey's numerous cavalry. He therefore withdrew immediately from his third line a cohort from each legion (six cohorts), in order to form a fourth line, placed it to receive Pompey's cavalry and showed it what it had to do. Then he explained fully to these cohorts that the success of the day depended on their valor. At the same time he ordered the entire army, and in particular the third line, not to move without his command, reserving to himself authority to give the signal by means of the standard when he thought it opportune.

"Cæsar then went through his lines to exhort his men to do well, and seeing them full of ardor, had the signal given.

"Between the two armies there was only enough space to give each the necessary distance for the charge. But Pompey had given his men orders to await the

[1] Cæsar's legions in battle order were in three lines: four cohorts in the first line, two in the second, and three in the third. In this way the cohorts of a legion were, in battle, always supported by cohorts of the same legion.

charge without stirring, and to let Cæsar's army break
its ranks upon them.　He did this, they say, on the advice of C. Triarius, as a method of meeting the force
of the first dash of Cæsar's men.　He hoped that their
battle order would be broken up and his own·soldiers,
well disposed in ranks, would have to fight with sword
in hand only men in disorder.　He thought that this
formation would best protect his troops from the force
of the fall of heavy javelins.　At the same time he
hoped that Cæsar's soldiers charging at the run would
be out of breath and overcome with fatigue at the moment of contact.　Pompey's immobility was an error
because there is in every one an animation, a natural
ardor that is instilled by the onset to the combat.　Generals ought not to check but to encourage this ardor.
It was for this reason that, in olden times, troops
charged with loud shouts, all trumpets sounding, in
order to frighten the enemy and encourage themselves.

　" In the meanwhile, our soldiers, at the given signal
advanced with javelins in hand; but having noticed that
Pompey's soldiers were not running towards them, and
taught by experience and trained by previous battles,
they slowed down and stopped in the midst of their
run, in order not to arrive out of breath and worn out.
Some moments after, having taken up their run again,
they launched their javelins, and immediately afterwards, according to Cæsar's order drew their swords.
The Pompeians conducted themselves perfectly.　They
received the darts courageously; they did not stir before
the dash of the legions; they preserved their lines, and,
having dispatched their javelins, drew their swords.

　" At the same time Pompey's entire cavalry dashed
from the left wing, as had been ordered, and the mass

of his archers ran from all parts of the line. Our cavalry did not await the charge, but fell back a little. Pompey's cavalry became more pressing, and commenced to reform its squadrons and turn our exposed flank. As soon as Cæsar saw this intention, he gave the signal to the fourth line of six cohorts. This line started directly and, standards low, they charged the Pompeian cavalry with such vigor and resolution that not a single man stood his ground. All wheeled about and not only withdrew in full flight, but gained the highest mountains as fast as they could. They left the archers and slingers without their defense and protection. These were all killed. At the same time the cohorts moved to the rear of Pompey's left wing, which was still fighting and resisting, and attacked it in rear.

" Meanwhile, Cæsar had advanced his third line, which up to this moment had been kept quietly at its post. These fresh troops relieved those that were fatigued. Pompey's men, taken in rear, could no longer hold out and all took to flight.

" Cæsar was not in error when he put these cohorts in a fourth line, particularly charged with meeting the cavalry, and urged them to do well, since their effort would bring victory. They repulsed the cavalry. They cut to pieces the slingers and archers. They turned Pompey's left wing, and this decided the day.

" When Pompey saw his cavalry repulsed and that portion of the army upon which he had counted the most seized with terror, he had little confidence in the rest. He quit the battle and galloped to his camp, where, addressing his centurians who were guarding the prætorian gate, he told them in a loud voice heard by the sol-

diers: ' Guard well the camp and defend it vigorously
in case of attack; as for myself, I am going to make
the tour of the other gates and assure their defense. '

"That said, he retired to the prætorium, despairing
of success and awaiting events.

"After having forced the enemy to flee to his entrenchments, Cæsar, persuaded that he ought not to
give the slightest respite to a terrorized enemy, incited
his soldiers to profit by their advantage and attack the
camp. Although overcome by the heat, for the struggle was prolonged into the middle of the day, they did
not object to greater fatigue and obeyed. The camp
was at first well defended by the cohorts on watch and
especially by the Thracians and barbarians. The men
who had fled from the battle, full of fright and overcome with fatigue, had nearly all thrown their arms
and colors away and thought rather more of saving
themselves than of defending the camp. Even those
who defended the entrenchments were unable long to
resist the shower of arrows. Covered with wounds,
they abandoned the place, and led by their centurions
and tribunes, they took refuge as quickly as they could
in the high mountains near the camp.

" Cæsar lost in this battle but two hundred soldiers,
but nearly thirty of the bravest centurions were killed
therein. Of Pompey's army fifteen thousand perished,
and more than twenty-four thousand took refuge in the
mountains. As Cæsar had invested the mountains with
entrenchments, they surrendered the following day."

Such is Cæsar's account. His action is so clearly
shown that there is scarcely any need of comment.

Initially Cæsar's formation was in three lines. This
was the usual battle order in the Roman armies. without
being absolute, however, since Marius fought with two

only. But, as we have said, according to the occasion, the genius of the chief decided the battle formation. There is no reason to suppose that Pompey's army was in a different order of battle.

To face that army, twice as large as his, Cæsar, if he had had to preserve the disposition of cohorts in ten ranks, would have been able to form but one complete line, the first, and a second, half as numerous, as a reserve. But he knew the bravery of his troops, and he knew the apparent force of deep ranks to be a delusion. He did not hesitate to diminish his depth in order to keep the formation and morale of three-fifths of his troops intact, until the moment of their engagement. In order to be even more sure of the third line of his reserve, and in order to make sure that it would not be carried away by its enthusiasm for action, he paid it most particular attention. Perhaps, the text is doubtful, he kept it at double the usual distance in rear of the fighting lines.

Then, to guard against a turning movement by Pompey's seven thousand cavalry and forty-two hundred slingers and archers, a movement in which Pompey placed the hopes of victory, Cæsar posted six cohorts that represented scarcely two thousand men. He had perfect confidence that these two thousand men would make Pompey's cavalry wheel about, and that his one thousand horsemen would then press the action so energetically that Pompey's cavalry would not even think of rallying. It happened so; and the forty-two hundred archers and slingers were slaughtered like sheep by these cohorts, aided, without doubt, by four-hundred foot [1] young and agile, whom Cæsar mixed with his

[1] Cæsar stated that in order to make up the numerical inferiority of his cavalry, he had chosen four hundred of the most

thousand horsemen and who remained at this task, leaving the horsemen, whom they had relieved, to pursue the terror-stricken fugitives.

Thus were seven thousand horsemen swept away and forty-two hundred infantrymen slaughtered without a struggle, all demoralized simply by a vigorous demonstration.

The order to await the charge, given by Pompey to his infantry, was judged too severely by Cæsar. Cæsar certainly was right as a general rule; the enthusiasm of the troops must not be dampened, and the initiative of the attack indeed gives to the assailant a certain moral influence. But with trusted soldiers, duly trained, one can try a stratagem, and the men of Pompey had proven their dependability by awaiting on the spot, without stirring, a vigorous enemy in good order, when they counted on meeting him in disorder and out of breath. Though it may not have led to success, the advice of Triarius was not bad. Even the conduct of Cæsar's men proves this. This battle shows the confidence of the soldier in the material rank in ancient combat, as assuring support and mutual assistance.

Notwithstanding the fact the Cæsar's soldiers had the initiative in the attack, the first encounter decided nothing. It was a combat on the spot, a struggle of several hours. Forty-five thousand good troops lost scarcely two hundred men in this struggle for, with like arms, courage and ability, Pompey's infantry ought

alert young men, from among those marching ahead of the standards, and by daily exercise had them accustomed to fighting between his horsemen. He had in this way obtained such results that his thousand riders dared, in open field, to cope with Pompey's seven thousand cavalry without becoming frightened at their number.

not to have lost in hand-to-hand fighting more than that of Cæsar's. These same forty-five thousand men gave way, and, merely between the battle field and their camp, twelve thousand were slaughtered.

Pompey's men had twice the depth of Cæsar's ranks, whose attack did not make them fall back a step. On the other hand their mass was unable to repel him, and he was fought on the spot. Pompey had announced to them, says Cæsar, that the enemy's army would be turned by his cavalry, and suddenly, when they were fighting bravely, step by step, they heard behind them the shouts of attack by the six cohorts of Cæsar, two thousand men.

Does it seem an easy matter for such a force to ward off this menace? No. The wing taken in rear in this way loses ground; more and more the contagion of fear spreads to the rest. Terror is so great that they do not think of re-forming in their camp, which is defended for a moment only by the cohorts on guard. Just as at Cannæ, their arms drop from their hands. But for the good conduct of the camp guards which permitted the fugitives to gain the mountains, the twenty-four thousand prisoners of the next day might have been corpses that very day.

Cannæ and Pharsalus, are sufficient to illustrate ancient combat. Let us, however, add some other characteristic examples, which we shall select briefly and in chronological order. They will complete our data.[1]

---

[1] Any one who wishes to read in extenso is referred to the fight of the ten thousand against Pharnabazus in Bithynia, Xenophon, par. 34, page 569, Lisken & Sauvan edition.— In Polybius, the battle of the Tecinus, Chapt. XIII, of Book III.— In Cæsar or those who followed him the battles against Scipio, Labienus, and Afranius, the Getæ and the Numidians, par. 61, page 282, and par. 69, 70, 71 and 72, pp. 283, 285, and 286, in the African war, Lisken & Sauvan edition.

Livy relates that in an action against some of the peoples in the neighborhood of Rome, I do not recall now which, the Romans did not dare to pursue for fear of breaking their ranks.

In a fight against the Hernici, he cites the Roman horsemen, who had not been able to do anything on horseback to break up the enemy, asking the consul for permission to dismount and fight on foot. This is true not only of Roman cavalrymen, for later on we shall see the best riders, the Gauls, the Germans, the Parthanians even, dismounting in order really to fight.

The Volsci, the Latini, the Hernici, etc., combined to fight the Romans; and as the action nears its end, Livy relates: " Finally, the first ranks having fallen, and carnage being all about them, they threw away their arms and started to scatter. The cavalry then dashed forward, with orders not to kill the isolated ones, but to harass the mass with their arrows, annoy it, to delay it, to prevent dispersion in order to permit the infantry to come up and kill."

In Hamilcar's engagement against the mercenaries in revolt, who up to then had always beaten the Carthaginians, the mercenaries endeavored to envelop him. Hamilcar surprised them by a new maneuver and defeated them. He marched in three lines: elephants, cavalry and light infantry, then heavily armed phalanxes. At the approach of the mercenaries who were marching vigorously towards him the two lines formed by the elephants, the cavalry and light infantry, turned about and moved quickly to place themselves on the flanks of the third line. The third line thus exposed met a foe which had thought only of pursuit, and which the surprise put to flight. It thus abandoned itself to the action of the elephants, horses and the light infantry who massacred the fugitives.

Hamilcar killed six thousand men, captured two thousand and lost practically nobody. It was a question as to whether he had lost a single man, since there had been no combat.

In the battle of Lake Trasimenus, the Carthaginians lost fifteen hundred men, nearly all Gauls; the Romans fifteen thousand and fifteen thousand prisoners. The battle raged for three hours.

At Zama, Hannibal had twenty thousand killed, twenty thousand prisoners; the Romans two thousand killed. This was a serious struggle in which Hannibal's third line alone fought. It gave way only under the attack on its rear and flank by the cavalry.

In the battle of Cynoscephalæ, between Philip and Flaminius, Philip pressed Flaminius with his phalanx thirty-two deep. Twenty maniples took the phalanx from behind. The battle was lost by Philip. The Romans had seven hundred killed; the Macedonians eighty thousand, and five thousand prisoners.

At Pydna, Æmilius Paulus against Perseus, the phalanx marched without being stopped. But gaps occurred from the resistance that it encountered. Hundreds penetrated into the gaps in the phalanx and killed the men embarrassed with their long pikes. They were effective only when united, abreast, and at shaft's length. There was frightful disorder and butchery; twenty thousand killed, five thousand captured out of forty-four thousand engaged! The historian does not deem it worth while to speak of the Roman losses.

After the battle of Aix against the Teutons, Marius surprised the Teutons from behind. There was frightful carnage; one hundred thousand Teutons and three hundred Romans killed.[1]

In Sulla's battle of Chæronea against Archelaus, a general of Mithridates, Sulla had about thirty thousand men, Archelaus, one hundred and ten thousand. Archelaus was beaten by being surprised from the rear. The Romans lost fourteen men, and killed their enemies until worn out in pursuit.

The battle of Orchomenus, against Archelaus, was a repetition of Chæronea.

Cæsar states that his cavalry could not fight the Britons without greatly exposing itself, because they pretended flight in order to get the cavalry away from the infantry and then, dashing from their chariots, they fought on foot with advantage.

A little less than two hundred veterans embarked on a boat which they ran aground at night so as not to be taken by superior naval forces. They reached an advantageous position and passed the night. At the break of day, Otacilius dispatched some four hundred horsemen and some infantry from the Alesio garrison against them. They defended themselves bravely; and having killed some, they rejoined Cæsar's troops without having lost a single man.

In Macedonia Cæsar's rear-guard was caught by Pompey's cavalry at the passage of the Genusus River, the banks of which were quite steep. Cæsar opposed Pompey's cavalry five to seven thousand strong, with his cavalry of six hundred to one thousand men, among which he had taken care to intermingle four hundred picked infantrymen. They did their duty so well that,

[1] In ancient combat, there was almost only, dead or lightly wounded. In action, a severe wound or one that incapacitated a man was immediately followed by the finishing stroke.

in the combat that followed, they repulsed the enemy, killed many, and fell back upon their own army without the loss of a single man.

In the battle of Thapsus in Africa, against Scipio, Cæsar killed ten thousand, lost fifty, and had some wounded.

In the battle under the walls of Munda in Spain, against one of Pompey's sons, Cæsar had eighty cohorts and eight thousand horsemen, about forty-eight thousand men. Pompey with thirteen legions had sixty thousand troops of the line, six thousand cavalry, six thousand light infantry, six thousand auxiliaries; in all, about eighty thousand men. The struggle, says the narrator, was valiantly kept up, step by step, sword to sword.[1]

In that battle of exceptional fury, which hung for a long time in the balance, Cæsar had one thousand dead, five hundred wounded; Pompey thirty-three thousand dead, and if Munda had not been so near, scarcely two miles away, his losses would have been doubled. The defensive works of Munda were constructed from dead bodies and abandoned arms.

In studying ancient combats, it can be seen that it was almost always an attack from the flank or rear, a surprise action, that won battles, especially against the Romans. It was in this way that their excellent tactics might be confused. Roman tactics were so excellent that a Roman general who was only half as good as his adversary was sure to be victorious. By surprise alone they could be conquered. Note Xanthippe,— Hannibal — the unexpected fighting methods of the Gauls, etc.

[1] Hand-to-hand, sword-to-sword, serious fighting at short distances, was rare then. Likewise in the duels of our day blades are rarely crossed in actual practice.

Indeed Xenophon says somewhere, " Be it agreeable or terrible, the less anything is foreseen, the more does it cause pleasure or dismay. This is nowhere better illustrated than in war where every surprise strikes terror even to those who are much the stronger."

But very few fighters armed with cuirass and shield were killed in the front lines.

Hannibal in his victories lost almost nobody but Gauls, his cannon-fodder, who fought with poor shields and without armor.

Nearly always driven in, they fought, nevertheless, with a tenacity that they never showed under any other command.

Thucydides characterizes the combat of the lightly armed, by saying: " As a rule, the lightly armed of both sides took to flight." [1]

In combat with closed ranks there was mutual pressure but little loss, the men not being at liberty to strike in their own way and with all their force.

Cæsar against the Nervii, saw his men, who in the midst of the action had instinctively closed in mass in order to resist the mass of barbarians, giving way under pressure. He therefore ordered his ranks and files to open, so that his legionaries, closed in mass, paralyzed and forced to give way to a very strong pressure, might be able to kill and consequently demoralize the enemy. And indeed, as soon as a man in the front rank of the Nervii fell under the blows of the legionaries, there was a halt, a falling back. Following an attack from the rear, and a mêlée, the defeat of the Nervii ensued.[2]

[1] To-day, it is the riflemen who do nearly all the work of destruction.

[2] Considering Cæsar's narrative what becomes of the mathematical theory of masses, which is still discussed? If that theory

had the least use, how could Marius ever have held out against the tide of the armies of the Cimbri and Teutons? In the battle of Pharsalus, the advice given by Triarius to Pompey's army, a counsel which was followed and which was from a man of experience, who had seen things close at hand, shows that the shock, the physical impulse of the mass was a by-word. They knew what to think of it.

CHAPTER V

MORALE IN ANCIENT BATTLE

WE now know the morale and mechanism of ancient fighting; the word mêlée employed by the ancients was many times stronger than the idea to be expressed; it meant a crossing of arms, not a confusion of men.

The results of battles, such as losses, suffice to demonstrate this, and an instant of reflection makes us see the error of the word mêlée. In pursuit it was possible to plunge into the midst of the fugitives, but in combat every one had too much need for the next man, for his neighbor, who was guarding his flanks and his back, to let himself be killed out of sheer wantonness by a sure blow from within the ranks of the enemy.[1]

In the confusion of a real mêlée, Cæsar at Pharsalus, and Hannibal at Cannæ, would have been conquered.

[1] The individual advance, in modern battle, in the midst of blind projectiles that do not choose, is much less dangerous than in ancient times, because it seldom goes up to the enemy.

At Pharsalus, the volunteer Crastinius, an old centurion, moved ahead with about a hundred men, saying to Cæsar: "I am going to act, general, in such a way that, living or dead, to-day you may have cause to be proud of me."

Cæsar, to whom these examples of blind devotion to his person were not displeasing, and whose troops had shown him that they were too mature, too experienced, to fear the contagion of this example, let Crastinius and his companions go out to be killed.

Such blind courage influences the action of the mass that follows. Probably for that reason, Cæsar permitted it. But against reliable troops, as the example of Crastinius proves, to move ahead in this way, against the enemy, is to go to certain death.

110

Their shallow ranks, penetrated by the enemy, would have had to fight two against one, they would even have been taken in rear in consequence of the breaking of their ranks.

Also has there not been seen, in troops equally reliable and desperate, that mutual weariness which brings about, with tacit accord, falling back for a breathing spell on both sides in order again to take up the battle?

How can this be possible with a mêlée?

With the confusion and medley of combatants, there might be a mutual extermination, but there would not be any victors. How would they recognize each other? Can you conceive two mixed masses of men or groups, where every one occupied in front can be struck with impunity from the side or from behind? That is mutual extermination, where victory belongs only to survivors; for in the mix-up and confusion, no one can flee, no one knows where to flee.

After all, are not the losses we have seen on both sides demonstration that there was no real mêlée?

The word is, therefore, too strong; the imagination of painters' and poets' has created the mêlée.

This is what happened:

At a charging distance troops marched towards the enemy with all the speed compatible with the necessity for fencing and mutual aid. Quite often, the moral impulse, that resolution to go to the end, manifested itself at once in the order and freedom of gait. That impulse alone put to flight a less resolute adversary.

It was customary among good troops to have a clash, but not the blind and headlong onset of the mass; the preoccupation [1] of the rank was very great, as the

[1] The men of the maniple, of the Roman company, mutually gave their word never to leave ranks, except to pick up an arrow,

behavior of Cæsar's troops at Pharsalus shows in their
slow march, timed by the flutes of Lacedæmonian battalions. At the moment of getting close to the enemy,
the dash slackened of its own accord, because the men
of the first rank, of necessity and instinctively, assured
themselves of the position of their supports, their neighbors in the same line, their comrades in the second, and
collected themselves together in order to be more the
masters of their movements to strike and parry. There
was a contact of man with man; each took the adversary
in front of him and attacked him, because by penetrating into the ranks before having struck him down, he
risked being wounded in the side by losing his flank
supports. Each one then hit his man with his shield,
expecting to make him lose his equilibrium, and at the
instant he tried to recover himself landed the blow.
The men in the second line, back of the intervals necessary for fencing in the first, were ready to protect
their sides against any one that advanced between them
and were prepared to relieve tired warriors. It was the
same in the third line, and so on.

Every one being supported on either side, the first
encounter was rarely decisive, and the fencing, the real
combat at close quarters, began.

If men of the first line were wounded quickly, if the
other ranks were not in a hurry to relieve or replace
them, or if there was hesitation, defeat followed. This
happened to the Romans in their first encounters with
the Gauls. The Gaul, with his shield, parried the first
thrust, brought his big iron sword swooping down with
fury upon the top of the Roman shield, split it and went
after the man. The Romans, already hesitating before

to save a comrade (a Roman citizen), or to kill an enemy.
(Livy).

the moral impulse of the Gauls, their ferocious yells, their nudeness, an indication of a contempt for wounds, fell then in a greater number than their adversaries and demoralization followed. Soon they accustomed themselves to this valorous but not tenacious spirit of their enemies, and when they had protected the top of their shields with an iron band, they no longer fell, and the rôles were changed.

The Gauls, in fact, were unable either to hold their ground against the better arms and the thrusts of the Romans, or against their individual superior tenacity, increased nearly tenfold by the possible relay of eight ranks of the maniple. The maniples were self-renewing. Whereas with the Gauls the duration of the combat was limited to the strength of a single man, on account of the difficulties of close or tumultuous ranks, and the impossibility of replacing losses when they were fighting at close quarters.

If the weapons were nearly alike, preserving ranks and thereby breaking down, driving back and confusing the ranks of the enemy, was to conquer. The man in disordered, broken lines, no longer felt himself supported, but vulnerable everywhere, and he fled. It is true that it is hardly possible to break hostile lines without doing the same with one's own. But the one who breaks through first, has been able to do so only by making the foe fall back before his blows, by killing or wounding. He has thereby raised his courage and that of his neighbor. He knows, he sees where he is marching; whilst the adversary overtaken as a consequence of the retreat or the fall of the troops that were flanking him, is surprised. He sees himself exposed on the flank. He falls back on a line with the rank in rear in order to regain support. But the lines in the

rear give way to the retreat of the first. If the withdrawal has a certain duration, terror comes as a result of the blows which drive back and mow down the first line. If, to make room for those pushed back, the last lines turn their backs, there is small chance that they will face the front again. Space has tempted them. They will not return to the fight.

Then by that natural instinct of the soldier to worry, to assure himself of his supports, the contagion of flight spreads from the last ranks to the first. The first, closely engaged, has been held to the fight in the meantime, under pain of immediate death. There is no need to explain what follows; it is butchery. (Cædes).

But to return to combat.

It is evident that the formation of troops in a straight line, drawn close together, existed scarcely an instant. Moreover each group of files formed in action was connected with the next group; the groups, like the individuals, were always concerned about their support. The fight took place along the line of contact of the first ranks of the army, a straight line, broken, curved, and bent in different directions according to the various chances of the action at such or such a point, but always restricting and separating the combatants of the two sides. Once engaged on that line, it was necessary to face the front under pain of immediate death. Naturally and necessarily every one in these first ranks exerted all his energy to defend his life.

At no point did the line become entangled as long as there was fighting, for, general or soldier, the effort of each one was to keep up the continuity of support all along the line, and to break or cut that of the enemy, because victory then followed.

We see then that between men armed with swords,

it was possible to have, and there was, if the combat was serious, penetration of one mass into the other, but never confusion, or a jumble of ranks, by the men forming these masses.[1]

Sword to sword combat was the most deadly. It presented the most sudden changes, because it was the one in which the individual valor and dexterity of the combatant had the greatest and most immediate influence. Other methods of combat were simpler.

Let us compare pikes and broadswords.

The close formation of men armed with pikes was irresistible so long as it was maintained. A forest of pikes fifteen to eighteen feet long kept you at a distance.[2] On the other hand it was easy to kill off the cavalry and light infantry about the phalanx, which was an unwieldly mass marching with a measured step, and which a mobile body of troops could always avoid. Openings in the phalanx might be occasioned by marching, by the terrain, by the thousand accidents of struggle, by the individual assault of brave men, by the wounded on the ground creeping under the high held pikes and cutting at the legs of the front rank. Men in the phalanx could scarcely see and even the first two lines hardly had a free position for striking. The men were armed with long lances, useless at close quarters, good only for combat at shaft's length (Polybius). They were struck with impunity by the groups [3]

---

[1] A small body of troops falling into a trap might present a sort of mêlée, for a second, the time necessary for its slaughter. In a rout it might be possible at some moment of the butchery to have conflict, a struggle of some men with courage, who want to sell their lives dearly. But this is not a real mêlée. Men are hemmed in, overwhelmed, but not thrown into confusion.

[2] The Greek phalanx.

[3] The Romans lost no one as their companies entered the openings in the phalanx.

which threw themselves into the intervals. And then, once the enemy was in the body of the phalanx, morale disappeared and it became a mass without order, a flock of panic-stricken sheep falling over each other.

In a mob hard-pressed men prick with their knives those who press them. The contagion of fear changes the direction of the human wave; it bends back upon itself and breaks to escape danger. If, then, the enemy fled before the phalanx there was no mêlée. If he gave way tactically before it and availing himself of gaps penetrated it by groups, still there was no mêlée or mixture of ranks. The wedge entering into a mass does not become intermingled with it.

With a phalanx armed with long pikes against a similar phalanx there was still less confusion. They were able to stand for a long time, if the one did not take the other in flank or in rear by a detached body of troops. In all ancient combat, even in victory achieved by methods which affected the morale, such methods are always effective, for man does not change.

It is unnecessary to repeat that in ancient conflicts, demoralization and flight began in the rear ranks.

We have tried to analyze the fight of infantry of the line because its action alone was decisive in ancient combat. The light infantry of both sides took to flight, as Thucydides states. They returned later to pursue and massacre the vanquished.[1]

In cavalry against cavalry, the moral effect of a mass charging in good order was of the greatest influence. We rarely see two cavalry organizations, neither of which breaks before such reciprocal action. Such ac-

---

[1] The Roman velites, light-armed soldiers, of the primitive legion before Marius, were required to stand for an instant in the intervals of the maniples, while awaiting the onset. They maintained, but only for an instant, the continuity of support.

tion was seen on the Tecinus and at Cannæ, engagements cited merely because they are very rare exceptions. And even in these cases there was no shock at full speed, but a halt face to face and then an engagement.

The hurricanes of cavalry of those days were poetic figures. They had no reality. In an encounter at full speed, men and horses would be crushed, and neither men nor horses wished such an encounter. The hands of the cavalrymen reined back, the instinct of men and horses was to slacken, to stop, if the enemy himself did not stop, and to make an about if he continued to advance. And if ever they met, the encounter was so weakened by the hands of the men, the rearing of the horses, the swinging of heads, that it was a face to face stop. Some blows were exchanged with the sword or the lance, but the equilibrium was too unstable, mutual support too uncertain for real sword play. Man felt himself too isolated. The moral pressure was too strong. Although not deadly, the combat lasted but a second, precisely because man felt himself, saw himself, alone and surrounded. The first men, who believed themselves no longer supported, could no longer endure uneasiness: they wheeled about and the rest followed. Unless the enemy had also turned, he then pursued at his pleasure until checked by other cavalry, which pursued him in turn.

There never was an encounter between cavalry and infantry. The cavalry harassed with its arrows, with the lance perhaps, while passing rapidly, but it never attacked.

Close conflict on horseback did not exist. And to be sure, if the horse by adding so much to the mobility of man gave him the means of menacing and charging with swiftness, it permitted him to escape with like rapidity when his menace did not shake the enemy. Man by using the horse, pursuant to his natural inclination and sane reasoning, could do as much damage as possible while risking the least possible. To riders without stirrups or saddle, for whom the throwing of the javelin was a difficult matter (Xenophon), combat was but a succession of reciprocal harassings, demonstrations, menaces, skirmishes with arrows. Each cavalry sought an opportunity to surprise, to intimidate, to avail itself of disorder, and to pursue either the cavalry or the infantry. Then " væ victis;" the sword worked.

Man always has had the greatest fear of being trampled upon by horses. That fear has certainly routed a hundred thousand times more men than the real encounter. This was always more or less avoided by the horse, and no one was knocked down. When two ancient cavalry forces wanted really to fight, were forced to it, they fought on foot (Note the Tecinus, Cannæ, examples of Livy). I find but little real fighting on horseback in all antiquity like that of Alexander the Great at the passage of the Granicus. Was even that fighting? His cavalry which traversed a river with steep banks defended by the enemy, lost eighty-five men; the Persian cavalry one thousand; and both were equally well armed!

The fighting of the Middle Ages revived the ancient battles except in science. Cavalrymen attacked each other perhaps more than the ancient cavalry did, for the reason that they were invulnerable: it was not sufficient to throw them down; it was necessary to kill when once they were on the ground. They knew, however, that their fighting on horseback was not important so far as results were concerned, for when they wished really to battle, they fought on foot. (Note the combat of the Thirty, Bayard, etc.)

The victors, arrayed in iron from head to foot, lost no one, the peasants did not count. If the vanquished was taken, he was not massacred, because chivalry had established a fraternity of arms between noblemen, the mounted warriors of different nations, and ransom replaced death.

If we have spoken especially of the infantry fight, it is because it was the most serious. On foot, on horseback, on the bridge of a vessel, at the moment of danger, the same man is always found. Any one who knows him well, deduces from his action in the past what his action will be in the future.

CHAPTER VI

Let us repeat now, what we said at the beginning of this study. Man does not enter battle to fight, but for victory. He does everything that he can to avoid the first and obtain the second. The continued improvement of all appliances of war has no other goal than the annihilation of the enemy. Absolute bravery, which does not refuse battle even on unequal terms, trusting only to God or to destiny, is not natural in man; it is the result of moral culture. It is infinitely rare, because in the face of danger the animal sense of self-preservation always gains the upper hand. Man calculates his chances, with what errors we are about to see.

Now, man has a horror of death. In the bravest, a great sense of duty, which they alone are capable of understanding and living up to, is paramount. But the mass always cowers at sight of the phantom, death. Discipline is for the purpose of dominating that horror by a still greater horror, that of punishment or disgrace. But there always comes an instant when natural horror gets an upper hand over discipline, and the fighter flees. " Stop, stop, hold out a few minutes, an instant more, and you are victor! You are not even

wounded yet,— if you turn your back you are dead! "
He does not hear, he cannot hear any more. He is
full of fear. How many armies have sworn to conquer or perish? How many have kept their oaths?
An oath of sheep to stand up against wolves. History
shows, not armies, but firm souls who have fought
unto death, and the devotion of Thermopylæ is therefore justly immortal.

Here we are again brought to the consideration of
essential truths, enunciated by many men, now forgotten or unknown.

To insure success in the rude test of conflict, it is
not sufficient to have a mass composed of valiant men
like the Gauls or the Germans.

The mass needs, and we give it, leaders who have
the firmness and decision of command proceeding from
habit and an entire faith in their unquestionable right
to command as established by tradition, law and society.

We add good arms. We add methods of fighting
suitable to these arms and those of the enemy and
which do not overtax the physical and moral forces of
man. We add also a rational decentralization that
permits the direction and employment of the efforts of
all even to the last man.

We animate with passion, a violent desire for independence, a religious fanaticism, national pride, a love
of glory, a madness for possession. An iron discipline, which permits no one to escape action, secures
the greatest unity from top to bottom, between all the
elements, between the commanding officers, between
the commanding officers and men, between the soldiers.

Have we then a solid army? Not yet. Unity,
that first and supreme force of armies, is sought by

enacting severe laws of discipline supported by powerful passions. But to order discipline is not enough.
A vigilance from which no one may escape in combat
should assure the maintenance of discipline. Discipline itself depends on moral pressure which actuates
men to advance from sentiments of fear or pride.
But it depends also on surveillance, the mutual supervision of groups of men who know each other well.

A wise organization insures that the personnel of
combat groups changes as little as possible, so that
comrades in peace time maneuvers shall be comrades
in war. From living together, and obeying the same
chiefs, from commanding the same men, from sharing
fatigue and rest, from coöperation among men who
quickly understand each other in the execution of warlike movements, may be bred brotherhood, professional knowledge, sentiment, above all unity. The duty
of obedience, the right of imposing discipline and the
impossibility of escaping from it, would naturally
follow.

And now confidence appears.

It is not that enthusiastic and thoughtless confidence
of tumultous or unprepared armies which goes up to
the danger point and vanishes rapidly, giving way to a
contrary sentiment, which sees treason everywhere.
It is that intimate confidence, firm and conscious, which
does not forget itself in the heat of action and which
alone makes true combatants.

Then we have an army; and it is no longer difficult
to explain how men carried away by passions, even
men who know how to die without flinching, without
turning pale, really strong in the presence of death,
but without discipline, without solid organization, are

vanquished by others individually less valiant, but firmly, jointly and severally combined.

One loves to picture an armed mob upsetting all obstacles and carried away by a blast of passion.

There is more imagination than truth in that picture. If the struggle depended on individuals, the courageous, impassioned men, composing the mob would have more chance of victory. But in any body of troops, in front of the enemy, every one understands that the task is not the work of one alone, that to complete it requires team work. With his comrades in danger brought together under unknown leaders, he feels the lack of union, and asks himself if he can count on them. A thought of mistrust leads to hesitation. A moment of it will kill the offensive spirit.

Unity and confidence cannot be improvised. They alone can create that mutual trust, that feeling of force which gives courage and daring. Courage, that is the temporary domination of will over instinct, brings about victory.

Unity alone then produces fighters. But, as in everything, there are degrees of unity. Let us see whether modern is in this respect less exacting than ancient combat.

In ancient combat there was danger only at close quarters. If the troops had enough morale (which Asiatic hordes seldom had) to meet the enemy at broadsword's length, there was an engagement. Whoever was that close knew that he would be killed if he turned his back; because, as we have seen, the victors lost but few and the vanquished were exterminated. This simple reasoning held the men and made them fight, if it was but for an instant.

Neglecting the exceptional and very rare circumstances, which may bring two forces together, action to-day is brought on and fought out from afar. Danger begins at great distances, and it is necessary to advance for a long time under fire which at each step becomes heavier. The vanquished loses prisoners, but often, in dead and in wounded, he does not lose more than the victor.

Ancient combat was fought in groups close together, within a small space, in open ground, in full view of one another, without the deafening noise of present day arms. Men in formation marched into an action that took place on the spot and did not carry them thousands of feet away from the starting point. The surveillance of the leaders was easy, individual weakness was immediately checked. General consternation alone caused flight.

To-day fighting is done over immense spaces, along thinly drawn out lines broken every instant by the accidents and the obstacles of the terrain. From the time the action begins, as soon as there are rifle shots, the men spread out as skirmishers or, lost in the inevitable disorder of a rapid march,[1] escape the supervision of their commanding officers. A considerable number conceal themselves [2]; they get away from the engagement and diminish by just so much the material and moral effect and confidence of the brave ones who remain. This can bring about defeat.

[1] A result forced by the improvement of war appliances.

[2] In troops without cohesion, this movement begins at fifty leagues from the enemy. Numbers enter the hospitals without any other complaint than the lack of morale, which very quickly becomes a real disease. A Draconian discipline no longer exists; cohesion alone can replace it.

But let us look at man himself in ancient combat and in modern. In ancient combat: — I am strong, apt, vigorous, trained, full of calmness, presence of mind; I have good offensive and defensive weapons and trustworthy companions of long standing. They do not let me be overwhelmed without aiding me. I with them, they with me, we are invincible, even invulnerable. We have fought twenty battles and not one of us remained on the field. It is necessary to support each other in time; we see it clearly; we are quick to replace ourselves, to put a fresh combatant in front of a fatigued adversary. We are the legions of Marius, fifty thousand who have held out against the furious avalanches of the Cimbri. We have killed one hundred and forty thousand, taken prisoner sixty thousand, while losing but two or three hundred of our inexperienced soldiers.

To-day, as strong, firm, trained, and courageous as I am, I can never say; I shall return. I have no longer to do with men, whom I do not fear, I have to do with fate in the form of iron and lead. Death is in the air, invisible and blind, whispering, whistling. As brave, good, trustworthy, and devoted as my companions may be, they do not shield me. Only,— and this is abstract and less immediately intelligible to all than the material support of ancient combat,— only I imagine that the more numerous we are who run a dangerous risk, the greater is the chance for each to escape therefrom. I also know that, if we have that confidence which none of us should lack in action, we feel, and we are, stronger. We begin more resolutely, are ready to keep up the struggle longer, and therefore finish it more quickly.

We finish it! But in order to finish it, it is necessary to advance, to attack the enemy,[1] and infantryman or troopers, we are naked against iron, naked against lead, which cannot miss at close range. Let us advance in any case, resolutely. Our adversary will not stand at the point-blank range of our rifle, for the attack is never mutual, we are sure of that. We have been told so a thousand times. We have seen it. But what if matters should change now! Suppose the enemy stands at point-blank range! What of that?

How far this is from Roman confidence!

In another place we have shown that in ancient times to retire from action was both a difficult and perilous matter for the soldier. To-day the temptation is much stronger, the facility greater and the peril less.

Now, therefore, combat exacts more moral cohesion, greater unity than previously. A last remark on the difficulty of obtaining it will complete the demonstration.

Since the invention of fire arms, the musket, the rifle, the cannon, the distances of mutual aid and support have increased among the different arms.[2]

Besides, the facility of communications of all kinds permits the assembling on a given territory of enormous forces. For these reasons, as we have stated, battle fields have become immense.

[1] It is a troublesome matter to attack men who shoot six to eight shots a minute, no matter how badly aimed. Will he have the last word then, who has the last cartridge, who knows best how to make the enemy use his cartridges without using his own?

The reasoning is always the same. With arrows: Let us use up their arrows. With the club: Let us break their clubs. But how? That is always the question. In matters of war, above all, precept is easy; accomplishment is difficult.

[2] The more one imagines he is isolated, the more has he need of morale.

Supervision becomes more and more difficult. Direction being more distant tends more often to escape from the supreme commanders and the subordinate leaders. The certain and inevitable disorder, which a body of troops always presents in action, is with the moral effect of modern appliances, becoming greater every day. In the midst of the confusion and the vacillation of firing lines, men and commanding officers often lose each other.

Troops immediately and hotly engaged, such as companies and squads, can maintain themselves only if they are well-organized and serve as supports or rallying points to those out of place. Battles tend to become now, more than they have ever been, the battles of men.

This ought not to be true! Perhaps. But the fact is that it is true.

Not all troops are immediately or hotly engaged in battle. Commanding officers always try to keep in hand, as long as possible, some troops capable of marching, acting at any moment, in any direction. To-day, like yesterday, like to-morrow, the decisive action is that of formed troops. Victory belongs to the commander who has known how to keep them in good order, to hold them, and to direct them.

That is incontrovertible.

But commanders can hold out decisive reserves only if the enemy has been forced to commit his.

In troops which do the fighting, the men and the officers closest to them, from corporal to battalion commander, have a more independent action than ever. As it is alone the vigor of that action, more independent than ever of the direction of higher commanders, which leaves in the hands of higher commanders available forces which can be directed at a decisive moment.

that action becomes more preponderant than ever. Battles, now more than ever, are battles of men, of captains. They always have been in fact, since in the last analysis the execution belongs to the man in ranks. But the influence of the latter on the final result is greater than formerly. From that comes the maxim of to-day: The battles of men.

Outside of the regulations on tactics and discipline, there is an evident necessity for combating the hazardous predominance of the action of the soldier over that of the commander. It is necessary to delay as long as possible, that instant which modern conditions tend to hasten — the instant when the soldier gets from under the control of the commander.

This completes the demonstration of the truth stated before: Combat requires to-day, in order to give the best results, a moral cohesion, a unity more binding than at any other time.[1] It is as true as it is clear, that, if one does not wish bonds to break, one must make them elastic in order to strengthen them.

[1] Are not naval battles above all the battles of captains? All captains endeavor to promote a feeling of solidarity which will cause them all to fight unitedly on the day of action. Trafalgar — Lissa.

In 1588, the Duke of Medina Sidonia, preparing for a naval engagement, sent three commanders on light vessels to the advance-guard and three to the rearguard, with executioners, and ordered them to have every captain hanged who abandoned the post that had been assigned to him for the battle.

In 1702, the English Admiral Benbow, a courageous man, was left almost alone by his captains during three days of fighting. With an amputated leg and arm, before dying, he had four brought to trial. One was acquitted, three were hanged; and from that instant dates the inflexible English severity towards commanders of fleets and vessels, a severity necessary in order to force them to fight effectively.

Our commanders of battalions, our captains, our men, once under fire, are more at sea than these commanders of vessels.

CHAPTER VII

ANY other deductions on this subject must come from the meditations of the reader. To be of value in actual application such deductions should be based upon study of modern combat, and that study cannot be made from the accounts of historians alone.

The latter show the action of troop units only in a general way. Action in detail and the individual action of the soldier remain enveloped in a cloud of dust, in narratives as in reality. Yet these questions must be studied, for the conditions they reveal should be the basis of all fighting methods, past, present and future.

Where can data on these questions be found?

We have very few records portraying action as clearly as the report on the engagement at the Pont de l'Hôpital by Colonel Bugeaud. Such stories in even greater detail, for the smallest detail has its importance, secured from participants and witnesses who knew how to see and knew how to remember, are what is necessary in a study of the battle of to-day.

The number of killed, the kind and the character of wounds, often tell more than the longest accounts. Sometimes they contradict them. We want to know how man in general and the Frenchman in particular fought yesterday. Under the pressure of danger, impelled by the instinct for self-preservation, did he follow, make light of, or forget the methods prescribed or recommended? Did he fight in the manner imposed upon him, or in that indicated to him by his instinct or by his knowledge of warfare?

When we have the answers to these questions we shall be very near to knowing how he will conduct himself to-morrow, with and against appliances far more destructive to-day than those of yesterday. Even now, knowing that man is capable only of a given quantity of terror, knowing that the moral effect of destruction is in proportion to the force applied, we are able to predict that, to-morrow less than ever will studied methods be practicable. Such methods are born of the illusions of the field of fire and are opposed to the teachings of our own experience. To-morrow, more than ever, will the individual valor of the soldier and of small groups, be predominant. This valor is secured by discipline.

The study of the past alone can give us a true perception of practical methods, and enable us to see how the soldier will inevitably fight to-morrow.

So instructed, so informed, we shall not be confused; because we shall be able to prescribe beforehand such methods of fighting, such organization, such dispositions as are seen to be inevitable. Such prescriptions may even serve to regulate the inevitable. At any rate they will serve to reduce the element of chance by enabling the commanding officer to retain control as long as possible, and by releasing the individual only at the moment when instinct dominates him.

This is the only way to preserve discipline, which has a tendency to go to pieces by tactical disobedience at the moment of greatest necessity.

It should be understood that the prescriptions in

question have to do with dispositions before action; with methods of fighting, and not with maneuvers.

Maneuvers are the movements of troops in the theater of action, and they are the swift and ordered movement on the scene of action of tactical units of all sizes. They do not constitute action. Action follows them.

Confusion in many minds between maneuvers and action brings about doubt and mistrust of our regulation drills. These are good, very good as far as they go, inasmuch as they give methods of executing all movements, of taking all possible formations with rapidity and good order.

To change them, to discuss them, does not advance the question one bit. They do not affect the problem of positive action. Its solution lies in the study of what took place yesterday, from which, alone, it is possible to deduce what will happen to-morrow.

This study must be made, and its result set forth. Each leader, whose worth and authority has been tested in war and recognized by armies, has done something of the sort. Of each of these even might be said, " He knew the soldier; he knew how to make use of him."

The Romans, too, had this knowledge. They obtained it from continuous experience and profound reflexion thereon.

Experience is not continuous to-day. It must be carefully gathered. Study of it should be careful and the results should stimulate reflexion, especially in men of experience. Extremes meet in many things. In ancient times at the point of the pike and sword, armies have conquered similar armies twice their size. Who knows if, in these days of perfected long-range arms of destruction, a small force might not secure, by a happy combination of good sense or genius with morale and appliances, these same heroic victories over a greater force similarly armed? [1]

In spite of the statements of Napoleon I, his assumption that victory is always on the side of the strongest battalions was costly.

[1] The effect of surprise would certainly not last long to-day However, to-day wars are quickly decided.

PART II
MODERN BATTLE

CHAPTER I

1. *Ancient and Modern Battle*

I HAVE heard philosophers reproached for studying too exclusively man in general and neglecting the race, the country, the era, so that their studies of him offer little of real social or political value. The opposite criticism can be made of military men of all countries. They are always eager to expound traditional tactics and organization suitable to the particular character of their race, always the bravest of all races. They fail to consider as a factor in the problem, man confronted by danger. Facts are incredibly different from all theories. Perhaps in this time of military reorganization it would not be out of place to make a study of man in battle and of battle itself.

The art of war is subjected to many modifications by industrial and scientific progress. But one thing does not change, the heart of man. In the last analysis, success in battle is a matter of morale. In all matters which pertain to an army, organization, discipline and tactics, the human heart in the supreme moment of battle is the basic factor. It is rarely taken into account; and often strange errors are the result. Witness the carbine, an accurate and long range weapon, which has never given the service expected of it, because it was used mechanically without considering the human heart. We must consider it!

With improvement in weapons, the power of de-

135

struction increases, the moral effect of such weapons increases, and courage to face them becomes rarer. Man does not, cannot change. What should increase with the power of material is the strength of organization, the unity of the fighting machine. Yet these are most neglected. A million men at maneuvers are useless, if a sane and reasoned organization does not assure their discipline, and thereby their reliability, that is, their courage in action.

Four brave men who do not know each other will not dare to attack a lion. Four less brave, but knowing each other well, sure of their reliability and consequently of mutual aid, will attack resolutely. There is the science of the organization of armies in a nutshell.

At any time a new invention may assure victory. Granted. But practicable weapons are not invented every day, and nations quickly put themselves on the same footing as regards armament. The determining factor, leaving aside generals of genius, and luck, is the quality of troops, that is, the organization that best assures their esprit, their reliability, their confidence, their unity. Troops, in this sense, means soldiers. Soldiers, no matter how well drilled, who are assembled haphazard into companies and battalions will never have, have never had, that entire unity which is born of mutual acquaintanceship.

In studying ancient battle, we have seen what a terrible thing battle is. We have seen that man will not really fight except under disciplinary pressure. Even before having studied modern battle, we know that the only real armies are those to which a well thought out and rational organization gives unity throughout battle. The destructive power of improved firearms becomes greater. Battle becomes more open, hindering supervision, passing beyond the vision of the commander and even of subordinate officers. In the same degree, unity should be strengthened. The organization which assures unity of the combatants should be better thought out and more rational. The power of arms increases, man and his weaknesses remain the same. What good is an army of two hundred thousand men of whom only one-half really fight, while the other one hundred thousand disappear in a hundred ways? Better to have one hundred thousand who can be counted upon.

The purpose of discipline is to make men fight in spite of themselves. No army is worthy of the name without discipline. There is no army at all without organization, and all organization is defective which neglects any means to strengthen the unity of combatants. Methods cannot be identical. Draconian discipline does not fit our customs. Discipline must be a state of mind, a social institution based on the salient virtues and defects of the nation.

Discipline cannot be secured or created in a day. It is an institution, a tradition. The commander must have absolute confidence in his right to command. He must be accustomed to command and proud to command. This is what strengthens discipline in armies commanded by an aristocracy in certain countries.

The Prussians do not neglect the homogenity and consequent unity of organization. They recognize its value. Hessian regiments are composed, the first year, of one-third Hessians, two-thirds Prussians, to control the racial tendencies of troops of a recently annexed country; the second year, of two-thirds Hessians, one-third Prussians; the third year, all Hessians with their own officers.

The Americans have shown us what happens in mod-

ern battle to large armies without cohesion. With
them the lack of discipline and organization has had
the inevitable result. Battle has been between hidden
skirmishers, at long distance, and has lasted for days,
until some faulty movement, perhaps a moral exhaustion, has caused one or the other of the opposing forces
to give way.

In this American War, the mêlées of Agincourt are
said to have reappeared, which merely means a mêlée
of fugitives. But less than ever has there been close
combat.

To fight from a distance is instinctive in man.
From the first day he has worked to this end, and he
continues to do so. It was thought that with long
range weapons close combat might return. On the
contrary troops keep further off before its effects.

The primitive man, the Arab, is instability incarnate.
A breath, a nothing, governs him at each instant in war.
The civilized man, in war, which is opposed to civiliza-
tion, returns naturally to his first instincts.

With the Arab war remains a matter of agility and
cunning. Hunting is his principal pastime and the
pursuit of wild beasts teaches the pursuit of man.
General Daumas depicts Arabs as cavaliers. What
more chivalrous warfare than the night surprise and
sack of a camp! Empty words!!

It is commonly said that modern war is the most
recondite of things, requiring experts. War, so long
as man risks his skin in it, will always be a matter of
instinct.

Ancient battle resembled drill. There is no such resemblance in modern battle. This greatly disconcerts
both officers and soldiers.

Ancient battles were picnics, for the victors, who lost nobody. Not so to-day.

Artillery played no part in ancient battle.

The invention of firearms has diminished losses in battle. The improvement of firearms continues to diminish losses. This looks like a paradox. But statistics prove it. Nor is it unreasonable.

Does war become deadlier with the improvement of weapons? Not at all. Man is capable of standing before a certain amount of terror; beyond that he flees from battle. The battle of Pharsalus lasted some four hours. Cæsar broke his camp, which is done in the morning; then the formation for battle; then the battle, etc. And he says that his troops were tired, the battle having lasted up to noon. This indicates that he considered it long.

For the middle ages, consult Froissart. The knights in the Battle of the Thirty were armed for battle on foot which they preferred in a serious affair, that is to say in a restricted space. There was a halt, a rest in the combat, when the two parties became exhausted. The Bretons, at this rest, were twenty-five against thirty. The battle had lasted up to exhaustion without loss by the English! Without Montauban the battle would have been terminated by complete and mutual exhaustion and without further losses. For the greater the fatigue, the less strength remained for piercing the armor. Montauban was at the same time felon and hero; felon because he did a thing not permitted by the code of combat; hero, because, if the Bretons had not ably profited by the disorder, he would have been killed when he entered the English formation alone. At the end of the contest the Bretons had four killed, the Eng-

lish eight.   Four of the killed were overcome by their
armor.

Explain how, under Turenne, men held much longer
under fire than to-day.   It is perfectly simple.   Man is
capable of standing before only a certain amount of
terror.   To-day there must be swallowed in five minutes what took an hour under Turenne.   An example
will be given.

With the present arms, whose usage is generally
known, the instruction of the soldier is of little importance.   It does not make the soldier.   Take as an example the case of the peasants of the Vendée.   Their
unity and not individual instruction made them soldiers,
whose value could not be denied.   Such unity was natural in people of the same village of the same com-
mune, led in battle by their own lords, their own priests,
etc.

The greater the perfection of weapons, the more
dreadful becomes modern battle, and discipline becomes
more difficult to maintain.

The less mobile the troops, the deadlier are battles.
Bayonet attacks are not so easily made to-day, and
morale consequently is less affected, man fearing man
more than death.   Astonishing losses seem to have been
suffered without breaking by Turenne's armies.   Were
the casualty reports submitted by the captains of those
days correct?

Frederick liked to say that three men behind the
enemy were worth more than fifty in front of him, for
moral effect.   The field of action to-day is more extensive than in Frederick's time.   Battle is delivered on
more accidented terrain, as armies with great mobility
do not need any particular terrain to fight on.

The nature of ancient arms required close order.

Modern arms require open order, and they are at the same time of such terrible power that against them too often discipline is broken. What is the solution? Have your combatants opened out? Have them well acquainted with each other so as to have unity. Have reserves to threaten with, held with an iron hand.

Modern weapons have a terrible effect and are almost unbearable by the nervous system. Who can say that he has not been frightened in battle? Discipline in battle becomes the more necessary as the ranks become more open, and the material cohesion of the ranks not giving confidence, it must spring from a knowledge of comrades, and a trust in officers, who must always be present and seen. What man to-day advances with the confidence that rigid discipline and pride in himself gave the Roman soldier, even though the contest is no longer with man but with fate?

To-day the artillery is effective at great distances. There is much liberty of movement for the different arms. The apparent liasion between arms is lessened. This has its influence on morale. There is another advantage in reliable troops, in that they can be extended more widely, and will consequently suffer smaller losses and be in better morale for close conflict.

The further off one is, the more difficult it is to judge of the terrain. Consequently the greater is the necessity for scouting, for reconnoitering the terrain by skirmishers. This is something that the Duke of Gramont forgot at Nordlingen, and which is often forgotten; but it constitutes another important reason for the use of skirmishers.

The formation in rank is a disciplinary measure against the weakness of man in the face of danger. This weakness is greater to-day in that the moral action of weapons is more powerful, and that the material rank has the inherent lack of cohesion of open order. However, open order is necessary to economize losses and permit the use of weapons. Thus to-day there is greater necessity than ever for the rank, that is for discipline, not for the geometrical rank. It is at the same time more necessary and doubly difficult to attain.

In ancient battle unity existed, at least with the Greeks and the Romans. The soldier was known to his officer and comrades; they saw that he fought.

In modern armies where losses are as great for the victor as for the vanquished, the soldier must more often be replaced. In ancient battle the victor had no losses. To-day the soldier is often unknown to his comrades. He is lost in the smoke, the dispersion, the confusion of battle. He seems to fight alone. Unity is no longer insured by mutual surveillance. A man falls, and disappears. Who knows whether it was a bullet or the fear of advancing further that struck him! The ancient combatant was never struck by an invisible weapon and could not fall in this way. The more difficult surveillance, the more necessary becomes the individuality of companies, sections, squads. Not the least of their boasts should be their ability to stand a roll call at all times.

The ancients often avoided hand to hand conflict, so terrible were its consequences. In modern combat, there never is hand to hand conflict if one stands fast.

From day to day close combat tends to disappear. It is replaced by fire action; above all by the moral action of maneuvers. Dispersion brings us back to the necessity for the unity which was an absolute necessity in ancient battle.

Strategy is a game. The first strategist, long before Napoleon, was Horace with his three enemies.

The size of the battle field permits, less than ever, holding units together; the rôle of the general is much more difficult: many more chances are left to fate. Thus the greater the necessity for the best troops who know best their trade, who are most dependable and of greatest fortitude. To diminish the effect of luck, it is necessary to hold longer, to wait for help from a distance. Battles resolve themselves into battles of soldiers. The final decision is more difficult to obtain. There is a strange similarity in battle at one league to battle at two paces. The value of the soldier is the essential element of success. Let us strengthen the soldier by unity.

Battle has more importance than ever. Communication facilities such as the telegraph, concentration facilities such as the railroad, render more difficult such strategic surprises as Ulm and Jena. The whole forces of a country can thus be united. So united, defeat becomes irreparable, disorganization greater and more rapid.

In modern combat the mêlée really exists more than in ancient battle. This appears paradoxical. It is true nevertheless of the mêlée taken in the sense of a mixed up affair where it is infinitely difficult to see clearly.

Man, in the combat of our days, is a man who, hardly knowing how to swim, is suddenly thrown into the sea.

The good quality of troops will more than ever secure victory.

As to the comparative value of troops with cohesion

and of new troops, look at the Zouaves of the Guard or the Grenadiers at Magenta, and the 55th at Solferino.[1]

Nothing should be neglected to make the battle order stronger, man stronger.

2. *Moral Elements in Battle*

When, in complete security, after dinner, in full physical and moral contentment, men consider war and battle they are animated by a noble ardor that has nothing in common with reality. How many of them, however, even at that moment, would be ready to risk their lives? But oblige them to march for days and weeks to arrive at the battle ground, and on the day of battle oblige them to wait minutes, hours, to deliver it. If they were honest they would testify how much the physical fatigue and the mental anguish that precede action have lowered their morale, how much less eager to fight they are than a month before, when they arose from the table in a generous mood.

Man's heart is as changeable as fortune. Man shrinks back, apprehends danger in any effort in which he does not foresee success. There are some isolated characters of an iron temper, who resist the tendency; but they are carried away by the great majority (Bismarck).

Examples show that if a withdrawal is forced, the army is discouraged and takes flight (Frederick). The brave heart does not change.

Real bravery, inspired by devotion to duty, does not know panic and is always the same. The bravery sprung from hot blood pleases the Frenchman more. He understands it, it appeals to his vanity; it is a char-

[1] See Appendix VI. (Historical documents). (Editor's note).

acteristic of his nature. But it is passing; it fails him at times, especially when there is nothing for him to gain in doing his duty.

The Turks are full of ardor in the advance. They carry their officers with them. But they retreat with the same facility, abandoning their officers.

Mediocre troops like to be led by their shepherds. Reliable troops like to be directed, with their directors alongside of them or behind. With the former the general must be the leader on horseback; with the latter, the manager.

Warnery did not like officers to head a charge. He thought it useless to have them killed before the others. He did not place them in front and his cavalry was good.

General Leboeuf did not favor the proposed advance into battle with platoon leaders in front of the center of their platoons. The fear exists that the fall of the captain will demoralize the rest. What is the solution? Leboeuf must have known that if the officer is not in front of his command, it will advance less confidently, that, with us, all officers are almost always in advance. Practice is stronger than any theory. Therefore fit theories to it. In column, put the chiefs of platoon on the flank where they can see clearly.

Frightfulness! Witness the Turks in the Polish wars. What gave power to the Turks in their wars with Poland was not so much their real strength as their ferocity. They massacred all who resisted; they massacred without the excuse of resistance. Terror preceded them, breaking down the courage of their enemies. The necessity to win or to submit to extreme peril brought about cowardice and submission, for fear of being conquered.

Turenne said, " You tremble, body. . . ." The instinct of self-preservation can then make the strongest tremble. But they are strong enough to overcome their emotion, the fear of advancing, without even losing their heads or their coolness. Fear with them never becomes terror; it is forgotten in the activities of command. He who does not feel strong enough to keep his heart from ever being gripped by terror, should never think of becoming an officer.

The soldiers themselves have emotion. The sense of duty, discipline, pride, the example of their officers and above all their coolness, sustain them and prevent their fear from becoming terror. Their emotion never allows them to sight, or to more than approximately adjust their fire. Often they fire into the air. Cromwell knew this very well, dependable as his troops were, when he said, " Put your trust in God and aim at their shoe laces."

What is too true is that bravery often does not at all exclude cowardice, horrible devices to secure personal safety, infamous conduct.

The Romans were not mighty men, but men of discipline and obstinacy. We have no idea of the Roman military mind, so entirely different from ours. A Roman general who had as little coolness as we have would have been lost. We have incentives in decorations and medals that would have made a Roman soldier run the gauntlet.

How many men before a lion, have the courage to look him in the face, to think of and put into practice measures of self-defense? In war when terror has seized you, as experience has shown it often does, you are as before a lion. You fly trembling and let yourself be eaten up. Are there so few really brave men among so many soldiers? Alas, yes! Gideon was lucky to find three hundred in thirty thousand.

Napoleon said, " Two Mamelukes held three Frenchmen; but one hundred French cavalry did not fear the same number of Mamelukes; three hundred vanquished the same number; one thousand French beat fifteen hundred Mamelukes. Such was the influence of tactics, order and maneuver." In ordinary language, such was the great moral influence of unity, established by discipline and made possible and effective in battle by organization and mutual support. With unity and sensible formation men of an individual value one-third less beat those who were individually their betters. That is the essential, must be the essential, point in the organization of an army. On reflection, this simple statement of Napoleon's seems to contain the whole of battle morale. Make the enemy believe that support is lacking; isolate; cut off, flank, turn, in a thousand ways make his men believe themselves isolated. Isolate in like manner his squadrons, battalions, brigades and divisions; and victory is yours. If, on account of bad organization, he does not anticipate mutual support, there is no need of such maneuver; the attack is enough.

Some men, such as Orientals, Chinese, Tartars, Mongols do not fear death. They are resigned to it at all times. Why is it that they can not stand before the armies of the western people? It is lack of organization. The instinct of self-preservation which at the last moment dominates them utterly, is not opposed by discipline. We have often seen fanatic eastern peoples, implicitly believing that death in battle means a happy and glorious resurrection, superior in numbers, give way before discipline. If attacked confidently, they are crushed by their own weight. In close combat the dagger is better than the bayonet, but instinct is too strong for such people.

What makes the soldier capable of obedience and direction in action, is the sense of discipline. This includes: respect for and confidence in his chiefs; confidence in his comrades and fear of their reproaches and retaliation if he abandons them in danger; his desire to go where others do without trembling more than they; in a word, the whole of esprit de corps. Organization only can produce these characteristics. Four men equal a lion.

Note the army organizations and tactical formations on paper are always determined from the mechanical point of view, neglecting the essential coefficient, that of morale. They are almost always wrong.

Esprit de corps is secured in war. But war becomes shorter and shorter and more and more violent. Consequently, secure esprit de corps in advance.

Mental acquaintanceship is not enough to make a good organization. A good general esprit is needed. All must work for battle and not merely live, quietly going through with drills without understanding their application. Once a man knows how to use his weapon and obey all commands there is needed only occasional drill to brush up those who have forgotten. Marches and battle maneuvers are what is needed.

The technical training of the soldier is not the most difficult. It is necessary for him to know how to use and take care of his weapon; to know how to move to the right and to the left, forward, to the rear, at command, to charge and to march with full pack. But this does not make the soldier. The Vendeans, who knew little of this, were tough soldiers.

It is absolutely necessary to change the instruction, to

reduce it to the necessary minimum and to cut out all the superfluities with which peacetime laborers overload it each year. To know the essential well is better than having some knowledge of a lot of things, many of them useless. Teach this the first year, that the second, but the essential from the beginning! Also instruction should be simple to avoid the mental fatigue of long drills that disgust everybody.

Here is a significant sentence in Colonel Borbstæd's enumeration of the reasons for Prussian victory over the Austrians in 1866, " It was . . . because each man, being trained, knew how to act promptly and confidently in all phases of battle." This is a fact.

To be held in a building, at every minute of the day to have every movement, every attitude under a not too intelligent surveillance is indeed to be harried. This incessant surveillance weakens the morale of both the watched and the watcher. What is the reason for this incessant surveillance which has long since exceeded shipboard surveillance? Was not that strict enough?

3. *Material and Moral Effect.*

The effect of an army, of one organization on another, is at the same time material and moral. The material effect of an organization is in its power to destroy, the moral effect in the fear that it inspires.

In battle, two moral forces, even more than two material forces, are in conflict. The stronger conquers, The victor has often lost by fire more than the vanquished. Moral effect does not come entirely from destructive power, real and effective as it may be. It comes, above all, from its presumed, threatening power, present in the form of reserves threatening to renew the battle, of troops that appear on the flank, even of a determined frontal attack.

Material effect is greater as instruments are better (weapons, mounts, etc.), as the men know better how to use them, and as the men are more numerous and stronger, so that in case of success they can carry on longer.

With equal or even inferior power of destruction he will win who has the resolution to advance, who by his formations and maneuvers can continually threaten his adversary with a new phase of material action, who, in a word has the moral ascendancy. Moral effect inspires fear. Fear must be changed to terror in order to vanquish.

When confidence is placed in superiority of material means, valuable as they are against an enemy at a distance, it may be betrayed by the actions of the enemy. If he closes with you in spite of your superiority in means of destruction, the morale of the enemy mounts with the loss of your confidence. His morale dominates yours. You flee. Entrenched troops give way in this manner.

At Pharsalus, Pompey and his army counted on a cavalry corps turning and taking Cæsar in the rear. In addition Pompey's army was twice as numerous. Cæsar parried the blow, and his enemy, who saw the failure of the means of action he counted on, was demoralized, beaten, lost fifteen thousand men put to the sword (while Cæsar lost only two hundred) and as many prisoners.

Even by advancing you affect the morale of the enemy. But your object is to dominate him and make him retreat before your ascendancy, and it is certain that everything that diminishes the enemy's morale adds to your resolution in advancing. Adopt then a formation which permits your destructive agency, your skirmishers, to help you throughout by their material action and to this degree diminish that of the enemy.

Armor, in diminishing the material effect that can be suffered, diminishes the dominating moral effect of fear. It is easy to understand how much armor adds to the moral effect of cavalry action, at the critical moment. You feel that thanks to his armor the enemy will succeed in getting to you.

It is to be noted that when a body actually awaits the attack of another up to bayonet distance (something extraordinarily rare), and the attacking troop does not falter, the first does not defend itself. This is the massacre of ancient battle.

Against unimaginative men, who retain some coolness and consequently the faculty of reasoning in danger, moral effect will be as material effect. The mere act of attack does not completely succeed against such troops. (Witness battles in Spain and Waterloo). It is necessary to destroy them, and we are better at this than they by our aptitude in the use of skirmishers and above all in the mad dash of our cavalry. But the cavalry must not be treated, until it comes to so consider itself, as a precious jewel which must be guarded against injury. There should be little of it, but it must be good.

" Seek and ye shall find " not the ideal but the best method that exists. In maneuvers skirmishers, who have some effect, are returned to ranks to execute fire in two ranks which never killed anybody. Why not put your skirmishers in advance? Why sound trum-

pet calls which they neither hear no understand? That
they do not is fortunate, for each captain has a different
call sounded. Example: at Alma, the retreat, etc.[1]

The great superiority of Roman tactics lay in their
constant endeavor to coördinate physical and moral effect. Moral effect passes; finally one sees that the
enemy is not so terrible as he appeared to be. Physical effect does not. The Greeks tried to dominate.
The Romans preferred to kill, and kill they did. They
followed thereby the better method. Their moral effect was aided by their reliable and deadly swords.

What moral force is worth to a nation at war is
shown by examples. Pichegru played the traitor; this
had great influence at home and we were beaten. Napoleon came back; victory returned with him.

But at that we can do nothing without good troops,
not even with a Napoleon. Witness Turenne's army
after his death. It remained excellent in spite of conflict between and the inefficiency of its two leaders.
Note the defensive retreat across the Rhine; the regiment in Champagne attacked in front by infantry and
taken in the rear by cavalry. One of the prettiest feats
of the art of war.

In modern battle, which is delivered with combatants so far apart, man has come to have a horror of
man. He comes to hand to hand fighting only to
defend his body or if forced to it by some fortuitous
encounter. More than that! It may be said that he
seeks to catch the fugitive only for fear that he will
turn and fight.

Guilbert says that shock actions are infinitely rare.
Here, infinity is taken in its exact mathematical sense.
Guilbert reduces to nothing, by deductions from prac-

[1] See Appendix VI. (Historical documents). (Editor's note).

tical examples, the mathematical theory of the shock of one massed body on another. Indeed the physical impulse is nothing. The moral impulse which estimates the attacker is everything. The moral impulse lies in the perception by the enemy of the resolution that animates you. They say that the battle of Amstetten was the only one in which a line actually waited for the shock of another line charging with the bayonets. Even then the Russians gave way before the moral and not before the physical impulse. They were already disconcerted, wavering, worried, hesitant, vacillating, when the blow fell. They waited long enough to receive bayonet thrusts, even blows with the rifle (in the back, as at Inkerman).[1]

This done, they fled. He who calm and strong of heart awaits his enemy, has all the advantage of fire. But the moral impulse of the assailant demoralizes the assailed. He is frightened; he sets his sight no longer; he does not even aim his piece. His lines are broken without defense, unless indeed his cavalry, waiting halted, horsemen a meter apart and in two ranks, does not break first and destroy all formation.

With good troops on both sides, if an attack is not prepared, there is every reason to believe that it will fail. The attacking troops suffer more, materially, than the defenders. The latter are in better order, fresh, while the assailants are in disorder and already have suffered a loss of morale under a certain amount of punishment. The moral superiority given by the offensive movement may be more than compensated by the good order and integrity of the defenders, when the assailants have suffered losses. The slightest reaction by the defense may demoralize the attack. This

[1] See Appendix VI. (Historical documents). (Editor's note).

is the secret of the success of the British infantry in Spain, and not their fire by rank, which was as ineffective with them as with us.

The more confidence one has in his methods of attack or defense, the more disconcerted he is to see them at some time incapable of stopping the enemy. The effect of the present improved fire arm is still limited, with the present organization and use of riflemen, to point blank ranges. It follows that bayonet charges (where bayonet thrusts never occur), otherwise attacks under fire, will have an increasing value, and that victory will be his who secures most order and determined dash. With these two qualities, too much neglected with us, with willingness, with intelligence enough to keep a firm hold on troops in immediate support, we may hope to take and to hold what we take. Do not then neglect destructive effort before using moral effect. Use skirmishers up to the last moment. Otherwise no attack can succeed. It is true it is haphazard fire, nevertheless it is effective because of its volume.

This moral effect must be a terrible thing. A body advances to meet another. The defender has only to remain calm, ready to aim, each man pitted against a man before him. The attacking body comes within deadly range. Whether or not it halts to fire, it will be a target for the other body which awaits it, calm, ready, sure of its effect. The whole first rank of the assailant falls, smashed. The remainder, little encouraged by their reception, disperse automatically or before the least indication of an advance on them. Is this what happens? Not at all! The moral effect of the assault worries the defenders. They fire in the air if at all. They disperse immediately before the assailants who are even encouraged by this fire now that it is over. It quickens them in order to avoid a second salvo.

It is said by those who fought them in Spain and at Waterloo that the British are capable of the necessary coolness. I doubt it nevertheless. After firing, they made swift attacks. If they had not, they might have fled. Anyhow the English are stolid folks, with little imagination, who try to be logical in all things. The French with their nervous irritability, their lively imagination, are incapable of such a defense.

Anybody who thinks that he could stand under a second fire is a man without any idea of battle. (Prince de Ligne).

Modern history furnishes us with no examples of stonewall troops who can neither be shaken nor driven back, who stand patiently the heaviest fire, yet who retire precipitately when the general orders the retreat. (Bismarck).

Cavalry maneuvers, like those of infantry, are threats. The most threatening win. The formation in ranks is a threat, and more than a threat. A force engaged is out of the hand of its commander. I know, I see what it does, what it is capable of. It acts; I can estimate the effect of its action. But a force in formation is in hand; I know it is there, I see it, feel it. It may be used in any direction. I feel instinctively that it alone can surely reach me, take me on the right, on the left, throw itself into a gap, turn me. It troubles me, threatens me. Where is the threatened blow going to fall?

The formation in ranks is a serious threat, which may at any moment be put into effect. It awes one in a terrible fashion. In the heat of battle, formed troops do more to secure victory than do those actively engaged. This is true, whether such a body actually exists or whether it exists only in the imagination of the enemy. In an indecisive battle, he wins who can show, and merely show, battalions and squadrons in hand. They inspire the fear of the unknown.

From the taking of the entrenchments at Fribourg up to the engagement at the bridge of Arcola, up to Solferino, there occur a multitude of deeds of valor, of positions taken by frontal attack, which deceive every one, generals as well as civilians, and which always cause the same mistakes to be made. It is time to teach these folks that the entrenchments at Fribourg were not won by frontal attack, nor was the bridge of Arcola (see the correspondence of Napoleon I), nor was Solferino.

Lieutenant Hercule took fifty cavalry through Alpon, ten kilometers on the flank of the Austrians at Arcola, and the position that held us up for three days, was evacuated. The evacuation was the result of strategic, if not of tactical, moral effect. General or soldier, man is the same.

Demonstrations should be made at greater or less distance, according to the morale of the enemy. That is to say, battle methods vary with the enemy, and an appropriate method should be employed in each individual case.

We have treated and shall treat only of the infantryman. In ancient as in modern battle, he is the one who suffers most. In ancient battle, if he is defeated, he remains because of his slowness at the mercy of the victor. In modern battle the mounted man moves swiftly through danger, the infantryman has to walk. He even has to halt in danger, often and for long periods of time. He who knows the morale of the infantryman, which is put to the hardest proof, knows the morale of all the combatants.

4. *The Theory of Strong Battalions.*

To-day, numbers are considered the essential. Napoleon had this tendency (note his strength reports). The Romans did not pay so much attention to it. What they paid most attention to was to seeing that everybody fought. We assume that all the personnel present with an army, with a division, with a regiment on the day of battle, fights. Right there is the error.

The theory of strong battalions is a shameful theory. It does not reckon on courage but on the amount of human flesh. It is a reflection on the soul. Great and small orators, all who speak of military matters to-day, talk only of masses. War is waged by enormous masses, etc. In the masses, man as an individual disappears, the number only is seen. Quality is forgotten, and yet to-day as always, quality alone produces real effect. The Prussians conquered at Sadowa with made soldiers, united, accustomed to discipline. Such soldiers can be made in three or four years now, for the material training of the soldier is not indeed so difficult.

Cæsar had legions that he found unseasoned, not yet dependable, which had been formed for nine years.

Austria was beaten because her troops were of poor quality, because they were conscripts.

Our projected organization will give us four hundred thousand good soldiers. But all our reserves will be without cohesion, if they are thrown into this or that organization on the eve of battle, At a distance, numbers of troops without cohesion may be impressive, but close up they are reduced to fifty or twenty-five per cent. who really fight. Wagram was not too well executed. It illustrated desperate efforts that had for once a moral effect on an impressionable enemy. But for once only. Would they succeed again?

The Cimbrians gave an example [1] and man has not changed. Who to-day is braver than they were? And they did not have to face artillery, nor rifles.

Originally Napoleon found as an instrument, an army with good battle methods, and in his best battles, combat followed these methods. He himself prescribed, at least so they say, for he misrepresented at Saint Helena, the methods used at Wagram, at Eylau, at Waterloo, and engaged enormous masses of infantry which did not give material effect. But it involved a frightful loss of men and a disorder that, after they had once been unleashed, did not permit of the rallying and reëmployment that day of the troops engaged. This was a barbaric method, according to the Romans, amateurish, if we may say such a thing of such a man; a method which could not be used against experienced and well trained troops such as d'Erlon's corps at Waterloo. It proved disastrous.

Napoleon looked only at the result to be attained. When his impatience, or perhaps the lack of experience and knowledge in his officers and soldiers, forbade his continued use of real attack tactics, he completely sacrificed the material effect of infantry and even that of cavalry to the moral effect of masses. The personnel of his armies was too changing. In ancient battle victory cost much less than with modern armies, and the same soldiers remained longer in ranks. At the end

[1] See Appendix VI. (Historical documents). (Editor's note).

of his campaigns, when he had soldiers sixty years old, Alexander had lost only seven hundred men by the sword. Napoleon's system is more practicable with the Russians, who naturally group together, mass up, but it is not the most effective. Note the mass formation at Inkerman.[1]

What did Napoleon I do? He reduced the rôle of man in battle. and depended instead on formed masses. We have not such magnificent material.

Infantry and cavalry masses showed, toward the end of the Empire, a tactical degeneracy resulting from the wearing down of their elements and the consequent lowering of standards of morale and training. But since the allies had recognized and adopted our methods, Napoleon really had a reason for trying something so old that it was new to secure that surprise which will give victory once. It can give victory only once however, tried again surprise will be lacking. This was sort of a desperate method which Napoleon's supremacy allowed him to adopt when he saw his prestige waning.

When misfortune and lack of cannon fodder oppressed him, Napoleon became again the practical man not blinded by his supremacy. His entire good sense, his genius, overcame the madness to conquer at all price, and we have his campaign of 1814.

General Ambert says: " Without military traditions, almost without a command, these confused masses (the American armies of the Civil War) struck as men struck at Agincourt and Crecy." At Agincourt and Crecy, we struck very little, but were struck a lot. These battles were great slaughters of Frenchmen, by English and other Frenchmen, who did not greatly

[1] See Appendix VI. (Historical documents). (Editor's note).

suffer themselves. In what, except in disorder, did the American battles resemble these butcheries with the knife? The Americans were engaged as skirmishers at a distance of leagues. In seeking a resemblance the general has been carried away by the mania for phrase-making.

Victory is always for the strong battalions. This is true. If sixty determined men can rout a battalion, these sixty must be found. Perhaps only as many will be found as the enemy has battalions (Note Gideon's proportion of three hundred to thirty thousand of one to one hundred.) Perhaps it would be far and away better, under these circumstances, to fight at night.

5. Combat Methods

Ancient battle was fought in a confined space. The commander could see his whole force. Seeing clearly, his account should have been clear, although we note that many of these ancient accounts are obscure and incomplete, and that we have to supplement them. In modern battle nobody knows what goes on or what has gone on, except from results. Narrations cannot enter into details of execution.

It is interesting to compare tales of feats of arms, narrated by the victor (so-called) or the vanquished. It is hard to tell which account is truthful, if either. Mere assurance may carry weight. Military politics may dictate a perversion of the facts for disciplinary, moral or political reasons. (Note Sommo-Sierra.)

It is difficult even to determine losses, the leaders are such consummate liars. Why is this?

It is bewildering to read a French account and then

a foreign account of the same event, the facts stated are so entirely different. What is the truth? Only results can reveal it, such results as the losses on both sides. They are really instructive if they can be gotten at.

I believe that under Turenne there was not existent to the same degree a national pride which tended to hide unpleasant truths. The troops in contending armies were often of the same nation.

If national vanity and pride were not so touchy about recent occurrences, still passionately debated, numerous lessons might be drawn from our last wars. Who can speak impartially of Waterloo, or Waterloo so much discussed and with such heat, without being ashamed? Had Waterloo been won, it would not have profited us. Napoleon attempted the impossible, which is beyond even genius. After a terrible fight against English firmness and tenacity, a fight in which we were not able to subdue them, the Prussians appear. We would have done no better had they not appeared, but they did, very conveniently to sustain our pride. They were confronted. Then the rout began. It did not begin in the troops facing the Prussians but in those facing the English, who were exhausted perhaps, but not more so than their enemies. This was the moral effect of an attack on their right, when they had rather expected reinforcements to appear. The right conformed to the retrograde movement. And what a movement it was!

Why do not authorities acknowledge facts and try to formulate combat methods that conform to reality? It would reduce a little the disorder that bothers men not warned of it. They jump perhaps from the frying pan into the fire. I have known two colonels, one of them a very brave man, who said, " Let soldiers alone before the enemy. They know what to do better than you do." This is a fine statement of French confidence! That they know better than you what should be done. Especially in a panic, I suppose!

A long time ago the Prince de Ligne justified battle formations, above all the famous oblique formation. Napoleon decided the question. All discussions of formations is pedantry. But there are moral reasons for the power of the depth formation.

The difference between practice and theory is incredible. A general, who has given directions a thousand times on the battle field, when asked for directions, gives this order, " Go there, Colonel." The colonel, a man of good sense, says, " Will you explain, sir? What point do you want me to guide on? How far should I extend? Is there anybody on my right? On my left?" The general says, " Advance on the enemy, sir. It seems to me that that ought to be enough. What does this hesitation mean?" But my dear general, what are your orders? An officer should know where his command is, and the command itself should know. Space is large. If you do not know where to send your troops, and how to direct them, to make them understand where they are to go, to give them guides if necessary, what sort of general are you?"

What is our method for occupying a fortified work, or a line? We have none! Why not adopt that of Marshal Saxe? Ask several generals how they would do it. They will not know.

There is always mad impatience for results, without considering the means. A general's ability lies in judging the best moment for attack and in knowing how to prepare for it. We took Melegnano without artillery, without maneuver, but at what a price! At Waterloo the Hougoumont farm held us up all day, cost us dear and disorganized us into a mad mob, until Napoleon finally sent eight mortars to smash and burn the château. This is what should have been done at the commencement of the general attack.

A rational and ordered method of combat, or if not ordered, known to all, is enough to make good troops, if there is discipline be it understood. The Portugese infantry in the Spanish War, to whom the English had taught their method of combat, almost rivalled the English infantry. To-day who has formulated method? Who has a traditional method? Ask the generals. No two will agree.

We have a method, a manner rather, that accords with the national tendency, that of skirmishers in large numbers. But this formation is nowhere formulated. Before a campaign it is decried. Properly so, for it degenerates rapidly into a flock of lost sheep. Consequently troops come to the battle field entirely unused to reality. All the leaders, all the officers, are confused and unoriented. This goes so far that often generals are found who have lost their divisions or brigades; staff officers who have lost their generals and their divisions both; and, although this is more easily understood, many company officers who have lost their commands. This is a serious matter, which might cost us dear in a prolonged war in which the enemy gains experience. Let us hope that experience will lead us, not to change the principle. but to modify and form in a practical way our characteristic battle

method of escaping by advancing. The brochure of
the Prince of Prussia shows that, without having
fought us, the Prussians understand our methods.

There are men such as Marshal Bugeaud who are
born warriors in character, mental attitude, intelligence
and temperament. They recommend and show by
example, such as Colonel Bugeaud's battles in 1815 at
the Hospital bridge, tactics entirely appropriate to their
national and personal characters. Note Wellington
and the Duke of York among the English. But the
execution of tactics such as Bugeaud's requires officers
who resemble their commanders, at least in courage and
decisions. All officers are not of such temper. There
is need then of prescribed tactics conforming to the
national character, which may serve to guide an ordinary officer without requiring him to have the exceptional ability of a Bugeaud. Such prescribed tactics
would serve an officer as the perfectly clear and well
defined tactics of the Roman legion served the legion
commander. The officer could not neglect them without failing in his duty. Of course they will not make
him an exceptional leader. But, except in case of ut-
ter incapacity they will keep him from entirely failing in his task, from making absurd mistakes. Nor
will they prevent officers of Bugeaud's temper from
using their ability. They will on the contrary help
them by putting under their command men prepared
for the details of battle, which will not then come to
them as a surprise.

This method need not be as completely dogmatic as
the Roman. Our battle is too varying an affair. But
some clearly defined rules, established by experience,
would prevent the gross errors of inefficients. (Such
as causing skirmishers to fall back when the formed

rank fires, and consequently allowing them to carry with them in their retreat, the rank itself.) They would be useful aids to men of coolness and decision.

The laying down of such tactics would answer the many who hold that everything is improvised on the battle field and who find no better improvisation than to leave the soldier to himself. (See above.)

We should try to exercise some control over our soldiers, who advance by flight (note the Vendeans) or escape by advancing, as you like. But if something unexpected surprises them, they flee as precipitately.

Invention is less needed than verification, demonstration and organization of proper methods. To verify; observe better. To demonstrate; try out and describe better. To organize, distribute better, bearing in mind that cohesion means discipline. I do not know who put things that way; but it is truer than ever in this day of invention.

With us very few reason or understand reason, very few are cool. Their effect is negligible in the disorder of the mass; it is lost in numbers. It follows that we above all need a method of combat, sanely thought out in advance. It must be based on the fact that we are not passively obedient instruments, but very nervous and restless people, who wish to finish things quickly and to know in advance where we are going. It must be based on the fact that we are very proud people, but people who would all skulk if we were not seen, and who consequently must always be seen, and act in the presence of our comrades and of the officers who supervise us. From this comes the necessity for organizing the infantry company solidly. It is the infantryman on whom the battle has the most violent effect, for he is always most exposed; it is he therefore who must be the most solidly supported. Unity must be secured by a mutual acquaintanceship of long standing between all elements.

If you only use combat methods that require leaders without fear, of high intelligence, full of good sense, of esprit, you will always make mistakes. Bugeaud's method was the best for him. But it is evident, in his fight at the Hospital bridge that his battalion commanders were useless. If he had not been there, all would have been lost. He alone, omnipresent, was capable of resolute blows that the others could not execute. His system can be summed up in two phrases; always attack even when on the defensive; fire and take cover only when not attacked. His method was rational, considering his mentality and the existing conditions, but in carrying it into execution he judged his officers and soldiers by himself and was deceived. No dogmatic principles can be drawn from his method, nor from any other. Man is always man. He does not always possess ability and resolution. The commander must make his choice of methods, depending on his troops and on himself.

The essential of tactics is: the science of making men fight with their maximum energy. This alone can give an organization with which to fight fear. This has always been true.

We must start here and figure mathematically. Mathematics is the dominant science in war, just as battle is its only purpose. Pride generally causes refusal to acknowledge the truth that fear of being vanquished is basic in war. In the mass, pride, vanity, is responsible for this dissimulation. With the tiny number of absolutely fearless men, what is responsible is their ignorance of a thing they do not feel.

There is however, no real basis but this, and all real tactics are based on it. Discipline is a part of tactics, is absolutely at the base of tactics, as the Romans showed. They excelled the Gauls in intelligence, but not in bravery.

To start with: take battalions of four companies, four platoons each, in line or in column. The order of battle may be: two platoons deployed as skirmishers, two companies in reserve, under command of the battalion commander. In obtaining a decision destructive action will come from skirmishers. This action should be directed by battalion commanders, but such direction is not customary. No effect will be secured from skirmishers at six hundred paces. They will never, never, never, be nicely aligned in front of their battalions, calm and collected, after an advance. They will not, even at maneuvers. The battalion commander ought to be advanced enough to direct his skirmishers. The whole battalion, one-half engaged, one-half ready for any effort, ought to remain under his command, under his personal direction as far as possible. In the advance the officers, the soldiers, are content if they are merely directed; but, when the battle becomes hot, they must see their commander, know him to be near. It does not matter even if he is without initiative, incapable of giving an order. His presence creates a belief that direction exists, that orders exist, and that is enough.

When the skirmishers meet with resistance, they fall back to the ranks. It is the rôle of reserves to support and reinforce the line, and above all, by a swift charge to cut the enemy's line. This then falls back and the skirmishers go forward again, if the advance is resumed. The second line should be in the formation,

battalions in line or in column, that hides it best.
Cover the infantry troops before their entry into action; cover them as much as possible and by any means;
take advantage of the terrain; make them lie down.
This is the English method in defense of heights, in-
stanced in Spain and at Waterloo. Only one bugle to
each battalion should sound calls. What else is there
to be provided for?

Many haughty generals would scream protests like
eagles if it were suggested that they take such precautions for second line battalions or first line troops not
committed to action. Yet this is merely a sane measure to insure good order without the slightest implica-
tion of cowardice.[1]

With breech-loading weapons, the skirmishers on the
defensive fire almost always from a prone position.
They are made to rise with difficulty, either for retreat
or for advance. This renders the defense more tenacious . . .

[1] It is true that such measures are recommended in camps of
instruction and in publications. But in maneuvers they are
neglected in the mania for alignment, and in that other mad
desire of generals to mix in details which do not concern them.

CHAPTER II

1. *Masses — Deep Columns*

STUDY of the effect of columns brings us to the consideration of mass operations in general. Read this singular argument in favor of attacks by battalions in close columns: " A column cannot stop instantly without a command. Suppose your first rank stops at the instant of shock: the twelve ranks of the battalion, coming up successively, would come in contact with it, pushing it forward. . . . Experiments made have shown that beyond the sixteenth the impulsion of the ranks in rear has no effect on the front, it is completely taken up by the fifteen ranks already massed behind the first. . . . To make the experiment, march at charging pace and command halt to the front rank without warning the rest. The ranks will precipitate themselves upon each other unless they be very attentive, or unless, anticipating the command, they check themselves unconsciously while marching."

But in a real charge, all your ranks are attentive, restless, anxious about what is taking place at the front and, if the latter halts, if the first line stops, there will be a movement to the rear and not to the front. Take a good battalion, possessed of extraordinary calmness and coolness, thrown full speed on the enemy, at one hundred and twenty steps to the minute. To-day it would have to advance under a fire of five shots a min-

169

ute! At this last desperate moment if the front rank stops, it will not be pushed, according to the theory of successive impulses, it will be upset. The second line will arrive only to fall over the first and so on. There should be a drill ground test to see up to what rank this falling of the pasteboard figures would extend.

Physical impulse is merely a word. If the front rank stops it will let itself fall and be trampled under foot rather than cede to the pressure that pushes it forward. Any one experienced in infantry engagements of to-day knows that is just what happens. This shows the error of the theory of physical impulse — a theory that continues to dictate as under the Empire (so strong is routine and prejudice) attacks in close column. Such attacks are marked by absolute disorder and lack of leadership. Take a battalion fresh from barracks, in light marching order; intent only on the maneuver to be executed. It marches in close column in good order; its subdivisions are full four paces apart. The non-commissioned officers control the men. But it is true that if the terrain is slightly accidented, if the guide does not march with mathematical precis-cision, the battalion in close column becomes in the twinkling of an eye a flock of sheep. What would happen to a battalion in such a formation, at one hundred paces from the enemy? Nobody will ever see such an instance in these days of the rifle.

If the battalion has marched resolutely, if it is in good order, it is ten to one that the enemy has already withdrawn without waiting any longer. But suppose the enemy does not flinch? Then the man of our days, naked against iron and lead, no longer controls himself. The instinct of preservation controls him absolutely. There are two ways of avoiding or diminishing the danger; they are to flee or to throw one-self upon it. Let us rush upon it. Now, however small the intervals of space and time that separate us from the enemy, instinct shows itself. We rush forward, but . . . generally, we rush with prudence, with a tendency to let the most urgent ones, the most intrepid ones, pass on. It is strange, but true, that the nearer we approach the enemy, the less we are closed up. Adieu to the theory of pressure. If the front rank is stopped, those behind fall down rather than push it. Even if this front rank is pushed, it will itself fall down rather than advance. There is nothing to wonder at, it is sheer fact. Any pushing is to the rear. (Battle of Diernstein.)

To-day more than ever flight begins in the rear, which is affected quite as much as the front.

Mass attacks are incomprehensible. Not one out of ten was ever carried to completion and none of them could be maintained against counter-attacks. They can be explained only by the lack of confidence of the generals in their troops. Napoleon expressly condemns in his memoirs such attacks. He, therefore, never ordered them. But when good troops were used up, and his generals believed they could not obtain from young troops determined attacks in tactical formation, they came back to the mass formation, which belongs to the infancy of the art, as a desperate resort.

If you use this method of pressing, of pushing, your force will disappear as before a magician's wand.

But the enemy does not stand; the moral pressure of danger that precedes you is too strong for him. Otherwise, those who stood and aimed even with empty rifles, would never see a charge come up to them. The

first line of the assailant would be sensible of death
and no one would wish to be in the first rank.   Therefore, the enemy never merely stands; because if he
does, it is you that flee.   This always does away with
the shock.   The enemy entertains no smaller anxiety
than yours.   When he sees you near, for him also
the question is whether to flee or to advance.   Two
moral impulses are in conflict.

This is the instinctive reasoning of the officer and
soldier, " If these men wait for me to close with them,
it means death.   I will kill, but I will undoubtedly be
killed.   At the muzzle of the gun-barrel the bullet
can not fail to find its mark.   But if I can frighten
them, they will run away.   I can shoot them and bayonet in the back.   Let us make a try at it."   The trial
is made, and one of the two forces, at some stage of the
advance, perhaps only at two paces, makes an about
and gets the bayonet in the back.

Imagination always sees loaded arms and this fancy
is catching.

The shock is a mere term.   The de Saxe, the Bugeaud
theory: " Close with the bayonet and with fire action
at close quarters.   That is what kills people and the
victor is the one who kills most," is not founded on
fact.   No enemy awaits you if you are determined,
and never, never, never, are two equal determinations
opposed to each other.   It is well known to everybody,
to all nations, that the French have never met any one
who resisted a bayonet charge.

The English in Spain, marching resolutely in face
of the charges of the French in column, have always
defeated them. . . . The English were not dismayed
at the mass.   If Napoleon had recalled the defeat of
the giants of the Armada by the English vessels, he

might not have ordered the use of the d'Erlon column.

Blücher in his instructions to his troops, recalled that the French have never held out before the resolute march of the Prussians in attack column . . .

Suvaroff used no better tactics. Yet his battalions in Italy drove us at the point of their bayonets.

Each nation in Europe says: " No one stands his ground before a bayonet charge made by us." All are right. The French, no more than others, resist a resolute attack. All are persuaded that their attacks are irresistable; that an advance will frighten the enemy into flight. Whether the bayonet be fixed or in the scabbard makes no difference. . . .

There is an old saying that young troops become uneasy if any one comes upon them in a tumult and in disorder; the old troops, on the contrary, see victory therein. At the commencement of a war, all troops are young. Our impetuosity pushes us to the front like fools . . . the enemy flees. If the war lasts, everybody becomes inured. The enemy no longer troubles himself when in front of troops charging in a disordered way, because he knows and feels that they are moved as much by fear as by determination. Good order alone impresses the enemy in an attack, for it indicates real determination. That is why it is necessary to secure good order and retain it to the very last. It is unwise to take the running step prematurely, because you become a flock of sheep and leave so many men behind that you will not reach your objective. The close column is absurd; it turns you in advance into a flock of sheep, where officers and men are jumbled together without mutual support. It is then necessary to march as far as possible in such order as best permits the action of the non-commissioned officers, the action of unity, every one marching in front of eye-witnesses, in the open. On the other hand, in closed columns man marches unobserved and on the slightest pretext he lies down or remains behind. Therefore, it is best always to keep the skirmishers in advance or on the flanks, and never to recall them when in proximity to the enemy. To do so establishes a counter current that carries away your men. Let your skirmishers alone. They are your lost children; they will know best how to take care of themselves.

To sum up: there is no shock of infantry on infantry. There is no physical impulse, no force of mass. There is but a moral impulse. No one denies that this moral impulse is stronger as one feels better supported, that it has greater effect on the enemy as it menaces him with more men. From this it follows that the column is more valuable for the attack than the deployed order.

It might be concluded from this long statement that a moral pressure, which always causes flight when a bold attack is made, would not permit any infantry to hold out against a cavalry charge; never, indeed, against a determined charge. But infantry must resist when it is not possible to flee, and until there is complete demoralization, absolute terror, the infantry appreciates this. Every infantryman knows it is folly to flee before cavalry when the rifle is infallible at point-blank, at least from the rider's point of view. It is true that every really bold charge ought to succeed. But whether man is on foot or on horseback, he is always man. While on foot he has but himself to force; on horseback he must force man and beast to march against the enemy. And mounted, to flee is so easy. (Remark by Varney).

We have seen than in an infantry mass those in rear are powerless to push those in front unless the danger is greater in rear. The cavalry has long understood this. It attacks in a column at double distance rather than at half-distance, in order to avoid the frightful confusion of the mass. And yet, the allurement of mathematical reasoning is such that cavalry officers, especially the Germans, have seriously proposed attacking infantry by deep masses, so that the units in rear might give impulse to those in front. They cite the proverb. " One nail drives the other." What can you say to people who talk such nonsense? Nothing, except, " Attack us always in this way."

Real bayonet attacks occurred in the Crimean war. (Inkerman).[1] They were carried out by a small force against a larger one. The power of mass had no influence in such cases. It was the mass which fell back, turned tail even before the shock. The troops who made the bold charge did nothing but strike and fire at backs. These instances show men unexpectedly finding themselves face to face with the enemy, at a distance at which a man can close fearlessly without falling out on the way breathless. They are chance encounters. Man is not yet demoralized by fire; he must strike or fall back. . . . Combat at close quarters does not exist. At close quarters occurs the ancient carnage when one force strikes the other in the back.

Columns have absolutely but a moral effect. They are threatening dispositions . . .

The mass impulse of cavalry has long been discredited. You have given up forming it in deep ranks although cavalry possesses a speed that would bring on more of a push upon the front at a halt than the

[1] See Appendix VI. (Historical documents.) (Editor's note.)

last ranks of the infantry would bring upon the first. Yet you believe in the mass action of infantry!

As long as the ancient masses marched forward, they did not lose a man and no one lay down to avoid the combat. Dash lasted up to the time of stopping; the run was short in every case. In modern masses, in French masses especially, the march can be continued, but the mass loses while marching under fire. Moral pressure, continually exterted during a long advance, stops one-half of the combatants on the way. To-day, above all in France, man protests against such use of his life. The Frenchman wants to fight, to return blow for blow. If he is not allowed to, this is what happens. It happened to Napoleon's masses. Let us take Wagram, where his mass was not repulsed. Out of twenty-two thousand men, three thousand to fifteen hundred reached the position. Certainly the position was not carried by them, but by the material and moral effect of a battery of one hundred pieces, cavalry, etc., etc. Were the nineteen thousand missing men disabled? No. Seven out of twenty-two, a third, an enormous proportion may have been hit. What became of the twelve thousand unaccounted for? They had lain down on the road, had played dummy in order not to go on to the end. In the confused mass of a column of deployed battalions, surveillance, difficult enough in a column at normal distances, is impossible. Nothing is easier than dropping out through inertia; nothing more common.

This thing happens to every body of troops marching forward, under fire, in whatever formation it may be. The number of men falling out in this way, giving up at the least opportunity, is greater as formation is less fixed and the surveillance of officers and comrades more difficult. In a battalion in closed column, this kind of temporary desertion is enormous; one-half of the men drop out on the way. The first platoon is mingled with the fourth. They are really a flock of sheep. No one has control, all being mixed. Even if, in virtue of the first impulse, the position is carried, the disorder is so great that if it is counter-attacked by four men, it is lost.

The condition of morale of such masses is fully described in the battle of Cæsar against the Nervii, Marius against the Cimbri.[1]

What better arguments against deep columns could there be than the denials of Napoleon at St. Helena?

2. *Skirmishers — Supports — Reserves — Squares.*

This is singular. The cavalry has definite tactics, Essentially it knows how it fights. The infantry does not.

Our infantry no longer has any battle tactics; the initiative of the soldier rules. The soldiers of the First Empire trusted to the moral and passive action of masses. To-day, the soldiers object to the passive action of masses. They fight as skirmishers, or they march to the front as a flock of sheep of which three-fourths seek cover enroute, if the fire is heavy. The first method, although better than the second, is bad unless iron discipline and studied and practical methods of fighting insure maintaining strong reserves. These should be in the hands of the leaders and officers for support purposes, to guard against panics, and to finish by the moral effect of a march on the enemy, of flank menaces, etc., the destructive action of the skirmishers.

[1] See Appendix VI. (Historical documents.) (Editor's note.)

To-day when the ballistic arm is so deadly, so effective, a unit which closes up in order to fight is a unit in which morale is weakened.

Maneuver is possible only with good organization; otherwise it is no more effective than the passive mass or a rabble in an attack.

In ancient combat, the soldier was controlled by the leader in engagements; now that fighting is open, the soldier cannot be controlled. Often he cannot even be directed. Consequently it is necessary to begin an action at the latest possible moment, and to have the immediate commanders understand what is wanted, what their objectives are, etc.

In the modern engagement, the infantryman gets from under our control by scattering, and we say: a soldier's war. Wrong, wrong. To solve this problem, instead of scattering to the winds, let us increase the number of rallying points by solidifying the companies. From them come battalions; from battalions come regiments.

Action in open order was not possible nor evident under Turenne. The majority of the soldiers that composed the army, were not held near at hand, in formation. They fought badly. There was a general seeking for cover. Note the conduct of the Americans in their late war.

The organization of the legion of Marshal Saxe shows the strength of the tendency toward shock action as opposed to fire action.

The drills, parades and firing at Potsdam were not the tactics of Old Fritz. Frederick's secret was promptitude and rapidity of movement. But they were popularly believed to be his means. People were fond of them, and are yet. The Prussians for all their leaning toward parade, mathematics, etc., ended by adopting the best methods. The Prussians of Jena were taken in themselves by Frederick's methods. But since then they have been the first to strike out in a practical way, while we, in France, are still laboring at the Potsdam drills.

The greater number of generals who fought in the last wars, under real battle conditions, ask for skirmishers in large units, well supported. Our men have such a strong tendency to place themselves in such units even against the will of their leaders, that they do not fight otherwise.

A number of respectable authors and military men advocate the use of skirmishers in large bodies, as being dictated by certain necessities of war. Ask them to elucidate this mode of action, and you will see that this talk of skirmishers in large bodies is nothing else but an euphemism for absolute disorder. An attempt has been made to fit the theory to the fact. Yet the use of skirmishers in large bodies is absurd with Frenchmen under fire, when the terrain and the sharpness of the action cause the initiative and direction to escape from the commanders, and leave it to the men, to small groups of soldiers.

Arms are for use. The best disposition for material effect in attack or defense is that which permits the easiest and most deadly use of arms. This disposition is the scattered thin line. The whole of the science of combat lies then in the happy, proper combination, of the open order, scattered to secure destructive effect, and a good disposition of troops in formation as supports and reserves, so as to finish by moral effect the action of the advanced troops. The proper combination varies with the enemy, his morale and the terrain. On the other hand, the thin line can have good order only with a severe discipline, a unity which our men attain from pride. Pride exists only among people who know each other well, who have esprit de corps, and company spirit. There is a necessity for an organization that renders unity possible by creating the real individuality of the company.

Self-esteem is unquestionably one of the most powerful motives which moves our men. They do not wish to pass for cowards in the eyes of their comrades. If they march forward they want to distinguish themselves. After every attack, formation (not the formation of the drill ground but that adopted by those rallying to the chief, those marching with him,) no longer exists. This is because of the inherent disorder of every forward march under fire. The bewildered men, even the officers, have no longer the eyes of their comrades or of their commander upon them, sustaining them. Self-esteem no longer impels them, they do not hold out; the least counter-offensive puts them to rout.

The experience of the evening ought always to serve the day following; but as the next day is never identical with the evening before, the counsel of experience can not be applied to the latter. When confused battalions shot at each other some two hundred paces for some time with arms inferior to those of our days, flight commenced at the wings. Therefore, said experience, let us reënforce the wings, and the battalion was placed between two picked companies. But it was found that the combat methods had been transformed. The elite companies were then reassembled into picked corps and the battalion, weaker than ever, no longer had reënforced wings. Perhaps combat in open order predominates, and the companies of light infantrymen being, above all, skirmishers, the battalion again is no longer supported. In our day the use of deployed battalions as skirmishers is no longer possible; and one of the essential reasons for picked companies is the strengthening of the battalion.

The question has been asked; Who saved the French army on the Beresina and at Hanau? The Guard, it is true. But, outside of the picked corps, what was the French army then? Droves, not troops. Abnormal times, abnormal deeds. The Beresina, Hanau, prove nothing to-day.

With the rapid-firing arms of infantry to-day, the advantage belongs to the defense which is completed by offensive movements carried out at opportune times.

Fire to-day is four or five times more rapid even if quite as haphazard as in the days of muzzle loaders. Everybody says that this renders impossible the charges of cavalry against infantry which has not been completely thrown into disorder, demoralized. What then must happen to charges of infantry, which marches while the cavalry charges?

Attacks in deep masses are no longer seen. They are not wise, and never were wise. To advance to the attack with a line of battalions in column, with large intervals and covered by a thick line of skirmishers, when the artillery has prepared the terrain, is very well. People with common sense have never done otherwise. But the thick line of skirmishers is essential. I believe that is the crux of the matter.

But enough of this. It is simple prudence for the artillery to prepare the infantry action by a moment's conversation with the artillery of the enemy infantry. If that infantry is not commanded by an imbecile, as it sometimes is, it will avoid that particular conversation the arguments of which would break it up, although they may not be directed precisely in its direction. All other things being equal, both infantries suffer the same losses in the artillery duel. The proportion does not vary, however complete the artillery preparation. One infantry must always close with another under rapid fire from troops in position, and such a fire is, to-day more than ever, to the advantage of the defense. Ten men come towards me; they are at four hundred meters; with the ancient arm, I have time to kill but two before they reach me; with rapid fire, I have time to kill four or five. Morale does not increase with losses. The eight remaining might reach me in the first case; the five or six remaining will certainly not in the second.

If distance be taken, the leader can be seen, the file-closers see, the platoon that follows watches the preceding. Dropping out always exists, but it is less extensive with an open order, the men running more risks of being recognized. Stragglers will be fewer as the companies know each other better, and as the officers and men are more dependable.

It is difficult, if not impossible, to get the French infantry to make use of its fire before charging. If it fires, it will not charge, because it will continue to fire. (Bugeaud's method of firing during the advance is good.) What is needed, then, is skirmishers, who deliver the only effective fire, and troops in formation who push the skirmishers on, in themselves advancing to the attack.

The soldier wants to be occupied, to return shot for shot. Place him in a position to act immediately, individually. Then, whatever he does, you have not wholly lost your authority over him.

Again and again and again, at drill, the officers and non-commissioned officer ought to tell the private: "This is taught you to serve you under such circumstances." Generals, field officers, ought to tell officers the same thing. This alone can make an instructed army like the Roman army. But to-day, who of us can explain page for page, the use of anything ordered by our tactical regulations except the school of the skirmisher? "Forward," "retreat," and "by the flank," are the only practical movements under fire. But the others should be explained. Explain the position of "carry arms" with the left hand. Explain the ordinary step. Explain firing at command in the school of the battalion. It is well enough for the school of the platoon, because a company can make use thereof, but a battalion never can.

Everything leads to the belief that battle with present arms will be, in the same space of time, more deadly than with ancient ones. The trajectory of the projectile reaching further, the rapidity of firing being four times as great, more men will be put out of commission in less time. While the arm becomes more deadly, man does not change, his morale remains capable of certain efforts and the demands upon it become stronger. Morale is overtaxed; it reaches more rapidly the maximum of tension which throws the soldier to the front or rear. The rôle of commanders is to maintain morale, to direct those movements which men instinctively execute when heavily engaged and under the pressure of danger.

Napoleon I said that in battle, the rôle of skirmishers

is the most fatiguing and most deadly. This means that under the Empire, as at present, the strongly engaged infantry troops rapidly dissolved into skirmishers. The action was decided by the moral agency of the troops not engaged, held in hand, capable of movement in any direction and acting as a great menace of new danger to the adversary, already shaken by the destructive action of the skirmishers. The same is true to-day. But the greater force of fire arms requires, more than ever, that they be utilized. The rôle of the skirmisher becomes preëminently the destructive rôle; it is forced on every organization seriously engaged by the greater moral pressure of to-day which causes men to scatter sooner.

Commanders-in-chief imagine formed battalions firing on the enemy and do not include the use of skirmishers in drill. This is an error, for they are necessary in drill and everywhere, etc. The formed rank is more difficult to utilize than ever. General Leboeuf used a very practical movement of going into battle, by platoons, which advance to the battle line in echelon, and can fire, even if they are taken in the very act of the movement. There is always the same dangerous tendency toward mass action even for a battalion in maneuver. This is an error. The principles of maneuver for small units should not be confused with those for great units. Emperor Napoleon did not prescribe skirmishers in flat country. But every officer should be reduced who does not utilize them to some degree.

The rôle of the skirmisher becomes more and more predominant. He should be so much the more watched and directed as he is used against more deadly arms, and, consequently, is more disposed to escape from all control, from all direction. Yet under such battle conditions formations are proposed which send skirmishers six hundred paces in advance of battalions and which give the battalion commander the mission of watching and directing (with six companies of one hundred and twenty men) troops spread over a space of three hundred paces by five hundred, at a minimum. To advance skirmishers six hundred paces from their battalion and to expect they will remain there is the work of people who have never observed.

Inasmuch as combat by skirmishers tends to predominate and since it becomes more difficult with the increase of danger, there has been a constant effort to bring into the firing line the man who must direct it. Leaders have been seen to spread an entire battalion in front of an infantry brigade or division so that the skirmishers, placed under a single command, might obey a general direction better. This method, scarcely practicable on the drill-ground, and indicating an absolute lack of practical sense, marks the tendency. The authors of new drills go too far in the opposite direction. They give the immediate command of the skirmishers in each battalion to the battalion commander who must at the same time lead his skirmishers and his battalion. This expedient is more practical than the other. It abandons all thought of an impossible general control and places the special direction in the right hands. But the leadership is too distant, the battalion commander has to attend to the participation of his battalion in the line, or in the ensemble of other battalions of the brigade or division, and the particular performance of his skirmishers. The more difficult, confused, the engagement becomes, the more simple and clear ought to be the rôles of each one. Skirmishers are in need of a firmer hand than ever to direct and maintain

them, so that they may do their part. The battalion
commander must be entirely occupied with the rôle of
skirmishers, or with the rôle of the line. There should
be smaller battalions, one-half the number in reserve,
one-half as skirmisher battalions. In the latter the
men should be employed one-half as skirmishers and
one-half held in reserve. The line of skirmishers will
then gain steadiness.

Let the battalion commander of the troops of the
second line entirely occupy himself with his battalion.

The full battalion of six companies is to-day too unwieldy for one man. Have battalions of four companies of one hundred men each, which is certainly quite
sufficient considering the power of destruction which
these four companies place in the hands of one man.
He will have difficulty in maintaining and directing
these four companies under the operation of increasingly powerful modern appliances. He will have difficulty in watching them, in modern combat, with the
greater interval between the men in line that the use of
the present arms necessitates. With a unified battalion
of six hundred men, I would do better against a battalion of one thousand Prussians, than with a battalion
of eight hundred men, two hundred of whom are immediately taken out of my control.

Skirmishers have a destructive effect; formed troops
a moral effect. Drill ground maneuvers should prepare for actual battle. In such maneuvers, why, at the
decisive moment of an attack, should you lighten the
moral anxiety of the foe by ceasing his destruction, by
calling back your skirmishers? If the enemy keeps his
own skirmishers and marches resolutely behind them,
you are lost, for his moral action upon you is aug-

mented by his destructive action against which you have kindly disarmed yourself.

Why do you call back your skirmishers? Is it because your skirmishers hinder the operation of your columns, block bayonet charges? One must never have been in action to advance such a reason. At the last moment, at the supreme moment when one or two hundred meters separate you from the adversary, there is no longer a line. There is a fearless advance, and your skirmishers are your forlorn hope. Let them charge on their own account. Let them be passed or pushed forward by the mass. Do not recall them. Do not order them to execute any maneuver for they are not capable of any, except perhaps, that of falling back and establishing a counter-current which might drag you along. In these moments, everything hangs by a thread. Is it because your skirmishers would prevent you from delivering fire? Do you, then, believe in firing, especially in firing under the pressure of approaching danger, before the enemy? If he is wise, certainly he marches preceded by skirmishers, who kill men in your ranks and who have the confidence of a first success, of having seen your skirmishers disappear before them. These skirmishers will certainly lie down before your unmasked front. In that formation they easily cause you losses, and you are subjected to their destructive effect and to the moral effect of the advance of troops in formation against you. Your ranks become confused; you do not hold the position. There is but one way of holding it, that is to advance, and for that, it is necessary at all costs to avoid firing before moving ahead. Fire opened, no one advances further.

Do you believe in opening and ceasing fire at the

will of the commander as on the drill ground? The commencement of fire by a battalion, with the present arms especially, is the beginning of disorder, the moment where the battalion begins to escape from its leader. While drilling even, the battalion commanders, after a little lively drill, after a march, can no longer control the fire.

Do you object that no one ever gets within two hundred meters of the enemy? That a unit attacking from the front never succeeds? So be it! Let us attack from the flank. But a flank is always more or less covered. Men are stationed there, ready for the blow. It will be necessary to pick off these men.

To-day, more than ever, no rapid, calm firing is possible except skirmish firing.

The rapidity of firing has reduced six ranks to two ranks. With reliable troops who have no need of the moral support of a second rank behind them, one rank suffices to-day. At any rate, it is possible to await attack in two ranks.

In prescribing fire at command, in seeking to minimize the rôle of skirmishers instead of making it predominate, you take sides with the Germans. We are not fitted for that sort of game. If they adopt fire at command, it is just one more reason for our finding another method. We have invented, discovered the skirmisher; he is forced upon us by our men, our arms, etc. He must be organized.

In fire by rank, in battle, men gather into small groups and become confused. The more space they have, the less will be the disorder.

Formed in two ranks, each rank should be still thinner. All the shots of the second line are lost. The men should not touch; they should be far apart. The second rank in firing from position at a supreme moment, ought not to be directly behind the first. The men ought to be echeloned behind the first. There will always be firing from position on any front. It is necessary to make this firing as effective and as easy as possible. I do not wish to challenge the experiences of the target range but I wish to put them to practical use.

It is evident that the present arms are more deadly than the ancient ones; the morale of the troops will therefore be more severely shaken. The influence of the leader should be greater over the combatants, those immediately engaged. If it seems rational, let colonels engage in action, with the battalions of their regiment in two lines. One battalion acts as skirmishers; the other battalion waits, formed ready to aid the first. If you do not wish so to utilize the colonels, put all the battalions of the regiment in the first line, and eventually use them as skirmishers. The thing is inevitable; it will be done in spite of you. Do it yourself at the very first opportunity.

The necessity of replenishing the ammunition supply so quickly used up by the infantry, requires engaging the infantry by units only, which can be relieved by other units after the exhaustion of the ammunition supply. As skirmishers are exhausted quickly, engage entire battalions as skirmishers, assisted by entire battalions as supports or reserves. This is a necessary measure to insure good order. Do not throw into the fight immediately the four companies of the battalion. Up to the crucial moment, the battalion commander ought to guard against throwing every one into the fight.

There is a mania, seen in our maneuver camps, for

completely covering a battle front, a defended position, by skirmishers, without the least interval between the skirmishers of different battalions. What will be the result? Initially a waste of men and ammunition. Then, difficulty in replacing them.

Why cover the front everywhere? If you do, then what advantage is there in being able to see from a great distance? Leave large intervals between your deployed companies. We are no longer only one hundred meters from the enemy at the time of firing. Since we are able to see at a great distance we do not risk having the enemy dash into these intervals unexpectedly. Your skirmisher companies at large intervals begin the fight, the killing. While your advance companies move ahead, the battalion commander follows with his formed companies, defilading them as much as possible. He lets them march. If the skirmishers fight at the halt, he supervises them. If the commanding officer wishes to reënforce his line, if he wants to face an enemy who attempts to advance into an interval, if he has any motive for doing it, in a word, he rushes new skirmishers into the interval. Certainly, these companies have more of the forward impulse, more dash, if dash is needed, than the skirmishers already in action. If they pass the first skirmishers, no harm is done. There you have echelons already formed. The skirmishers engaged, seeing aid in front of them, can be launched ahead more easily.

Besides, the companies thrown into this interval are a surprise for the enemy. That is something to be considered, as is the fact that so long as there is fighting at a halt, intervals in the skirmish lines are fit places for enemy bullets. Furthermore, these companies remain in the hands of their leaders. With the present

method of reënforcing skirmishers — I am speaking of
the practical method of the battlefield, not of theory —
a company, starting from behind the skirmishers engaged, without a place in which to deploy, does not find
anything better to do than to mingle with the skirmishers. Here it doubles the number of men, but in doing
so brings disorder, prevents the control of the commanders and breaks up the regularly constituted groups.
While the closing up of intervals to make places for
new arrivals is good on the drill ground, or good before
or after the combat, it never works during battle.

No prescribed interval will be kept exactly. It will
open, it will close, following the fluctuations of the
combat. But the onset, during which it can be kept, is
not the moment of brisk combat; it is the moment of
the engagement, of contact, consequently, of feeling
out. It is essential that there remain space in which
to advance. Suppose you are on a plain, for in a maneuver one starts from the flat terrain. In extending
the new company it will reënforce the wings of the
others, the men naturally supporting the flanks of their
comrades. The individual intervals will lessen in order
to make room for the new company. The company
will always have a well determined central group, a
rallying point for the others. If the interval has disappeared there is always time to employ the emergency
method of doubling the ranks in front; but one must
not forget, whatever the course taken, to preserve good
order.

We cannot resist closing intervals between battalions;
as if we were still in the times of the pikemen when,
indeed, it was possible to pass through an interval!
To-day, the fighting is done ten times farther away, and
the intervals between battalions are not weak points.

They are covered by the fire of the skirmishers, as well covered by fire as the rest of the front, and invisible to the enemy.

Skirmishers and masses are the formations for action of poorly instructed French troops. With instruction and unity there would be skirmishers supported and formation in battalion columns at most.

Troops in close order can have only a moral effect, for the attack, or for a demonstration. If you want to produce a real effect, use musketry. For this it is necessary to form a single line. Formations have purely moral effect. Whoever counts on their material, effective action against reliable, cool troops, is mistaken and is defeated. Skirmishers alone do damage. Picked shots would do more if properly employed.

In attacking a position, start the charge at the latest possible moment, when the leader thinks he can reach the objective not all out of breath. Until then, it has been possible to march in rank, that is under the officers, the rank not being the mathematical line, but the grouping in the hands of the leader, under his eye. With the run comes confusion. Many stop, the fewer as the run is shorter. They lie down on the way and will rejoin only if the attack succeeds, if they join at all. If by running too long the men are obliged to stop in order to breathe and rest, the dash is broken, shattered. At the advance, very few will start. There are ten chances to one of seeing the attack fail, of turning it into a joke, with cries of " Forward with fixed bayonet," but none advancing, except some brave men who will be killed uselessly. The attack vanishes finally before the least demonstration of the foe. An unfortunate shout, a mere nothing, can destroy it.

Absolute rules are foolish, the conduct of every

charge being an affair requiring tact. But so regulate by general rules the conduct of an infantry charge that those who commence it too far away can properly be accused of panic. And there is a way. Regulate it as the cavalry charge is regulated, and have a rearguard in each battalion of non-commissioned officers, of most reliable officers, in order to gather together, to follow close upon the charge, at a walk, and to collect all those who have lain down so as not to march or because they were out of breath. This rearguard might consist of a small platoon of picked shots, such as we need in each battalion. The charge ought to be made at a given distance, else it vanishes, evaporates. The leader who commences it too soon either has no head, or does not want to gain his objective.

The infantry of the line, as opposed to élite commands, should not be kept in support. The least firm, the most impressionable, are thus sent into the road stained with the blood of the strongest. We place them, after a moral anxiety of waiting, face to face with the terrible destruction and mutilation of modern weapons. If antiquity had need of solid troops as supports, we have a greater need of them. Death in ancient combat was not as horrible as in the modern battle where the flesh is mangled, slashed by artillery fire. In ancient combat, except in defeat, the wounded were few in number. This is the reply to those who wish to begin an action by chasseurs, zouaves, etc.

He, general or mere captain, who employs every one in the storming of a position can be sure of seeing it retaken by an organized counter-attack of four men and a corporal.

In order that we may have real supervision and responsibility in units from companies to brigades, the supporting troops ought to be of the same company, the same battalion, the same brigade, as the case may be.   Each brigade ought to have its two lines, each battalion its skirmishers, etc.

The system of holding out a reserve as long as possible for independent action when the enemy has used his own, ought to be applied downwards.   Each battalion should have its own, each regiment its own, firmly maintained.

There is more need than ever to-day, for protecting the supporting forces, the reserves.   The power of destruction increases, the morale remains the same.   The tests of morale, being more violent than previously, ought to be shorter, because the power of morale has not increased.   The masses, reserves, the second, the first lines, should be protected and sheltered even more than the skirmishers.

Squares sometimes are broken by cavalry which pursues the skirmishers into the square.   Instead of lying down, they rush blindly to their refuge which they render untenable and destroy.   No square can hold out against determined troops. . . . But!

The infantry square is not a thing of mechanics, of mathematical reasoning; it is a thing of morale.   A platoon in four ranks, two facing the front, two the rear, its flanks guarded by the extreme files that face to the flank, and conducted, supported by the non-commissioned officers placed in a fifth rank, in the interior of the rectangle, powerful in its compactness and its fire, cannot be dislodged by cavalry.   However, this platoon will prefer to form a part of a large square, it will consider itself stronger, because of numbers, and indeed it will be, since the feeling of force pervades this whole force.   This feeling is power in war.

People who calculate only according to the fire delivered, according to the destructive power of infantry, would have it fight deployed against cavalry. They do not consider that although supported and maintained, although such a formation seem to prevent flight, the very impetus of the charge, if led resolutely, will break the deployment before the shock arrives. It is clear that if the charge is badly conducted, whether the infantry be solid or not, it will never reach its objective. Why? Moral reasons and no others make the soldier in a square feel himself stronger than when in line. He feels himself watched from behind and has nowhere to flee.

3. *Firing.*

It is easy to misuse breech-loading weapons, such as the rifle. The fashion to-day is to use small intrenchments, covering battalions. As old as powder. Such shelter is an excellent device on the condition, however, that behind it, a useful fire can be delivered.

Look at these two ranks crouched under the cover of a small trench. Follow the direction of the shots. Even note the trajectory shown by the burst of flame. You will be convinced that, under such conditions, even simple horizontal firing is a fiction. In a second, there will be wild firing on account of the noise, the crowding, the interference of the two ranks. Next everybody tries to get under the best possible cover. Good-by firing.

It is essential to save ammunition, to get all possible efficiency from the arm. Yet the official adoption of fire by rank insures relapsing into useless firing at random. Good shots are wasted, placed where it is impossible for them to fire well.

Since we have a weapon that fires six times more rapidly than the ancient weapon, why not profit by it to cover a given space with six times fewer riflemen than formerly? Riflemen placed at greater intervals, will be less bewildered, will see more clearly, will be better watched (which may seem strange to you), and will consequently deliver a better fire than formerly. Besides, they will expend six times less ammunition. That is the vital point. You must always have ammunition available, that is to say, troops which have not been engaged. Reserves must be held out. This is hard to manage perhaps. It is not so hard to manage, however, as fire by command.

What is the use of fire by rank? By command? It is impracticable against the enemy, except in extraordinary cases. Any attempt at supervision of it is a joke! File firing? The first rank can shoot horizontally, the only thing required; the second rank can fire only into the air. It is useless to fire with our bulky knapsacks interfering so that our men raise the elbow higher than the shoulder. Learn what the field pack can be from the English, Prussians, Austrians, etc. . . . Could the pack not be thicker and less wide? Have the first rank open; let the second be checkerwise; and let firing against cavalry be the only firing to be executed in line.

One line will be better than two, because it will not be hindered by the one behind it. One kind of fire is practicable and efficient, that of one rank. This is the fire of skirmishers in close formation.

The king's order of June 1st, 1776, reads (p. 28): " Experience in war having proved that three ranks fire standing, and the intention of his majesty being to prescribe only what can be executed in front of the enemy,

he orders that in firing, the first man is never to put his
knee on the ground, and that the three ranks fire standing at the same time." This same order includes instructions on target practice, etc.

Marshal de Gouvion-Saint Cyr says that conserva-
tively one-fourth of the men who are wounded in an
affair are put out of commission by the third rank.
This estimate is not high enough if it concerns a unit
composed of recruits like those who fought at Lützen
and Bautzen. The marshal mentions the astonishment
of Napoleon when he saw the great number of men
wounded in the hand and forearm. This astonishment
of Napoleon's is singular. What ignorance in his marshals not to have explained such wounds! Chief Surgeon Larrey, by observation of the wounds, alone exon-
erated our soldiers of the accusation of self-inflicted
wounds. The observation would have been made
sooner, had the wounds heretofore been numerous.
That they had not been can be explained only by the
fact that while the young soldiers of 1813 kept instinctively close in ranks, up to that time the men must have
spaced themselves instinctively, in order to be able to
shoot. Or perhaps in 1813, these young men might
have been allowed to fire a longer time in order to distract them and keep them in ranks, and not often allowed to act as skirmishers for fear of losing them.
Whilst formerly, the fire by rank must have been much
rarer and fire action must have given way almost
entirely to the use of skirmishers.

Fire by command presupposes an impossible coolness.
Had any troops ever possessed it they would have
mowed down battalions as one mows down corn stalks.
Yet it has been known for a long time, since Frederick,
since before Frederick, since the first rifle. Let troops

get the range calmly, let them take aim together so that
no one disturbs or hinders the other. Have each one
see clearly, then, at a signal, let them all fire at once.
Who is going to stand against such people? But did
they aim in those days? Not so accurately, possibly,
but they knew how to shoot waist-high, to shoot at the
feet. They knew how to do it. I do not say they did
it. If they had done so, there would not have been any
need of reminding them of it so often. Note Cromwell's favorite saying, " Aim at their shoe-laces; " that
of the officers of the empire, " Aim at the height of the
waist." Study of battles, of the expenditure of bullets, show us no such immediate terrible results. If
such a means of destruction was so easy to obtain, why
did not our illustrious forbears use it and recommend
it to us? (Words of de Gouvion-Saint-Cyr.)

Security alone creates calmness under fire.

In minor operations of war, how many captains are
capable of tranquilly commanding their fire and maneuvering with calmness?

Here is a singular thing. You hear fire by rank
against cavalry seriously recommended in military lectures. Yet not a colonel, not a battalion commander,
not a captain, requires this fire to be executed in maneuvers. It is always the soldier who forces the firing.
He is ordered to shoot almost before he aims for fear
he will shoot without command. Yet he ought to feel
that when he is aiming, his finger on the trigger, his
shot does not belong to him, but rather to the officer
who ought to be able to let him aim for five minutes,
if advisable, examining, correcting the positions, etc.
He ought, when aiming, always be ready to fire upon
the object designated, without ever knowing when it
will please his commander to order him to fire.

Fire at command is not practicable in the face of the enemy. If it were, the perfection of its execution would depend on the coolness of the commander and the obedience of the soldier. The soldier is the more easily trained.

The Austrians had fire by command in Italy against cavalry. Did they use it? They fired before the command, an irregular fire, a fire by file, with defective results.

Fire by command is impossible. But why is firing by rank at will impossible, illusory, under the fire of the enemy? Because of the reasons already given and, for this reason: that closed ranks are incompatible with fire-arms, on account of the wounding caused by the latter in ranks. In closed ranks, the two lines touching elbows, a man who falls throws ten men into complete confusion. There is no room for those who drop and, however few fall, the resulting disorder immediately makes of the two ranks a series of small milling groups. If the troops are young, they become a disordered flock before any demonstration. (Caldiero, Duhesme.) If the troops have some steadiness, they of themselves will make space: they will try to make way for the bullets: they will scatter as skirmishers with small intervals. (Note the Grenadier Guards at Magenta.)[1]

With very open ranks, men a pace apart, whoever falls has room, he is noticed by a lesser number, he drags down no one in his fall. The moral impression on his comrades is less. Their courage is less impaired. Besides, with rapid fire everywhere, spaced ranks with no man in front of another, at least permit horizontal fire. Closed ranks permit it hardly in the first rank, whose ears are troubled by the shots from the men be-

[1] See Appendix II. (Historical documents.) (Editor's note.)

hind. When a man has to fire four or five shots a
minute, one line is certainly more solid than two, because, while the firing is less by half, it is more than
twice as likely to be horizontal fire as in the two-rank
formation. Well-sustained fire, even with blank cartridges, would be sufficient to prevent a successful
charge. With slow fire, two ranks alone were able to
keep up a sufficiently continuous fusillade. With rapid
fire, a single line delivers more shots than two with
ancient weapons. Such fire, therefore, suffices as a
fusillade.

Close ranks, while suitable for marching, do not lend
themselves to firing at the halt. Marching, a man likes
a comrade at his side. Firing, as if he felt the flesh
attracting the lead, he prefers being relatively isolated,
with space around him. Breech-loading rifles breed
queer ideas. Generals are found who say that rapid
firing will bring back fire at command, as if there ever
were such a thing. They say it will bring back salvo
firing, thus permitting clear vision. As if such a thing
were possible! These men have not an atom of common sense.

It is singular to see a man like Guibert, with practical
ideas on most things, give a long dissertation to demonstrate that the officers of his time were wrong in aiming
at the middle of the body, that is, in firing low. He
claims this is ridiculous to one who understands the
trajectory of the rifle. These officers were right.
They revived the recommendations of Cromwell, because they knew that in combat the soldier naturally
fires too high because he does not aim, and because the
shape of the rifle, when it is brought to the shoulder,
tends to keep the muzzle higher than the breech.
Whether that is the reason or something else, the fact

is indisputable. It is said that in Prussian drills all the bullets hit the ground at fifty paces. With the arms of that time and the manner of fighting, results would have been magnificent in battle if the bullets had struck fifty paces before the enemy instead of passing over his head.

Yet at Mollwitz, where the Austrians had five thousand men disabled, the Prussians had over four thousand.

Firing with a horizontal sector, if the muzzle be heavy, is more deadly than firing with a vertical sector.

4. *Marches. Camps. Night Attacks.*

From the fact that infantry ought always to fight in thin formation, scattered, it does not follow that it ought to be kept in that order. Only in column is it possible to maintain the battle order. It is necessary to keep one's men in hand as long as possible, because once engaged, they no longer belong to you.

The disposition in closed mass is not a suitable marching formation, even in a battalion for a short distance. On account of heat, the closed column is intolerable, like an unventilated room. Formation with half-distances is better. (Why? Air, view, etc.)

Such a formation prevents ready entry of the column into battle in case of necessity or surprise. The half-divisions not in the first line are brought up, the arms at the order, and they can furnish either skirmishers or a reserve for the first line which has been deployed as skirmishers.

At Leuctra, Epaminondas diminished, by one-half, the depth of his men; he formed square phalanxes of fifty men to a side. He could have very well dispensed

with it, for the Lacedæmanian right was at once
thrown into disorder by its own cavalry which was
placed in front of that wing. The superior cavalry of
Epaminondas overran not only the cavalry but the infantry that was behind it. The infantry of Epaminondas, coming in the wake of his cavalry finished the
work. Turning to the right, the left of Epaminondas
then took in the flank the Lacedæmonian line. Menaced also in front by the approaching echelons of
Epaminondas, this line became demoralized and took
to flight. Perhaps this fifty by fifty formation was
adopted in order to give, without maneuver, a front of
fifty capable of acting in any direction. At Leuctra,
it simply acted to the right and took the enemy in the
flank and in reverse.

Thick woods are generally passed through in close
column. There is never any opening up, with subsequent closing on the far side. The resulting formation
is as confused as a flock of sheep.

In a march through mountains, difficult country, a
bugler should be on the left, at the orders of an intelligent officer who indicates when the halt seems necessary for discipline in the line. The right responds and
if the place has been judged correctly an orderly formation is maintained. Keep in ranks. If one man
steps out, others follow. Do not permit men to leave
ranks without requiring them to rejoin.

In the rear-guard it is always necessary to have pack
mules in an emergency; without this precaution, considerable time may be lost. In certain difficult places
time is thus lost every day.

In camp, organize your fatigue parties in advance;
send them out in formation and escorted.

Definite and detailed orders ought to be given to

the convoy, and the chief baggage-master ought to supervise it, which is rarely the case.

It is a mistake to furnish mules to officers and replace them in case of loss or sickness. The officer overloads the mule and the Government loses more thereby than is generally understood. Convoys are endless owing to overloaded mules and stragglers. If furnished money to buy a mule the officer uses it economically because it is his. If mules are individually furnished to officers instead of money, the officer will care for his beast for the same reason. But it is better to give money only, and the officer, if he is not well cared for on the march has no claim against the Government.

Always, always, take Draconian measures to prevent pillage from commencing. If it begins, it is difficult ever to stop it. A body of infantry is never left alone. There is no reason for calling officers of that arm inapt, when battalions although established in position are not absolutely on the same line, with absolutely equal intervals. Ten moves are made to achieve the exact alignment which the instructions on camp movements prescribe. Yet designating a guiding battalion might answer well enough and still be according to the regulations.

Why are not night attacks more employed to-day, at least on a grand scale? The great front which armies occupy renders their employment more difficult, and exacts of the troops an extreme aptitude in this kind of surprise tactics (found in the Arabs, Turcos, Spahis), or absolute reliability. There are some men whose knowledge of terrain is wonderful, with an unerring eye for distance, who can find their way through places at night which they have visited only in the day time.

Utilizing such material for a system of guides it would be possible to move with certainty. These are simple means, rarely employed, for conducting a body of troops into position on the darkest night. There is, even, a means of assuring at night the fire of a gun upon a given point with as much precision as in plain day.

CHAPTER III

1. *Cavalry and Modern Appliances.*

They say that cavalry is obsolete; that it can be of no use in battles waged with the weapons of today. Is not infantry affected in the same way?

Examples drawn from the last two wars are not conclusive. In a siege, in a country which is cut off, one does not dare to commit the cavalry, and therefore takes from it its boldness, which is almost its only weapon.

The utility of cavalry has always been doubted. That is because its cost is high. It is little used, just because it does cost. The question of economy is vital in peace times. When we set a high value upon certain men, they are not slow to follow suit, and to guard themselves against being broken. Look at staff officers who are almost never broken (reduced), even when their general himself is.

With new weapons the rôle of cavalry has certainly changed less than any other, although it is the one which is most worried about. However, cavalry always has the same doctrine: Charge! To start with, cavalry action against cavalry is always the same. Also against infantry. Cavalry knows well enough today, as it has always known, that it can act only against infantry which has been broken. We must leave aside epic legends that are always false, whether

205

they relate to cavalry or infantry. Infantry cannot say as much of its own action against infantry. In this respect there is a complete anarchy of ideas. There is no infantry doctrine.

With the power of modern weapons, which forces you to slow down if it does not stop you, the advance under fire becomes almost impossible. The advantage is with the defensive. This is so evident that only a a madman could dispute it. What then is to be done? Halt, to shoot at random and cannonade at long range until ammunition is exhausted? Perhaps. But what is sure, is that such a state of affairs makes maneuver necessary. There is more need than ever for maneuver at a long distance in an attempt to force the enemy to shift, to quit his position. What maneuver is swifter than that of cavalry? Therein is its rôle.

The extreme perfection of weapons permits only individual action in combat, that is action by scattered forces. At the same time it permits the effective employment of mass action out of range, of maneuvers on the flank or in the rear of the enemy in force imposing enough to frighten him.

Can the cavalry maneuver on the battle field? Why not? It can maneuver rapidly, and above all beyond the range of infantry fire, if not of artillery fire. Maneuver being a threat, of great moral effect, the cavalry general who knows how to use it, can contribute largely to success. He arrests the enemy in movement, doubtful as to what the cavalry is going to attempt. He makes the enemy take some formation that keeps him under artillery fire for a while, above all that of light artillery if the general knows how to use it. He increases the enemy's demoralization and thus is able to rejoin his command.

Rifled cannon and accurate rifles do not change cavalry tactics at all. These weapons of precision, as the word precision indicates, are effective only when all battle conditions, all conditions of aiming, are ideal. If the necessary condition of suitable range is lacking, effect is lacking. Accuracy of fire at a distance is impossible against a troop in movement, and movement is the essence of cavalry action. Rifled weapons fire on them of course, but they fire on everybody.

In short, cavalry is in the same situation as anybody else.

What response is there to this argument? Since weapons have been improved, does not the infantryman have to march under fire to attack a position? Is the cavalryman not of the same flesh? Has he less heart than the infantryman? If one can march under fire, cannot the other gallop under it?

When the cavalryman cannot gallop under fire, the infantryman cannot march under it. Battles will consist of exchanges of rifle shots by concealed men, at long range. The battle will end only when the ammunition is exhausted.

The cavalryman gallops through danger, the infantryman walks. That is why, if he learns, as it is probable he will, to keep at the proper distance, the cavalryman will never see his battle rôle diminished by the perfection of long range fire. An infantryman will never succeed by himself. The cavalryman will threaten, create diversions, worry, scatter the enemy's fire, often even get to close quarters if he is properly supported. The infantryman will act as usual. But more than ever will he need the aid of cavalry in the attack. He who knows how to use his cavalry with audacity will inevitably be the victor. Even though the cavalryman offers a larger target, long range weapons will paralyze him no more than another.

The most probable effect of artillery of today, will be to increase the scattering in the infantry, and even in the cavalry. The latter can start in skirmisher formation at a distance and close in while advancing, near its objective. It will be more difficult to lead; but this is to the advantage of the Frenchman.

The result of improving the ballistics of the weapon, for the cavalry as for the infantry (there is no reason why it should be otherwise for the cavalry), will be that a man will flee at a greater distance from it, and nothing more.

Since the Empire, the opinion of European armies is that the cavalry has not given the results expected of it.

It has not given great results, for the reason that we and others lacked real cavalry generals. He is, it seems, a phenomenon that is produced only every thousand years, more rarely than a real general of infantry. To be a good general, whether of infantry or cavalry, is an infinitely rare thing, like the good in everything. The profession of a good infantry general is as difficult as, perhaps more difficult than, that of a good cavalry general. Both require calmness. It comes more easily to the cavalryman than to the foot soldier who is much more engaged. Both require a like precision, a judgment of the moral and physical forces of the soldier; and the morale of the infantryman, his constitution, is more tried than is the case with the horseman.

The cavalry general, of necessity, sees less clearly; his vision has its limits. Great cavalry generals are rare. Doubtless Seidlitz could not, in the face of the development of cannon and rifle, repeat his wonders. But there is always room for improvement. I believe there is much room for improvement.

We did not have under the Empire a great cavalry general who knew how to handle masses. The cavalry was used like a blind hammer that strikes heavily and not always accurately. It had immense losses. Like the Gauls, we have a little too much confidence in the " forward, forward, not so many methods." Methods do not hinder the forward movement. They prepare the effect and render it surer and at the same time less costly to the assailant. We have all the Gallic brutality. (Note Marignano, where the force of artillery and the possibility of a turning movement around a village was neglected). What rare things infantry and cavalry generals are!

A leader must combine resolute bravery and impetuosity with prudence and calmness; a difficult matter!

The broken terrain of European fields no longer permits, we are told, the operation of long lines, of great masses of cavalry. I do not regret it. I am struck more with the picturesque effect of these hurricanes of cavalry in the accounts of the Empire than with the results obtained. It does not seem to me that these results were in proportion to the apparent force of the effort and to the real grandeur of the sacrifices. And indeed, these enormous hammers (a usual figure), are hard to handle. They have not the sure direction of a weapon well in hand. If the blow is not true, recovery is impossible, etc. However, the terrain does not to-day permit the assembling of cavalry in great masses. This compelling reason for new methods renders any other reason superfluous.

Nevertheless, the other reasons given in the ministerial observations of 1868, on the cavalry service, seems to me excellent. The improvement of appliances, the extension of battle fields, the confidence to the infantry and the audacity to the artillery that the immediate support of the cavalry gives, demand that this arm be in every division in sufficient force for efficient action.

I, therefore, think it desirable for a cavalry regiment to be at the disposal of a general commanding a division. Whatever the experiences of instruction centers, they can not change in the least my conviction of the merit of this measure in the field.

2. *Cavalry Against Cavalry.*

Cavalry action, more than that of infantry, is an affair of morale.

Let us study first the morale of the cavalry engagement in single combat. Two riders rush at each other. Are they going to direct their horses front against front? Their horses would collide, both would be forced to their feet, while running the chance of being crushed in the clash or in the fall of their mounts. Each one in the combat counts on his strength, on his skill, on the suppleness of his mount, on his personal courage; he does not want a blind encounter, and he is right. They halt face to face, abreast, to fight man to man; or each passes the other, thrusting with the sabre or lance; or each tries to wound the knee of the adversary and dismount him in this way. But as each is trying to strike the other, he thinks of keeping out of the way himself, he does not want a blind encounter that does away with the combat. The ancient battles, the cavalry engagements, the rare cavalry combats of our days, show us nothing else.

Discipline, while keeping the cavalrymen in the ranks, has not been able to change the instinct of the rider. No more than the isolated man is the rider in the line willing to meet the shock of a clash with the enemy. There is a terrible moral effect in a mass moving forward. If there is no way to escape to the right or to the left, men and horses will avoid the clash by stopping face to face. But only preëminently brave troops, equally seasoned in morale, alike well led and swept along, animated alike, will meet face to face. All these conditions are never found united on either side, so the thing is never seen. Forty-nine times out of fifty, one of the cavalry forces will hesitate, bolt, get into disorder, flee before the fixed purpose of the other. Three quarters of the time this will happen at a distance, before they can see each other's eyes. Often they will get closer. But always, always, the stop, the backward movement, the swerving of horses, the confusion, bring about fear or hesitation. They lessen the shock and turn it into instant flight. The resolute assailant does not have to slacken. He has not been able to overcome or turn the obstacles of horses not yet in flight, in this uproar of an impossible about face executed by routed troops, without being in disorder himself. But this disorder is that of victory, of the advance, and a good cavalry does not trouble itself about it. It rallies in advancing, while the vanquished one has fear at its heels.

On the whole, there are few losses. The engagement, if there is one, is an affair of a second. The proof is that in this action of cavalry against cavalry, the conquered alone loses men, and he loses generally few. The battle against infantry is alone the really deadly struggle. Like numbers of little chasseurs have

routed heavy cuirassiers.   How could they have done
so if the others had not given way before their determination?   The essential factor was, and always is,
determination.

The cavalry's casualties are always much less than
those of the infantry both from fire and from disease.
Is it because the cavalry is the aristocratic arm?   This
explains why in long wars it improves much more than
the infantry.

As there are few losses between cavalry and cavalry,
so there is little fighting.

Hannibal's Numidians, like the Russian Cossacks,
inspired a veritable terror by the incessant alarms they
caused.   They tired out without fighting and killed
by surprise.

Why is the cavalry handled so badly? — It is true
that infantry is not used better.— Because its rôle is
one of movement, of morale, of morale and movement
so united, that movement alone, often without a charge
or shock action of any sort can drive the enemy into
retreat, and, if followed closely, into rout.   That is a
result of the quickness of cavalry.   One who knows
how to make use of this quickness alone can obtain such
results.

All writers on cavalry will tell you that the charge
pushed home of two cavalry bodies and the shock at
top speed do not exist.   Always before the encounter,
the weaker runs away, if there is not a face to face
check.   What becomes then of the MV^2?   If this
famous MV^2 is an empty word, why then crush your
horses under giants, forgetting that in the formula besides M there is V^2.   In a charge, there is M, there is
V^2, there is this and that.   There is resolution, and I
believe, nothing else that counts!

Cohesion and unity give force to the charge. Alignment is impossible at a fast gait where the most rapid
pass the others. Only when the moral effect has been
produced should the gait be increased to take advantage of it by falling upon an enemy already in disorder,
in the act of fleeing. The cuirassiers charge at a trot.
This calm steadiness frightens the enemy into an about
face. Then they charge at his back, at a gallop.

They say that at Eckmühl, for every French cuiras-
sier down, fourteen Austrians were struck in the back.
Was it because they had no back-plate? It is evident
that it was because they offered their backs to the
blows.

Jomini speaks of charges at a trot against cavalry at
a gallop. He cites Lasalle who used the trot and who,
seeing cavalry approach at a gallop, would say: " There
are lost men." Jomini insists on the effect of shock.
The trot permits that compactness which the gallop
breaks up. That may be true. But the effect is moral
above all. A troop at the gallop sees a massed squadron coming towards it at a trot. It is surprised at first
at such coolness. The material impulse of the gallop
is superior; but there are no intervals, no gaps through
which to penetrate the line in order to avoid the shock,
the shock that overcomes men and horses. These men
must be very resolute, as their close ranks do not permit
them to escape by about facing. If they move at such
a steady gait, it is because their resolution is also firm
and they do not feel the need of running away, of
diverting themselves by the unchecked speed of the
unrestrained gallop, etc.[1]

[1] A propos of gaps: At the battle of Sempach thirteen hundred
badly armed Swiss opposed three thousand Lorraine knights
in phlanxes. The attack of the Swiss in a formation was
ineffective, and they were threatened with envelopment. But

Galloping men do not reason these things out, but they know them instinctively. They understand that they have before them a moral impulse superior to theirs. They become uneasy, hesitate. Their hands instinctively turn their horses aside. There is no longer freedom in the attack at a gallop. Some go on to the end, but three-fourths have already tried to avoid the shock. There is complete disorder, demoralization, flight. Then begins the pursuit at a gallop by the men who attacked at the trot.

The charge at a trot exacts of leaders and men complete confidence and steadfastness. It is the experience of battle only that can give this temper to all. But this charge, depending on a moral effect, will not always succeed. It is a question of surprise. Xenophon [1] recommended, in his work on cavalry operations, the use of surprise, the use of the gallop when the trot is customary, and vice-versa. " Because," he says, " agreeable or terrible, the less a thing is foreseen, the more pleasure or fright does it cause. This is nowhere seen better than in war, where every surprise strikes terror even to the strongest."

As a general rule, the gallop is and should be necessary in the charge; it is the winning, intoxicating gait, for men and horses. It is taken up at such a distance as may be necessary to insure its success, whatever it may cost in men and horses. The regulations are correct in prescribing that the charge be started close up. If the troopers waited until the charge was ordered, they would always succeed. I say that strong men, moved by pride or fear, by taking up too soon the

Arnold von Winkelried created a gap; the Swiss penetrated and the massacre followed.

[1] See Appendix II. (Historical documents.) (Editor's note.)

charge against a firm enemy, have caused more charges to fail than to succeed. Keeping men in hand until the command " charge," seizing the precise instant for this command, are both difficult. They exact of the energetic leader domination over his men and a keen eye, at a moment when three out of four men no longer see anything, so that good cavalry leaders, squadron leaders in general are very rare. Real charges are just as rare.

Actual shock no longer exists. The moral impulse of one of the adversaries nearly always upsets the other, perhaps far off, perhaps a little nearer. Were this " a little nearer," face to face, one of the two troops would be already defeated before the first saber cut and would disentangle itself for flight. With actual shock, all would be thrown into confusion. A real charge on the one part or the other would cause mutual extermination. In practice the victor scarcely loses any one.

Observation demonstrates that cavalry does not close with cavalry; its deadly combats are those against infantry alone.

Even if a cavalryman waits without flinching, his horse will wish to escape, to shrink before the collision. If man anticipates, so does the horse. Why did Frederick like to see his center closed in for the assault? As the best guarantee against the instincts of man and horse.

The cavalry of Frederick had ordinarily only insignificant losses: a result of determination.

The men want to be distracted from the advancing danger by movement. The cavalrymen who go at the enemy, if left to themselves, would start at a gallop, for fear of not arriving, or of arriving exhausted and

material for carnage. The same is true of the Arabs.
Note what happened in 1864 to the cavalry of General
Martineau. The rapid move relieves anxiety. It is
natural to wish to lessen it. But the leaders are there,
whom experience, whom regulations order to go slowly,
then to accelerate progressively, so as to arrive with
the maximum of speed. The procedure should be the
walk, then the trot, after that the gallop, then the
charge. But it takes a trained eye to estimate distance
and the character of the terrain, and, if the enemy approaches, to pick the point where one should meet him.
The nearer one approaches, the greater among the
troops is the question of morale. The necessity of
arriving at the greatest speed is not alone a mechanical
question, since indeed one never clashes, it is a moral
necessity. It is necessary to seize the moment at which
the uneasiness of one's men requires the intoxication
of the headlong charging gallop. An instant too late,
and a too great anxiety has taken the upper hand and
caused the hands of the riders to act on the horses; the
start is not free; a number hide by remaining behind.
An instant too soon: before arrival the speed has
slowed down; the animation, the intoxication of the
run, fleeting things, are exhausted. Anxiety takes the
upper hand again, the hands act instinctively, and even
if the start were unhampered, the arrival is not.

Frederick and Seidlitz were content when they saw
the center of the charging squadron three and four
ranks deep. It was as if they understood that with
this compact center, as the first lines could not escape
to the right or left, they were forced to continue
straight ahead.

In order to rush like battering-rams, even against
infantry, men and horses ought to be watered and fresh

(Ponsomby's cavalry at Waterloo). If there is ever contact between cavalry, the shock is so weakened by the hands of the men, the rearing of the horses, the swinging of heads, that both sides come to a halt.

Only the necessity for carrying along the man and the horse at the supreme moment, for distracting them, necessitates the full gallop before attacking the enemy, before having put him to flight.

Charges at the gallop of three or four kilometers, suppose horses of bronze.

Because morale is not studied and because historical accounts are taken too literally, each epoch complains that cavalry forces are no longer seen charging and fighting with the sword, that too much prudence dictates running away instead of clashing with the enemy.

These plaints have been made ever since the Empire, both by the allies, and by us. But this has always been true. Man was never invulnerable. The charging gait has almost always been the trot. Man does not change. Even the combats of cavalry against cavalry today are deadlier than they were in the lamented days of chivalry.

The retreat of the infantry is always more difficult than that of the cavalry; the latter is simple. A cavalry repulsed and coming back in disorder is a foreseen, an ordinary happening; it is going to rally at a distance. It often reappears with advantage. One can almost say, in view of experience, that such is its rôle. An infantry that is repelled, especially if the action has been a hot one and the cavalry rushes in, is often disorganized for the rest of the day.

Even authors who tell you that two squadrons never collide, tell you continually: " The force of cavalry is in the shock." In the terror of the shock, Yes. In the shock, No! It lies only in determination. It is a mental and not a mechanical condition.

Never give officers and men of the cavalry mathematical demonstrations of the charge. They are good only to shake confidence. Mathematical reasoning shows a mutual collapse that never takes place. Show them the truth. Lasalle with his always victorious charge at a trot guarded against similar reasonings, which might have demonstrated to him mathematically that a charge of cuirassiers at a trot ought to be routed by a charge of hussars at a gallop. He simply told them: " Go resolutely and be sure that you will never find a daredevil determined enough to come to grips with you." It is necessary to be a daredevil in order to go to the end. The Frenchman is one above all. Because he is a good trooper in battle, when his commanders themselves are daredevils he is the best in Europe. (Note the days of the Empire, the remarks of Wellington, a good judge). If moreover, his leaders use a little head work, that never harms anything. The formula of the cavalry is R (Resolution) and R, and always R, and R is greater than all the MV^2 in the world.

There is this important element in the pursuit of cavalry by cavalry. The pursued cannot halt without delivering himself up to the pursuer. The pursuer can always see the pursued. If the latter halts and starts to face about the pursuer can fall upon him before he is faced, and take him by surprise. But the pursued does not know how many are pursuing him. If he alone halts two pursuers may rush on him, for they see ahead of them and they naturally attack whoever tries to face about. For with the about face danger again confronts them. The pursuit is often instigated by the fear that the enemy will turn. The material fact that once in flight all together cannot turn again without risking being surprised and overthrown, makes the flight continuous. Even the bravest flee, until sufficient distance between them and the enemy, or some other circumstances such as cover or supporting troops, permits of a rally and a return to the offensive. In this case the pursuit may turn into flight in its turn.

Cavalry is insistent on attacking on an equal front. Because, if with a broader front, the enemy gives way before it, his wings may attack it and make it the pursued instead of the pursuer. The moral effect of resolution is so great that cavalry, breaking and pursuing a more numerous cavalry, is never pursued by the enemy wings. However the idea that one may be taken in rear by forces whom one has left on the flanks in a position to do so, has such an effect that the resolution necessary for an attack under these circumstances is rare.

Why is it that Colonel A—— does not want a depth formation for cavalry, he who believes in pressure of the rear ranks on the first? It is because at heart he is convinced that only the first rank can act in a cavalry charge, and that this rank can receive no impression, no speeding up, from those behind it.

There is debate as to the advantage of one or two ranks for the cavalry. This again is a matter of morale. Leave liberty of choice, and under varying conditions of confidence and morale one or the other will be adopted. There are enough officers for either formation.

It is characteristic of cavalry to advance further than infantry and consequently it exposes its flanks

more. It then needs more reserves to cover its flanks
and rear than does infantry. It needs reserves to protect and to support the pursuers who are almost always
pursued when they return. With cavalry even more
than infantry victory belongs to the last reserves held
intact. The one with the reserves is always the one
who can take the offensive. Tie to that, and no one
can stand before you.

With room to maneuver cavalry rallies quickly. In
deep columns it cannot.

The engagement of cavalry lasts only a moment. It
must be reformed immediately. With a roll call at
each reforming, it gets out of hand less than the infantry, which, once engaged, has little respite. There
should be a roll call for cavalry, and for infantry after
an advance, at each lull. There should be roll calls at
drill and in field maneuvers, not that they are necessary but in order to become habituated to them. Then
the roll call will not be forgotten on the day of action,
when very few think of what ought to be done.

In the confusion and speed of cavalry action, man
escapes more easily from surveillance. In our battles
his action is increasingly individual and rapid. The
cavalryman should not be left too free; that would be
dangerous. Frequently in action troops should be
reformed and the roll called. It would be an error not
to do so. There might be ten to twenty roll calls in a
day. The officers, the soldiers, would then have a
chance to demand an accounting from each man, and
might demand it the next day.

Once in action, and that action lasts, the infantryman of today escapes from the control of his officers.
This is due to the disorder inherent in battle, to deployment, to the absence of roll calls, which cannot be held

in action. Control, then, can only be in the hands of his comrades. Of modern arms infantry is the one in which there is the greatest need for cohesion.

Cavalry always fights very poorly and very little. This has been true from antiquity, when the cavalry-man was of a superior caste to the infantryman, and ought to have been braver.

Anybody advancing, cavalry or infantry, ought to scout and reconnoiter as soon as possible the terrain on which it acts. Condé forgot this at Neerwinden. The 55th forgot it at Solferino.[1] Everybody forgets it. And from the failure to use skirmishers and scouts, come mistakes and disasters.

The cavalry has a rifle for exceptional use. Look out that this exception does not become the rule. Such a tendency has been seen. At the battle of Sicka, the first clash was marred by the lack of dash on the part of a regiment of Chasseurs d'Afrique, which after being sent off at the gallop, halted to shoot. At the second clash General Bugeaud charged at their head to show them how to charge.

A young Colonel of light cavalry, asked carbines for his cavalry. "Why? So that if I want to recon-noiter a village I can sound it from a distance of seven or eight hundred meters without losing anybody." What can you say to a man advancing such ideas? Certainly the carbine makes everybody lose common sense.

The work of light cavalry makes it inevitable that they be captured sometimes. It is impossible to get news of the enemy without approaching him. If one man escapes in a patrol, that is enough. If no one comes back, even that fact is instructive. The cavalry

---

[1] See Appendix II. (Historical documents.) (Editor's note.)

is a priceless object that no leader wants to break. However it is only by breaking it that results can be obtained.

Some authors think of using cavalry as skirmishers, mounted or dismounted. I suppose they advance holding the horse by the bridle? This appears to be to be an absurdity. If the cavalryman fires he will not charge. The African incident cited proves that. It would be better to give the cavalryman two pistols than a carbine.

The Americans in their vast country where there is unlimited room, used cavalry wisely in sending it off on distant forays to cut communications, make levies, etc. What their cavalry did as an arm in battle is unknown. The cavalry raids in the American war were part of a war directed against wealth, against public works, against resources. It was war of destruction of riches, not of men. The raiding cavalry had few losses, and inflicted few losses. The cavalry is always the aristocratic arm which loses very lightly, even if it risks all. At least it has the air of risking all, which is something at any rate. It has to have daring and daring is not so common. But the merest infantry engagements in equal numbers costs more than the most brilliant cavalry raid.

3. *Cavalry Against Infantry.*

Cavalry knows how to fight cavalry. But how it fights infantry not one cavalry officer in a thousand knows. Perhaps not one of them knows. Go to it then gaily, with general uncertainty!

A military man, a participant in our great wars, recommends as infallible against infantry in line the charge from the flank, horse following horse. He

would have cavalry coming up on the enemy's left, pass
along his front and change direction so as to use its
arms to the right. This cavalryman is right. Such
charges should give excellent results, the only deadly
results. The cavalryman can only strike to his right,
and in this way each one strikes. Against ancient infantry such charges would have been as valuable as
against modern infantry. This officer saw with his
own eyes excellent examples of this attack in the wars
of the Empire. I do not doubt either the facts he
cites or the deductions he makes. But for such
charges there must be officers who inspire absolute
confidence in their men and dependable and experienced
soldiers. There is necessary, in short, an excellent
cavalry, seasoned by long wars, and officers and men
of very firm resolution. So it is not astonishing that
examples of this mode of action are rare. They always will be. They always require a head for the
charge, an isolated head, and when he is actually about
to strike, he will fall back into the formation. It
seems to him that lost in the mass he risks less than
when alone. Everybody is willing to charge, but only
if all charge together. It is a case of belling the
cat.

The attack in column on infantry has a greater
moral action than the charge in line. If the first and
second squadrons are repulsed, but the infantry sees a
third charging through the dust, it will say " When is
this going to stop? " And it will be shaken.

An extract from Folard: "Only a capable officer
is needed to get the best results from a cavalry which
has confidence in its movement, which is known to be
good and vigorous, and also is equipped with excellent
weapons. Such cavalry will break the strongest bat-

talions, if its leader has sense enough to know its power and courage enough to use this power."

Breaking is not enough, and is a feat that costs more than it is worth if the whole battalion is not killed or taken prisoner, or at least if the cavalry is not immediately followed by other troops, charged with this task.

At Waterloo our cavalry was exhausted fruitlessly, because it acted without artillery or infantry support.

At Krasno, August 14, 1812, Murat, at the head of his cavalry could not break an isolated body of ten thousand Russian infantry which continually held him off by its fire, and retired tranquilly across the plain.

The 72nd was upset by cavalry at Solferino.

From ancient days the lone infantryman has always had the advantage over the lone cavalryman. There is no shadow of a doubt about this in ancient narrations. The cavalryman only fought the cavalryman. He threatened, harassed, troubled the infantryman in the rear, but he did not fight him. He slaughtered him when put to flight by other infantry, or at least he scattered him and the light infantry slaughtered him.

Cavalry is a terrible weapon in the hands of one who knows how to use it. Who can say that Epaminondas could have defeated the Spartans twice without his Thessalonian cavalry,

Eventually rifle and artillery fire deafen the soldier; fatigue overpowers him; he becomes inert; he hears commands no longer. If cavalry unexpectedly appears, he is lost. Cavalry conquers merely by its appearance. (Bismarck or Decker).

Modern cavalry, like ancient cavalry, has a real effect only on troops already broken, on infantry engaged with infantry, on cavalry disorganized by artillery fire or by a frontal demonstration. But against such troops its action is decisive. In such cases its action is certain and gives enormous results. You might fight all day and lose ten thousand men, the enemy might lose as many, but if your cavalry pursues him, it will take thirty thousand prisoners. Its rôle is less knightly than its reputation and appearance, less so than the rôle of infantry. It always loses much less than infantry. Its greatest effect is the effect of surprise, and it is thereby that it gets such astonishing results.

What formation should infantry, armed with modern weapons, take to guard against flank attacks by cavalry? If one fires four times as fast, if the fire is better sustained, one needs only a quarter as many men to guard a point against cavalry. Protection might be secured by using small groups, placed the range of a rifle shot apart and flanking each other, left on the flank of the advance. But they must be dependable troops, who will not be worried by what goes on behind them.

4. *Armor and Armament.*

An armored cavalry is clearly required for moral reasons.

Note this with reference to the influence of cuirassiers (armored cavalrymen) on morale. At the battle of Renty, in 1554, Tavannes, a marshal, had with him his company armored in steel. It was the first time that such armor had been seen. Supported by some hundreds of fugitives who had rallied, he threw himself at the head of his company, on a column of two thousand German cavalry who had just thrown both infantry and cavalry into disorder. He chose his time so well that he broke and carried away these two thousand Germans, who fell back and broke the twelve hundred light horsemen who were supporting them. There followed a general flight, and the battle was won.

General Renard says "The decadence of cavalry caused the disappearance of their square formations in battle, which were characteristic in the seventeenth century." It was not the decadence of the cavalry but the abandonment of the cuirass and the perfecting of the infantry weapon to give more rapid fire. When cuirassiers break through they serve as examples, and emulation extends to others, who another time try to break through as they did.

Why cuirassiers? Because they alone, in all history, have charged and do charge to the end.

To charge to the end the cuirassiers need only half the courage of the dragoons, as their armor raises their morale one half. But since the cuirassiers have as much natural courage as the dragoons, for they are all the same men, it is proper to count the more on their action. Shall we have only one kind of cavalry? Which? If all our cavalry could wear the cuirass and at the same time do the fatiguing work of light cavalry, if all our horses could in addition carry the cuirass through such work, I say that there should be only cuirassiers. But I do not understand why the morale given by the cuirass should be lightly done away with, merely to have one cavalry without the cuirass.

A cavalryman armored completely and his horse partially, can charge only at a trot.

On the appearance of fire arms, cavalry, according to General Ambert, an author of the past, covered itself with masses of armor resembling anvils rather

than with cuirasses. It was at that time the essential
arm. Later as infantry progressed the tactics changed,
it needed more mobility. Permanent armies began to
be organized by the State. The State thought less
of the skin of the individual than of economy and
mobility and almost did away with cuirassiers. The
cuirass has always given, and today more than ever it
will give, confidence to the cavalryman. Courage,
dash, and speed have a value beyond that of mere mass.
I leave aside mathematical discussions which seem to
me to have nothing in common with battle conditions.
I would pick to wear the cuirass the best men in the
army, big chested, red-blooded, strong limbed, the foot
chasseurs. I would organize a regiment of light
cuirassiers for each of our divisions. Men and horses,
such a cavalry would be much more robust and active
than our present cuirassiers. If our armored cavalry
is worth more than any other arm by its dash in battle,
this cavalry would be worth twice as much. But how
would these men of small stature get into the saddle?
To this serious objection I answer, " They will arrange it." And this objection, which I do not admit,
is the only one that can be made against the organization of a light armored cavalry, an organization that
is made imperative by the improvement in weapons.
The remainder of those chasseur battalions which furnish cuirassiers, should return to the infantry, which
has long demanded them, and hussars and dragoons,
dismounted in the necessary number will also be wel-
comed by the infantry.

As for the thrust, the thrust is deadlier than the
cut. You do not have to worry about lifting your
arm; you thrust. But it is necessary that the cavalryman be convinced that to parry a vertical cut is folly.

This can be done by his officers, by those who have had experience, if there are any such in peace times. This is not easy. But in this respect, as in all others, the advantage lies with the brave. A cavalry charge is a matter of morale above all. It is identical in its methods, its effects, with the infantry charge. All the conditions to be fulfilled in the charge (walk, trot, gallop, charge, etc.) have a reason bearing on morale. These reasons have already been touched on.

Roman discipline and character demand tenacity. The hardening of the men to fatigue, and a good organization, giving mutual support, produced that tenacity, against which the bravest could not stand. The exhausting method of powerful strokes used by the Gauls could not last long against the skillful, terrible and less fatiguing method of fighting by the thrust.

The Sikh cavalrymen of M. Nolan armed with dragoon sabers sharpened by themselves, liked the cut. They knew nothing about methods of swordsmanship; they did not practice. They said " A good saber and a willingness to use it are enough." True, True!

There is always discussion as to the lance or the saber. The lance requires skillful vigorous cavalrymen, good horsemen, very well drilled, very adroit, for the use of the lance is more difficult than that of the straight sword, especially if the sword is not too heavy. Is not this an answer to the question? No matter what is done, no matter what methods are adopted, it must always be remembered that our recruits in war time are sent into squadrons as into battalions, with a hasty and incomplete training. If you give them lances, most of them will just have sticks in their hands, while a straight sword at the end of a strong arm is at the same time simple and terrible. A short trident spear, with three short points just long enough to kill but not only enough to go through the body, would remain in the body of the man and carry him along. It would recoil on the cavalryman who delivered the blow, he would be upset by the blow himself. But the dragoon must be supported by the saddle, and as he had kept hold of the shaft he would be able to disengage the fork which had pierced the body some six inches. No cavalry of equal morale could stand against a cavalry armed with such forked spears.

As between forks and lances, the fork would replace the lance. That is, of course, for beginners in mounted fencing. But the fork! It would be ridiculous, not military!

With the lance one always figures without the horse, whose slightest movement diverts the lance so much. The lance is a weapon frightful even to the mounted man who uses it properly. If he sticks an enemy at the gallop, he is dismounted, torn off by the arm attached to the lance which remains in the body of his enemy.

Cavalry officers and others who seek examples in " Victories and Conquests," in official reports, in " Bazancourt " are too naïve. It is hard to get at the truth. In war, in all things, we take the last example which we have witnessed. And now we want lances, which we do not know how to use, which frighten the cavalryman himself and pluck him from the saddle if he sticks anybody. We want no more cuirasses; we want this and that. We forget that the last example gives only a restricted number of instances relating to the matter in question.

It appears, according to Xenophon, that it was not easy to throw the dart from horseback. He constantly recommends obtaining as many men as possible who know how to throw the dart. He recommends leaning well back to avoid falling from the horse in the charge. In reading Xenophon it is evident that there was much falling from the horse.

It appears that in battle there is as great difficulty in handling the saber as in handling the bayonet. Another difficulty for the cavalryman lies in the handling of the musket. This is seen in the handling of the regulation weapon of the spahis. There is only one important thing for the cavalryman, to be well seated. Men should be on horseback for hours at a time, every day, from their arrival in the organization. If the selection of those who know something about horses was not neglected in the draft, and if such men were made cavalrymen, the practical training of the greater number would be much more rapidly concluded. I do not speak of the routine of the stable. Between mounted drills, foot drills might be gone through with in a snappy, free fashion, without rigidity, with daily increasing speed. Such drills would instruct cavalrymen more rapidly than the restricted method employed.

A dragoon horse carries in campaign with one day's food three hundred and eight pounds, without food or forage two hundred and seventy seven pounds. How can such horses carry this and have speed?

Seek the end always, not the means! Make a quarter of your cavalrymen into muleteers, a quarter of your horses into pack animals. You will thus secure, for the remaining three quarters unquestioned vigor. But how will you make up these pack trains? You will have plenty of wounded horses after a week of campaign.

CHAPTER IV

IF artillery did not have a greater range than the rifle, we could not risk separating it far from its support, as it would have to wait until the enemy was but four or five hundred paces away to fire on him. But the more its range is increased, the further away it can be placed from its support.

The greater the range of artillery, the greater freedom of action from the different arms, which no longer have to be side by side to give mutual support.

The greater the range of artillery, the easier it is to concentrate its fire. Two batteries fifteen hundred meters apart can concentrate on a point twelve hundred meters in front of and between them. Before the range was so long they had to be close together, and the terrain did not always lend itself to this.

Furthermore, do not support a piece by placing infantry just behind or alongside of it, as is done three-quarters of the time at maneuvers. On the contrary hide the infantry to the right or left and far behind, cover it without worrying too much about distance and let the artillery call for help if they think that the piece is in danger of being lost. Why should infantry be placed too close, and consequently have its advance demoralized? This will throw away the greatest advantage that we Frenchmen have in defense, that of defending ourselves by advancing, with morale unim-

231

paired, because we have not suffered heavy losses at a
halt.   There is always time to run to the defense of
artillery.   To increase the moral effect advance your
supports in formation.   Skirmishers can also be
swiftly scattered among the batteries.   These skirmishers, in the midst of the guns will not have to fear
cavalry.   Even if they are assailed by infantry it will
not be such a terrible thing.   The engagement will
merely be one between skirmishers, and they will be
able to take cover behind the pieces, firing against the
enemy who is coming up in the open.

Guibert, I believe, held that artillery should not
worry whether it was supported or not; that it should
fire up to the last minute, and finally abandon the
pieces, which supporting troops might or might not re-
capture.   These supporting troops should not be too
close.   It is easier to defend pieces, to take them back
even, by advancing on an enemy dispersed among
them, than to defend them by standing fast after having participated in the losses suffered by the artillery
under fire.   (Note the English in Spain.   The system
of having artillery followed by infantry platoons is
absurd.)

Artillery in battle has its men grouped around the
pieces, stationary assembly points, broadly distributed,
each one having its commander and its cannoneers,
who are always the same.   Thus there is in effect a
roll call each time artillery is put into battery.   Artillery carries its men with it; they cannot be lost nor
can they hide.   If the officer is brave, his men rarely
desert him.   Certainly, in all armies, it is in the artillery that the soldier can best perform his duty.

As General Leboeuf tells us, four batteries of artillery can be maneuvered, not more.   That is all right.

Here is the thing in a nut-shell. Four battalions is a big enough command for a colonel. A general has eight battalions. He gets orders, General, do so and so." He orders, " Colonel, do so and so." So that without any maneuvers being laid down for more than four battalions, as many battalions as you like can be maneuvered and drilled.

CHAPTER V

THERE are plenty of carefree generals, who are never worried nor harassed. They do not bother about anything. They say, " I advance. Follow me." The result is an incredible disorder in the advance of columns. If ten raiders should fall on the column with a shout, this disorder would become a rout, a disaster. But these gentlemen never bother with such an eventuality. They are the great men of the day, until the moment that some disaster overwhelms them.

Cavalry is no more difficult to work with than infantry. According to some military authors, a cavalry general ought to have the wisdom of the phoenix. The perfect one should have. So should the perfect infantry general. Man on horseback and man afoot is always the same man. Only, the infantry general rarely has to account for the losses in his command, which may have been due to faulty or improper handling. The cavalry general does have to do this. (We shall lay aside the reasons why.) The infantry general has six chances for real battle to one for the cavalry general. These are the two reasons why, from the begginning of a war, more initiative is found in infantry than in cavalry generals. General Bugeaud might have made a better cavalry general than an infantry general. Why? Because he had immediate decision and firm resolution. There is more need for resolution in the infantryman than in the cavalryman.

234

Why? There are many reasons, which are matters of opinion.

In short, the infantryman is always more tired than the cavalryman. His morale is therefore harder to keep up. I believe therefore that a good infantry general is rarer than one of cavalry. Also, the resolution of an infantry general does not have to last for a moment only; it has to endure for a long, long time.

Good artillery generals are common. They are less concerned with morale than with other things, such as material results. They have less need to bother about the morale of their troops, as combat discipline is always better with them than with the other arms. This is shown elsewhere.

Brigadier generals ought to be in their prescribed places. Very well, but the most of them are not and never have been. They were required to be in place at the battle of Moscow, but, as they were so ordered there, it is evident that they were not habitually in place. They are men; and their rank, it seems to them, ought to diminish rather than increase the risks they have to run. And, then, in actual engagement, where is their prescribed place?

When one occupies a high command there are many things which he does not see. The general-in-chief, even a division commander, can only escape this failing by great activity, moved by strict conscientiousness and aided by clairvoyance. This failing extends to those about him, to his heads of services. These men live well, sleep well; the same must be true of all! They have picked, well-conditioned horses; the roads are excellent! They are never sick; the doctors must be exaggerating sickness! They have attendants and doctors; everybody must be well looked after! Something happens which shows abominable negligence, common enough in war. With a good heart and a full belly they say, " But this is infamous, unheard of! It could nót have happened! It is impossible! etc."

To-day there is a tendency, whose cause should be sought, on the part of superiors to infringe on the authority of inferiors. This is general. It goes very high and is furthered by the mania for command, inherent in the French character. It results in lessening the authority of subordinate officers in the minds of their soldiers. This is a grave matter, as only the firm authority and prestige of subordinate officers can maintain discipline. The tendency is to oppress subordinates; to want to impose on them, in all things, the views of the superior; not to admit of honest mistakes, and to reprove them as faults; to make everybody, even down to the private, feel that there is only one infallible authority. A colonel, for instance, sets himself up as the sole authority with judgment and intelligence. He thus takes all initiative from subordinate officers, and reduces them to a state of inertia, coming from their lack of confidence in themselves and from fear of being severely reproved. How many generals, before a regiment, think only of showing how much they know! They lessen the authority of the colonel. That is nothing to them. They have asserted their superiority, true or false; that is the essential. With cheeks puffed out, they leave, proud of having attacked discipline.

This firm hand which directs so many things is absent for a moment. All subordinate officers up to this moment have been held with too strong a hand, which has kept them in a position not natural to them. Immediately they are like a horse, always kept on a tight rein, whose rein is loosened or missing. They cannot in an instant recover that confidence in themselves, that has been painstakingly taken away from them without their wishing it. Thus, in such a moment conditions become unsatisfactory, the soldier very quickly feels that the hand that holds him vacillates.

"Ask much, in order to obtain a little," is a false saying, a source of errors, an attack on discipline. One ought to obtain what one asks. It is only necessary to be moderately reasonable and practical.

In following out this matter, one is astonished at the lack of foresight found in three out of four officers. Why? Is there anything so difficult about looking forward a little? Are three-quarters of the officers so stupid? No! It is because their egoism, generally frankly acknowledged, allow them to think only of who is looking at them. They think of their troops by chance perhaps, or because they have to. Their troops are never their preoccupation, consequently they do not think about them at all. A major in command of an organization in Mexico, on his first march in a hot country, started without full canteens, perhaps without canteens at all, without any provision for water, as he might march in France. No officer in his battalion called his attention to the omission, nor was more foresighted than he. In this first march, by an entire lack of foresight in everything, he lost, in dead, half of his command. Was he reduced? No! He was made a lieutenant-colonel.

Officers of the general staff learn to order, not to command. "Sir, I order," a popular phrase, applies to them.

The misfortune is not that there is a general staff,

but that it has achieved command. For it always has commanded, in the name of its commanders it is true, and never obeyed, which is its duty. It commands in fact. So be it! But just the same it is not supposed to.

Is it the good quality of staffs or that of combatants that makes the strength of armies? If you want good fighting men, do everything to excite their ambition, to spare them, so that people of intelligence and with a future will not despise the line but will elect to serve in it. It is the line that gives you your high command, the line only, and very rarely the staff. The staff, however, dies infrequently, which is something. Do they say that military science can only be learned in the general staff schools? If you really want to learn to do your work, go to the line.

To-day, nobody knows anything unless he knows how to argue and chatter. A peasant knows nothing, he is a being unskilled even in cultivating the soil. But the agriculturist of the office is a farmer emeritus, etc. Is it then believed that there is ability only in the general staff? There is the assurance of the scholar there, of the pedagogue who has never practiced what he preaches. There is book learning, false learning when it treats of military matters. But knowledge of the real trade of a soldier, knowledge of what is possible, knowledge of blows given and received, all these are conspicuously absent.

Slowness of promotion in the general staff as compared to its rapidity in the line might make many men of intelligence, of head and heart, pass the general staff by and enter the line to make their own way. To be in the line would not then be a brevet of imbecility. But to-day when general staff officers rank the best of

the line, the latter are discouraged and rather than
submit to this situation, all who feel themselves fitted
for advancement want to be on the general staff. So
much the better? So much the worse. Selection is
only warranted by battle.

How administrative deceits, in politics or elsewhere,
falsify the conclusions drawn from a fact!

In the Crimea one hundred per cent. of the French
operated upon succumbed, while only twenty-seven per
cent. of the English operated upon died. That was
attributed to the difference in temperament! The
great cause of this discrepancy was the difference in
care. Our newspapers followed the self-satisfied and
rosy statements given out by our own supply depart-
ment. They pictured our sick in the Crimea lying in
beds and cared for by sisters of charity. The fact is
that our soldiers never had sheets, nor mattresses, nor
the necessary changes of clothes in the hospitals; that
half, three-quarters, lay on mouldy straw, on the
ground, under canvass. The fact is, that such were
the conditions under which typhus claimed twenty-five
to thirty thousand of our sick after the siege; that
thousands of pieces of hospital equipment were offered
by the English to our Quartermaster General, and that
he refused them! Everybody ought to have known
that he would! To accept such equipment was to acknowledge that he did not have it. And he ought to
have had it. Indeed he did according to the newspapers and the Quartermaster reports. There were
twenty-five beds per hospital so that it could be said,
"We have beds!" Each hospital had at this time
five hundred or more sick.

These people are annoyed if they are called hypo-
crites. While our soldiers were in hospitals, without

anything, so to speak, the English had big, well-venti-
lated tents, cots, sheets, even night stands with urinals.
And our men had not even a cup to drink from! Sick
men were cared for in the English hospitals. They
might have been in ours, before they died, which they
almost always did.

It is true that we had the typhus and the English
had not. That was because our men in tents had the
same care as in our hospitals, and the English the same
care as in their hospitals.

Read the war reports of supply departments and
then go unexpectedly to verify them in the hospitals
and storehouses. Have them verified by calling up
and questioning the heads of departments, but question
them conscientiously, .without dictating the answers.
In the Crimea, in May of the first year, we were no
better off than the English who complained so much,
Who has dared to say, however, that from the time
they entered the hospital to the time that they left it,
dead, evacuated, or cured, through fifteen or twenty
days of cholera or typhus, our men lay on the same
plank, in the same shoes, drawers, shirts and clothing
that they brought in with them? They were in a state
of living putrefaction that would by itself have killed
well men! The newspapers chanted the praises of the
admirable French administration. The second winter
the English had no sick, a smaller percentage than in
London. But to the eternal shame of the French command and administration we lost in peace time, twenty-
five to thirty thousand of typhus and more than one
thousand frozen to death. Nevertheless, it appeared
that we had the most perfect administration in the
world, and that our generals, no less than our administration, were full of devoted solicitude to provide all

the needs of the soldier. That is an infamous lie, and is known as such, let us hope.

The Americans have given us a good example. The good citizens have gone themselves to see how their soldiers were treated and have provided for them themselves. When, in France, will good citizens lose faith in this best of administrations which is theirs? When will they, confident in themselves, do spontaneously, freely, what their administration cannot and never will be able to do?

The first thing disorganized in an army is the administration. The simplest foresight, the least signs even of order disappear in a retreat. (Note Russia-Vilna).

In the Crimea, and everywhere more or less, the doctor's visit was without benefit to the patient. It was made to keep up his spirits, but could not be followed by care, due to lack of personnel and material. After two or three hours of work, the doctor was exhausted.

In a sane country the field and permanent hospitals ought to be able to handle one-fifth of the strength at least. The hospital personnel of to-day should be doubled. It is quickly cut down, and it ought to have time, not only to visit the sick, but to care for them, feed them, dose and dress them, etc.

CHAPTER VI

MAN's admiration for the great spectacles of nature is the admiration for force. In the mountains it is mass, a force, that impresses him, strikes him, makes him admire. In the calm sea it is the mysterious and terrible force that he divines, that he feels in that enormous liquid mass; in the angry sea, force again. In the wind, in the storm, in the vast depth of the sky, it is still force that he admires.

All these things astounded man when he was young. He has become old, and he knows them. Astonishment has turned to admiration, but always it is the feeling of a formidable force which compels his admiration. This explains his admiration for the warrior.

The warrior is the ideal of the primitive man, of the savage, of the barbarian. The more people rise in moral civilization, the lower this ideal falls. But with the masses everywhere the warrior still is and for a long time will be the height of their ideals. This is because man loves to admire the force and bravery that are his own attributes. When that force and bravery find other means to assert themselves, or at least when the crowd is shown that war does not furnish the best examples of them, that there are truer and more exalted examples, this ideal will give way to a higher one.

Nations have an equal sovereignty based on their

242

existence as states. They recognize no superior juris-
diction and call on force to decide their differences.
Force decides. Whether or not might was right, the
weaker bows to necessity until a more successful effort
can be made. (Prud'homme). It is easy to understand Gregory VII's ideas on the subject.

In peace, armies are playthings in the hands of
princes. If the princes do not know anything about
them, which is usually the case, they disorganize them.
If they understand them, like the Prince of Prussia,
they make their armies strong for war.

The King of Prussia and the Prussian nobility,
threatened by democracy, have had to change the passion for equality in their people into a passion for
domination over foreign nations. This is easily done,
when domination is crowned with success, for man,
who is merely the friend of equality is the lover of
domination. So that he is easily made to take the
shadow for the substance. They have succeeded.
They are forced to continue with their system. Otherwise their status as useful members of society would be
questioned and they would perish as leaders in war.
Peace spells death to a nobility. Consequently nobles
do not desire it, and stir up rivalries among peoples,
rivalries which alone can justify their existence as
leaders in war, and consequently as leaders in peace.
This is why the military spirit is dead in France. The
past does not live again. In the spiritual as in
the physical world, what is dead is dead. Death comes
only with the exhaustion of the elements, the conditions which are necessary for life. For these reasons
revolutionary wars continued into the war with Prussia. For these reasons if we had been victorious we
would have found against us the countries dominated

by nobilities, Austria, Russia, England. But with us vanquished, democracy takes up her work in all European countries, protected in the security which victory always gives to victors. This work is slower but surer than the rapid work of war, which, exalting rivalries, halts for a moment the work of democracy within the nations themselves. Democracy then takes up her work with less chance of being deterred by rivalry against us. Thus we are closer to the triumph of democracy than if we had been victors. French democracy rightfully desires to live, and she does not desire to do so at the expense of a sacrifice of national pride. Then, since she will still be surrounded for a long time by societies dominated by the military element, by the nobility, she must have a dependable army. And, as the military spirit is on the wane in France, it must be replaced by having noncommissioned officers and officers well paid. Good pay establishes position in a democracy, and to-day none turn to the army, because it is too poorly paid. Let us have well paid mercenaries. By giving good pay, good material can be secured, thanks to the old warrior strain in the race. This is the price that must be paid for security.

The soldier of our day is a merchant. So much of my flesh, of my blood, is worth so much. So much of my time, of my affections, etc. It is a noble trade, however, perhaps because man's blood is noble merchandise, the finest that can be dealt in.

M. Guizot says "Get rich!" That may seem cynical to prudes, but it is truly said. Those who deny the sentiment, and talk to-day so loftily, what do they advise? If not by words, then by example they counsel the same thing; and example is more contagious.

Is not private wealth, wealth in general, the avowed ambition sought by all, democrats and others? Let us be rich, that is to say, let us be slaves of the needs that wealth creates.

The Invalides in France, the institutions for pensioners, are superb exhibits of pomp and ostentation. I wish that their founding had been based on ideas of justice and Christianity and not purely on military-political considerations. But the results are disastrous to morality. This collection of weaklings is a school of depravity, where the invalided soldier loses in vice his right to respect.

Some officers want to transform regiments into permanent schools for officers of all ranks, with a two-hour course each day in law, military art, etc. There is little taste for military life in France; such a procedure would lessen it. The leisure of army life attracts three out of four officers, laziness, if you like. But such is the fact. If you make an officer a schoolboy all his life he will send his profession to the devil, if he can. And those who are able to do so, will in general be those who have received the best education. An army is an extraordinary thing, but since it is necessary, there should be no astonishment that extraordinary means must be taken to keep it up; such as offering in peace time little work and a great deal of leisure. An officer is a sort of aristocrat, and in France we have no finer ideal of aristocratic life than one of leisure. This is not a proof of the highest ideals, nor of firmness of character. But what is to be done about it?

From the fact that military spirit is lacking in our nation (and officers are with greater difficulty than ever recruited in France) it does not follow that we shall not have to engage in war. Perhaps the contrary is true.

It is not patriotic to say that the military spirit is dead in France? The truth is always patriotic. The military spirit died with the French nobility, perished because it had to perish, because it was exhausted, at the end of its life. That only dies which has no longer the sap of life, and can no longer live. If a thing is merely sick it can return to health. But who can say that of the French nobility? An aristocracy, a nobility that dies, dies always by its own fault; because it no longer performs its duties; because it fails in its task; because its functions are of no more value to the state; because there is no longer any reason for its existence in a society, whose final tendency is to suppress its functions.

After 1789 had threatened our patriotism, the natural desire for self-protection revived the military spirit in the nation and in the army. The Empire developed this movement, changed the defensive military spirit to the offensive, and used it with increasing effect up to 1814 or 1815. The military spirit of the July Restoration was a reminiscence, a relic of the Empire, a form of opposition to government by liberalism instead of democracy. It was really the spirit of opposition and not the military spirit, which is essentially conservative.

There is no military spirit in a democratic society, where there is no aristocracy, no military nobility. A democratic society is antagonistic to the military spirit.

The military spirit was unknown to the Romans. They made no distinction between military and civil duties. I think that the military air dates from the time that the profession of arms became a private profession, from the time of the bravos, the Italian condottieri, who were more terrifying to civilians than to the enemy. When the Romans said "cedant arma togæ," they did not refer to civil officials and soldiers; the civil officials were then soldiers in their turn; professional soldiers did not exist. They meant "might gives way to right."

Machiavelli quotes a proverb, "War makes thieves and peace has them hanged." The Spaniards in Mexico, which has been in rebellion for forty years, are more or less thieves. They want to continue to ply the trade. Civil authority exists no longer with them, and they would look on obedience to such an authority as shameful. It is easy to understand the difficulty of organizing a peaceful government in such a country. Half the population would have to hang the other half. The other half does not want to be hanged.

We are a democratic society; we become less and less military. The Prussian, Russian, Austrian aristocracies which alone make the military spirit of those states, feel in our democratic society an example which threatens their existence, as nobility, as aristocracy. They are our enemies and will be until they are wiped out, until the Russian, Austrian and Prussian states become democratic societies, like ours. It is a matter of time.

The Prussian aristocracy is young. It has not been degenerated by wealth, luxury and servility of the court. The Prussian court is not a court in the luxurious sense of the word. There is the danger.

Meanwhile Machiavelian doctrines not being forbidden to aristocracies, these people appeal to German Jingoism, to German patriotism, to all the passions

which move one people who are jealous of another.
All this is meant to hide under a patriotic exterior
their concern for their own existence as an aristocracy,
as a nobility.

The real menace of the day is czarism, stronger than
the czars themselves, which calls for a crusade to drive
back Russia and the uncultured Slav race.

It is time that we understood the lack of power in
mob armies; that we recall to mind the first armies of
the revolution that were saved from instant destruction only by the lack of vigor and decision in European
cabinets and armies. Look at the examples of revolu-
tionaries of all times, who have all to gain and cannot
hope for mercy. Since Spartacus, have they not
always been defeated? An army is not really strong
unless it is developed from a social institution. Spartacus and his men were certainly terrible individual
fighters. They were gladiators used to struggle and
death. They were prisoners, barbarian slaves en-
raged by their loss of liberty, or escaped serfs, all men
who could not hope for mercy. What more terrible
fighters could be imagined? But discipline, leadership,
all was improvised and could not have the firm discipline coming down from the centuries and drawn from
the social institutions of the Romans. They were
conquered. Time, a long time, is needed to give to
leaders the habit of command and confidence in their
authority — to the soldiers confidence in their leaders
and in their fellows. It is not enough to order discipline. The officers must have the will to enforce it,
and its vigorous enforcement must instill subordination in the soldiers. It must make them fear it more
than they fear the enemy's blows.

How did Montluc fight, in an aristocratic society?

Montluc shows us, tells us. He advanced in the van
of the assault, but in bad places he pushed in front of
him a soldier whose skin was not worth as much as
was his. He had not the slightest doubt or shame
about doing this. The soldier did not protest, the pro-
priety of the act was so well established. But you,
officers, try that in a democratic army, such as we have
commenced to have, such as we shall later have!

In danger the officer is no better than the soldier.
The soldier is willing enough to advance, but behind
his officer. Also, his comrades' skin is no more
precious than is his, they must advance too. This
very real concern about equality in danger, which seeks
equality only, brings on hesitation and not resolution.
Some fools may break their heads in closing in, but
the remainder will fire from a distance. Not that this
will cause fewer losses, far from it.

Italy will never have a really firm army. The Italians are too civilized, too fine, too democratic in a certain sense of the word. The Spaniards are the same.
This may cause laughter, but it is true.

The French are indeed worthy sons of their fathers,
the Gauls. War, the most solemn act in the life of a
nation, the gravest of acts, is a light thing to them.
The good Frenchman lets himself be carried away, in-
flamed by the most ridiculous feats of arms into the
wildest enthusiasm. Moreover he interprets the word
" honor " in a fashion all his own. An expedition is
commenced without sufficient reason, and good Frenchmen, who do not know why the thing is done, disap-
prove. But presently blood is spilled. Good sense
and justice dictate that this spilled blood should taint
those responsible for an unjust enterprise. But jingoism says " French blood has been spilled: Honor is at

stake!" And millions of gold, which is the unit of labor, millions of men, are sacrificed to a ridiculous high-sounding phrase.

Whence comes this tendency toward war which characterizes above all the good citizen, the populace, who are not called upon personally to participate? The military man is not so easily swayed. Some hope for promotion or pension, but even they are sobered by their sense of duty. It comes from the romance that clothes war and battle, and that has with us ten times more than elsewhere, the power of exciting enthusiasm in the people. It would be a service to humanity and to one's people to dispell this illusion, and to show what battles are. They are buffooneries, and none the less buffooneries because they are made terrible by the spilling of blood. The actors, heroes in the eyes of the crowd, are only poor folk torn between fear, discipline and pride. They play some hours at a game of advance and retreat, without ever meeting, closing with, even seeing closely, the other poor folks, the enemy, who are as fearful as they but who are caught in the same web of circumstance.

What should be considered is how to organize an army in a country in which there is at the same time national and provincial feeling. Such a country is France, where there is no longer any necessity for uniting national and provincial feeling by mixing up the soldiers. In France, will the powerful motif of pride, which comes from the organization of units from particular provinces, be useful? From the fusion of varying elements comes the character of our troops, which is something to be considered. The make-up of the heavy cavalry should be noted. It has perhaps

too many Germans and men from the northern provinces.

French sociability creates cohesion in French troops
more quickly than could be secured in troops in other
nations. Organization and discipline have the same
purpose. With a proud people like the French, a rational organization aided by French sociability can
often secure desired results without it being necessary
to use the coercion of discipline.

Marshal de Gouvion-Saint Cyr said, " Experienced
soldiers know and others ought to know that French
soldiers once committed to the pursuit of the enemy
will not return to their organization that day until
forced back into it by the enemy. During this time
they must be considered as lost to the rest of the
army."

At the beginning of the Empire, officers, trained in
the wars of the Revolution by incessant fighting, possessed great firmness. No one would wish to purchase
such firmness again at the same price. But in our
modern wars the victor often loses more than the
vanquished, apart from the temporary loss in prisoners.
The losses exceed the resources in good men, and discourage the exhausted, who appear to be very numerous, and those who are skilled in removing themselves
from danger. Thus we fall into disorder. The Duke
of Fezensac, testifying of other times, shows us the
same thing that happens to-day. Also to-day we depend only on mass action, and at that game, despite the
cleverest strategic handling, we must lose all, and do.

French officers lack firmness but have pride. In
the face of danger they lack composure, they are disconcerted, breathless, hesitant, forgetful, unable to

think of a way out.   They call, " Forward, forward."
This is one of the reasons why handling a formation
in line is difficult, especially since the African campaigns where much is left to the soldier.

The formation in rank is then an ideal, unobtainable
in modern war, but toward which we should strive.
But we are getting further away from it.   And then,
when habit loses its hold, natural instinct resumes its
empire.   The remedy lies in an organization which will
establish cohesion by the mutual acquaintanceship of
all.   This will make possible mutual surveillance,
which has such power over French pride.

It might be said that there are two kinds of war,
that in open country, and in the plain, and that of posts
garrisoning positions in broken country.   In a great
war, with no one occupying positions, we should be
lost immediately.   Marshal Saxe knew us well when
he said that the French were best for a war of position.
He recognized the lack of stability in the ranks.

On getting within rifle range the rank formation
tends to disappear.   You hear officers who have been
under fire say " When you get near the enemy, the
men deploy as skirmishers despite you.   The Russians
group under fire.   Their holding together is the hud-
dling of sheep moved by fear of discipline and of danger."   There are then two modes of conduct under
fire, the French and the Russian.

The Gauls, seeing the firmness of the Roman formation, chained themselves together, making the first
rank unbreakable and tying living to dead.   This forbade the virtue they had not divined in the Roman
formation, the replacement of wounded and exhausted
by fresh men.   From this replacement came the firm-

ness which seemed so striking to the Gauls. The rank continually renewed itself.

Why does the Frenchman of to-day, in singular contrast to the Gaul, scatter under fire? His natural intelligence, his instinct under the pressure of danger causes him to deploy.

His method must be adopted. In view of the impossibility to-day of the Roman Draconian discipline which put the fear of death behind the soldier, we must adopt the soldier's method and try to put some order into it. How? By French discipline and an organization that permits of it.

Broken, covered country is adapted to our methods. The zouaves at Magenta could not have done so well on another kind of ground.[1]

Above all, with modern weapons, the terrain to be advanced over must be limited in depth.

How much better modern tactics fit the impatient French character! But also how necessary it is to guard against this impatience and to keep supports and reserves under control.

It should be noted that German or Gallic cavalry was always better than Roman cavalry, which could not hold against it, even though certainly better armed. Why was this? Because decision, impetuosity, even blind courage, have more chance with cavalry than with infantry. The defeated cavalry is the least brave cavalry. (A note for our cavalry here!) It was easier for the Gauls to have good cavalry than it is for us, as fire did not bother them in the charge.

The Frenchman has more qualities of the cavalryman than of the infantryman. Yet French infantry

[1] See Appendix II. (Historical documents.) (Editor's note.)

appears to be of greater value. Why? Because the use of cavalry on the battlefield requires rare decision and the seizing of the crucial opportunity. If the cavalryman has not been able to show his worth, it is the fault of his leaders. French infantry has always been defeated by English infantry. In cavalry combat the English cavalry has always fled before the French in those terrible cavalry battles that are always flights. Is this because in war man lasts longer in the cavalry and because our cavalrymen were older and more seasoned soldiers than our infantry? This does not apply to us only. If it is true for our cavalrymen, it is also true for the English cavalrymen. The reason is that on the field of battle the rôle of the infantryman against a firm adversary requires more coolness and nerve than does the rôle of the cavalryman. It requires the use of tactics based on an understanding of the national characteristics of ourselves and of our enemies. Against the English the confidence in the charge that is implanted in our brains, was completely betrayed. The rôle of cavalry against cavalry is simpler. The French confidence in the charge makes good fighting cavalry, and the Frenchman is better fitted than any other for this rôle. Our cavalry charge better than any other. That is the whole thing, on the battle field it is understood. As they move faster than infantry, their dash, which has its limits, is better preserved when they get up to the enemy.

The English have always fled before our cavalry. This proves that, strong enough to hold before the moral impulse of our infantry, they were not strong enough to hold before the stronger impulse of cavalry.

We ought to be much better cavalrymen than infantrymen, because the essential in a cavalryman is a fearless impetuosity. That is for the soldier. The cavalry leader ought to use this trait without hesitation, at the same time taking measures to support it and to guard against its failings. The attack is always, even on the defensive, an evidence of resolution, and gives a moral ascendancy. Its effect is more immediate with cavalry, because the movements of cavalry are more rapid and the moral effect has less time to be modified by reflection. To insure that the French cavalry be the best in Europe, and a really good cavalry, it needs but one thing, to conform to the national temperament, to dare, to dare, and to advance.

One of the singular features of French discipline is that on the road, especially in campaign the methods of punishment for derelictions become illusory, impractical. In 1859 there were twenty-five thousand skulkers in the Army in Italy. The soldier sees this immediately and lack of discipline ensues. If our customs do not permit of Draconian discipline, let us replace that moral coercion by another. Let us insure cohesion by the mutual acquaintanceship of men and officers; let us call French sociability to our aid.

With the Romans discipline was severest and most rigidly enforced in the presence of the enemy. It was enforced by the soldiers themselves. To-day, why should not the men in our companies watch discipline and punish themselves. They alone know each other, and the maintenance of discipline is so much to their interest as to encourage them to stop skulking. The twenty-five thousand men who skulked in Italy, all wear the Italian medal. They were discharged with certificates of good conduct. This certificate, in campaign should be awarded by the squad only. In place of that, discipline must be obtained somehow, and it is placed as an additional burden on the officer. He above all has to uphold it. He is treated without regard for his dignity. He is made to do the work of the non-commissioned officer. He is used as fancy dictates.

This cohesion which we hope for in units from squad to company, need not be feared in other armies. It cannot develop to the same point and by the same methods with them as with us. Their make-up is not ours, their character is different. This individuality of squads and companies comes from the make-up of our army and from French sociability.

Is it true that the rations of men and horses are actually insufficient in campaign? This is strange economy! To neglect to increase the soldier's pay five centimes! It would better his fare and prevent making of an officer a trader in vegetables in order to properly feed his men. Yet millions are squandered each year for uniforms, geegaws, shakos, etc!

If a big army is needed, it ought to cost as little as possible. Simplicity in all things! Down with all sorts of plumes! Less amateurs! If superfluous trimmings are not cut down it will be unfortunate! What is the matter with the sailor's uniform? Insignificant and annoying details abound while vital details of proper footgear and instruction, are neglected. The question of clothing for campaign is solved by adopting smocks and greatcoats and by doing away with headquarters companies! This is the height of folly. I suppose it is because our present uniforms need specialists to keep them in condition, and smocks and greatcoats do not!

APPENDIX I

1. *Introduction.*

It may be said that the history of the development of infantry fire is none too plain, even though fire action to-day, in Europe, is almost the sole means of destruction used by that arm.

Napoleon said, " The only method of fire to be used in war is fire at will." Yet after such a plain statement by one who knew, there is a tendency to-day to make fire at command the basis of infantry battle tactics.

Is this correct? Experience only can determine. Experience is gained; but nothing, especially in the trade of war, is sooner forgotten than experience. So many fine things can be done, beautiful maneuvers executed, ingenious combat methods invented in the confines of an office or on the maneuver ground. Nevertheless let us try to hold to facts.

Let us consider, in the study of any kind of fire, a succinct history of small arms; let us see what kind of fire is used with each weapon, attempting at the same time to separate that which has actually happened from the written account.

2. *Succinct History of the Development of Small Arms, from the Arquebus to Our Rifle.*

The arquebus in use before the invention of powder gave the general design to fire arms. The arquebus marks then the transition from the mechanically thrown missile to the bullet.

The tube was kept to direct the projectile, and the bow and string were replaced by a powder chamber and ignition apparatus.

[1] Written in 1869. (Editor's note.)

257

This made a weapon, very simple, light and easy to charge; but the small caliber ball thrown from a very short barrel, gave penetration only at short distances.

The barrel was lengthened, the caliber increased, and a more efficient, but a less convenient arm resulted. It was indeed impossible to hold the weapon in aiming·position and withstand the recoil at the moment of firing.

To lessen recoil there was attached to the bottom of the barrel a hook to catch on a fixed object at the moment of discharge. This was called a hook arquebus.

But the hook could only be used under certain circumstances. To give the arm a point of support on the body, the stock was lengthened and inclined to permit sighting. This was the petrinal or poitrinal. The soldier had in addition a forked support for the barrel.

In the musket, which followed, the stock was again modified and held against the shoulder. Further the firing mechanism was improved.

The arm had been fired by a lighted match; but with the musket, the arm becoming lighter and more portable, there came the serpentine lock, the match-lock, then the wheel-lock, finally the Spanish lock and the flint-lock.

The adoption of the flint-lock and the bayonet produced the rifle, which Napoleon regarded as the most powerful weapon that man possesses.

But the rifle in its primitive state had defects. Loading was slow; it was inaccurate, and under some circumstances it could not be fired.

How were these defects remedied?

As to the loading weakness, Gustavus Adolphus, understanding the influence on morale of rapid loading and the greater destruction caused by the more rapid fire, invented the cartridge for muskets. Frederic, or some one of his time, the name marks the period, replaced wooden by cylindrical iron ramrods. To prime more quickly a conical funnel allowed the powder to pass from the barrel into the firing-pan. These two last improvements saved time in two ways, in priming and in loading. But it was the adoption of the breech-loader that brought the greatest increase in rapidity of fire.

These successive improvements of the weapon, all tending to increase the rapidity of fire, mark the most remarkable military periods of modern times:

    cartridges — Gustavus Adolphus
    iron ramrod — Frederic
    improved vent (adopted by the soldiers if not pre-
        scribed by competent orders) — wars of the Re-
        public and of the Empire,
    breech-loading — Sadowa.

Accuracy was sacrificed to rapidity of fire. This will be explained later. Only in our day has the general use of rifling and of elongated projectiles brought accuracy to the highest point. In our times, also, the use of fulminate has assured fire under all conditions.

We have noted briefly the successive improvements in fire arms, from the arquebus to the rifle.

Have the methods of employment made the same progress?

3. *Progressive Introduction of Fire-Arms Into the Arma-
    ment of the Infantryman.*

The revolution brought about by powder, not in the art of war but in that of combat, came gradually. It developed along with the improvement of fire arms. Those arms gradually became those of the infantryman.

Thus, under Francis I, the proportion of infantrymen carrying fire arms to those armed with pikes was one to three or four.

At the time of the wars of religion arquebusiers and pikemen were about equal in number.

Under Louis XIII, in 1643, there were two fire-arms to one pike; in the war of 1688, four to one; finally pikes disappeared.

At first men with fire-arms were independent of other combatants, and functioned like light troops in earlier days.

Later the pikes and the muskets were united in constituent elements of army corps.

The most usual formation was pikes in the center, muskets on the wings.

Sometimes the pikemen were in the center of their respective companies, which were abreast.

Or, half the musketeers might be in front of the pikemen, half behind. Or again, all the musketeers might be behind the kneeling pikemen. In these last two cases fire covered the whole front.

Finally pike and musket might alternate.

These combinations are found in treatises on tactics. But we do not know, by actual examples, how they worked in battle, nor even whether all were actually employed.

4. *The Classes of Fire Employed With Each Weapon.*

When originally some of the infantry were armed with the long and heavy arquebus in its primitive state, the feebleness of their fire caused Montaigne to say, certainly on military authority, " The arms have so little effect, except on the ears, that their use will be discontinued." Research is necessary to find any mention of their use in the battles of that period.[1]

However we find a valuable piece of information in Brantôme, writing of the battle of Pavia.

" The Marquis de Pescani won the battle of Pavia with Spanish arquebusiers, in an irregular defiance of all regulation and tradition by employing a new formation. Fifteen hundred arquebusiers, the ablest, the most experienced, the cleverest, above all the most agile and devoted, were selected by the Marquis de Pescani, instructed by him on new lines, and practiced for a long time. They scattered by squads over the battlefield, turning, leaping from one place to another with great speed, and thus escaped the cavalry charge. By this new method of fighting, unusual, astonishing, cruel and unworthy, these arquebusiers greatly hampered the operations of the French cavalry, who were com-

[1] It is hard to determine what method of fire, at command or at will, was used. But what we find in the works of the best military authorities, from Montecuculli to Marshal Saxe, is general opposition to the replacement of the pike by the rifle. All predicted the abandonment of the rifle for the pike, and the future always proved them wrong. They ignored experience. They could not understand that stronger than all logic is the instinct of man, who prefers long range to close fighting, and who, having the rifle would not let it go, but continually improved it.

pletely lost. For they, joined together and in mass, were brought to earth by these few brave and able arquebusiers. This irregular and new method of fighting is more easily imagined than described. Any one who can try it out will find it is good and useful; but it is necessary that the arquebusiers be good troops, very much on the jump (as the saying is) and above all reliable."

It should be borne in mind, in noting the preceding, that there is always a great difference between what actually occurred, and the description thereof (made often by men who were not there, and God knows on what authority). Nevertheless, there appears in these lines of Brantôme a first example of the most destructive use of the rifle, in the hands of skirmishers.

During the religious wars, which consisted of skirmishes and taking and retaking garrisoned posts, the fire of arquebusiers was executed without order and individually, as above.

The soldier carried the powder charges in little metal boxes hung from a bandoleer. A finer, priming, powder was contained in a powder horn; the balls were carried in a pouch. At the onset the soldier had to load his piece. It was thus that he had to fight with the match arquebus. This was still far from fire at command.

However this presently appeared. Gustavus Adolphus was the first who tried to introduce method and coördination into infantry fire. Others, eager for innovations, followed in his path. There appeared successively, fire by rank, in two ranks, by subdivision, section, platoon, company, battalion, file fire, parapet fire, a formal fire at will, and so many others that we can be sure that all combinations were tried at this time.

Fire by ranks was undoubtedly the first of these; it will give us a line on the others.

Infantry was formed six deep. To execute fire by rank all ranks except the last knelt. The last rank fired and reloaded. The rank in front of it then rose and did the same thing, as did all other ranks successively. The whole operation was then recommenced.

Thus the first group firing was executed successively by ranks.

Montecuculli said, " The musketeers are ranged six deep, so that the last rank has reloaded by the time the first has fired, and takes up the fire again, so that the enemy has to face continuous fire."

However, under Condé and Turenne, we see the French army use only fire at will.

It is true that at this time fire was regarded only as an accessory. The infantry of the line which, since the exploit of the Flemish, the Swiss and the Spaniards, had seen their influence grow daily, was required for the charge and the advance and consequently was armed with pikes.

In the most celebrated battles of these times, Rocroi, Nordlingen, Lens, Rethel and the Dunes, we see the infantry work in this way. The two armies, in straight lines, commenced by bombarding each other, charged with their cavalry wings, and advanced with their infantry in the center. The bravest or best disciplined infantry drove back the other, and often, if one of its wings was victorious, finished by routing it. No marked influence of fire is found at this time. The tradition of Pescani was lost.

Nevertheless fire-arms improved; they became more effective and tended to replace the pike. The use of the pike obliged the soldier to remain in ranks, to fight only in certain cases, and exposed him to injury without being able to return blow for blow. And, this is exceedingly instructive, the soldier had by this time an instinctive dislike of this arm, which often condemned him to a passive rôle. This dislike necessitated giving high pay and privilege to obtain pikemen. And in spite of all at the first chance the soldier threw away his pike for a musket.

The pikes themselves gradually disappeared before fire-arms; the ranks thinned to permit the use of the latter. Four rank formation was used, and fire tried in that order, by rank, by two ranks, upright, kneeling, etc.

In spite of these attempts, we see the French army in combat, notably at Fontenoy, still using fire at will, the soldier leaving ranks to fire and returning to load.

It can be stated, in spite of numerous attempts at adoption, that no fire at command was used in battle up to the days of Frederick.

Already, under William, the Prussian infantry was noted for the rapidity and continuity of its fire. Frederick further increased the ability of his battalions to fire by decreasing their depth. This fire, tripled by speed in loading, became so heavy that it gave Prussian battalions a superiority over others of three to one.

The Prussians recognized three kinds of fire, at a halt, in advancing, and in retreat. We know the mechanics of fire at a halt, the first rank kneeling. Of fire in advancing Guibert says: " What I call marching fire, and which anybody who thinks about it must find as ill advised as I do, is a fire I have seen used by some troops. The soldiers, in two ranks, fire in marching, but they march of course at a snail's pace. This is what Prussian troops call fire in advancing. It consists in combined and alternating volleys from platoons, companies, half battalions or battalions. The parts of the line which have fired advance at the double, the others at the half step."

In other methods of fire, as we have said, the Prussian battalion was in three ranks, the first kneeling. The line delivered salvos, only at command.

However, the theory of executing fire by salvo in three ranks did not bother Frederick's old soldiers. We will see presently how they executed it on the field of battle.

Be that as it may, Europe was impressed with these methods and tended to adopt them. D'Argenson provided for them in the French army and introduced fire at command. Two regulations prescribing this appeared, in 1753 and 1755. But in the war which followed, Marshal de Broglie, who undoubtedly had experience and as much common sense as M. D'Argenson, prescribed fire at will. All infantry in his army was practiced in it during the winter of 1761–1762.

Two new regulations succeeded the preceding, in 1764 and 1776. The last prescribed fire in three ranks at command, all ranks upright.[1]

Thus we come to the wars of the Revolution, with regula-

[1] The danger arising from this kind of fire, led to proposals to put the smallest men in the front rank, the tallest in the rear rank.

tions calling for fire at command, which was not executed in battle.

Since these wars, our armies have always fought as skirmishers. In speaking of our campaigns, fire at command is never mentioned. It was the same under the Empire, in spite of numerous essays from the Boulogne school and elsewhere. At the Boulogne school, fire at command by ranks was first tried by order of Napoleon. This fire, to be particularly employed against cavalry — in theory it is superb — does not seem to have been employed. Napoleon says so himself, and the regulations of 1832, in which some influence of soldiers of the Empire should be found, orders fire in two ranks or at will, by bodies of men, to the exclusion of all others.

According to our military authority, on the authority of our old officers, fire at command did not suit our infantry; yet it lived in the regulations. General Fririon (1822) and de Gouvion-Saint-Cyr (1829) attacked this method. Nothing was done. It remained in the regulations of 1832, but without being ordered in any particular circumstances. It appeared there for show purposes, perhaps.

On the creation of the chasseurs d'Orléans, fire by rank was revived. But neither in our African campaigns nor in our last two wars in the Crimea and Italy can a single example of fire at command be found. It practice it was believed to be impracticable. It was known to be entirely ineffective and fell into disrepute.

But to-day, with the breech-loading rifle, there is a tendency to believe it practicable and to take it up with new interest. Is this more reasonable than in the past? Let us see.

5. *Methods of Fire Used in the Presence of the Enemy; Methods Recommended or Ordered But Impractical. Use and Efficacy of Fire at Command.*

Undoubtedly at the Potsdam maneuvers the Prussian infantry used only salvos executed admirably. An unbelievable discipline kept the soldier in place and in line. Barbaric punishments were incorporated in the military code. Blows, the whip, executions, punished the slightest derelictions. Even N. C. O.'s were subjected to blows with the flat of the sword. Yet all this was not enough on the field of battle; a complete rank of non-commissioned officer file closers was also needed to hold the men to their duty.

M. Carion-Nisas said, " These file-closers hook their halberds together and form a line that cannot be broken." In spite of all this, after two or three volleys, so says General Renard, whom we believe more than charitable, there is no power of discipline which can prevent regular fire from breaking into fire at will.

But let us look further, into Frederick's battles. Let us take the battle of Mollwitz, in which success was specifically laid to fire at command, half lost, then won by the Prussian salvos.

" The Austrian infantry had opened fire on the lines of the Prussians, whose cavalry had been routed. It was necessary to shake them to insure victory. The Austrians still used wooden ramrods. Their fire came slowly, while the Prussian fire was thunderous, five or six shots to the rifle per minute. The Imperial troops, surprised and disconcerted by this massed fire, tried to hurry. In their hurry many broke their fragile ramrods. Confusion spread through the ranks, and the battle was lost."

But, if we study actual conditions of the period, we see that things did not happen in such an orderly sequence.

Firing started, and it is said that it was long and deadly. The Prussians iron ramrods gave them the advantage over an enemy whose ramrods were wooden, harder to manipulate and easily broken. However, when the order to advance was given to the Prussians, whole battalions stood fast; it was impossible to budge them. The soldiers tried to escape the fire and got behind each other, so that they were thirty or forty deep.

Here are men who exhibit under fire an admirable calm, an immovable steadiness. Each instant they hear the dead heavy sound of a bullet striking. They see, they feel, around them, above them, between their legs, their comrades fall and writhe, for the fire is deadly. They have the power in their hands to return blow for blow, to send back to the enemy the death that hisses and strikes about them. They

do not take a false step; their hands do not close instinctively
on the trigger. They wait, imperturbably, the order of their
chiefs — and what chiefs! These are the men who at the
command " forward," lack bowels, who huddle like sheep one
behind the other. Are we to believe this?

Let us get to the truth of the matter. Frederick's veterans,
in spite of their discipline and drill, are unable to follow the
methods taught and ordered. They are no more able to
execute fire at command than they are to execute the ordered
advance of the Potsdam maneuver field. They use fire at
will. They fire fast from instinct — stronger than their
discipline — which bids them send two shots for one. Their
fire becomes indeed, a thunderous roll, not of salvos, but of
rapid fire at will. Who fires most, hits most, so the soldier
figures. So indeed did Frederick, for he encouraged fire in
this same battle of Mollwitz; he thereafter doubled the number of cartridges given the soldier, giving him sixty instead
of thirty.

Furthermore, if fire at command had been possible, who
knows what Frederick's soldiers would have been capable
of? They would have cut down battalions like standing
grain. Allowed to aim quietly, no man interfering with
another, each seeing clearly — then at the signal all firing
together. Could anything hold against them? At the first
volley the enemy would have broken and fled, under the
penalty of annihilation in case they stayed. However, if we
look at the final result at Mollwitz, we see that the number
of killed is about the same on the side that used fire at command as on the side that did not. The Prussians lost 960
dead, the Austrians 966.

But they say that if fire was not more deadly, it was because sight-setting was then unknown. What if it was?
There was no adjustment of fire perhaps, but there were
firing regulations; aiming was known. Aiming is old. We
do not say it was practiced; but it was known, and often
mentioned. Cromwell often said, " Put your confidence in
God, my children, and fire at their shoe-laces."

Do we set our sights better to-day? It is doubtful. If
the able soldiers of Cromwell, of Frederick, of the Republic
and of Napoleon could not set their sights — can we?

Thus this fire at command, which was only possible rarely and to commence action, was entirely ineffective.

Hardy spirits, seeing the slight effect of long range firing in battle, counselled waiting till the enemy was at twenty paces and driving him back with a volley. You do not have to sight carefully at twenty paces. What would be the result?

" At the battle of Castiglione," says Marshal Saxe, " the Imperial troops let the French approach to twenty paces, hoping to destroy them by a volley. At that distance they fired coolly and with all precautions, but they were broken before the smoke cleared. At the battle of Belgrade (1717) I saw two battalions who at thirty paces, aimed and fired at a mass of Turks. The Turks cut them up, only two or three escaping. The Turkish loss in dead was only thirty-two."

No matter what the Marshal says, we doubt that these men were cool. For men who could hold their fire up to such a near approach of the enemy, and fire into masses, would have killed the front rank, thrown the others into confusion, and would never have been cut up as they were. To make these men await, without firing, an enemy at twenty or thirty paces, needed great moral pressure. Controlled by discipline they waited, but as one waits for the roof to fall, for a bomb to explode, full of anxiety and suppressed emotion. When the order is given to raise the arms and fire the crisis is reached. The roof falls, the bomb explodes, one flinches and the bullets are fired into the air. If anybody is killed it is an accident.

This is what happened before the use of skirmishers. Salvos were tried. In action they became fire at will. Directed against troops advancing without firing they were ineffective. They did not halt the dash of the assault, and the troops who had so counted on them fled demoralized. But when skirmishers were used, salvos became impossible. Armies who held to old methods learned this to their cost.

In the first days of the Revolution our troops, undrilled and not strictly disciplined, could not fight in line. To advance on the enemy, a part of the battalion was detached as skirmishers. The remainder marched into battle and was engaged without keeping ranks. The combat was sustained by groups fighting without formal order. The art was to support by reserves the troops advanced as skirmishers. The skirmishers always began the action, when indeed they did not complete it.

To oppose fire by rank to skirmishers was fools' play.

Skirmishers necessarily opposed each other. Once this method was adopted, they were supported, reinforced by troops in formation. In the midst of general firing fire at command became impossible and was replaced by fire at will.

Dumouriez, at the battle of Jemmapes, threw out whole battalions as skirmishers, and supporting them by light cavalry, did wonders with them. They surrounded the Austrian redoubts and rained on the cannoneers a hail of bullets so violent that they abandoned their pieces.

The Austrians, astounded by this novel combat method, vainly reinforced their light troops by detachments of heavy infantry. Their skirmishers could not resist our numbers and impetuosity, and presently their line, beaten by a storm of bullets, was forced back. The noise of battle, the firing, increased; the defeated troops, hearing commands no longer, threw down their arms and fled in disorder.

So fire in line, heavy as it may be, cannot prevail against the power of numerous detachments of skirmishers. A rain of bullets directed aimlessly is impotent against isolated men profiting by the slightest cover to escape the fire of their adversaries, while the deployed battalions offer to their rifles a huge and relatively harmless target. The dense line, apparently so strong, withers under the deadly effect of the fire of isolated groups, so feeble in appearance. (General Renard.)

The Prussians suffered in the same way at Jena. Their lines tried fire at command against our skirmishers. You might as well fire on a handful of fleas.

They tell us of the English salvos at Sainte-Euphémie, in Calabria, and later in Spain. In these particular cases they could be used, because our troops charged without first sending out skirmishers.

The battle of Sainte-Euphémie only lasted half an hour; it was badly conceived and executed, " And if," says General

Duhesme, "the advancing battalions had been preceded by detachments of skirmishers who had already made holes in enemy ranks, and, on close approach, the heads of columns had been launched in a charge, the English line would not have conserved that coolness which made their fire so effective and accurate. Certainly it would not have waited so long to loose its fire, if it had been vigorously harassed by skirmishers.'

An English author, treating of the history of weapons, speaks of the rolling fire, well directed, of the English troops. He makes no mention of salvos. Perhaps we were mistaken, and in our accounts have taken the fire of a battalion for the formal battalion fire at command of our regulations.

The same tendency appears more clearly in the work on infantry of the Marquis de Chambray, who knew the English army well. He says that the English in Spain used almost entirely fire in two ranks. They employed battalion fire only when attacked by our troops without skirmishers, firing on the flanks of our columns. And he says "The fire by battalion, by half battalion and by platoon is is limited to the target range. The fire actually most used in war is that in two ranks, the only one used by the French." Later he adds "Experience proves fire in two ranks the only one to be used against the enemy." Before him Marshal Saxe wrote "Avoid dangerous maneuvers, such as fire by platoon, which have often caused shameful defeats." These statements are as true now as then.

Fire at command, by platoon, by battalion, etc., is used in case the enemy having repulsed skirmishers and arrived at a reasonable range either charges or opens fire for effect himself. If the latter, fire is reciprocal and lasts until one or the other gives way or charges. If the enemy charges. what happens? He advances preceded by skirmishers who deliver a hail of bullets. You wish to open fire, but the voices of your officers are lost. The noise of artillery, of small arms, the confusion of battle, the shrieks of the wounded, distract the soldiers' attention. Before you have delivered your command the line is ablaze. Then try to stop your soldiers. While there is a cartridge left, they will fire.

The enemy may find a fold of ground that protects him; he may adopt in place of his deployed order columns with wide intervals between, or otherwise change his dispositions. The changing incidents of battle are hidden by smoke and the troops in front, from the view of the officers behind. The soldiers will continue to fire and the officers can do nothing about it.

All this has been said already, has been gone into, and fire at command has been abandoned. Why take it up again? It comes to us probably from the Prussians. Indeed the reports of their general staff on their last campaign, of 1866, say that it was very effectively employed, and cite many examples.

But a Prussian officer who went through the campaign in the ranks and saw things close up, says, " In examining the battles of 1866 for characteristics, one is struck by a feature common to all, the extraordinary extension of front at the expense of depth. Either the front is spun out into a single long thin line, or it is broken into various parts that fight by themselves. Above all the tendency is evident to envelop the enemy by extending the wings. There is no longer any question of keeping the original order of battle. Different units are confused, by battle, or even before battle. Detachments and large units of any corps are composed of diverse and heterogeneous elements. The battle is fought almost exclusively by columns of companies, rarely of half-battalions. The tactics of these columns consists in throwing out strong detachments of skirmishers. Gradually the supports are engaged and deployed. The line is broken, scattered, like a horde of irregular cavalry. The second line which has held close order tries to get up to the first promptly, first to engage in the fight, also because they suffer losses from the high shots directed at the first line. It suffers losses that are heavy as it is compact and supports them with impatience as it does not yet feel the fever of battle. The most of the second line then forces entry into the first, and, as there is more room on the wings, it gravitates to the wings. Very often even the reserve is drawn in, entirely, or so largely that it cannot fulfill its mission. In fact, the fighting of the first two lines is a

series of combats between company commands and the
enemy each command faces. Superior officers cannot follow on horseback all the units, which push ahead over all
sorts of ground. They have to dismount and attach themselves to the first unit of their command met. Unable to
manipulate their whole command, in order to do something.
they command the smaller unit. It is not always better commanded at that. Even generals find themselves in this situation."

Here is something we understand better. It is certainly
what occurs.

As for the instances cited in the general staff reports,
they deal with companies or half-battalions at most. Not
withstanding the complacency with which they are cited,
they must have been rare, and the exception should not be
taken as establishing a rule.

6. *Fire at Will — Its Efficacy.*

Thus fire at command, to-day as in the past, is impractical
and consequently not actually used in battle. The only means
employed are fire at will and the fire of skirmishers. Let
us look into their efficacy.

Competent authorities have compiled statistics on this
point.

Guibert thinks that not over two thousand men are killed
or wounded by each million cartridges used in battle.

Gassendi assures us that of three thousand shots only one
is a hit.

Piobert says that the estimate, based on the result of long
wars, is that three to ten thousand cartridges are expended
for each man hit.

To-day, with accurate and long range weapons, have things
changed much? We do not think so. The number of bullets
fired must be compared with the number of men dropped,
with a deduction made for the action of artillery, which
must be considered.

A German author has advanced the opinion that with the
Prussian needle rifle the hits are 60% of the shots fired.
But then how explain the disappointment of M. Dreyse. the
happy inventor of the needle rifle, when he compared Prus-

sian and Austrian losses. This good old gentleman was disagreeably astonished at seeing that his rifle had not come up to his expectations.

Fire at will, as we shall presently show, is a fire to occupy the men in the ranks but its effect is not great. We could give many examples; we only cite one, but it is conclusive.

"Has it not been remarked," says General Duhesme, "that, before a firing line there is raised a veil of smoke which on one side or the other hides the troops from view, and makes the fire of the best placed troops uncertain and practically without effect? I proved it conclusively at the battle of Caldiero, in one of the successive advances that occurred on my left wing. I saw some battalions, which I had rallied, halted and using an individual fire which they could not keep up for long. I went there. I saw through the smoke cloud nothing but flashes, the glint of bayonets and the tops of grenadier's caps. We were not far from the enemy however, perhaps sixty paces. A ravine separated us, but it could not be seen. I went into the ranks, which were neither closed nor aligned, throwing up with my hand the soldiers' rifles to get them to cease firing and to advance. I was mounted, followed by a dozen orderlies. None of us were wounded, nor did I see an infantryman fall. Well then! Hardly had our line started when the Austrians, heedless of the obstacle that separated us, retreated."

It is probable that had the Austrians started to move first, the French would have given way. It was veterans of the Empire, who certainly were as reliable as our men, who gave this example of lack of coolness.

In ranks, fire at will is the only possible one for our officers and men. But with the excitement, the smoke, the annoying incidents, one is lucky to get even horizontal fire, to say nothing of aimed fire.

In fire at will, without taking count of any trembling, men interfere with each other. Whoever advances or who gives way to the recoil of his weapon deranges the shot of his neighbor. With full pack, the second rank has no loophole; it fires in the air. On the range, spacing men to the extremty of the limits of formation, firing very slowly, men are found who are cool and not too much bothered by the crack of discharge in their ears, who let the smoke pass and seize a loophole of pretty good visibility, who try, in a word, not to lose their shots. And the percentage results show much more regularity than with fire at command.

But in front of the enemy fire at will becomes in an instant haphazard fire. Each man fires as much as possible, that is to say, as badly as possible. There are physical and mental reasons why this is so.

Even at close range, in battle, the cannon can fire well. The gunner, protected in part by his piece, has an instant of coolness in which to lay accurately. That his pulse is racing does not derange his line of sight, if he has will power. The eye trembles little, and the piece once laid, remains so until fired.

The rifleman, like the gunner, only by will-power keeps his ability to aim. But the excitement in the blood, of the nervous system, opposes the immobility of the weapon in his hands. No matter how supported, a part of the weapon always shares the agitation of the man. He is instinctively in haste to fire his shot, which may stop the departure of the bullet destined for him. However lively the fire is, this vague reasoning, unformed as it is in his mind, controls with all the force of the instinct of self preservation. Even the bravest and most reliable soldiers then fire madly.

The greater number fire from the hip.

The theory of the range is that with continual pressure on the trigger the shot surprises the firer. But who practices it under fire?

However, the tendency in France to-day is to seek only accuracy. What good will it do when smoke, fog, darkness, long range, excitement, the lack of coolness, forbid clear sight?

It is hard to say, after the feats of fire at Sebastopol, in Italy, that accurate weapons have given us no more valuable service than a simple rifle. Just the same, to one who has seen, facts are facts. But — see how history is written. It has been set down that the Russians were beaten at Inkermann by the range and accuracy of weapons of the French troops. But the battle was fought in thickets and wooded country, in a dense fog. And when the weather cleared, our soldiers, our chasseurs were out of ammunition and borrowed from the Russian cartridge boxes, amply provided with cartridges for round, small calibered bullets. In either case there could have been no accurate fire. The facts are that the Russians were beaten by superior morale; that unaimed fire, at random, there perhaps more than elsewhere, had the only material effect.

When one fires and can only fire at random, who fires most hits most. Or perhaps it is better said that who fires least expects to be hit most.

Frederick was impressed with this, for he did not believe in the Potsdam maneuvers. The wily Fritz looked on fire as a means to quiet and occupy the undependable soldiers and it proved his ability that he could put into practice that which might have been a mistake on the part of any other general officer. He knew very well how to count on the effect of his fire, how many thousand cartridges it took to kill or wound an enemy. At first his soldiers had only thirty cartridges. He found the number insufficient, and after Mollwitz gave them sixty.

To-day as in Frederick's day, it is rapid random fire, the only one practicable, which has given prestige to the Prussians. This idea of rapid fire was lost after Frederck, but the Prussians have recovered it to-day by exercising common sense. However our veterans of the Empire had preserved this idea, which comes from instinct. They enlarged their vents, scornful of flare backs, to avoid having to open the chamber and prime. The bullet having a good deal of clearance when the cartridge was torn and put in the gun, with a blow of the butt on the ground they had their arms charged and primed.

But to-day as then, in spite of skill acquired in individual fire, men stop aiming and fire badly as soon as they are grouped into platoons to fire.

Prussian officers, who are practical men, know that adjustment of sights is impracticable in the heat of action, and that in fire by volleys troops tend to use the full sight. So in the war of 1866 they ordered their men to fire very low, almost without sighting, in order to profit by ricochets.

7. *Fire by Rank Is a Fire to Occupy the Men in Ranks.*

But if fire at will is not effective, what is its use? As we have already said its use is to occupy the men in the ranks.

In ordinary fire the act of breathing alone, by the movement it communicates to the body greatly annoys men in firing. How then can it be claimed that on the field of battle, in rank, men can fire even moderately well when they fire only to soothe themselves and forget danger?

Napoleon said " The instinct of man is not to let himself be killed without defending himself." And indeed man in combat is a being in whom the instinct of self preservation dominates at times all other sentiments. The object of discipline is to dominate this instinct by a greater terror of shame or of punishment. But it is never able entirely to attain this object; there is a point beyond which it is not effectual. This point reached, the soldier must fire or he will go either forward or back. Fire is then, let us say, a safety vent for excitement.

In serious affairs it is then difficult, if not impossible, to control fire. Here is an example given by Marshal Saxe:

" Charles XII, King of Sweden, wished to introduce into his infantry the method of charging with the bayonet. He spoke of it often, and it was known in the army that this was his idea. Finally at the battle of —— against the Russians, when the fighting started he went to his regiment of infantry, made it a fine speech, dismounted before the colors, and himself led the regiment to the charge. When he was thirty paces from the enemy the whole regiment fired, in spite of his orders and his presence. Otherwise, it did very well and broke the enemy. The king was so annoyed that all he did was pass through the ranks, remount his horse, and go away without saying a word."

So that, if the soldier is not made to fire, he will fire anyway to distract himself and forget danger. The fire of Frederick's Prussians had no other purpose. Marshal Saxe saw this. " The speed with which the Prussans load their rifles," he tells us, " is advantageous in that it occupies the soldier and forbids reflection while he is in the presence of the enemy. It is an error to believe that the five last victories gained by the nation in its last war were due to fire. It has been noted that in most of these actions there were more Prussians killed by rifle fire than there were of their enemies."

It would be sad to think the soldier in line a firing machine. Firing has been and always will be his principal object, to fire as many shots in as short a time as possible. But the victor is not always the one who kills the most; he is fortunate who best knows how to overcome the morale of his enemy.

The coolness of men cannot be counted on. And as it is necessary above all to keep up their morale one ought to try above all to occupy and soothe them. This can best be done by frequent discharges. There will be little effect, and it would be absurd to expect them to be calm enough to fire slowly, adjust their ranges and above all sight carefully.

8. *The Deadly Fire Is the Fire of Skirmishers.*

In group firing, when the men are grouped into platoons or battalions, all weapons have the same value, and if it is assumed to-day that fire must decide engagements, the method of fighting must be adopted which gives most effect to the weapon. This is the employment of skirmishers.

It is this class of fire, indeed, which is deadliest in war. We could give many examples but we shall be content with the two following instances, taken from General Duhesme.

" A French officer who served with the Austrians in one of the recent wars," says General Duhesme, " told me that from the fire of a French battalion one hundred paces from them, his company lost only three or four men, while in the same time they had had more than thirty killed or wounded by the fire of a group of skirmishers in a little wood on their flank three hundred paces away."

" At the passage of the Minico, in 1801, the 2nd battalion of the 91st received the fire of a battalion of Bussi's regiment without losing a man; the skirmishers of that same organization killed more than thirty men in a few minutes while protecting the retreat of their organization."

The fire of skirmishers is then the most deadly used in war, because the few men who remain cool enough to aim are not otherwise annoyed while employed as skirmishers. They will perform better as they are better hidden, and better trained in firing.

The accuracy of fire giving advantages only in isolated fire, we may consider that accurate weapons will tend to make fighting by skirmishers more frequent and more decisive.

For the rest, experience authorizes the statement that the use of skirmishers is compulsory in war. To day all troops seriously engaged become in an instant groups of skirmishers and the only possible precise fire is from hidden snipers.

However, the military education which we have received, the spirit of the times, clouds with doubt our mind regarding this method of fighting by skirmishers. We accept it regretfully. Our personal experience being incomplete, insufficient, we content ourselves with the supposition that gives us satisfaction. The war of skirmishers, no matter how thoroughly it has been proven out, is accepted by constraint, because we are forced by circumstance to engage our troops by degrees, in spite of ourselves, often unconsciously. But, be it understood, to-day a successive engagement is necessary in war.

However, let us not have illusions as to the efficacy of the fire of skirmishers. In spite of the use of accurate and long range weapons, in spite of all training that can be given the soldier, this fire never has more than a relative effect, which should not be exaggerated.

The fire of skirmishers is generally against skirmishers. A body of troops indeed does not let itself be fired on by skirmishers without returning a similar fire. And it is absurd to expect skirmishers to direct their fire on a body protected by skirmishers. To demand of troops firing individually, almost abandoned to themselves, that they do not answer the shots directed at them, by near skirmishers, but aim at a distant body, which is not harming them, is to ask an impossible unselfishness.

As skirmishers men are very scattered. To watch the adjustment of ranges is difficult. Men are practically left alone. Those who remain cool may try to adjust their range, but it is first necessary to see where your shots fall, then, if the terrain permits this and it will rarely do so, to distinguish them from shots fired at the same time by your neighbors. Also these men will be more disturbed, will fire faster and less accurately, as the fight is more bitter, the enemy stauncher; and perturbation is more contagious than coolness.

The target is a line of skirmishers, a target offering so little breadth and above all depth, that outside of point blank fire, an exact knowledge of the range is necessary to secure effect. This is impossible, for the range varies at each instant with the movements of the skirmishers.[1]

Thus, with skirmishers against skirmishers, there are scattered shots at scattered targets. Our fire of skirmishers, marching, on the target range, proves this, although each man knows exactly the range and has time and the coolness to set his sights. It is impossible for skirmishers in movement to set sights beyond four hundred meters, and this is pretty extreme, even though the weapon is actually accurate beyond this.

Also, a shot is born. There are men, above all in officer instructors at firing schools, who from poor shots become excellent shots after years of practice. But it is impossible to give all the soldiers such an education without an enormous consumption of ammunition and without abandoning all other work. And then there would be no results with half of them.

To sum up, we find that fire is effective only at point

[1] Nothing is more difficult than to estimate range; in nothing is the eye more easily deceived. Practice and the use of instruments cannot make a man infallible. At Sebastopol, for two months, a distance of one thousand to twelve hundred meters could not be determined by the rifle, due to inability to see the shots. For three months it was impossible to measure by ranging shots, although all ranges were followed through, the distance to a certain battery which was only five hundred meters away, but higher and separated from us by a ravine. One day, after three months, two shots at five hundred meters were observed in the target. This distance was estimated by everybody as over one thousand meters; it was only five hundred. The village taken and the point of observation changed, the truth became evident.

blank. Even in our last wars there have been very few circumstances in which men who were favored with coolness and under able leadership have furnished exceptions. With these exceptions noted, we can say that accurate and long range weapons have not given any real effect at a range greater than point blank.

There has been put forward, as proof of the efficacy of accurate weapons the terrible and decisive results obtained by the British in India, with the Enfield rifle. But these results have been obtained because the British faced comparatively poorly armed enemies. They had then the security, the confidence, the ensuing coolness necessary for the use of accurate weapons. These conditions are completely changed when one faces an enemy equally well armed, who consequently, gives as good as he gets.

9. *Absolute Impossibility of Fire at Command.*

Let us return to fire at command, which there is a tendency to-day to have troops execute in line.

Can regular and efficient fire be hoped for from troops in line? Ought it to be hoped for?

No, for man cannot be made over, and neither can the line.

Even on the range or on the maneuver field what does this fire amount to?

In fire at command, on the range, all the men in the two ranks come to the firing position simultaneously, everybody is perfectly quiet. Men in the front rank consequently are not deranged by their neighbors. Men in the second rank are in the same situation. The first rank being set and motionless they can aim through the openings without more annoyance than those in the first rank.

Fire being executed at command, simultaneously, no weapon is deranged at the moment of firing by the movements of the men. All conditions are entirely favorable to this kind of fire. Also as the fire is ordered with skill and coolness by an officer who has perfectly aligned his men (a thing rare even on the drill ground) it gives percentage results greater than that of fire at will executed with the minutest precautions, results that are sometimes astonishing.

But fire at command, from the extreme coolness that it demands of all, of the officer certainly more than of the soldier, is impracticable before the enemy except under exceptional circumstances of picked officers, picked men, ground, distance, safety, etc. Even in maneuvers its execution is farcical. There is not an organization in which the soldiers do not hurry the command to fire in that the officers are so afraid that their men will anticipate the command that they give it as rapidly as possible, while the pieces are hardly in firing position, often while they are still in motion.

The prescription that the command to fire be not given until about three seconds after coming to the firing position may give good results in the face of range targets. But it is not wise to believe that men will wait thus for long in the face of the enemy.

It is useless to speak of the use of the sight-leaf before the enemy, in fire attempted by the same officers and men who are so utterly lacking, even on the maneuver ground. We have seen a firing instructor, an officer of coolness and assurance, who on the range had fired trial shots every day for a month, after this month of daily practice fire four trial shots at a six hundred meter range with the sight leaf at point blank.

Let us not pay too much attention to those who in military matters base everything on the weapon and unhesitating assume that the man serving it will adopt the usage provided and ordered in their regulations. The fighting man is flesh and blood. He is both body and soul; and strong as the soul may often be it cannot so dominate the body that there is no revolt of the flesh, no mental disturbance, in the face of destruction. Let us learn to distrust mathematics and material dynamics as applied to battle principles. We shall learn to beware of the illusions drawn from the range and the maneuver field.

There experience is with the calm, settled, unfatigued, attentive, obedient soldier, with an intelligent and tractable man instrument in short. And not with the nervous, easily swayed, moved, troubled, distrait, excited, restless being, not even under self-control, who is the fighting man from general to private. There are strong men, exceptions, but they are rare.

These illusions nevertheless, stubborn and persistent, always repair the next day the most damaging injuries inflicted on them by reality. Their least dangerous effect is to lead to prescribing the impracticable, as if ordering the impracticable were not really an attack on discipline, and did not result in disconcerting officers and men by the unexpected and by surprise at the contrast between battle and the theories of peace-time training.

Battle of course always furnishes surprises. But it furnishes less in proportion as good sense and the recognition of the truth have had their effect on the training of the fighting man.

Man in the mass, in a disciplined body organized for combat, is invincible before an undisciplined body. But against a similarly disciplined body he reverts to the primitive man who flees before a force that is proved stronger, or that he feels stronger. The heart of the soldier is always the human heart. Discipline holds enemies face to face a little longer, but the instinct of self-preservation maintains its empire and with it the sense of fear.

Fear!

There are chiefs, there are soldiers who know no fear, but they are of rare temper. The mass trembles, for the flesh cannot be suppressed. And this trembling must be taken into account in all organization, discipline, formation, maneuver, movement, methods of action. For in all of these the soldier tends to be upset, to be deceived, to under-rate himself and to exaggerate the offensive spirit of the enemy.

On the field of battle death is in the air, blind and invisible, making his presence known by fearful whistlings that make heads duck. During this strain the recruit hunches up, closes in, seeking aid by an instinctive unformulated reasoning. He figures that the more there are to face a danger the greater each one's chances of escaping. But he soon sees that flesh attracts lead. Then, possessed by terror, inevitably he retreats before the fire, or "he escapes by advancing," in the picturesque and profound words of General Burbaki.

The soldier escapes from his officer, we say. Yes, he escapes! But is it not evident that he escapes because up

to this moment nobody has bothered about his character, his
temperament, the impressionable and exciteable nature of
man? In prescribed methods of fighting he has always
been held to impossibilities. The same thing is done to-day.
To-morrow, as yesterday, he will escape.

There is of course a time when all the soldiers escape,
either forward, or to the rear. But the organization, the
combat methods should have no other object than to delay
as long as possible this crisis. Yet they hasten it.

All our officers fear, quite justifiably from their experience, that the soldier will too rapidly use his cartridges in
the face of the enemy. This serious matter is certainly
worthy of attention. How to stop this useless and dangerous
waste of ammunition ·is the question. Our soldiers show
little coolness. Once in danger they fire, fire to calm themselves, to pass the time; they cannot be stopped.

There are some people you cannot embarrass. With the
best faith in the world they say, "What is this? You are
troubled about stopping the fire of your soldiers? That is
not difficult. You find that they show little coolness, and
shoot despite their officers, in spite even of themselves? All
right, require of them and their officers methods of fire that
demand extremes of coolness, calm and assurance, even in
maneuver. They cannot give a little? Ask a lot and you
will get it. There you have a combat method nobody has
ever heard of, simple, beautiful, and terrible."

This is indeed a fine theory. It would make the wily
Frederick who surely did not believe in these maneuvers,
laugh until he cried.[1]

This is to escape from a difficulty by a means always
recognized as impossible, and more impossible than ever
to-day.

Fearing that the soldier will escape from command, c?n

[1] His war instructions prove this. His best generals, Zieten,
Warnery, knew of such methods, saw nothing practicable in
them and guarded against them in war as indeed he did himself.
But Europe believed him, tried to imitate his maneuvers on the
field of battle, and aligned her troops to be beaten by him. This
is what he was after. He even deceived the Prussians. But
they came back to sound methods after 1808, in 1813 and afterwards.

not better means be found to hold him than to require of him and his officer, impracticable fire? This, ordered and not executed by the soldiers, and even by the officers, is an attack on the discipline of the unit. "Never order the impossible," says discipline, "for the impossible becomes then a disobedience."

How many requisites there are to make fire at command possible, conditions among the soldiers, among their officers. Perfect these conditions, they say. All right, perfect their training, their discipline, etc.; but to obtain fire at command it is necessary to perfect their nerves, their physical force, their moral force, to make bronze images of them, to do away with excitement, with the trembling of the flesh. Can any one do this?

Frederick's soldiers were brought, by blows of the baton, to a terrible state of discipline. Yet their fire was fire at will. Discipline had reached its limits.

Man in battle, let us repeat again, is a being to whom the instinct of self-preservation at times dominates everything else. Discipline, whose purpose is to dominate this instinct by a feeling of greater terror, can not wholly achieve it. Discipline goes so far and no farther.

We cannot deny the existence of extraordinary instances when discipline and devotion have raised man above himself. But these examples are extraordinary, rare. They are admired as exceptions, and the exception proves the rule.

As to perfection, consider the Spartans. If man was ever perfected for war it was he; and yet he has been beaten, and fled.

In spite of training, moral and physical force has limits. The Spartans, who should have stayed to the last man on the battle field, fled.

The British with their phlegmatic coolness and their terrible rolling fire, the Russians, with that inertia that is called their tenacity, have given way before attack. The German has given way, he who on account of his subordination and stability has been called excellent war material.

Again an objection is raised. Perhaps with recruits the method may be impracticable. But with veterans — But with whom is war commenced? Methods are devised precisely for young and inexperienced troops.

They ask, also, if the Prussians used this method of fire
successfully in the last war, why should not we do as well?
Supposing that the Prussians actually did use it, and this is
far from being proved, it does not follow that it is practicable
for us. This mania for borrowing German tactics is not
new, although it has always been properly protested against.
Marshal Luchner said, " No matter how much they tor-
ment their men, fortunately they will never make them
Prussians." Later de Gouvion-Saint-Cyr said, " The men are
drilled in various exercises believed necessary to fit them
for war, but there is no question of adopting exercises to
suit the French military genius, the French character and
temperament. It has not been thought necessary to take
this into account; it has been easier to borrow German
methods."

To follow preconceived tactics is more the part of the
phlegmatic German than it is ours. The Germans obey well
enough, but the point is that they try to follow tactics
which are contrary to nature. The Frenchman cannot.
More spontaneous, more exciteable and impressionable, less
calm and obedient, he has in our last wars promptly and
completely violated both the letter and the spirit of the regulations. " The German," said a Prussian officer, " has sentiments of duty and obedience. He submits to severe discipline. He is full of devotion, although not animated by a
lively mind. Easy by nature, rather heavy than active, in-
tellectually calm, reflective, without dash or divine fire, wishing but not mad to conquer, obeying calmly and conscientiously, but mechanically and without enthusiasm, fighting
with a resigned valor, with heroism, he may let himself be
sacrificed uselessly, but he sells his life dearly. Without
warlike tendencies, not bellicose, unambitious, he is yet excellent war material on account of his subordination and
stability. What must be inculcated in him is a will of his
own, a personal impulse to send him forward." According
to this unflattering portrait, which we believe a little extreme,
even if by a compatriot, it is possible that the Germans can
be handled in tactics impossible with French. However,
did they actually use these tactics? Remember the urgent
warning of Blücher to his brigade commanders, not to let
bayonet attacks break down into fusillades. Note the article

in the present Prussian firing regulations, which prescribes trial shots before each fire delivered, " so as to dissipate the kind of excitement that possesses the soldier when his drill has been interrupted for some time."

In conclusion, if fire at command was impossible with the ancient rifle, it is more so to-day, for the simple reason that trembling increases as the destructive power increases. Under Turenne, lines held longer than to-day, because the musket was in use and the battle developed more slowly. To-day when every one has the rapid fire rifle, are things easier? Alas no! Relations between weapons and the man are the same. You give me a musket, I fire at sixty paces, a rifle, at two hundred; a chessepot, at four hundred. But I have perhaps less coolness and steadiness than at the old sixty paces, for with the rapidity of fire the new weapon is more terrible at four hundred paces, for me as well as for the enemy, than was the musket at sixty paces. And is there even more fire accuracy? No. Rifles were used before the French revolution, and yet this perfectly well known weapon was very rarely seen in war, and its efficacy, as shown in those rare cases, was unsatisfactory. Accurate fire with it at combat distances of from two hundred to four hundred meters was illusory, and it was abandoned in favor of the old rifle. Did the foot chasseurs know fire at command? Picked troops, dependable, did they use it? Yet it would have been a fine method of employing their weapons. To-day we have weapons that are accurate at six hundred to seven hundred meters. Does that mean that accurate fire at seven hundred meters is possible? No. If your enemy is armed as we are, fire at seven hundred meters will show the same results that have been shown for four hundred meters. The same losses will be suffered, and the coolness shown will be the same — that is, it will be absent. If one fire three times as fast, three times as many men will fall, and it will be three times as difficult to preserve coolness. Just as formerly it was impossible to execute fire at command, so it is to-day. Formerly no sight-setting was possible; it is no better to-day.

But if this fire is impossible, why attempt it? Let us remain always in the realm of the possible or we shall make sad mistakes. " In our art," said General Daine, " theorists abound; practical men are very rare. Also when the moment of action arrives, principles are often found to be confused, application impossible, and the most erudite officers remain inactive, unable to use the scientific treasures that they have amassed."

Let us then, practical men, seek for possible methods. Let us gather carefully the lessons of their experience, remembering Bacon's saying, " Experience excels science."

APPENDIX II

1. *Cavalry.*

An Extract from Xenophon.

" The unexpectedness of an event accentuates it, be it pleasant or terrible. This is nowhere seen better than in war, where surprise terrorizes even the strongest.

" When two armies are in touch or merely separated by the field of battle, there are first, on the part of the cavalry, skirmishes, thrusts, wheels to stop or pursue the enemy, after which usually each goes cautiously and does not put forth its greatest effort until the critical part of the conflict. Or, having commenced as usual, the opposite is done and one moves swiftly, after the wheel, either to flee or to pursue. This is the method by which one can, with the least possible risk, most harm the enemy, charging at top speed when supported, or fleeing at the same speed to escape the enemy. If it is possible in these skirmishes to leave behind, formed in column and unobserved four or five of the bravest and best mounted men in each troop they may be very well employed to fall on the enemy at the moment of the wheel.

2. *Marius Against the Cimbrians.*

Extract from Plutarch's " Life of Marius."

" Boiorix, king of the Cimbrians, at the head of a small troop of cavalry, approached Marius' camp and challenged him to fix a day and place to decide who would rule the country. Marius answered that Romans did not ask their enemies when to fight, but that he was willing to satisfy the Cimbrians. They agreed then to give battle in three days on the plain of Verceil, a convenient place for the Romans to deploy their cavalry and for the barbarians to

287

extend their large army. The two opponents on the day set
were in battle formation. Catulus had twenty thousand
three hundred men. Marius had thirty-two thousand, placed
on the wings and consequently on either side of those of
Catulus, in the center. So writes Sylla, who was there.
They say that Marius gave this disposition to the two parts
of his army because he hoped to fall with his two wings
on the barbarian phalanxes and wished the victory to
come only to his command, without Catulus taking any part
or even meeting with the enemy. Indeed, as the front of
battle was very broad, the wings were separated from the
center, which was broken through. They add that Catulus
reported this disposition in the explanation that he had to
make and complained bitterly of Marius' bad faith. The
Cimbrian infantry came out of its positions in good order
and in battle array formed a solid phalanx as broad as it was
wide, thirty stades or about eighteen thousand feet. Their
fifteen thousand horsemen were magnificently equipped.
Their helmets were crowned by the gaping mouths of savage
beasts, above which were high plumes which looked like
wings. This accentuated their height. They were protected by iron cuirasses and had shields of an astonishing
whiteness. Each had two javelins to throw from a distance,
and in close fighting they used a long heavy sword.

"In this battle the cavalry did not attack the Romans in
front, but, turning to the right they gradually extended with
the idea of enclosing the Romans before their infantry and
themselves. The Roman generals instantly perceived the
ruse. But they were not able to restrain their men, one of
whom, shouting that the enemy was flying, led all the others
to pursue. Meanwhile the barbarian infantry advanced like
the waves of a great sea.

"Marius washed his hands, raised them to heaven, and
vowed to offer a hecatomb to the gods. Catulus for his
part, also raised his hands to heaven and promised to con-
secrate the fortune of the day. Marius also made a sacrifice, and, when the priest showed him the victim's entrails,
cried, "Victory is mine." But, as the two armies were set
in motion, something happened, which, according to Sylla,
seemed divine vengeance on Marius. The movements of
such a prodigious multitude raised such a cloud of dust that

the two armies could not see each other. Marius, who had advanced first with his troops to fall on the enemy's formation, missed it in the dust, and having passed beyond it, wandered for a long time in the plain. Meanwhile fortune turned the barbarians toward Catulus who had to meet their whole attack with his soldiers, among whom was Sylla. The heat of the day and the burning rays of the sun, which was in the eyes of the Cimbrians, helped the Romans. The barbarions, reared in cold wooded places, hardened to extreme cold, could not stand the heat. Sweating, panting, they shaded their faces from the sun with their shields. The battle occurred after the summer solstice, three days before the new moon of the month of August, then called Sextilis. The cloud of dust sustained the Romans' courage by concealing the number of the enemy. Each battalion advancing against the enemy in front of them were engaged, before the sight of such a great horde of barbarians could shake them. Furthermore, hardship and hard work had so toughened them that in spite of the heat and impetuousness with which they attacked, no Roman was seen to sweat or pant. This, it is said, is testified to by Catulus himself in eulogizing the conduct of his troops.

" Most of the enemy, above all the bravest, were cut to pieces, for, to keep the front ranks from breaking, they were tied together by long chains attached to their belts. The victors pursued the fugitives to their entrenched camp.

" The Romans took more than sixty thousand Cimbrians prisoners, and killed twice as many."

3. *The Battle of the Alma.*

Extract from the correspondence of Colonel Ardant du Picq. A letter sent from Huy, February 9, 1869, by Captain de V——, a company officer in the attack division.

" My company, with the 3rd, commanded by Captain D—— was designated to cover the battalion.

" At eight or nine hundred meters from the Alma, we saw a sort of wall, crowned with white, whose use we could not understand. Then, at not more than three hundred meters, this wall delivered against us a lively battalion fire and deployed at the run. It was a Russian battalion whose

uniform, partridge-gray or chestnut-gray color, with white
helmet, had, with the help of a bright sun, produced the illusion. This, parenthetically, showed me that this color is
certainly the most sensible, as it can cause such errors.[1] We
replied actively, but there was effect on neither side because
the men fired too fast and too high . . . The advance was
then taken up, and I don't know from whom the order can
have come . . . We went on the run, crossing the river easily
enough, and while we were assembling to scramble up the
hill we say the rest of the battalion attacking, without order,
companies mixed up, crying, " Forward," singing, etc. We
did the same, again took up the attack, and were lucky enough
to reach the summit of the plateau first. The Russians,
astounded, massed in a square. Why? I suppose that,
turned on the left, attacked in the center, they thought themselves surrounded, and took this strange formation. At this
moment a most inopportune bugle call was sounded by order
of Major De M —— commanding temporarily a battalion of
foot chasseurs. This officer had perceived the Russian
cavalry in motion and believed that its object was to charge
us, while, on the contrary it was maneuvering to escape
the shells fired into it while in squadron formation by the
Megere, a vessel of the fleet. This order given by bugle signal was executed as rapidly as had been the attack, such is
the instinct of self-preservation which urges man to flee
danger, above all when ordered to flee. Happily a level-
headed officer, Captain Daguerre, seeing the gross mistake,
commanded " Forward " in a stentorian tone. This halted
the retreat and caused us again to take up the attack. The
attack made us masters of the telegraph-line, and the battle
was won. At this second charge the Russians gave, turned,
and hardly any of them were wounded with the bayonet.
So then a major commanding a battalion, without orders,

[1] It is noted here that French uniforms are of an absurd color,
serving only to take the eye at a review. So the chasseurs, in
black, are seen much further than a rifleman of the line in his
gray coat. The red trousers are seen further than the gray —
thus gray ought to be the basic color of the infantry uniform,
above all that of skirmishers.

At night fall the Russians came up to our trenches without
being seen by any one, thanks to their partridge-gray coats.

sounds a bugle call and endangers success. A simple Captain commands " Forward," and decides the victory. This is the history of yesterday, which may be useful to-morrow.

It appears from this that, apart from the able conception of the commander-in-chief, the detail of execution was abominable, and that to base on successes new rules of battle would lead to lamentable errors. Let us sum up:

First: A private chasseur d'Afrique gave the order to attack;

Second: The troops went to the attack mixed up with each other. We needed nearly an hour merely to reform the brigade. This one called, that one congratulated himself, the superior officers cried out, etc., etc.; there was confusion that would have meant disaster if the cavalry charge which was believed to threaten us, had been executed. Disorder broke out in the companies at the first shot. Once engaged, commanders of organizations no longer had them in hand, and they intermingled, so that it was not easy to locate oneself;

Third: There was no silence in ranks. Officers, non-commissioned officers and soldiers commanded, shouted, etc.; the bugles sounded the commands they heard coming from nobody knew where;

Fourth: There was no maneuvering from the first shot to the last. I do not remember being among my own men; it was only at the end that we found each other. Zouaves, chasseurs, soldiers of the 20th line formed an attack group — that was all. About four o'clock there was a first roll call. About a third of the battalion was missing at nine at night there was a second roll call. Only about fifty men were missing, thirty of whom were wounded. Where the rest were I do not know.

Fifth: To lighten the men, packs had been left on the plain at the moment fire opened, and as the operation had not been worked out in advance, no measures were taken to guard them. In the evening most of the men found their packs incomplete, lacking all the little indispensables that one cannot get in the position in which we were

It is evidently a vital necessity to restrain the individual initiative of subordinates and leave command to the chiefs, and above all to watch the training of the soldiers who are always ready, as they approach, to run on the enemy with the bayonet. I have always noted that if a body which is charged does not hold firm, it breaks and takes flight, but that if it holds well, the charging body halts some paces away before it strikes. I shall tell you something notable that I saw at Castel-Fidardo. They talk a lot of the bayonet. For my part I only saw it used once, in the night, in a trench. Also it is noted that in the hospital, practically all the wounds treated were from fire, rarely from the bayonet.

4. *The Battle of the Alma.*

Extract from the correspondence of Colonel A. du Picq. Letters dated in November, 1868, and February, 1869, sent from Rennes by Captain P—— of the 17th battalion of foot chasseurs, with remarks by the colonel and responses of Captain P——.

First letter from Captain P——

" . . . It is there that I had time to admire the coolness of my brave Captain Daguerre, advancing on a mare under the enemy's eyes, and observing imperturbable, like a tourist, all the movements of our opponents.

"I will always pay homage to his calm and collected bravery. . . . "
Remarks by the colonel.

"Did not Captain Daguerre change the bugle call 'Retreat,' ordered by —— to the bugle call 'Forward ?'"
Answer of Captain P——

"In fact, when protected in the wood by pieces of wall we were firing on the Russians, we heard behind us the bugle sounding 'Retreat' at the order of ——. At this moment my captain, indignant, ordered 'Forward' sounded to reëstablish confidence which had been shaken by the distraction or by the inadvertance of ——."

5. *The Battle of Inkermann.*

Extract from the correspondence of Colonel Ardant du Picq. First: Letter sent from Lyon, March 21, 1869, by Major de G——, 17th Line Regiment.

" . . . The 1st Battalion of the 7th Light Regiment had

hardly arrived close to the telegraph when it received a new order to rush to the help of the English army, which, too weak to hold such a large army, had been broken in the center of its line and driven back on its camps.

" The 1st Battalion of the 7th Light Regiment, Major Vaissier, had the honor to arrive first in the presence of the Russians, after moving three kilometers on the run. Received by the enthusiastic cheers of the English, it formed for battle, then carried away by burning cries of ' Forward, with the bayonet ' from its brave major it threw itself headlong, on the Russian columns, which broke.

" For two hours the 1st Battalion of the 7th Light Regiment, a battalion of the 6th Line Regiment, four companies of the 3rd Battalion of foot chasseurs, five companies of Algerian chasseurs held the head of the Russian army which continued to debouch in massed columns from the ravine and plateau of Inkermann.

" Three times the battalion of the 7th Light Regiment was obliged to fall back some paces to rally. Three times it charged with the bayonet, with the same ardor and success.

" At four in the afternoon the Russians were in rout, and were pursued into the valley of Inkermann.

" On this memorable day all the officers, non-commissioned officers and soldiers of the 7th Light Regiment performed their duty nobly, rivalling each other in bravery and self-sacrifice."

Second: Notes on Inkermann, which Colonel A. du Picq indicates come from the letters of Captain B —— (these letters are missing).

" In what formation were the Russians? In column, of which the head fired, and whose platoons tried to get from behind the mead to enter into action?

" When Major Vaissier advanced was he followed by every one? At what distance? In what formation were the attackers? in disordered masses? in one rank? in two? in mass? Did the Russians immediately turn tail, receiving shots and the bayonet in the back? did they fall back on the mass which itself was coming up? What was the duration of this attack against a mass, whose depth prevented its falling back?

" Did we receive bayonet wounds?

" Did we fall back before the active reaction of the mass
or merely because, after the first shock, the isolated soldiers fell back to find companions and with them a new confidence?

" Was the second charge made like the first one? Was
the 6th Line Regiment engaged as the first support of the
7th Light Regiment? How were the Zouaves engaged?"

6. *The Battle of Magenta.*

Extract from the correspondence of Colonel Ardant du Picq.
Letters from Captain C——, dated August 23, 1868.

" At Magenta I was in Espinasse's division, of Marshal
MacMahon's corps. This division was on the extreme left
of the troops that had passed the Ticino at Turbigo and was
moving on Magenta by the left bank. Close to the village
a fusillade at close range apprised us that the enemy was before us. The country, covered with trees, hedges, and
vines, had hidden them.

" Our 1st Battalion and the 2nd Foreign Regiment drove
the Austrians into Magenta.

" Meanwhile the 2nd and 3rd Battalions of Zouaves, with
which I was, remained in reserve, arms stacked, under control of the division commander. Apparently quite an interval had been left between Espinasse's division and la Mot-
terouge's, the 1st of the corps, and, at the moment of engagement, at least an Austrian brigade had entered the gap,
and had taken in flank and rear the elements of our
division engaged before Magenta. Happily the wooded country concealed the situation or I doubt whether our troops
engaged would have held on as they did. At any rate the
two reserve battalions had not moved. The fusillade extended to our right and left as if to surround us; bullets
already came from our right flank. The General had put
five guns in front of us, to fire on the village, and at the
same time I received the order to move my section to the
right, to drive off the invisible enemy who was firing on us.
I remember that I had quit the column with my section when
I saw a frightened artillery captain run toward us, crying
'General, General, we are losing a piece!' The general

answered, ' Come! Zouaves, packs off.' At these words, the two battalions leaped forward like a flock of sheep, dropping packs everywhere. The Austrians were not seen at first. It was only after advancing for an instant that they were seen. They were already dragging off the piece that they had taken. At the sight of them our men gave a yell and fell on them. Surprise and terror so possessed the Austrians, who did not know that we were so near, that they ran without using their arms. The piece was retaken; the regimental standard was captured by a man in my company. About two hundred prisoners were taken, and the Austrian regiment — Hartmann's 9th Infantry — was dispersed like sheep in flight, five battalions of them. I believe that had the country not been thick the result might have been different. The incident lasted perhaps ten minutes.

" The two battalions took up their first position. They had had no losses, and their morale was in the clouds. After about an hour General Espinasse put himself at the head of the two battalions and marched us on the village. We were in column of platoons with section intervals. The advance was made by echelon, the 2nd Battalion in front, the 3rd a little in rear, and a company in front deployed as skirmishers.

" At one hundred and fifty paces from the Austrians, wavering was evident in their lines; the first ranks threw themselves back on those in rear. At that instant the general ordered again, ' Come! Packs off. At the double!' Everybody ran forward, shedding his pack where he was.

" The Austrians did not wait for us. We entered the village mixed up with them. The fighting in houses lasted quite a while. Most of the Austrians retired. Those who remained in the houses had to surrender. I found myself, with some fifty officers and men, in a big house from which we took four hundred men and five officers, Colonel Hauser for one.

" My opinion is that we were very lucky at Magenta. The thick country in which we fought, favored us in hiding our inferior number from the Austrians. I do not believe we would have succeeded so well in open country. In the gun episode the Austrians were surprised, stunned. Those whom we took kept their arms in their hands, without either abandoning them or using them. It was a typical Zouave attack, which, when it succeeds, has astonishing results; but if one is not lucky it sometimes costs dearly. Note the 3rd Zouaves at Palestro, the 1st Zouaves at Marignano. General Espinasse's advance on the village, at the head of two battalions, was the finest and most imposing sight I have ever seen. Apart from that advance, the fighting was always by skirmishers and in large groups."

7. *The Battle of Solferino.*

Extract from the correspondence of Colonel Ardant du Picq. Letters from Captain C——.

" The 55th infantry was part of the 3rd division of the 4th corps.

" Coming out of Medole, the regiment was halted on the right of the road and formed, as each company arrived, in close column. Fascines were made.

" An aide-de-camp came up and gave an order to the Colonel.

" The regiment was then put on the road, marched some yards and formed in battalion masses on the right of the line of battle. This movement was executed very regularly although bullets commenced to find us. Arms were rested, and we stayed there, exposed to fire, without doing anything, not even sending out a skirmisher. For that matter, during the whole campaign, it seemed to me that the skirmisher school might never have existed.

" Then up came a Major of Engineers, from General Niel, to get a battalion from the regiment. The 3rd battalion being on the left received the order to march. The major commanding ordered ' by the left flank,' and we marched by the flank, in close column, in the face of the enemy, up to Casa-Nova Farm, I believe, where General Niel was.

" The battalion halted a moment, faced to the front, and closed a little.

" ' Stay here,' said General Niel; ' you are my only reserve ! '

" Then the general, glancing in front of the farm, said to

the major, after one or two minutes, ' Major, fix bayonets,
sound the charge, and forward ! '

" This last movement was still properly executed at the
start. and for about one hundred yards of advance.

" Shrapnel annoyed the battalion, and the men shouldered
arms to march better.

" At about one hundred yards from the farm, the cry
' Packs down,' came from I do not know where. The cry
was instantly repeated in the battalion. Packs were thrown
down, anywhere, and with wild yells the advance was renewed, in the wildest disorder.

" From that moment, and for the rest of the day, the 3rd
Battalion as a unit disappeared.

" Toward the end of the day, after an attempt had been
made to get the regiment together, and at the end of half
an hour of backing and filling, there was a roll-call.

" The third company of grenadiers had on starting off in
the morning one hundred and thirty-two to one hundred
and thirty-five present. At this first roll-call, forty-seven
answered, a number I can swear to, but many of the men
were still hunting packs and rations. The next day at rev-
ille roll-call, ninety-three or four answered. Many came
back in the night.

" This was the strength for many days I still remember,
for I was charged with company supply from June 25th.

" As additional bit of information — it was generally
known a few days later that at least twenty men of the 4th
company of grenadiers were never on the field of battle.
Wounded of the company, returned for transport to Medole,
said later that they had seen some twenty of the company
together close to Medole, lying in the grass while their
comrades fought. They even gave some names, but could
not name them all. The company had only been formed for
the war on April 19th, and had received that same day forty-
nine new grenadiers and twenty-nine at Milan, which made
seventy-eight recruits in two months. None of these men
were tried or punished. Their comrades rode them hard,
that was all."

8. *Mentana.*

Extract from the correspondence of Colonel Ardant du Picq. Letters from Captain C——, dated August 23, 1868.

"November 3, at two in the morning, we took up arms to go to Monte-Rotondo. We did not yet know that we would meet the Garibaldians at Mentana.

"The Papal army had about three thousand men, we about two thousand five hundred. At one o'clock the Papal forces met their enemies. The Zouaves attacked vigorously, but the first engagements were without great losses on either side. There is nothing particular in this first episode. The usual thing happened, a force advances and is not halted by the fire of its adversary who ends by showing his heels. The papal Zouaves are marked by no ordinary spirit. In comparing them with the soldiers of the Antibes legion, one is forced to the conclusion that the man who fights for an idea fights better than one who fights for money. At each advance of the papal forces, we advanced also. We were not greatly concerned about the fight, we hardly thought that we would have to participate, not dreaming that we could be held by the volunteers. However, that did not happen.

"It was about three o'clock. At that time three companies of the battalion were employed in protecting the artillery — three or four pieces placed about the battle-field. The head of the French column was then formed by the last three companies of the battalion, one of the 1st Line Regiment; the other regiments were immediately behind. Colonel Fremont of the 1st Line Regiment, after having studied the battle-field, took two chasseur companies, followed by a battalion of his regiment and bore to the right to turn the village.

"Meanwhile the 1st Line Regiment moved further to the right in the direction of Monte-Rotondo, against which at two different times it opened a fire at will which seemed a veritable hurricane. Due to the distance or to the terrain the material result of the fire seemed to be negligible. The moral result must have been considerable, it precipitated a flood of fugitives on the road from Mentana to Monte-Rotondo, dominated by our sharpshooters, who opened on the fugitives a fire more deadly than that of the chassepots. We stayed in the same position until night, when we retired to a position near Mentana, where we bivouacked.

"My company was one of the two chasseur companies which attacked on the right with the 1st Line Regiment. My company had ninety-eight rifles (we had not yet received the chassepots). It forced the volunteers from solidly held positions where they left a gun and a considerable number of rifles. In addition, it put nearly seventy men out of action, judging by those who remained on the field. It had one man slightly wounded, a belt and a carbine broken by bullets.

"There remained with the general, after our movement to the right, three companies of chasseurs, a battalion of the 29th, and three of the 59th. I do not include many elements of the Papal army which had not been engaged. Some of my comrades told me of having been engaged with a chasseur company of the 59th in a sunken road, whose sides had not been occupied; the general was with this column. Having arrived close to the village, some shots either from the houses or from enemy sharpshooters, who might easily have gotten on the undefended flanks, provoked a terrible fusilade in the column. In spite of the orders and efforts of the officers, everybody fired, at the risk of killing each other, and this probably happened. It was only when some men, led by officers, were able to climb the sides of the road that this firing ceased. I do not think that this was a well understood use of new arms.

"The fusillade of the 1st Line Regiment against Monte-Rotondo was not very effective, I believe negligible. I do not refer to the moral result, which was great.

"The Garibaldians were numerous about Monte-Rotondo. But the terrain like all that around Italian villages was covered with trees, hedges, etc. Under these conditions, I believe that the fire of sharpshooters would have been more effective than volleys, where the men estimate distances badly and do not aim."

GENERAL CARL VON CLAUSEWITZ

PRINCIPLES OF WAR

Carl von Clausewitz

Translated and edited with an introduction

by

Hans W. Gatzke

CONTENTS

INTRODUCTION

Carl von Clausewitz, spiritual father of the German army, has long been recognized as one of the greatest and most original writers on the subject of war. "Only if we understand the nature of warfare in the spirit of Clausewitz can we hope to maintain our existence in case necessity should once again force the sword into our hands." These words introduced to the German army and the German people in 1936 a new edition of Clausewitz' essay, "The Most Important Principles For The Conduct Of War." With equal, if not greater validity, they may serve to introduce the English translation of the same essay.

Clausewitz' life was that of a soldier. It was rarely happy, never easy, and it did not see the fulfillment of his fondest hope: to gain a position of sufficient influence, that he might translate into reality his ideas on the theory and conduct of war.

Born in 1780, a son of a retired Prussian officer, he joined the army when he was only twelve years old. After participating in the War of the First Coalition against France in 1793-94, he spent several trying and uneventful years as officer in the small garrison of Neuruppin. He made use of this period to complete the defective education of his early years, studying in particular the writings of King Frederick II of Prussia, whose character and concept of duty he deeply admired.

In 1801 he entered the "War School" (Kriegs-schüle), a training school for officers at Berlin. Insufficient preparation as well as financial hardship made life very difficult, adding an element of pessimism to his already overly sensitive character. After a while, however, one of his instructors, the great Scharnhorst, recognized Clausewitz' brilliance and outstanding ability and gave him the encouragement and friendship he needed. As a result Clausewitz became one of his best pupils, and in 1803, on Scharnhorst's recommendation, he became aide-de-camp to Prince August of Prussia. As such he accompanied his royal master in the campaign of 1806 against Napoleon, and was taken prisoner by the French.

After his return to Germany in 1807 he worked in close collaboration with Scharnhorst, whose ideas on military theory and on the necessity of reforming the Prussian army he shared. The influence of Scharnhorst on Clausewitz was profound, and after the death of the great reformer in 1813, Clausewitz considered himself in many respects the intellectual heir of the "father and friend" of his spirit. In 1810, again on Scharnhorst's recommendation, he was attached (as major) to the Prussian General Staff, and was given a position at the "General War School" (Allgemeine Kriegsschule). This school, founded in 1810, was an outgrowth of the earlier schools of officers and eventually developed into the famous "War Academy" (Kriegsakademie). It was at this time that Clausewitz became a close friend of General Gneisenau, who, like Scharnhorst, was one

of the leading figures of the Prussian army, and
Marshal Blücher's chief of staff in the campaigns
against Napoleon. A proof that Clausewitz' ability
was recognized is the fact that he was also appointed military instructor of the Prussian crown
prince, Frederick William.

These were the years which saw the phenomenal
rise of Napoleon. Clausewitz, though a great admirer of Napoleon the soldier, was deeply opposed
to Napoleon the conquering dictator. Therefore,
when his King, Frederick William III, concluded
a treaty with France in 1812, Clausewitz followed
the example of many of his fellow-officers and
left the service of his country, after publicly and
courageously defending his step. On his way to
Russia, to join the army of Tsar Alexander I
against Napoleon, he completed the memorandum
which he had written for the military instruction
of his royal pupil, entitled: "The Most Important
Principles For The Conduct Of War To Complete
My Course Of Instruction Of His Royal Highness
The Crown Prince," the translation of which is
given in this book.

While in Russia he served as intermediary between Tsar Alexander and the Prussian General
Yorck, negotiating the Convention of Tauroggen
which eventually brought Prussia back to the side
of the powers allied against Napoleon. Clausewitz
took part in the Wars of Liberation, first with the
Russian army and later as colonel in the army of
his own country. Like his friend Scharnhorst, he

was never entrusted with the actual conduct of a major military operation, but had to content himself with staff duties. As chief of staff of the third army corps, under General Thielemann, he took part in the Waterloo Campaign, and remained in this position, after peace was concluded, until 1818.

It is doubtful whether Clausewitz would have made a successful leader of armies, considering his reserve and shyness, which gave him the reputation of being cold and conceited. He was too sensitive, too much of the intellectual perhaps, aware of the manifold aspects of a problem, to possess the singleness of purpose which he himself demanded from a military leader. On the other hand, his boundless energy and his sense of reality made him eager to transform into action his thought on things military. The impossibility of doing so accounts for much of his unhappiness and dissatisfaction.

In 1818 he was promoted Major-General and called to Berlin to become head of the Prussian War School, a position which he held until shortly before his death. His duties, unfortunately, were limited to the administration of the school and offered little opportunity for an improvement of the curriculum along the lines of his revolutionary ideas on warfare. Finding himself deprived of all other outlets, Clausewitz turned to writing as the only means of expressing and developing his ideas. It was during this period that he wrote the bulk of his military works, especially his most famous, entitled VOM KRIEGE ("On War").

While still in the midst of his writing, he was made chief of artillery inspection at Breslau, and shortly afterwards chief of staff to Field Marshal Gneisenau's army of observation which had been sent to Posen during the Polish rebellion of 1830. Clausewitz was happy to escape his fruitless administrative duties, but the sudden death of his friend Gneisenau brought new unhappiness. Much overworked, as always, he returned to Germany in 1831. There he came down with a serious attack of cholera, caught during his stay in Posen, and on November 16, 1831, he died, "pushing aside his life like a heavy burden."

The writings of Clausewitz were published only after his death. He had been aware that they constituted "a revolution in the thought of war," and his sensitive nature feared the misunderstanding and immature criticism of his contemporaries. His widow, Marie von Clausewitz, understanding companion and collaborator for twenty years, published the ten volumes of his collected works between 1832 and 1837.

The first three of these, entitled VOM KRIEGE, contain the sum and substance of Clausewitz' thought "On War," and constitute, in the words of Count Schlieffen, "in content and form the greatest work on war ever written." The book is incomplete, and in many of its specific details and illustrations it has been outdated by the tremendous technical developments since Clausewitz' time. Yet, inasmuch as it was not intended to be a specific instruction for the conduct of military operations but rather a philosophical appraisal of war, it possesses a timeless quality which makes it as vital today as ever.

Clausewitz was aware that the French Revolution and its heir, Napoleon, had profoundly affected the character and methods of warfare. War was no longer a careful process of maneuvering for positions with small, expensive armies, trying to reach a decision by the less bloody and costly method of interrupting the enemy's lines of supply. War had become a contest of mass armies in which elements of speed and concentrated, superior effort (forgotten since the days of Frederick the Great) were once again decisive. "Victory is purchased by blood," and complete victory is assured only through destruction of the enemy's forces. Such is Clausewitz' unlimited war of annihilation, his absolute war. "War is an act of violence, pushed to its utmost bounds." This act of violence, moreover, is not divorced from the political life of a nation, it is not an abnormal situation, but merely the forceful realization of a political aim, "a mere continuation of policy by other means." Therefore it must be dictated by political considerations, and military leadership of a state must be subordinated to its political leadership.

Clausewitz' work, in his own words, is the result of "thought and observation, philosophy and experience." To back up his generalizations he refers continually to actual campaigns, many of which he had thoroughly studied and in some of which he had himself participated. But to consider him merely the interpreter of the achievements of others, especially of Napoleon, would be to overlook the originality of his thought as well as the flexibility of his ideas. He was well aware that warfare would again change, as it had done so often in the past.

A large part of Clausewitz' book "On War" is devoted to an evaluation of the moral factors involved in warfare. These sections, in which he treats what might be called the "psychological aspects" of war, have been considered his most unique and enduring contributions. In contrast to the emphasis which 18th century warfare and military theory placed on material forces and mathematical calculations, he stresses the necessity of such intangible qualities as courage, audacity, and self-sacrifice, showing himself perfectly aware of the extreme importance of army morale and public opinion. Exceptional qualities of character, a deep devotion to duty, and a well-rounded personality are the prerequisites of military leadership. They are necessary to overcome the frictions inherent in war and to reach "heroic decisions based on reason," which are the truest expression of superior leadership.

Clausewitz' desire to write a book on war "which would not be forgotten in two or three years" was fulfilled. He wrote a classic which has made a deep and lasting impression, not only on the army of his own country, but on that of other nations as well. (Parts of his writings were translated into English as early as 1843!) His ideas were first put into effect by Helmuth von Moltke, chief of staff of the Prussian army after 1857; and Prussia's success in the wars of 1866 and 1870-71 was considered proof of the validity of Clausewitz' teachings. Moltke's second successor, Count Schlieffen, was likewise a great admirer and disciple of Clausewitz. Moltke, who had been at the War School under Clausewitz, recognized that certain adjustments had to be made in the application of Clausewitz' theories, because of the technical, social, and economic developments of the Industrial Revolution. Both he and Schlieffen realized, for example, that Clausewitz' decision in favor of concentrated frontal attack was no longer feasible, because of the defensive power of modern weapons, and proposed instead to defeat the enemy by strategic turning moves (*e.g.*, Schlieffen's famous Plan of 1905). Such open-minded and broad interpretation of Clausewitz' principles endows them with lasting significance, no matter how modern conditions may differ from those during the age of Napoleon and Clausewitz. In 1937, upon publication of the 15th edition of VOM KRIEGE, the German Minister of War, General von Blomberg, wrote: "In spite of all changes of military organization and technique, Clausewitz' book 'On War' remains for all times the basis for any meaningful development of the art of war."

As appendix to the third volume of VOM KRIEGE, we find the memorandum, mentioned above, written for the military instruction of the Prussian crown prince. Though by no means comparable in scope and significance to the main work, it has nevertheless aroused sufficient interest to be published repeatedly in a separate edition. A French translation appeared toward the end of the last century, when the influence of Clausewitz made itself felt in the French army, notably through Marshal Foch. (Also at this time the French École Supérieure de Guerre was founded on the model of the German Kriegsakademie.) Later, during the First World War, an abbreviated version of the memorandum was published in the United States. The interest shown in the little essay is due to the fact that it contains, in brief form, many of the ideas later expressed in Clausewitz' major work. Like nothing else, therefore, it may serve as an introduction to his theories on the nature and conduct of war. Its brevity, moreover, should not blind us to the vital significance of its contents, which supply enough food for thought "to occupy the whole life of an officer."

The Germans thought enough of the memorandum to republish it in 1936, with an introduction by General Friedrich von Cochenhausen, military writer and instructor at the German Academy for Aerial Warfare. It is significant that a General of

Aviation, which is considered the most modern and revolutionary branch of the armed services, found the memorandum worthy of publication. From this recent edition, considerably more complete than any of the earlier ones (including even the one published in Clausewitz' collected works), the present book has been translated.

Cochenhausen stressed the revolutionary features of Clausewitz' theories, but pointed out that some of his ideas, especially on tactics, are out of date, due to the technical advances of the last century. The sections he thought no longer applicable to modern warfare have been indicated in the German edition by italics, a practice which has been maintained throughout this translation.

But most parts of the little essay still have great current value and "might have been written today." This is true, for example, of the chapter dealing with the influence of terrain on warfare. Still more important and typical is Clausewitz' constant stress on the moral elements of warfare. His language, that of a man who also wrote romantic poetry, may sometimes sound strange to modern ears. But his advice: "Be audacious and cunning in your plans, firm and persevering in their execution, determined to find a glorious end," will never lose its significance.

HANS W. GATZKE

Cambridge, Massachusetts
September 1, 1942

THE MOST IMPORTANT PRINCIPLES
FOR THE CONDUCT OF WAR

These principles, though the result of long thought and continuous study of the history of war, have none the less been drawn up hastily, and thus will not stand severe criticism in regard to form. In addition, only the most important subjects have been picked from a great number, since a certain brevity was necessary. These principles, therefore, will not so much give complete instruction to Your Royal Highness, as they will stimulate and serve as a guide for your own reflections.

CARL VON CLAUSEWITZ

I. PRINCIPLES FOR WAR IN GENERAL

1. The theory of warfare tries to discover how we may gain a preponderance of physical forces and material advantages at the decisive point. As this is not always possible, theory also teaches us to calculate moral factors: the likely mistakes of the enemy, the impression created by a daring action, . . . yes, even our own desperation. None of these things lie outside the realm of the theory and art of war, which is nothing but the result of reasonable reflection on all the possible situations encountered during a war. We should think very frequently of the most dangerous of these situations and familiarize ourselves with it. Only thus shall we reach heroic decisions based on reason, which no critic can ever shake.

Any person who may present this matter differently to Your Royal Highness is a pedant, whose views will only be harmful to you. In the decisive moments of your life, in the turmoil of battle, you will some day feel that this view alone can help where help is needed most, and where a dry pedantry of figures will forsake you.

2. Whether counting on physical or moral advantages, we should always try, in time of war, to have the probability of victory on our side. But this is not always possible. Often we must act AGAINST this probability, SHOULD THERE BE NOTHING BETTER TO DO. Were we to despair here, we would abandon the use of reason just when it be-

comes most necessary, when everything seems to be conspiring against us.

Therefore, even when the likelihood of success is against us, we must not think of our undertaking as unreasonable or impossible; for it is always reasonable, if we do not know of anything better to do, and if we make the best use of the few means at our disposal.

We must never lack the calmness and firmness, which are so hard to preserve in time of war. Without them the most brilliant qualities of mind are wasted. We must therefore familiarize ourselves with the thought of an honorable defeat. We must always nourish this thought within ourselves, and we must get completely used to it. Be convinced, Most Gracious Master, that without this firm resolution no great results can be achieved in the most successful war, let alone in the most unsuccessful.

Certainly this thought frequently occupied the mind of Frederick II during his first Silesian wars. Because he was familiar with it he undertook his attack near Leuthen, on that memorable fifth of December, and not because he believed that his oblique formation would very likely beat the Austrians.[1]

3. In any specific action, in any measure we may undertake, we always have the choice between the most audacious and the most careful solution. Some people think that the theory of war always

[1] See notes beginning on page 70.

advises the latter. That assumption is false. If the theory does advise anything, it is the nature of war to advise the most decisive, that is, the most audacious. Theory leaves it to the military leader, however, to act according to his own courage, according to his spirit. of enterprise, and his self-confidence. Make your choice, therefore, according to this inner force; but never forget that no military leader has ever become great without audacity.

II. TACTICS OR THE THEORY OF COMBAT

War is a combination of many distinct engagements. Such a combination may or may not be reasonable, and success depends very much on this. Yet the engagement itself is for the moment more important. For only a combination of successful engagements can lead to good results. The most important thing in war will always be the art of defeating our opponent in combat. To this matter Your Royal Highness can never turn enough attention and thought. I think the following principles the most important:

1. General Principles For Defense

1. To keep our troops covered as long as possible. Since we are always open to attack, except when we ourselves are attacking, we must at every instant be on the defensive and thus should place our forces as much under cover as possible.

2. Not to bring all our troops into combat immediately. With such action all wisdom in conducting a battle disappears. It is only with troops left at our disposal that we can turn the tide of battle.

3. To be little or not at all concerned about the extent of our front. This in itself is unimportant, and an extension of the front limits the depth of our formation (that is the number of corps which are lined up one behind the other). Troops which

are kept in the rear are always available. We can use them either to renew combat at the same point, or to carry the fight to other neighboring points. This principle is a corollary of the previous one.

4. The enemy, while attacking one section of the front, often seeks to outflank and envelop us at the same time. The army-corps [2] which are kept in the background can meet this attempt and thus make up for the support usually derived from obstacles in the terrain. They are better suited for this than if they were standing in line and extending the front. For in this case the enemy could easily outflank them. This principle again is a closer definition of the second.

5. If we have many troops to hold in reserve, only part of them should stand directly behind the front. The rest we should put obliquely behind.

From this position they in turn can attack the flank of the enemy columns which are seeking to envelop us.

6. A fundamental principle is never to remain completely passive, but to attack the enemy frontally and from the flanks, even while he is attacking us. We should, therefore, defend ourselves on a given front merely to induce the enemy to deploy his forces in an attack on this front. Then we in turn attack with those of our troops which we have kept back. The art of entrenchment, as Your Royal Highness expressed so excellently at one time, shall serve the defender not to defend

himself more securely behind a rampart, but to attack the enemy more successfully. This idea should be applied to any passive defense. Such defense is nothing more than a means by which to attack the enemy most advantageously, in a terrain chosen in advance, where we have drawn up our troops and have arranged things to our advantage.

7. This attack from a defensive position can take place the moment the enemy actually attacks, or while he is still on the march. I can also, at the moment the attack is about to be delivered, withdraw my troops, luring the enemy into unknown territory and attacking him from all sides. The formation in depth—*i.e.*, the formation in which only two-thirds or half or still less of the army is drawn-up in front and the rest directly or obliquely behind and hidden, if possible—is very suitable for all these moves. This type of formation is, therefore, of immense importance.

8. If, for example, I had two divisions, I would prefer to keep one in the rear. If I had three, I would keep at least one in the rear, and if four probably two. If I had five, I should hold at least two in reserve and in many cases even three, etc.

9. At those points where we remain passive we must make use of the art of fortification. This should be done with many independent works, completely closed and with very strong profiles.

10. In our plan of battle we must set this great aim: the attack on a large enemy column and its

complete destruction. If our aim is low, while that
of the enemy is high, we will naturally get the
worst of it. We are penny-wise and pound-foolish.

11. Having set a high goal in our plan of defense
(the annihilation of an enemy column, etc.), we
must pursue this goal with the greatest energy and
with the last ounce of our strength. In most cases
the aggressor will pursue his own aim at some other
point. While we fall upon his right wing, for example, he will try to win decisive advantages with
his left. Consequently, if we should slacken before
the enemy does, if we should pursue our aim with
less energy than he does, he will gain his advantage
completely, while we shall only half gain our's.
He will thus achieve preponderance of power; the
victory will be his, and we shall have to give up
even our partly gained advantages. If Your Royal
Highness will read with attention the history of
the battles of Ratisbon and Wagram, all this will
seem true and important.[2]

In both these battles the Emperor Napoleon attacked with his right wing and tried to hold out
with his left. The Archduke Charles did exactly
the same. But, while the former acted with great
determination and energy, the latter was wavering
and always stopped half-way. That is why the
advantages which Charles gained with the victorious part of his army were without consequence,
while those which Napoleon gained at the opposite end were decisive.

12. Let me sum up once more the last two principles. Their combination gives us a maxim which should take first place among all causes of victory in the modern art of war: "Pursue one great decisive aim with force and determination."

13. If we follow this and fail, the danger will be even greater, it is true. But to increase caution at the expense of the final goal is no military art. It is the wrong kind of caution, which, as I have said already in my "General Principles," is contrary to the nature of war. For great aims we must dare great things. When we are engaged in a daring enterprise, the right caution consists in not neglecting out of laziness, indolence, or carelessness those measures which help us to gain our aim. Such was the case of Napoleon, who never, because of caution, pursued great aims in a timid or half-hearted way.

If you remember, Most Gracious Master, the few defensive battles that have ever been won, you will find that the best of them have been conducted in the spirit of the principles voiced here. For it is the study of the history of war which has given us these principles.

At Minden, Duke Ferdinand suddenly appeared where the enemy did not expect him and took the offensive, while at Tannhausen he defended himself passively behind earthworks.[4] At Rossbach Frederick II threw himself against the enemy at an unexpected point and an unexpected moment.[5]

At Liegnitz the Austrians found the King at night in a position very different from that in which they had seen him the previous day. He fell with his whole army upon one enemy column and defeated it before the others could start fighting.[6]

At Hohenlinden Moreau had five divisions in his frontline and four directly behind and on his flanks. He outflanked the enemy and fell upon his right wing before it could attack.[7]

At Ratisbon Marshal Davout defended himself passively, while Napoleon attacked the fifth and sixth army-corps with his right wing and beat them completely.

Though the Austrians were the real defenders at Wagram, they did attack the emperor on the second day with the greater part of their forces. Therefore Napoleon can also be considered a defender. With his right wing he attacked, outflanked and defeated the Austrian left wing. At the same time he paid little attention to his weak left wing (consisting of a single division), which was resting on the Danube. Yet through strong reserves (*i.e.*, formation in depth), he prevented the victory of the Austrian right wing from having any influence on his own victory gained on the Russbach. He used these reserves to retake Aderklaa.

Not all the principles mentioned earlier are clearly contained in each of these battles, but all are examples of active defense.

The mobility of the Prussian army under Frederick II was a means towards victory on which we can no longer count, since the other armies are at least as mobile as we are. On the other hand, outflanking was less common at that time and formation in depth, therefore, less imperative.

2. General Principles For Offense

1. We must select for our attack one point of the enemy's position (*i.e.*, one section of his troops —a division, a corps) and attack it with great superiority, leaving the rest of his army in uncertainty but keeping it occupied. This is the only way that we can use an equal or smaller force to fight with advantage and thus with a chance of success. The weaker we are, the fewer troops we should use to keep the enemy occupied at unimportant points, in order to be as strong as possible at the decisive point. Frederick II doubtlessly won the battle of Leuthen only because he massed his small army together in one place and thus was very concentrated, as compared to the enemy.[8]

2. We should direct our main thrust against an enemy wing by attacking it from the front and from the flank, or by turning it completely and attacking it from the rear. Only when we cut off the enemy's line of retreat are we assured of great success in victory.

3. Even though we are strong, we should still direct our main attack against one point only. In

that way we shall gain more strength at this point. For to surround an army completely is possible only in rare cases and requires tremendous physical or moral superiority. It is possible, however, to cut off the enemy's line of retreat at one point of his flank and thereby already gain great success.

4. Generally speaking, the chief aim is the certainty (high probability) of victory, that is, the certainty of driving the enemy from the field of battle. The plan of battle must be directed towards this end. For it is easy to change an indecisive victory into a decisive one through energetic pursuit of the enemy.

5. Let us assume that the enemy has troops enough on one wing to make a front in all directions. Our main force should try to attack the wing concentrically, so his troops find themselves assailed from all sides. Under these circumstances his troops will get discouraged much more quickly; they suffer more, get disordered—in short, we can hope to turn them to flight much more easily.

6. This encirclement of the enemy necessitates a greater deployment of forces in the front line for the aggressor than for the defender.

If the corps *a b c* should make a concentric attack on the section *e* of the enemy army, they should, of course, be next to each other. But we should never have so many forces in the front line that we have none in reserve. That would be a very great error which would lead to defeat, should the enemy be in the least prepared for an encirclement.

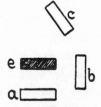

If *a b c* are the corps which are to attack section *e*, the corps *f g* must be held in reserve. With this formation in depth we are able to harass the same point continuously. And in case our troops should be beaten at the opposite end of the line, we do not need to give up immediately our attack at this end, since we still have reserves with which

to oppose the enemy. The French did this in the battle of Wagram. Their left wing, which opposed the Austrian right wing resting on the Danube, was extremely weak and was completely defeated. Even their center at Aderklaa was not very strong and was forced by the Austrians to retreat on the first day of battle. But all this did not matter, since Napoleon had such depth on his right wing, with which he attacked the Austrian left from the front and side, that he advanced against the Austrians at Aderklaa with a tremendous column of cavalry and horse-artillery; and, though he could not beat them, he at least was able to hold them there.

7. Just as on the defensive, we should choose as object of our offensive that section of the enemy's army whose defeat will give us decisive advantages.

8. As in defense, as long as any resources are left, we must not give up until our purpose has been reached. Should the defender likewise be active, should he attack us at other points, we shall be able to gain victory only if we surpass him in energy and boldness. On the other hand, should he be passive, we really run no great danger.

9. Long and unbroken lines of troops should be avoided completely. They would lead only to parallel attacks, which today are no longer feasible.

Each division makes its attack separately, though according to the directions of a higher command and thus in agreement with each other. Yet one division (8,000 to 10,000 men) is never formed into one single line, but into two, three, or even four. From this it follows that a long unbroken line is no longer possible.

10. The concerted attacks of the divisions and army corps should not be obtained by trying to

direct them from a central point, so that they maintain contact and even align themselves on each other, though they may be far apart or even separated by the enemy. This is a faulty method of bringing about cooperation, open to a thousand mischances. Nothing great can be achieved with it and we are certain to be thoroughly beaten by a strong opponent.

The true method consists in giving each commander of an army corps or a division the main direction of his march, and in pointing out the enemy as the objective and victory as the goal.

Each commander of a column, therefore, has the order to attack the enemy wherever he may find him and to do so with all his strength. He must not be made responsible for the success of his attack, for that would lead to indecision. But he is responsible for seeing that his corps will take part in battle with all its energy and with a spirit of self-sacrifice.

11. A well-organized, independent corps can withstand the best attack for some time (several hours) and thus can not be annihilated in a moment. Thus, even if it engaged the enemy prematurely and was defeated, its fight will not have been in vain. The enemy will unfold and expend his strength against this one corps, offering the rest a good chance for an attack.

The way in which a corps should be organized for this purpose will be treated later.

We therefore assure the cooperation of all forces by giving each corps a certain amount of independence, but seeing to it that each seeks out the enemy and attacks him with all possible self-sacrifice.

12. One of the strongest weapons of offensive warfare is the surprise attack. The closer we come to it, the more fortunate we shall be. The unexpected element which the defender creates through secret preparations and through the concealed disposition of his troops, can be counterbalanced on the part of the aggressor only by a surprise attack.

Such action, however, has been very rare in recent wars, partly because of the more advanced precautionary measures, partly because of the rapid conduct of campaigns. There seldom arises a long suspension of activities, which lulls one side into security and thus gives the other an opportunity to attack unexpectedly.

Under these circumstances—except for nightly assaults which are always possible (as at Hochkirch)[9]—we can surprise our opponent only by marching to the side or to the rear and then suddenly advancing again. Or, should we be far from the enemy, we can through unusual energy and activity arrive faster than he expects us.

13. The regular surprise attack (by night as at Hochkirch) is the best way to get the most out of a very small army. But the aggressor, who is

not as well acquainted with the terrain as the defender, is open to many risks. The less well one knows the terrain and the preparations of the enemy, the greater these risks become. In many instances, therefore, these attacks must be considered only as desperate means.

14. This kind of attack demands simpler preparations and a greater concentration of our troops than in the daytime.

3. Principles Governing The Use Of Troops

1. If we cannot dispense with firearms (and if we could, why should we bring them along?), we must use them to open combat. *Cavalry must not be used before the enemy has suffered considerably from our infantry and artillery. From this it follows:*

(a) *That we must place the cavalry behind the infantry. That we must not be easily led to use it in opening combat. Only when the enemy's disorder or his rapid retreat offer the hope of success, should we use our cavalry for an audacious attack.*

2. Artillery fire is much more effective than that of infantry. A battery of eight six-pounders takes up less than one-third of the front taken up

---

* The passages in italics on the following pages are those considered no longer applicable to modern warfare by General Friedrich von Cochenhausen, of the German Academy for Aerial Warfare.

by an infantry battalion; it has less than one-eighth the men of a battalion, and yet its fire is two to three times as effective. On the other hand, artillery has the disadvantage of being less mobile than infantry. This is true, on the whole, even of the lightest horse-artillery, for it cannot, like infantry, be used in any kind of terrain. *It is necessary, therefore, to direct the artillery from the start against the most important points, since it cannot, like infantry, concentrate against these points as the battle progresses. A large battery of 20 to 30 pieces usually decides the battle for that section where it is placed.*

3. From these and other apparent characteristics the following rules can be drawn for the use of the different arms:

(a) We should begin combat with the larger part of our artillery. Only when we have large masses of troops at our disposal should we keep horse and foot-artillery in reserve. *We should use artillery in great batteries massed against one point. Twenty to thirty pieces combined into one battery defend the chief part of our line, or shell that part of the enemy position which we plan to attack.*

(b) After this we use light infantry—either marksmen, riflemen, or fusileers—being careful not to put too many forces into play at the beginning. We try first to discover what lies ahead of us (for we can seldom see that clearly in advance), and which way the battle is turning, etc.

If this firing line is sufficient to counter-act the enemy's troops, and if there is no need to hurry, we should do wrong to hasten the use of our remaining forces. We must try to exhaust the enemy as much as possible with this preliminary skirmish.

(c) *If the enemy should lead so many troops into combat that our firing line is about to fall back, or if for some other reason we should no longer hesitate, we must draw up a full line of infantry. This will deploy between 100 and 200 paces from the enemy and will fire or charge, as matters may be.*

(d) *This is the main purpose of the infantry. If, at the same time, the battle-array is deep enough, leaving us another line of infantry (arranged in columns) as reserve, we shall be sufficiently master of the situation at this sector. This second line of infantry should, if possible, be used only in columns to bring about a decision.*

(e) *The cavalry should be as close behind the fighting troops during battle as is possible without great loss; that is, it should be out of the enemy's grape-shot or musket fire.*

*On the other hand, it should be close enough
to take quick advantage of any favorable
turn of battle.*

4. In obeying these rules more or less closely,
we should never lose sight of the following principle, which I cannot stress enough:

Never bring all our forces into play haphazardly
and at one time, thereby losing all means of directing the battle; but fatigue the opponent, if possible,
with few forces and conserve a decisive mass for
the critical moment. Once this decisive mass has
been thrown in, it must be used with the greatest
audacity.

*5. We should establish one battle-order (the
arrangement of troops before and during combat)
for the whole campaign or the whole war. This
order will serve in all cases when there is no time
for a special disposition of troops. It should, therefore, be calculated primarily for the defensive.
This battle-array will introduce a certain uniform-
ity into the fighting-method of the army, which
will be useful and advantageous. For it is inevitable
that a large part of the lower generals and other
officers at the head of small contingents have no
special knowledge of tactics and perhaps no outstanding aptitude for the conduct of war.*

*Thus there arises a certain methodism in war-
fare to take the place of art, wherever the latter
is absent. In my opinion this is to the highest degree the case in the French armies.*

6. *After what I have said about the use of weapons, this battle-order, applied to a brigade, would be approximately as follows:*

a-b is the line of light infantry, which opens combat and which in rough terrain serves to some extent as an advanced guard. Then comes the artillery, c-d, to be set up at advantageous points. As long as it is not set up, it remains behind the first line of infantry. e-f is the first line of infantry (in this case four battalions) whose purpose is to form into line and to open fire, and g-h are a few regiments of cavalry. i-k is the second line of infantry, which is held in reserve for the decisive stage of the battle, and l-m is its cavalry. A strong corps would be drawn up according *to the same principles and in a similar manner. At the same time, it is not essential that the battle-array be exactly like this. It may differ slightly provided that the above principles are followed. So, for instance, in ordinary battle-order the first line of cavalry g-h can remain with the second line of cavalry, l-m. It is to be advanced only in particular cases, when this position should prove to be too far back.*

7. The army consists of several such independent corps, which have their own general and staff. They are drawn up in line and behind each other, as described in the general rules for combat. *It should be observed at this point that, unless we are very weak in cavalry, we should create a special cavalry reserve, which, of course, is kept in the rear. Its purpose is as follows:*[10]

(a) *To fall upon the enemy when he is retreating from the field of battle and to attack the cavalry which he uses to cover up his retreat. Should we defeat the enemy's cavalry at this moment, great successes are inevitable, unless the enemy's infantry would perform miracles of bravery. Small detachments of cavalry would not accomplish this purpose.*

(b) *To pursue the enemy more rapidly, if he should be retreating unbeaten or if he should continue to retreat the day after a lost battle.*

Cavalry moves faster than infantry and has a more demoralizing effect on the retreating troops. Next to victory, the act of pursuit is most important in war.

(c) *To execute a great (strategic) turning move, should we need, because of the detour, a branch of the army which moves more rapidly than the infantry.*

In order to make this corps more independent, we should attach a considerable mass of horse-artillery; for a combination of several types of arms can only give greater strength.

8. *The battle-order of troops described thus far was intended for combat; it was the formation of troops for battle.*

The order of march is essentially as follows:

(a) Each independent corps (whether brigade or division) has its own advanced- and rear-guard and forms its own column. That, however, does not prevent several corps from marching one behind the other on the same road, and thus, as it were, forming a single column.

(b) The corps march according to their position in the general formation of battle. They march beside or behind each other, just as they would stand on the battle-field.

(c) *In the corps themselves the following order is invariably observed: the light infantry,*

with the addition of one regiment of cav-
alry, forming the advanced and rear-guard,
then the infantry, the artillery, and last the
remaining cavalry.

This order stands, whether we are moving against
the enemy—in which case it is the natural order—
or parallel with him. In the latter case we should
assume that those troops which in the battle forma-
tion were behind each other should march side by
side. But when we have to draw up the troops
for battle, there will always be sufficient time to
move the cavalry and the second line of infantry
either to the right or left.

4. Principles For The Use Of Terrain

1. The terrain (the ground or country) offers
two advantages in warfare.

The first is that it presents obstacles to the enemy's approach. These either make his advance
impossible at a given point, or force him to march
more slowly and to maintain his formation in columns, etc.

The second advantage is that obstacles in the
terrain enable us to place our troops under cover.

Although both advantages are very important,
I think the second more important than the first.
In any event, it is certain that we profit from it
more frequently, since in most cases even the simplest terrain permits us to place ourselves more

or less under cover. Formerly only the first of
these advantages was known and the second was
rarely used. But today the greater mobility of all
armies has led us to use the former less frequently,
and therefore the latter more frequently. The first
of these two advantages is useful for defense alone,
the second for both offense and defense.

2. The terrain as an obstacle to approach serves
chiefly to support our flank, and to strengthen our
front.

3. To support our flank it must be absolutely
impassable, such as a large river, a lake, an im-
penetrable morass. These obstacles, however, are
very rare, and a complete protection of our flank
is, therefore, hard to find. It is rarer today than
ever before, since we do not stay in one position
very long, but move about a great deal. Consequently we need more positions in the theatre of
war.

An obstacle to approach which is not wholly
impassable is really no *point d'appui* for our flank,
but only a reinforcement. In that case troops must
be drawn up behind it, and for them in turn it
becomes an obstacle to approach.

Yet it is always advantageous to secure our flank
in this way, for then we shall need fewer troops
at this point. But we must beware of two things:
first, of relying so completely on this protection
that we do not keep a strong reserve in the rear;
second, of surrounding ourselves on both flanks

with such obstacles, for, since they do not protect us completely, they do not always prevent
fighting on our flanks. They are, therefore, highly
detrimental to our defense, for they do not permit
us to engage easily in active defense on either wing.
We shall be reduced to defense under the most
disadvantageous conditions, with both flanks, *a d*
and *c b*, thrown back.

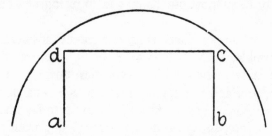

4. The observations just made furnish new arguments for the formation in depth. The less we can
find secure support for our flanks, the more corps
we must have in the rear to envelop those troops
of the enemy which are surrounding us.

5. All kinds of terrain, which cannot be passed
by troops marching in line, all villages, all en-
closures surrounded by hedges or ditches, marshy
meadows, finally all mountains which are crossed
only with difficulty, constitute obstacles of this
kind. We can pass them, but only slowly and
with effort. They increase, therefore, the power
of resistance of troops drawn up behind them.
Forests are to be included only if they are thickly

wooded and marshy. An ordinary timber-forest
can be passed as easily as a plain. But we must not
overlook the fact that a forest may hide the enemy.
If we conceal ourselves in it, this disadvantage af-
fects both sides. But it is very dangerous, and
thus a grave mistake, to leave forests on our front
or flank unoccupied, unless the forest can be traversed only by a few paths. Barricades built as
obstacles are of little help, since they can easily
be removed.

6. From all this it follows that we should use
such obstacles on one flank to put up a relatively
strong resistance with few troops, while executing
our planned offensive on the other flank. It is
very advantageous to combine the use of entrenchments with such natural obstacles, because then,
if the enemy should pass the obstacle, the fire from
these entrenchments will protect our weak troops
against too great superiority and sudden rout.

7. When we are defending ourselves, any obstacle on our front is of great value.

Mountains are occupied only for this reason.
For an elevated position seldom has any important
influence, often none at all, on the effectiveness
of arms. But if we stand on a height, the enemy,
in order to approach us, must climb laboriously.
He will advance but slowly, become separated, and
arrive with his forces exhausted. Given equal bravery and strength, these advantages may be decisive. On no account should we overlook the

moral effect of a rapid, running assault. It hardens
the advancing soldier against danger, while the
stationary soldier loses his presence of mind. *It is,
therefore, always very advantageous to put our first
line of infantry and artillery upon a mountain.*

Often the grade of the mountain is so steep, or
its slope so undulating and uneven, that it cannot
be effectively swept by gun-fire. In that case we
should not place our first line, but at the most
only our sharp-shooters, at the edge of the mountain. Our full line we should place in such a way
that the enemy is subject to its most effective fire
the moment he reaches the top and reassembles
his forces.

All other obstacles to approach, such as small
rivers, brooks, ravines, etc., serve to break the
enemy's front. He will have to re-form his lines
after passing them and thus will be delayed. These
obstacles must, therefore, be placed under our
most effective fire, *which is grape-shot (400 to
600 paces), if we have a great deal of artillery or
musket-shot (150 to 200 paces), if we have little
artillery at this point.*

8. It is, therefore, a basic law to place all obstacles to approach, which are to strengthen our
front, under our most effective fire. But it is important to notice that we must never completely
limit our resistance to this fire *but must hold ready
for a bayonet-charge an important part of our
troops (1/3 to 1/2) organized into columns. Should*

*we be very weak, therefore, we must place only
our firing-line, composed of riflemen and artillery,
close enough to keep the obstacle under fire. The
rest of our troops, organized into columns, we
should keep 600 to 800 paces back, if possible under cover.*

9. Another method of using these obstacles to
protect our front is to leave them a short distance
ahead. They are thus within the effective range
of our cannon (*1000 to 2000 paces*) and we can
attack the enemy's columns from all sides, as they
emerge. (Something like this was done by Duke
Ferdinand at Minden.[4]) In this way the obstacle
contributes to our plan of active defense, and this
active defense, of which we spoke earlier, will be
executed on our front.

10. Thus far we have considered the obstacles
of the ground and country primarily as connected
lines related to extended positions. It is still necessary to say something about isolated points.

On the whole we can defend single, isolated
points only by entrenchments or strong obstacles
of terrain. We shall not discuss the first here. The
only obstacles of terrain which can be held by
themselves are:

(a) Isolated, steep heights.

> Here entrenchments are likewise indis-
> pensable; for the enemy can always move
> against the defender with a more or less
> extended front. And the latter will always

end up by being taken from the rear, since
one is rarely strong enough to make front
towards all sides.

(b) Defiles.

By this term we mean any narrow path,
through which the enemy can advance only
against one point. Bridges, dams, and steep
ravines belong here.

We should observe that these obstacles
fall into two categories: either the aggressor
can in no way avoid them, as for example
bridges across large rivers, in which case the
defender can boldly draw up his whole
force so as to fire upon the point of crossing as effectively as possible. Or we are not
absolutely sure that the enemy can not turn
the obstacle, as with bridges across small
streams and most mountain defiles. In that
case it is necessary to reserve a considerable
part of our troops 1/3 to 1/2 for an attack
in close order.

(c) Localities, villages, small towns, etc.

With very brave troops, who fight en-
thusiastically, houses offer a unique defense
for few against many. But, if we are not
sure of the individual soldier, it is preferable
to occupy the houses, gardens, etc., only
with sharp-shooters and the entrances to the
village with cannons. The greater part of
our troops *(1/2 to 3/4) we should keep in*

close columns and hidden in the locality or behind it, so as to fall upon the enemy while he is invading.

11. These isolated posts serve in large operations partly as outposts, in which case they serve not as absolute defense but only as a delay to the enemy, and partly to hold points which are important for the combinations we have planned for our army. Also it is often necessary to hold on to a remote point in order to gain time for the development of active measures of defense which we may have planned. But, if a point is remote, it is *ipso facto* isolated.

12. Two more observations about isolated obstacles are necessary. The first is that we must keep troops ready behind them to receive detachments that have been thrown back. The second is that whoever includes such isolated obstacles in his defensive combinations should never count on them too much, no matter how strong the obstacle may be. On the other hand, the military leader to whom the defense of the obstacle has been entrusted must always try to hold out, even under the most adverse circumstances. For this there is needed a spirit of determination and self-sacrifice, which finds its source only in ambition and enthusiasm. We must, therefore, choose men for this mission who are not lacking in these noble qualities.

13. Using terrain to cover the disposition and advance of troops needs no detailed exposition.

We should not occupy the crest of the mountain which we intend to defend (as has been done so frequently in the past) but draw up behind it. We should not take our position in front of a forest, but inside or behind it; the latter only if we are able to survey the forest or thicket. *We should keep our troops in columns, so as to find cover more easily.* We must make use of villages, small thickets, and rolling terrain to hide our troops. For our advance we should choose the most intersected country, etc.

In cultivated country, which can be reconnoitered so easily, there is almost no region that can not hide a large part of the defender's troops if they have made clever use of obstacles. To cover the aggressor's advance is more difficult, since he must follow the roads.

It goes without saying that in using the terrain to hide our troops, we must never lose sight of the goal and combinations we have set for ourselves. Above all things we should not break up our battle-order completely, even though we may deviate slightly from it.

14. If we recapitulate what has been said about terrain, the following appears most important for the defender, *i.e.*, for the choice of positions:

(a) Support of one or both flanks.

(b) Open view on front and flanks.

(c) Obstacles to approach on the front.

(d) Masked disposition of troops. And finally

(e) Intersected country in the rear, to render pursuit more difficult in case of defeat. But no defiles too near (as at Friedland), since they cause delay and confusion.[11]

15. It would be pedantic to believe that all these advantages could be found in any position we may take up during a war. Not all positions are of equal importance: the most important are those in which we most likely may be attacked. It is here that we should try to have all these advantages, while in others we only need part.

16. The two main points which the aggressor should consider in regard to the choice of terrain are not to select too difficult a terrain for the attack, but on the other hand to advance, if possible, through a terrain in which the enemy can least survey our force.

17. I close these observations with a principle which is of highest significance, and which must be considered the keystone of the whole defensive theory:

NEVER TO DEPEND COMPLETELY ON THE STRENGTH OF THE TERRAIN AND CONSEQUENTLY NEVER TO BE ENTICED INTO PASSIVE DEFENSE BY A STRONG TERRAIN.

For if the terrain is really so strong that the aggressor cannot possibly expel us, he will turn it, which is always possible, and thus render the strongest terrain useless. We shall be forced into battle under very different circumstances, and in a completely different terrain, and we might as well not have included the first terrain in our plans. But if the terrain is not so strong, and if an attack within its confines is still possible, its advantages can never make up for the disadvantages of passive defense. All obstacles are useful, therefore, only for partial defense, in order that we may put up a relatively strong resistance with few troops and gain time for the offensive, through which we try to win a real victory elsewhere.

III. STRATEGY

This term means the combination of individual engagements to attain the goal of the campaign or war.

If we know how to fight and how to win, little more knowledge is needed. For it is easy to combine fortunate results. It is merely a matter of experienced judgment and does not depend on special knowledge, as does the direction of battle.

The few principles, therefore, which come up in this connection, and which depend primarily on the condition of the respective states and armies, can in their essential parts be very briefly summarized:

1. General Principles

1. Warfare has three main objects:
   - (a) To conquer and destroy the armed power of the enemy;
   - (b) To take possession of his material and other sources of strength, and
   - (c) To gain public opinion.

2. To accomplish the first purpose, we should always direct our principal operation against the main body of the enemy army or at least against an important portion of his forces. For only after defeating these can we pursue the other two objects successfully.

3. In order to seize the enemy's material forces we should direct our operations against the places

where most of these resources are concentrated: principal cities, storehouses, and large fortresses. On the way to these objectives we shall encounter the enemy's main force or at least a considerable part of it.

4. Public opinion is won through great victories and the occupation of the enemy's capital.

5. The first and most important rule to observe in order to accomplish these purposes, is to use our entire forces with the utmost energy. Any moderation shown would leave us short of our aim. Even with everything in our favor, we should be unwise not to make the greatest effort in order to make the result perfectly certain. For such effort can never produce negative results. Suppose the country suffers greatly from this, no lasting disadvantage will arise; for the greater the effort, the sooner the suffering will cease.

The moral impression created by these actions is of infinite importance. They make everyone confident of success, which is the best means for suddenly raising the nation's morale.

6. The second rule is to concentrate our power as much as possible against that section where the chief blows are to be delivered and to incur disadvantages elsewhere, so that our chances of success may increase at the decisive point. This will compensate for all other disadvantages.

7. The third rule is never to waste time. Unless important advantages are to be gained from hesita-

tion, it is necessary to set to work at once. By this speed a hundred enemy measures are nipped in the bud, and public opinion is won most rapidly.

Surprise plays a much greater role in strategy than in tactics. It is the most important element of victory. Napoleon, Frederick II, Gustavus Adolphus, Cæsar, Hannibal, and Alexander owe the brightest rays of their fame to their swiftness.

8. Finally, the fourth rule is to follow up our successes with the utmost energy.

Only pursuit of the beaten enemy gives the fruits of victory.

9. The first of these rules serves as a basis for the other three. If we have observed it, we can be as daring as possible with the last three, and yet not risk our all. For it provides us with the means of constantly creating new forces in our rear, and with fresh forces any misfortune can be remedied.

Therein lies the caution which deserves to be called wise, and not in taking each step forward with timidity.

10. Small states cannot wage wars of conquest in our times. But in defensive warfare even the means of small states are infinitely great. I am, therefore, firmly convinced that if we spare no effort to reappear again and again with new masses of troops, if we use all possible means of preparation and keep our forces concentrated at the main point, and if we, thus prepared, pursue a great

aim with determination and energy, we have done all that can be done on a large scale for the strategic direction of the war. And unless we are very unfortunate in battle we are bound to be victorious to the same extent that our opponent lags behind in effort and energy.

11. In observing these principles little depends on the form in which the operations are carried out. I shall try, nevertheless, to make clear in a few words the most important aspects of this question.

In tactics we always seek to envelop that part of the enemy against which we direct our main attack. We do this partly because our forces are more effective in a concentric than in a parallel attack, and further because we can only thus cut off the enemy from his line of retreat.

But if we apply this to the whole theatre of war (and consequently to the enemy's lines of communication), the individual columns and armies, which are to envelop the enemy, are in most cases too far away from each other to participate in one and the same engagement. The opponent will find himself in the middle and will be able to turn against the corps one by one and defeat them all with a single army. Frederick II's campaigns may serve as examples, especially those of 1757 and 1758.[12]

The individual engagement, therefore, remains the principal decisive event. Consequently, if we attack concentrically without having decisive superiority, we shall lose in battle all the advantages, which we expected from our enveloping attack on the enemy. For an attack on the lines of communication takes effect only very slowly, while victory on the field of battle bears fruit immediately.

In strategy, therefore, the side that is surrounded by the enemy is better off than the side which surrounds its opponent, especially with equal or even weaker forces.

Colonel Jomini was right in this, and if Mr. von Bülow has demonstrated the opposite with so much semblance of truth, it is only because he attributed too great an importance to the interruption of provisions and carelessly and completely denied the inevitable success of battle.[13]

To cut the enemy's line of retreat, however, strategic envelopment or a turning movement is very effective. But we can achieve this, if necessary, through tactical envelopment. A strategic move is, therefore, advisable only if we are so superior (physically and morally) that we shall be strong enough at the principal point to dispense with the detached corps.

The Emperor Napoleon never engaged in strategic envelopment, although he was often, indeed almost always, both physically and morally superior.[14]

Frederick II used it only once, in 1757, in his invasion of Bohemia.[15] To be sure, the result was

that the Austrians could not give battle until
Prague, and what good was the conquest of Bohemia as far as Prague without a decisive victory?
The battle of Kolin forced him to give up all this
territory again, which proves that battles decide
everything. At the same time he was obviously in
danger at Prague of being attacked by the whole
Austrian force, before Schwerin arrived. He would
not have run this risk had he passed through Saxony
with all his forces. In that case the first battle
would have been fought perhaps near Budin, on
the Eger, and it would have been as decisive as
that of Prague. The dislocation of the Prussian
army during the winter in Silesia and Saxony undoubtedly caused this concentric maneuver. It is
important to notice that circumstances of this kind
are generally more influential than the advantages
to be gained by the form of attack. For facility
of operations increases their speed, and the friction
inherent in the tremendous war-machine of an
armed power is so great in itself that it should not
be increased unnecessarily.

12. Moreover, the principle of concentrating
our forces as much as possible on the main point
diverts us from the idea of strategic envelopment
and the deployment of our forces follows automatically. I was right, therefore, in saying that the
form of this deployment is of little consequence.
There is, however, one case in which a strategic
move against the enemy's flank will lead to great

successes similar to those of a battle: if in a poor country the enemy has accumulated with great effort stores of supplies, on whose preservation his operations absolutely depend. In this case it may be advisable not to march our main forces against those of the enemy, but to attack his base of supply. For this, however, two conditions are essential:

(a) The enemy must be so far from his base that our threat will force him into a considerable retreat, and

(b) We must be able to obstruct his advance in the direction followed by his principal force with only a few troops (thanks to natural and artificial obstacles), so that he cannot make conquests somewhere else which will compensate for the loss of his base.

13. The provisioning of troops is a necessary condition of warfare and thus has great influence on the operations, especially since it permits only a limited concentration of troops and since it helps to determine the theatre of war through the choice of a line of operations.

14. The provisioning of troops is carried on, if a region possibly permits it, through requisitions at the expense of the region.

In the modern method of war armies take up considerably more territory than before. The creation of distinct, independent corps has made this possible, without putting ourselves at a disadvantage before an adversary who follows the old method of concentration at a single point (with from 70,000 to 100,000 men). For an independent corps, organized as they now are, can withstand for some time an enemy two or three times its superior. Then the others will arrive and, even if the first corps has already been beaten, it has not fought in vain, as we have had occasion to remark.

Today, therefore, the divisions and corps move into battle independently, marching side by side or behind each other and only close enough to take part in the same battle, if they belong to the same army.

This makes possible immediate provisioning without storehouses. The very organization of the corps with their General Staff and their Commissariat facilitates this.

15. If there are no MORE decisive motives (as for example the location of the enemy's main army), we choose the most fertile provinces for our operations; for facility of provisioning increases the speed of our actions. Only the situation of the enemy's main force which we are seeking out, only the location of his capital and the place of arms which we wish to conquer are more important than provisioning. All other considerations, such as the advantageous disposition of our forces, of which we have already spoken, are as a rule much less important.

16. In spite of these new methods of provision-

ing, it is quite impossible to do without any depots whatever. Therefore, even when the resources of the region are quite sufficient, a wise military leader does not fail to establish depots in his rear for unexpected emergencies and in order to be able to concentrate his forces at certain points. This precaution is of the sort which are not taken at the expense of the final goal.

2. *Defensive*

1. Politically speaking defensive war is a war which we wage for our independence. Strategically it is the kind of campaign in which we limit ourselves to fighting the enemy in a theatre of war which we have prepared for this purpose. Whether the battles which we wage in this theatre of war are offensive or defensive, makes no difference.

2. We adopt a strategic defensive mainly when the enemy is superior. Fortresses and intrenched camps, which constitute the chief preparations for a theatre of war, afford, of course, great advantages, to which may be added the knowledge of the terrain and the possession of good maps. A smaller army, or an army which is based on a smaller state and more limited resources, will be better able to withstand the enemy WITH these advantages than without them.

In addition there are the following two reasons which can lead us to choose a defensive war.

First, when the regions surrounding the theatre

of war render operations extremely difficult because of lack of provisions. In this case we avoid a disadvantage which the enemy is forced to undergo. This is the case now (1812) with the Russian army.

Second, when the enemy is superior in warfare. In a theatre of war which we have prepared, which we know, and in which all minor conditions are in our favor, war is easier to conduct, and we commit fewer mistakes. When lack of trust in our troops and generals forces us to wage defensive war, we often like to combine tactical with strategic defensive. In that case we fight battles in prepared positions because we are thus again exposed to fewer mistakes.

3. In defensive just as in offensive warfare, it is necessary to pursue a great aim: the destruction of the enemy army, either by battle or by rendering its subsistence extremely difficult. Thus we shall disorganize it and force it into a retreat, during which it will necessarily suffer great losses. Wellington's campaign in 1810 and 1811 is a good example.[16]

Defensive warfare, therefore, does not consist of waiting idly for things to happen. We must wait only if it brings us visible and decisive advantages. That calm before the storm, when the aggressor is gathering new forces for a great blow, is most dangerous for the defender.

If the Austrians after the battle of Aspern had

increased their forces threefold, as they might have and as the Emperor Napoleon did, then and only then would they have made good use of the lull which lasted until the battle of Wagram. This they did not do, and consequently the time was lost. It would have been wiser to profit from Napoleon's disadvantageous position, and to gather the fruits of the battle of Aspern.[17]

4. The purpose of fortifications is to keep a considerable part of the enemy's army occupied as siege troops, to give us an opportunity to defeat the rest of his army. Consequently, it is best to fight our battles behind our fortifications and not in front of them. But we must not stand by idly, while they are being conquered, as Bennigsen did during the siege of Danzig.[18]

5. Large rivers, across which it is difficult to throw a bridge (such as the Danube below Vienna and the Lower Rhine), offer a natural line of defense. But we should not distribute our forces evenly along the river bank in order to prevent any crossing whatsoever. That would be most dangerous. On the contrary, we should watch the river and fall upon the enemy from all sides the minute he crosses, while he has not yet reassembled his forces and is still restricted to a narrow space on the river bank. The battle of Aspern offers a good illustration. At Wagram the Austrians had yielded to the French too much territory without the slightest necessity, so that the

disadvantages inherent in a river crossing had disappeared.[19]

6. Mountains are the second obstacle which offers a good line of defense. There are two ways of using them. The first is to leave them in front of us, occupying them only with light troops and considering them, so to speak, a river which the enemy will have to cross. As soon as his separated columns emerge from the passes, we fall upon one of them with all our force. The second is to occupy the mountains ourselves. In that case we must defend each pass with just a small corps and keep an important part of the army (1/3-1/2) in reserve, in order to attack with superior forces one of the enemy columns that succeed in breaking through. We must not divide up this large reserve to prevent completely the penetration of any enemy columns, but must plan from the outset to fall only upon those columns which we suppose to be the strongest. If we thus defeat an important part of the attacking army, any other columns which have succeeded in breaking through will withdraw of their own accord.

In the midst of most mountain formations we find more or less elevated plains (plateaus) whose slopes are cut by ravines serving as means of access. Mountains, therefore, offer the defender a region in which he can move rapidly to the right or left, while the columns of the aggressor remain separated by steep, inaccessible ridges. Only mountains of this kind are well adapted for defensive warfare. If, on the other hand, their whole interior is rough and inaccessible, leaving the defender dispersed and divided, their defense by the bulk of the army is a dangerous undertaking. For under these circumstances all advantages are on the side of the aggressor, who can attack certain points with great superiority, and no pass, no isolated point is so strong that it cannot be taken within a day by superior forces.

7. In regard to mountain warfare in general, we should observe that everything depends on the skill of our subordinate officers and still more on the morale of our soldiers. Here it is not a question of skillful maneuvering, but of warlike spirit and whole-hearted devotion to the cause; for each man is left more or less to act independently. That is why national militias are especially suited for mountain warfare. While they lack the ability to maneuver, they possess the other qualities to the highest degree.

8. Finally, it should be observed that strategic defensive, though it is stronger than the offensive, should serve only to win the first important successes. If these are won and peace does not follow immediately, we can gain further successes only through the offensive. For if we remain continually on the defensive, we run the great risk of always waging war at our own expense. This no state can endure indefinitely. If it submits to the

blows of its adversary without ever striking back, it will very likely become exhausted and succumb. We must begin, therefore, using the defensive, so as to end more successfully by the offensive.

3. Offensive

1. The strategic offensive pursues the aim of the war directly, aiming straight at the destruction of the enemy's forces, while the strategic defensive seeks to reach this purpose indirectly. The principles of the offensive are therefore already contained in the "General Principles" of strategy. Only two points need be mentioned more fully.

2. The first is constant replacement of troops and arms. This is easier for the defender, because of the proximity of his sources of supply. The aggressor, although he controls in most cases a larger state, must usually gather his forces from a distance and therefore with great difficulty. Lest he find himself short of effectives, he must organize the recruiting of troops and the transport of arms a long time before they are needed. The roads of our lines of operation must be covered constantly with transports of soldiers and supplies. We must establish military stations along these roads to hasten this rapid transport.

3. Even under the most favorable circumstances and with greatest moral and physical superiority, the aggressor should foresee a possibility of great disaster. He therefore must organize on his lines

of operation strong points to which he can retreat with a defeated army. Such are fortresses with fortified camps or simply fortified camps.

Large rivers offer the best means of halting the pursuing enemy for a while. We must therefore secure our crossing by means of bridgeheads, surrounded by a number of strong redoubts.

We must leave behind us a number of troops for the occupation of these strong points as well as the occupation of the most important cities and fortresses. Their number depends on how much we have to be afraid of invasions or of the attitude of the inhabitants. These troops, together with reinforcements, form new corps, which, in case of success, follow the advancing army, but in case of misfortune, occupy the fortified points in order to secure our retreat.

Napoleon always took great care with these measures for the protection of the rear of his army, and therefore, in his most audacious operations, risked less than was usually apparent.

IV. APPLICATION OF THESE PRINCIPLES IN TIME OF WAR

The principles of the art of war are in themselves extremely simple and quite within the reach of sound common sense. Even though they require more special knowledge in tactics than in strategy, this knowledge is of such small scope, that it does not compare with any other subject in extent and variety. Extensive knowledge and deep learning are by no means necessary, nor are extraordinary intellectual faculties. If, in addition to experienced judgment, a special mental quality is required, it would be, after all that has been said, cunning or shrewdness. For a long time the contrary has been maintained, either because of false veneration for the subject or because of the vanity of the authors who have written about it. Unprejudiced reflection should convince us of this, and experience only makes this conviction stronger. As recently as the Revolutionary War we find many men who proved themselves able military leaders, yes, even military leaders of the first order, without having had any military education. In the case of Condé, Wallenstein, Suvorov, and a multitude of others[20] it is very doubtful whether or not they had the advantage of such education.

The conduct of war itself is without doubt very difficult. But the difficulty is not that erudition and great genius are necessary to understand the basic principles of warfare. These principles are within the reach of any well-organized mind, which is unprejudiced and not entirely unfamiliar with the subject. Even the application of these principles on maps or on paper presents no difficulty, and to have devised a good plan of operations is no great masterpiece. The great difficulty is this:

TO REMAIN FAITHFUL THROUGHOUT
TO THE PRINCIPLES WE HAVE LAID
DOWN FOR OURSELVES.

To call attention to this difficulty is the purpose of these closing remarks, and to give Your Royal Highness a clear idea of it I consider the most important object of this essay.

The conduct of war resembles the workings of an intricate machine with tremendous friction, so that combinations which are easily planned on paper can be executed only with great effort.

The free will and the mind of the military commander, therefore, find themselves constantly hampered, and one needs a remarkable strength of mind and soul to overcome this resistance. Many good ideas have perished because of this friction, and we must carry out more simply and moderately what under a more complicated form would have given greater results.

It may be impossible to enumerate exhaustively the causes of this friction; but the main ones are as follows:

1. Generally we are not nearly as well acquainted with the position and measures of the enemy as we assume in our plan of operations. The minute we begin carrying out our decision, a thousand doubts arise about the dangers which might develop if we have been seriously mistaken in our plan. A feeling of uneasiness, which often takes hold of a person about to perform something great, will take possession of us, and from this uneasiness to indecision, and from there to half measures are small, scarcely discernible steps.

2. Not only are we uncertain about the strength of the enemy, but in addition rumor (*i.e.*, all the news which we obtain from outposts, through spies, or by accident) exaggerates his size. The majority of people are timid by nature, and that is why they constantly exaggerate danger. All influences on the military leader, therefore, combine to give him a false impression of his opponent's strength, and from this arises a new source of indecision.

We cannot take this uncertainty too seriously, and it is important to be prepared for it from the beginning.

After we have thought out everything carefully in advance and have sought and found without prejudice the most plausible plan, we must not be ready to abandon it at the slightest provocation. On the contrary, we must be prepared to submit the reports which reach us to careful criticism, we must compare them with each other, and send out for more. In this way false reports are very often disproved immediately, and the first reports confirmed. In both cases we gain certainty and can make our decision accordingly. Should this certainty be lacking, we must tell ourselves that nothing is accomplished in warfare without daring; that the nature of war certainly does not let us see at all times where we are going; that what is probable will always be probable though at the moment it may not seem so; and finally, that we cannot be readily ruined by a single error, if we have made reasonable preparations.

3. Our uncertainty about the situation at a given moment is not limited to the conditions of the enemy only but of our own army as well. The latter can rarely be kept together to the extent that we are able to survey all its parts at any moment, and if we are inclined to uneasiness, new doubts will arise. We shall want to wait, and a delay of our whole plan will be the inevitable result.

We must, therefore, be confident that the general measures we have adopted will produce the results we expect. Most important in this connection is the trust which we must have in our lieutenants. Consequently, it is important to choose men on whom we can rely and to put aside all other considerations. If we have made appropriate preparations, taking into account all possible misfortunes, so that we shall not be lost immediately if they occur, we must boldly advance into the shadows of uncertainty.

4. If we wage war with all our strength, our subordinate commanders and even our troops (especially if they are not used to warfare) will frequently encounter difficulties which they declare insurmountable. They find the march too long, the fatigue too great, the provisions impossible. If we lend our ear to all these DIFFICULTIES, as Frederick II called them, we shall soon succumb completely, and instead of acting with force and determination, we shall be reduced to weakness and inactivity.

To resist all this we must have faith in our own insight and convictions. At the time this often has the appearance of stubbornness, but in reality it is that strength of mind and character which is called firmness.

5. The results on which we count in warfare are never as precise as is imagined by someone who has not carefully observed a war and become used to it.

Very often we miscalculate the march of a column by several hours, without being able to tell the cause of the delay. Often we encounter obstacles which were impossible to foresee. Often we intend to reach a certain place with our army and fall short of it by several hours. Often a small outpost which we have set up achieves much less than we expected, while an enemy outpost achieves much more. Often the resources of a region do not amount to as much as we expected, etc.

We can triumph over such obstacles only with very great exertion, and to accomplish this the leader must show a severity bordering on cruelty. Only when he knows that everything possible is always being done, can he be sure that these small difficulties will not have a great influence on his operations. Only then can he be sure that he will not fall too far short of the aim which he could have reached.

6. We may be sure that an army will never be in the condition supposed by someone following its operations from an armchair. If he is sympathetic to the army he will imagine it from a third to a half stronger and better than it really is. It is quite natural that the military commander will make the same mistake in planning his first operations. Consequently, he will see his army melt away as he never thought it would, and his cavalry and artillery become useless. What appeared possible and easy to the observer and to the commander at the opening of a campaign is often difficult and even impossible to carry out. If the military leader is filled with high ambition and if he pursues his aims with audacity and strength of will, he will reach them in spite of all obstacles; while an ordinary person would have found in the condition of his army a sufficient excuse for giving in.

Masséna proved at Genoa and in Portugal the influence of a strong-willed leader over his troops. At Genoa, the limitless exertion to which his strength of will, not to say his harshness, forced people, was crowned with success. In Portugal he at least retreated later than anyone else would have.[21]

Most of the time the enemy army is in the same position. For example, Wallenstein and Gustavus Adolphus at Nuremberg,[22] and Napoleon and Bennigsen after the battle of Eylau.[28] But while we do not see the condition of the enemy, our own is right before our eyes. The latter, therefore, makes a greater impression on ordinary people than the first, since sensuous impressions are stronger for such people than the language of reason.

7. The provisioning of troops, no matter how it is done, whether through storehouses or requisitions, always presents such difficulty that it must have a decisive influence on the choice of operations. It is often contrary to the most effective combination, and forces us to search for provisions when we would like to pursue victory and brilliant success. This is the main cause for the unwieldiness of the whole war machine which keeps the results so far beneath the flight of our great plans.

A general, who with tyrannical authority demands of his troops the most extreme exertions and the greatest privations, and an army which in the course of long wars has become hardened to such sacrifices will have a tremendous advantage over their adversaries and will reach their aim much faster in spite of all obstacles. With equally good plans, what a difference of result!

8. We cannot stress the following too much:

Visual impressions gained during actual combat are more vivid than those gained beforehand by mature reflection. But they give us only the outward appearance of things, which, as we know, rarely corresponds to their essence. We therefore run the risk of sacrificing mature reflection for first impression.

The natural timidity of humans, which sees only one side to everything, makes this first impression incline toward fear and exaggerated caution.

Therefore we must fortify ourselves against this impression and have blind faith in the results of our own earlier reflections, in order to strengthen ourselves against the weakening impressions of the moment.

These difficulties, therefore, demand confidence and firmness of conviction. That is why the study of military history is so important, for it makes us see things as they are and as they function. The principles which we can learn from theoretical instruction are only suited to facilitate this study and to call our attention to the most important elements in the history of war.

Your Royal Highness, therefore, must become acquainted with these principles in order to check them against the history of war, to see whether they are in agreement with it and to discover where they are corrected or even contradicted by the course of events.

In addition, only the study of military history is capable of giving those who have no experience of their own a clear impression of what I have just called the friction of the whole machine.

Of course, we must not be satisfied with its main conclusions, and still less with the reasoning of historians, but we must penetrate as deeply as possible into the details. For the aim of historians rarely is to present the absolute truth. Usually they wish to embellish the deeds of their army or to demonstrate the concordance of events with their imaginary rules. They invent history instead of writing it. We need not study much history for the purpose we propose. The detailed knowledge of a few individual engagements is more useful than the general knowledge of a great many campaigns. It is therefore more useful to read detailed accounts and diaries than regular works of history. An example of such an account, which cannot be surpassed, is the description of the defense of Menin in 1794, in the memoirs of General von Scharnhorst. This narrative, especially the part which tells of the sortie and break through the enemy lines, gives Your Royal

Highness an example of how to write military history.[24]

No battle in history has convinced me as much as this one that we must not despair of success in war until the last moment. It proves that the influence of good principles, which never manifests itself as often as we expect, can suddenly reappear, even under the most unfortunate circumstances, and when we have already given up hope of their influence.

A powerful emotion must stimulate the great ability of a military leader, whether it be ambition as in Caesar, hatred of the enemy as in Hannibal, or the pride in a glorious defeat, as in Frederick the Great.

Open your heart to such emotion. Be audacious and cunning in your plans, firm and persevering in their execution, determined to find a glorious end, and fate will crown your youthful brow with a shining glory, which is the ornament of princes, and engrave your image in the hearts of your last descendants.

NOTES

1. FREDERICK II ("the Great"), King of Prussia from 1740-1786, is one of the great military figures of history. The first half of his reign was largely devoted to war, with Austria under Maria Theresa as his chief adversary and Silesia as a major cause: the first and second SILESIAN WARS (1740-45) and the Seven Years' War (1756-63).

It was especially during the latter war, when Prussia, allied with England, had to fight the superior alliance of Austria, France, Russia, Sweden, and Saxony, that Frederick proved his unusual skill and audacity as a military leader. One of his most brilliant and decisive victories was won near the Silesian village of LEUTHEN (Dec. 5, 1757). This victory against a vastly superior Austrian army under Prince Charles of Lorraine was due to Frederick's military genius as well as the excellent morale of his officers and men. Before the battle, in the presence of his generals, the King delivered a famous address, which illustrates Clausewitz' point. It ended thus: "Gentlemen, the enemy stands behind his entrenchments, armed to the teeth. We must attack him and win, or else perish. Nobody must think of getting through any other way. If you do not like this you may hand in your resignation and go home."

(Other significant battles of the Seven Years' War, mentioned by Clausewitz, were the battles of Rossbach, Liegnitz, Prague, Kolin, Hochkirch, and Minden.)

2. The term "corps" as used throughout by Clausewitz does not refer to a specific army unit (such as a modern army-corps) but is used simply to describe any section of the army.

3. Both battles were part of Napoleon's campaign against Austria in 1809. At Eckmühl, near RATISBON, in Southern Germany, a French army under Napoleon and his Marshal Davout defeated a strong Austrian army on April 22. This paved the way for Napoleon's invasion of Austria, where at the village of WAGRAM, near Vienna, he succeeded in beating the Archduke Charles so thoroughly (July 5-6) that Austria had to ask for an armistice shortly afterwards.

(For further references to these battles see pages 20, 23, 55.)

4. Near MINDEN in Westphalia, DUKE FERDINAND OF BRUNSWICK, one of Frederick II's generals during the Seven Years' War, won a significant victory over the French under Marshal Contades. He had planned to attack the French positions in the early hours of August 1, 1759, when he received word that the French in turn were getting ready to attack him. He went through with his plans for mobilization, thus completely upsetting Contades' preparations for a surprise attack. In the ensuing battle the allied Prussian, English and Hanoverian troops won a decisive victory, which

resulted in the withdrawal of the French beyond the Rhine and Main rivers.

At the same time, about one-third of Ferdinand's army, organized as an independent corps under General von Wangenheim, was stationed to the left of the main army, near the village of TANNHAUSEN (also known as Thonhausen, or Thodthausen). This corps had not been informed of the impending attack of the French. An enemy corps under Broglie opened fire on Wangenheim's entrenchments around 5 A.M. It failed to follow up its surprise attack, however, thus enabling Wangenheim to draw up his troops and resist Broglie until the defeat of the main army under Contades forced the French to retreat.

5. At ROSSBACH, on November 5, 1757, FREDERICK II's army of 22,000 men defeated a combined French and German army twice its size, under the leadership of the incompetent Princes of Soubise (France) and Hildburghausen (Saxony). While his opponents, thinking he was beating a hasty retreat, began their pursuit, Frederick's excellently trained cavalry under General von Seydlitz suddenly attacked their right flank. The enemy, with no time to draw up in battle-formation, was completely dispersed and defeated.

The moral effect of Frederick's victory inside and outside of Germany was tremendous. It reestablished his reputation, which had suffered considerably after his defeat at Kolin (see note 15).

6. The Battle of LIEGNITZ, like those of Rossbach and Leuthen earlier, shows FREDERICK the Great's skill in defeating a superior force by using his highly mobile army in a concentrated attack, keeping the enemy as much in the dark about his intentions as possible.

Finding himself surrounded near Liegnitz (Saxony) by several Austrian armies numbering close to 100,000, he planned a careful withdrawal. During the night of August 14-15, 1760, he broke camp, leaving his fires burning, however, to deceive the enemy, who had planned a three-cornered attack for the morning of August 15. At dawn the Prussian King surprised one section of the Austrian army under Laudon on the river Katzbach, and defeated 30,000 men with an army half this size.

7. During Napoleon's campaign against the Second Coalition (Great Britain, Austria, and Russia), the French General MOREAU had concentrated his forces at the village of HOHENLINDEN, situated in the midst of a great forest on a plateau east of Munich. Despite the warnings of his generals, Archduke John of Austria entered the forest on Dec. 2, 1800, to seek the French. Meanwhile Moreau, hidden by the forest, moved part of his forces, outflanked the Austrians, and caught them between two fires. The Austrian army was thoroughly beaten, losing more than 20,000 men, and Moreau was free to continue his advance toward Vienna.

8. FREDERICK II achieved the necessary concentration of his forces by a peculiar battle-order known as "schiefe Schlachtordnung" (oblique formation). Though by no means new (it had been used occasionally since antiquity), it was Frederick who first applied this formation consistently in almost all his battles. In his *General Principles of Warfare*, written in 1748, Frederick described it as follows: "We 'refuse' one of our wings to the enemy and strengthen the wing with which we plan to attack." This would make possible the defeat of a vastly superior enemy: "An army of 100,000 men, thus attacked on its flank, can be beaten by 30,000 men." The most successful example of Frederick's use of this formation "in echelon" was the battle of Leuthen (see note 1).

9. At HOCHKIRCH, a village in Saxony, the Austrian army of Marshal Daun delivered a serious defeat to Frederick II's forces on October 14, 1758. Attacking at the crack of dawn, the Austrians caught the over-confident King of Prussia unprepared, and with a force of 78,000 they defeated his army of 40,000, inflicting heavy losses on the Prussians. About 9,000 men were lost and several of Frederick's generals were killed or wounded.

10. General Friedrich von Cochenhausen in his edition of this book points out that most of the rules dealing with this cavalry reserve, though no longer valid in modern warfare, can be applied almost word for word to mechanized units.

11. At FRIEDLAND, in East Prussia, a Russian army under Bennigsen was defeated by Napoleon, on June 14, 1807, during the war of the Third Coalition against France. The Russians were withdrawing along the right bank of the river Alle, towards Koenigsberg, when they met a single French corps under the command of Marshal Lannes. Bennigsen thought this an excellent chance for an attack, but Lannes held out until Napoleon arrived with his main army. The Emperor concentrated his attack on the Russian left wing, which was separated from the right wing by a ravine, and whose only possible retreat was through a narrow outlet between this ravine and the river. Napoleon's artillery, concentrating on this point, inflicted heavy losses on the Russians before they succeeded in gaining the other bank of the Alle.

12. During the Seven Years' War, Prussia found herself surrounded by enemies: Saxony and Austria to the south, France to the west, Sweden to the north, and Russia to the east. Frederick II overcame his difficult position by making full use of the advantages which fighting on the "inner line" offers to a highly mobile army led by a commander who does not shrink from taking the initiative: Without waiting to declare war he seized Saxony in 1756. His invasion of Bohemia in 1757 was checked by the Austrians at KOLIN (see note 14) and he had to fall back upon his own territories. From there he advanced with lightning

speed, first into Central Germany to defeat the
French at ROSSBACH (see note 5) and from there
back to Silesia, where he beat the Austrians at
LEUTHEN (see note 1). On August 25, 1758 he
defeated the Russians near ZORNDORF. Eventually,
however, the numerical superiority of his opponents became too great and Frederick was forced
to limit himself to a more defensive strategy, while
his tactics remained offensive.

13. Baron Antoine Henri JOMINI (1779-1869).
of Swiss origin, entered the French army in 1804
as aide-de-camp to Marshal Ney, and eventually
was attached to Napoleon's headquarters. When
he did not get the advancement he deserved, he
went to Russia in 1813, where he was made a general and became a close associate of Tsar Alexander I. He is famous for his very influential
writings on military theory, the chief of which,
Treatise on Grand Military Operations, was
published in 1805. His basic idea concerning
strategy was: "To lead the concentrated force
of our army to each important point on the theatre
of war and there to use these massed forces in
such a way that they attack only fractions of the
enemy army."

Baron Dietrich Heinrich VON BULOW (1757-
1807) had a varied and shiftless career as journal-
ist, businessman, preacher, and soldier. Toward
the end of his life he settled down long enough to
write a number of works on military theory and

strategy, the chief of which was *The Spirit of the New System of War* (1799). Though his restless life did not allow for careful research, his clear and independent mind made him one of the more influential writers on the subject, who established the use of many of our present day military terms. According to Bülow wars were not decided by victories gained on the battle-field, but rather by strategic manoeuvers against the enemy's "lines of operation" (*i.e.*, his system of provisioning). He held that "a corps surrounded by skirmishing infantry is one of the most pitiful objects." Clausewitz opposed the mechanical rigidity of Bülow's strategy, which overlooked completely the significant role played by less tangible moral factors.

14. This statement is only partly true for such battles as Jena, Ulm, Eckmühl, Marengo, and Wagram.

15. In the spring of 1757 FREDERICK the Great invaded Bohemia with three separate armies. Two of these advanced from Saxony (one led by the King himself) and a third from Silesia, under the command of the seventy-two year old Marshal SCHWERIN. The Austrian army under Prince Charles retreated before the invaders and took up a strong position near PRAGUE. Schwerin's army was late in arriving, and when it finally did, the Prussians defeated the Austrians (May 6, 1757), but allowed a large part of the Austrian forces to withdraw. On June 18, Frederick, though

outnumbered, once more attacked the Austrian army, this time under Marshal Daun, near KOLIN. He was thoroughly beaten, largely because of the numerical superiority of the Austrians and the ability and courage of Marshal Daun.

16. WELLINGTON'S CAMPAIGN OF 1810-1811 was part of the Peninsular War (1808-1813) to free Spain and Portugal from the domination of Napoleon. Just as in RUSSIA, during Napoleon's campaign of 1812, the inhabitants of the Peninsula voluntarily destroyed their possessions and stores of supplies, to make provisioning of the enemy impossible and to hasten his defeat. This policy of "scorched earth," as it is called today, was eminently successful in both cases.

17. In the vicinity of ASPERN and Essling, two villages near Vienna, Napoleon suffered a great military defeat on May 21-22, 1809. After winning against the Austrians near Ratisbon (see note 3), he had made his entry into Vienna on May 13th. The enemy's army, under Archduke Charles, had withdrawn to the north bank of the Danube, and Napoleon, in order to attack it, had to cross the river. In a murderous battle Charles defeated the French, who lost one of their ablest leaders, Marshal Lannes. After receiving vast reinforcements, Napoleon attempted another crossing on July 4. This time he was successful, and on July 5-6 he won the battle of WAGRAM, thus terminating Austria's premature war of liberation.

18. During the spring of 1807, Napoleon ordered his Marshal Lefebvre to lay siege to the city of Danzig. The siege, beginning in March, lasted into May. The Russian commander-in-chief, BENNIGSEN, who was stationed in the vicinity, remained passive throughout, even though the capitulation of Danzig gave Napoleon a valuable base and released a number of his troops, which he used to great advantage shortly afterwards in the battle of Friedland (see note 11).

19. See note 17.

20. Louis II de Bourbon, Prince of CONDÉ (1621-86), known as the "Great Condé," started on a brilliant military career in 1640, towards the end of the Thirty Years' War (1618-48). In 1643 he was made commander of the French forces against the Spaniards in northern France and won the decisive victory of Rocroy, which, at the age of 22 established him as one of the great military figures of history.

Albrecht von WALLENSTEIN (1583-1634), a Bohemian nobleman, was one of the outstanding military leaders of the Imperial catholic party during the Thirty Years' War, though his military education, according to Clausewitz' and our own standards, was brief and superficial. He saw two years of armed service (1604-1606) against the Turks and Hungarians, and from 1617 on he was commander of an increasing number of mercenaries (mostly hired at his own expense from a rapidly growing fortune), which he put at the disposal of the Emperor Ferdinand II. (See also note 22.)

Count Alexander SUVOROV (1729-1800) won fame as commander of the Russian forces during Catherine the Great's wars with Turkey (1768-74, 1787-92). In 1799, he was given supreme command over the Italian armies of the Second anti-French Coalition and succeeded in driving the French out of Italy.

21. Andre MASSÉNA, Prince of Essling, a distinguished French General and Marshal during the Revolutionary and Napoleonic Wars. In the spring of 1800, during the war of the Second Coalition, he was ordered by Napoleon to defend the Italian city of GENOA against the Austrians. The latter suddenly attacked, cut his army in two, and forced him to withdraw into the town with his remaining right wing. The Austrian general Ott laid siege to the city, and Masséna kept him occupied by constant sorties. In spite of the growing shortage of food he held out until June 4, enabling Napoleon to win the battle of Marengo.

In 1810 Masséna was made commander-in-chief of a French army of 70,000 invading PORTUGAL to drive the English under Wellington "into the sea." Again he had to pitch his will-power and determination against the terrible enemy of hunger. The British troops withdrew into the interior, leaving behind them a mountainous country bare of

provisions. Only one major battle was fought and
lost by the French (at Busaco). Most of the
French losses of 25,000 men were due to sickness
and starvation. It is largely because of Masséna's
skillful retreat, that not more troops were lost.

22. During the period of Swedish intervention
(1630-1632) in the Thirty Years' War, Albrecht
von WALLENSTEIN, the leader of the Catholic and
Imperial forces (see note 20) and King GUSTAVUS
ADOLPHUS of Sweden occupied positions opposite
each other near NUREMBERG in Southern Germany.
After Wallenstein had several times refused battle,
the Swedes attacked his camp on Sept. 3, 1632.
Fighting lasted into the night, inflicting heavy
losses on both sides, but Gustavus Adolphus did
not succeed in driving out Wallenstein.

23. Near EYLAU in East Prussia, a French army
under NAPOLEON and his Marshals Davout and
Ney claimed a victory over the Russians, led by
BENNIGSEN, on Feb. 8, 1807. The success of both
armies changed frequently during battle, due to
the various reinforcements they received, and at
nightfall neither of them had won a decisive victory; but the French losses exceeded those of the
Russians, who had lost more than a third of their
men. Bennigsen, however, realizing the exhaustion
of his troops and fearing further reinforcement of
the French army, withdrew, leaving Napoleon to
claim victory.

24. General Gerhard von SCHARNHORST (1755-

1813), known for his reforms of the Prussian army, was a close friend and teacher of Clausewitz'. While still a captain, he participated in the war of the First Coalition against revolutionary France, and was among the heroic defenders of the town of Menin in Flanders. He described his experiences in 1803 in a memorandum entitled *The Defense of the Town of Menin.*

For several days during April, 1794, a force of 2,000 men under General Hammerstein defended the fortified town against the attacks of 20,000 Frenchmen under General Moreau. When Hammerstein's munitions and supplies ran short and the town had gone up in flames, he led his troops in a successful break through the enemy's lines (April 30), losing more than one-fifth of his forces.

ANTOINE HENRI JOMINI

JOMINI

AND HIS

SUMMARY OF

THE ART OF WAR

A Condensed Version

Edited and with an

Introduction by

Brig. Gen. J. D. Hittle
U.S. Marine Corps, Ret.

CONTENTS

"They want war too methodical, too measured; I would make it brisk, bold, impetuous, perhaps sometimes even audacious."

JOMINI

INTRODUCTION

I

The military world that today burns gun-powder at the altar of Clausewitzian doctrine has all but forgotten Antoine Henri Jomini.

It is a strange paradox of military history that while Clausewitz is today's preeminent figure of military literature, it was less than a century ago that the name of Jomini was synonymous with military wisdom. The works of the Prussian, known to even the casual readers of military articles today, then were virtually unknown except to his devoted wife and a small group of leading military thinkers. The military world has gained greatly from the military and intellectual deification of Clausewitz, but it has deprived itself of more than a little knowledge by permitting the writings of Jomini to fall into discard and obsolescence.

Jomini, the native of Switzerland who soldiered in the Grand Armeé and later became a full general in the Imperial Army of the Russian Czar, is rightfully entitled to a place on the level with the foremost makers of modern military thought. No man in the history of war has exerted a greater influence on the development of modern warfare than Napoleon Bonaparte. No man has been more responsible for Napoleon's influence than Antoine Henri Jomini.

During the years that extended from the Alps to Waterloo, Napoleon fashioned the model of modern war. Applying the lessons of Alexander, Hannibal, and Caesar, borrowing from de Broglie and Bourcet, he proved by his victories that corps and divisions of infantry with its supporting arms had become permanent components of military organization. The basic features of his staff system, which had received such impetus from Pierre Bourcet and which were improved by Berthier and Thiebault, have endured to the present time. Against the background of the new concept of a "nation in arms," the Corsican wove the pattern of the war of movement based upon scientific and analytical planning, sound staff procedure, and the ascendency of the offensive.

The well-worn battlefields of the Old World were the test tubes in which Napoleon mixed the ingredients that produced our modern concept of war. The bloody fields that stretched from Fort Sumpter to Appomattox in the New World were the proving grounds of the Napoleonic concept of battle, for it was in our Civil War that the Confederate and Union generals applied the theories and methods that had brought victories to the First Empire.

It has been said with good reason that many a Civil War general went into battle with a sword in one hand and Jomini's *Summary of the Art of War* in the other. Napoleonic technique, characterized by the brilliant maneuvering of corps and divisions, became accepted and apparently permanent military doctrine during the years of our Civil War. And today our high command includes many generals who have studied and applied the lessons of Chancellorsville, The Wilderness, The March to the Sea, and Gettysburg.

In tracing our way back through the chain of Napoleonic influence, it becomes increasingly evident that Jomini's writings were the means by which Napoleonic technique was transfused into the military thought of the Civil War, which was so important in the development of the basic pattern of modern battlefield procedure. To appreciate properly the significance of Jomini's writings it is first necessary to understand Jomini the man—and that is a difficult task, for he was certainly not formed in the mold of ordinary men.

II

Antoine Henri Jomini was born in the Vaud canton, French Switzerland, in 1779. Several generations before his birth, his forebears had emigrated from Italy. After receiving the usual education afforded the son of a middle-class family, he began his life's work in a quite unexciting manner by entering the banking business in Paris. Soon Jomini convinced himself that the tedious life of a banker was not to be compared with the life afforded in the French Army, which, under Napoleon Bonaparte, was making history with its resounding victories against the enemies of the new France. It is difficult to say whether Jomini felt that war offered a more promising career than commerce, or whether he was drawn toward the army by the powerful magnetism of the new champion of French arms. Probably it was due to a combination of these two influences that young Jomini, at the age of seventeen, found himself in the French Army. While the youth of France were streaming to the Napoleonic standards, glad in their enthusiasm to be private soldiers under the command of the new leader, Jomini took a dim view of his chances of finding a marshal's baton in a private's knapsack and managed to begin his lifetime army career in a minor staff position handling routine matters of supply. There were more important positions in the Army, and Jomini set his sights on them. He was an ambitious man, burning with curiosity, and he had ability—a winning combination in any line of endeavor.

In addition to his ardent ambition, his self-confidence that at times made him many enemies, and his obvious ability, Jomini possessed one of the most penetrating military minds of his era. In the interval after the false Peace of Amiens Jomini produced his first significant military writing, a heavy treatise dealing with the campaigns of Frederick the Great. While it was far from qualifying as his greatest work, it served to advance his interests more than he could have expected from battlefield heroism. Jomini was successful in presenting a copy of the treatise to Napoleon, who, in one of his few periods of spare time, became interested in the work. Napoleon was quick to recognize that the writer was a man who sensed the true nature of the Napoleonic military method.

Napoleon was not wrong in his first appraisal of Jomini,

for it is upon his masterful interpretations of the Corsican's manner of war that Jomini's fame primarily rests. One of the healthy features of the Napoleonic armies was the fact that once ability was spotted, that ability was usually exploited by well merited promotion. In the youthful Swiss staff officer Napoleon saw a brilliant military mind. By 1806 Jomini (then 27 years old) had a regular colonel's commission, and in September of that year he received orders to report for duty on Napoleon's staff at Mainz.

III

In every man's life there is at least one big obstacle which he must surmount to achieve life's desires. Jomini, who most certainly did nothing on the small scale, had his obstacle and it was indeed an impressive one. The only person who blocked Jomini's path to a seat among the French high command was Berthier, Napoleon's chief of staff. The bitter feud that broke out between Berthier and Jomini, ending only with their deaths, was a result of a clash of intellect and temperament. Both possessed more than their share of these characteristics. In addition, each was ambitious—so much so that Berthier finally proved himself to be one of the most unsavory opportunists in history by deserting Napoleon after Leipzig (1813) and Jomini accepted a commission in the Russian Army after Bautzen, (1813), terminating his association with the French army under circumstances that provoked many of Napoleon's loyal supporters to cry "desertion" and "traitor." Whether these appellations were deserved is a question that still finds divided opinion among Napoleonic historians. It is quite a story in itself and we will look into it later.

So intense was the animosity between the two officers that after the battle of Wagram (1809), Jomini tendered his resignation rather than serve on the Imperial Staff, where Berthier would be his chief. A brilliant brain was something that Napoleon could use in more than one place in the Grand Armeé, so rather than have Jomini leave the French service, Napoleon assigned him to special duty in Paris for the purpose of writing a history of the Italian campaigns. The feud between Berthier and Jomini caused Napoleon much concern, yet he seemed to accept it as one of the prices of being served by men of intellect. He must have realized that ability and temperament usually go together, but he must also occasionally have felt more than a little disgust in being forced practically to play the part of a ballet master trying to keep star performers satisfied and working together.

The special assignment in Paris was not designed to put Jomini permanently on the shelf. Shortly before the battle of Lutzen, (1813), Napoleon ended the Paris assignment and ordered Jomini back to his former position as chief of staff for Marshal Ney. It was as chief of staff to the gallant Ney that Jomini distinguished himself as more than a military commentator and theorist. At the side of the Marshal he found himself in the midst of the greatest battles and campaigns of the Napoleonic Era.

By appointing Jomini as chief of staff to Ney Napoleon demonstrated his ability in making judicious assignments of chiefs of staff, which so often is the key to battle victories. Ney was a gallant, able, but quite impetuous leader, and he was far from being an intellectual general. By giving him Jomini as chief of staff Napoleon provided the military knowledge to complement the battle leadership of the Marshal. It proved to be a winning combination. At Bautzen Napoleon's orders to Ney were delayed, but Jomini, who more than once proved himself to be an amazingly accurate diviner of Napoleon's intentions,* advised a course of action which Ney executed and

---

* Jomini tells the story that at the end of a conference in which Napoleon was discussing the coming Jena (1806) campaign, Jomini asked if he might join Napoleon later at Bamberg. "Who told you that I'm going to Bamberg?" Napoleon is supposed to have asked with annoyance, believing his destination secret. "The map of Germany, Sire, and your campaigns of Marengo (1800) and Ulm (1805)," Jomini replied.

which eventually proved to be in accord with Napoleon's orders when they finally arrived.

Jomini, as Ney's chief of staff at Bautzen, held the rank of *general de brigade.* In recognition of his able work as chief of staff, Ney recommended Jomini for promotion to *general de division.* But such high rank was not destined to be Jomini's so long as he was in the French Army, nor as long as Berthier was Chief of the Imperial Staff. Berthier effectively blocked the promotion by countering it with an order to put Jomini under arrest for an alleged failure to submit certain reports on schedule. The irate Swiss could stand no more. Feeling that he could not combat the enemies of France as well as Berthier at the same time, he severed his association with the French Army and entered the service of Alexander of Russia.

While this was perhaps not exactly the soldierly thing to do, there were extenuating circumstances in Jomini's favor. He could not properly be termed a traitor to France, for he was a Swiss and was not bound by the ties of patriotism. Time and again he had demonstrated his high ability, only to see men of lesser ability receive their baton. He had more than once suffered what he probably rightfully considered to be indignities at the hands of Berthier. He could have bettered his personal position long before by accepting a much higher rank in the Russian Army. Yet he remained with the Grand Armeé, more or less content to be serving under the banner of Napoleon, whom even then he recognized to be one of history's greatest generals. The inconsiderate treatment he received after Bautzen proved to be the veritable last straw.

Probably the most interesting feature of the self-effected transfer from the French to the Russian Army involves the story of the Russian commission which Jomini accepted. Some few years previous to Bautzen, Alexander of Russia realized that his army could advantageously utilize a general of high intellectual ability and offered Jomini a commission as full general in the Russian army. Alexander sent the commission to Jomini. While he didn't accept it, neither did he return the commission. Through the following years of battle he carefully retained the proffered document, apparently in accordance with his theory of the proper and timely use of the strategic reserve. When, as a result of the bitter disappointment of not being promoted in spite of Marshal Ney's recommendation, he rode off to Russia, it was as if he had merely taken a long time to make up his mind and was at long last accepting Alexander's offer.

On entering the Russian Army Jomini changed his uniform and insignia of rank, but he did not change his thinking. In his new rank as general he continued his vigorous writing, and he labored to force Russian military thought onto a higher level. In his efforts to improve the collective Russian military mind he was instrumental in founding the Nicholas Military Academy in Moscow in 1832. The passing of years did not slacken the speed nor dull the sharpness of his pen, as he turned out volume after volume of military history and theory. The leaders of the great powers considered him much as a military consultant; his advice was sought on many a contemplated military enterprise.

IV

Jomini died in Paris in 1869. In the latter years of his life he had the pleasant satisfaction of knowing that he was looked upon as one of the foremost military minds in the world. His books were essentials of military education. It is said that a man must be happy to live long. Rank, wealth, prestige, and fame were definitely to his liking. But even more than that, the source of inner happiness that helped him live to be ninety years old could well have been the fact that in turning out his many books he had ample opportunity to drive numerous literary barbs deep into the military reputation of Berthier. To do that must have ben a source of never-ending joy to the old general.

Jomini was a very productive person with the pen, turning out. in the course of his career an impressive number of volumes dealing with both military history and theory. In addition to his many books he also managed to write a few pamphlets which usually were pointed replies to his critics. The historical works cover the operations of Frederick the Great, the Wars of the French Revolution, and the Napoleonic campaigns. All in all, his histories totaled twenty-seven volumes. Specifically, his more significant works are *Traité des Grandes Opérations Militaires* (eight volumes, Paris, 1804-1816), *Histoire Critique et Militaire des Guerres de la Révolution* (five volumes and atlas, Paris, 1806, and 15 volumes and 4 atlases, Paris, 1819-1824), *Vie Politique et Militaire de Napoléon* (four volumes, Paris, 1827), *Introduction a l'Étude des Grandes Combinations de la Stratégie et de la Tactique* (Paris, 1829), *Précis Politique et Militaire de la Campagne de* 1815 (Paris, 1839), and *Précis de l'Art de la Guerre* (two volumes, Paris, 1838, translated as the *Summary of the Art of War*).

His *Traité des Grandes Operations* was responsible for attracting Napoleon's attention to his talents. While his histories sometimes leaned toward the heavy side, they were usually less cumbersome reading than those written by his contemporaries and often proved to be easier reading than the prose of many of his successors in the field of military literature. Seldom, if ever, did his style approach the Teutonic heaviness that characterized the works of Clausewitz.

Jomini's writings are more than mere historical recitations or the printed results of theoretical dreaming. Napoleon was not wrong when he appraised Jomini as being a man who *thought* about war. He not only told what happened, but he continually sought to explain why certain courses of action were successful and why some failed. Always he seemed to be seeking the basic principles upon which successful war could be waged. He began his search for the basic principles in his first significant work, his *Traité*, in which he stated, "There have existed in all times fundamental principles on which depend good results in warfare . . . these principles are unchanging, independent of the kind of weapons, of historical time and of place." Today this thought is echoed by the teachers of the military art.

In his theoretical writings he utilized the modern and accepted educational technique of explaining by the use of examples. Unlike so many military theorists, he considered not only the "what" but also the "why" of his assertions. As one reads his works, particularly the later ones, it is possible to come to the conclusion that Jomini was actually writing as a teacher, endeavoring to make clear in the minds of his student readers the thoughts that he was propounding. Such could well be, for there were many years during which he was the foremost military authority of the western world, and his books were considered texts by those who studied military method. The pedagogical tenor of his writings in the *Summary* is no accident. Jomini intentionally wrote as a teacher. In one of his introductory explanations he asserts that the *Summary* is offered as "the book most suitable for the instruction of a prince or statesman." The manner in which he so clearly analyzed numerous Napoleonic actions will strike the military reader as amazingly similar in context and style to our modern military educational technique known as the "critique."

Throughout his long career of wielding both sword and pen, Jomini expounded his theories in terms of historically explained principles of war. His *Traité*, which, it should be remembered, was his first important work, contained many of his basic concepts of war. In the pages that flowed from his seldom-resting pen during the years following the publication of the *Traité* he continued to write much in the same vein. Even in his somewhat ponderous *Vie Politique et Militaire de Napoléon*, he did not permit his enthusiasm for Napoleonic technique to restrain him from "editorializing" on the Emperor's methods in terms of basic military principles. He points, quite pedagogically, to the fact that it was faulty staff work that endangered the Grand Armeé by crossing the main columns during the passage of the Danube prior to the Battle of Wagram. Nor was there any doubt in his mind that Ney's inaction at Charleroi (1815), or Napoleon's faulty transmission of orders to Vandamme, were clearly the results of improper administrative procedure. His summation of Napoleon's basic errors in the ill-fated Russian campaign is sharp, and on a high level of objective criticism seldom equaled in clarity and content by any military historian. Jomini's objective attitude toward Napoleon is clearly summarized by his statement: "One might say that he (Napoleon) was sent into this world to teach generals and statesmen what they ought to avoid. His victories teach what may be accomplished by activity, boldness, and skill; his disasters what might have been avoided by prudence." All his previous books seemed to be laying the ground work for his greatest theoretical treatise, the *Précis de l'Art de la Guerre* (*Summary of the Art of War*), published in 1838.

V

The *Summary* was in many ways the final consolidation of the doctrine and theory he had been expounding for better than a quarter of a century. All those ideas embodied in earlier books appear to be sifted carefully and evaluated in terms of his more mature and considered judgment before they found their way into the famous *Summary*. This book was recognized as an epic contribution to military thought. It was translated into practically all the important languages.

Jomini was admittedly intolerant of the loose military terminology of the early 19th Century. Because he realized that a clear definition of terms was a prerequisite to the development of sound military thought, definitions constitute an important feature of the "Summary." He confessed a mania for definitions but stoutly contended that he made a "merit of it."

Many of his definitions have been altered but little to the present time. For instance, Jomini defined the "theater of war" as embracing "all the countries in which two powers may assail each other, whether it belongs to themselves, their allies, or to weaker states who may be drawn into the war through fear or interest." Our Army's *Field Service Regulations** state, "The Theater of War comprises those areas of land, sea and air which are, or which may become, directly involved in the conduct of the war." Today's definition is more concise than Jomini's, yet there is considerable significance in the fact that both definitions contain the same two essential thoughts: that the "theater of war" includes the areas which *are* involved in the war as well as the areas which *might* be involved.

Strategy he defined as "the art of making war upon the map, and comprehends the whole of the theater of operations." The official U. S. Army dictionary explains strategy as "making plans and using military forces and equipment for the purpose of gaining and keeping the advantage over the enemy in combat operations . . . Strategy involves planning on a large scale." Again, in this definition, modern thought coincides very closely with the writings of Jomini penned well over a century ago. Now, as then, strategy refers basically to the broad aspects of war.

In the definition of tactics we find an even closer likeness in thought and wording. Jomini considered tactics as involving "the maneuvers of an army on the field of battle, or of combat, and the different formations for leading troops to the attack." The Army dictionary describes tactics as the "art of handling units in combat, planning and carrying out movements before and during battle, and using combat power on the field of battle."

If we make further comparisons between our current

---

* FM 100-5, *Field Service Regulations—Operations,* 15 June 1944.

Army publications and the writings of Jomini, we find that there is a readily apparent likeness, particularly in the manner in which the capabilities of the various arms are described; in some instances there is a surprising similarity in the wording of the descriptions. In writing his *Summary* Jomini considered each arm separately and stated its capabilities and limitations in general terms. The same literary device was followed in writing *Field Service Regulations*. Paragraph 25 of *FSR* voices the basic concept of modern military method, stressing the coordinated employment of all arms toward attaining the common battle goal. It says, "No one arm wins battles. The combined action of all arms and services is essential to success. The characteristics of each arm and service adapt it to the performance of its special functions. The higher commander coordinates and directs the action of all, exploiting their powers to attain the ends sought." Jomini anticipated this thought by writing, more than a hundred years ago, "I advise that the different arms be posted in conformity with the character of the ground, according to the object in view and the supposed designs of the enemy, and that they be used simultaneously in the manner best suited to them, care being taken to enable them to afford mutual support."

Such similarities in the technique of presenting basic military thought as well as in the nature of the thought expressed in both cases would appear to be more than coincidental. Indeed, it might well be said that modern *Field Service Regulations* are today's counterpart of the *Summary of the Art of War,* in which Jomini codified the fundamental battle doctrine that early in the 19th century emerged from the Napoleonic way of war. Much of what constitutes our current battle doctrine finds its written genesis in the words of General Jomini.

VI

The Napoleonic era produced the subject matter as well as the stimulation of military thought that resulted

in an increase in military writing. Foremost among the
new school of military authors emerging from the
Napoleonic era were Jomini (1779-1869) and Clausewitz
(1780-1831). These contemporaries, the Prussian and the
Swiss, present one of the most amazing studies of human
nature in modern military history, replete with striking
similarities and violent contrasts. Both were career
soldiers, both possessed analytical and penetrating intellects. Each had disappointments in his quest for high
rank and military fame, for Jomini failed to come even
close to independent command or a marshal's baton in
the Imperial Army and Clausewitz failed to achieve independent high command. Both spent the bulk of their
military years in the staff; each progressed from minor staff
assignments to positions as chiefs of staff of an army corps,
Jomini serving as chief of staff to Marshal Ney and Clausewitz performing the same duties in a Prussian army corps
participating in the battles of Ligny and Wavre in 1815.

Strangely, both were forced by circumstances to change
their allegiance and serve in a foreign army. Jomini left
the Grande Armeé to rid himself of Berthier, Clausewitz
left the Prussian army rather than be bound by terms of
the peace treaty between Frederick William III and Napoleon. Even more startling is the coincidence that, upon
renouncing his original loyalty, each joined the Russian
army, Jomini accepting service under the Czar after
Bautzen in 1813 and his Prussian contemporary going to
the Imperial Russian forces that same year. Jomini, however, remained in the Russian service for the remainder
of his military career, while Clausewitz, who entered on a
temporary basis, was back in the Prussian forces within
two years. Both fought the battles of the Napoleonic era
and both were, from the military and intellectual stand-
points, products of that period. The similarity of their
careers was further emphasized by the fact that their lives
were devoted to writing of war as they believed it
emerged from the era dominated by the Corsican. It is
with good reason that both Clausewitz and Jomini are

known to the readers of military literature as "Interpreters of Napoleon."

But the likenesses between the two go no further than the similarity of their careers. Their personalities clash in sharp differences. Clausewitz appears to have been a retiring individual, longing, as his wife described him, "for light and truth." His wife also called him free "from all petty vanity, from every feeling of restlessness, egotistical ambition." Indeed, there is strong evidence of the fact that his search for military truisms and his desire to contribute something worthwhile to military knowledge stemmed directly from his feelings that he had not been completely successful in his chosen profession.

Jomini, on the other hand, would probably be one of the first to admit that he was at least a little vain, was very restless, and was fired by ambition, although he would probably not concede that it was of an egotistical variety. In short, Clausewitz was retiring, almost to the point of being shy, and filled with a feeling of frustration; Jomini recognized himself as an authority (in this he was not alone, however), he loved acclaim, he loved being a soldier, and there is a strong reason to believe that instead of being free from vanity as was said of Clausewitz, he even loved Jomini.

It is only reasonable to expect that these great intellects, developing contemporaneously in the environment of the Napoleonic world, would produce theories of similar nature. This logical expectation would not be altogether erroneous. Careful comparison of their two greatest works—Jomini's *Summary of the Art of War* (1838) and Clausewitz's *On War* (first published shortly after Clausewitz's death in 1831)—discloses much common basic military theory. Many of the concepts popularly attributed to the mind of Clausewitz find their counterparts in the words of Jomini. The fundamental difference between Clausewitz and Jomini is that while the Prussian roamed in the psychological and philosophic domains of battle, peering into the metaphysical darkness whence come the intangible but nevertheless omni-present components of combat, Jomini was more concerned with the more immediate character of war as it *exists*, and so dealt more with the tangible, less with the philosophic. And yet when Jomini considered the intangible factors of war he was surprisingly close to Clausewitz, and when Clausewitz wrote of battle methods he was often on common ground with Jomini. Both wrote of tactical and strategical method, and each appreciated the great importance of morale; they were aware that battle was something fluid, changing, and subject to chance. Clausewitz advocated simplicity of plans and emphasized the friction of war. Likewise, to Jomini simplicity in battle planning was a cardinal virtue, for he postulated that "the more simple a decisive maneuver is, the more certain will be its success." Jomini's discussions of battlefield difficulties indicated that he was thoroughly aware of the fact that friction was an ever-present combat factor. It is significant that Jomini as well as Clausewitz frequently referred to the "drama" of war.

VII

One of the more popular misconceptions regarding the works of Jomini is the repeatedly voiced assertion that he thought of war in terms of geometrical formations and absolute rules. This opinion is not new, for Jomini was aware of the accusation when he wrote his famous *Summary*. He took extreme care to point out that his diagrams were "not to be understood precisely as the geometrical figures indicate them. A general who would expect to arrange his line of battle as regularly as upon paper or on a drill ground would be greatly mistaken, and would be likely to suffer defeat. This is particularly true as battles are now fought." Again he emphasized the fact that "these figures have never been of any other use than to indicate approximate arrangements." Numerous of his contemporaries as well as many of his successors in the field of military writing, have continued to describe Jomini as an advocate of geometrical battle methods. This he denied even as he wrote.

Military writers, past and present, who adhere to this false interpretation as the basic concept of Jomini's theory read only the words on the page and go no deeper than the printing ink. In attempting to explain the various maneuvers and formations Jomini, deliberately writing as a teacher, utilized diagrams drawn to present a fundamental picture of what he was writing. In a way he was misunderstood because he was ahead of his time, for in drawing pictures to represent his ideas he was employing visual aids, which constitute an essential part of modern educational technique. It is true that some of Jomini's diagrammed movements are no longer valid in terms of current battle doctrine, but it should be kept in mind that such movements are out-dated, not because they were "geometrical methods of war" but rather because of changes in weapons and technique.

Perhaps the writers who have labeled Jomini as an advocate of geometrical methods of war did so because they did not have the requisite professional military knowledge to understand correctly what his diagrams portrayed. It might be pointed out that some of the current annexes to operational and administrative orders possess a much more intricate geometric appearance than many of Jomini's diagrams. For instance, a present-day plan of fires for a weapons company or a landing diagram for an amphibious division, to mention only a few examples, would give a completely erroneous impression of rigidity and geometrical formalism if interpreted by a critic lacking the necessary professional knowledge to understand their proper usage.

There is one point, however, on which Jomini seems to follow geometrical thinking, in spite of his denouncement of that very thing. It involves the theory of what he refers to as "bases of operations" within the "theater of war." His "base" was what he termed the frontier of a state from which an army would launch its advance, whence it would draw its supplies and personnel replacements, and to where it could retreat if necessary. His arguments for adequate

bases are still valid, but the specifications for the proper
geometrical location of the base in relation to the enemy
base long ago drifted into obsolescence. It is in connection
with his discussion of the "base" and "zone" that Jomini
makes his most apparent slip toward the very narrow and
formal manner of thinking for which he so often and thoroughly condemned von Bulow and other of his predecessors
and contemporaries in military writing. Because his discussion of the "base" and "zone" (as well as some of his
dated examples of combat formations) comprise the more
obsolescent portions of his *Summary*, they have largely
been excluded from this condensed version of his book.

VIII

While Jomini dealt more with the practical aspects of
war than did Clausewitz, he was far from being one of the
materialistic school. He catalogued the different kinds of
wars and he recognized, as did Clausewitz, the importance
of political objectives in wars between nations.

The spirit of the "nation in arms" as exemplified by the
Napoleonic armies of a new France focused military attention upon morale as a great factor of war. Jomini was as
fully aware of the psychological and morale factors of war
as was Clausewitz. But even though Jomini attached great
value to morale, he evidenced a keen appreciation of the
manner in which it had to be fitted into the entire scheme
of combat, for he knew that by itself it was valueless in
modern war. Writing as a veteran of mighty and bloody
battles he likewise knew that spiritual enthusiasm had to
be mixed properly with strong discipline. Replying to
those who had over emphasized the power of high morale
he wrote, "A few Utopists have imagined that Napoleon
would have attained his end if, like Mohamet, he had
put himself at the head of an army of political dogmas,
and if, in place of the paradise of the Mussulmans, he
had promised to the masses those sweet liberties . . .
Although it be permitted us to believe that the support
of political dogmas is at times an excellent auxiliary,

it must not be forgotten that the Koran even would gain no more than a province at this day, for in order to effect this, cannon, shells, balls, gunpowder, and muskets are necessary." Here he was writing in the same vein as another great general who offered one of war's most practical admonitions, "Put your faith in God—but keep your powder dry."

While he never wrote as extensively as Clausewitz on the destruction of the enemy, Jomini does speak of operations which have as their objective the "destruction of armies," and he makes reference to "wars of extermination," which are definitely close to what the Prussian wrote about at great length. Jomini was as fully aware of the value of surprise as was Clausewitz, and he fully comprehended the advantages of the initiative. "A general," he said, "who stands motionless to receive his enemy, keeping strictly on the defensive, may fight ever so bravely, but he must give way when properly attacked." But in condemning the passive defense he stressed the power of the defensive-offensive strategy, explaining that the general who "awaits the enemy with the intent of launching a timely counter-attack will wrest from him (the enemy) and transfer to his own troops the moral effect always produced by onward movement when coupled with the certainty of throwing the main strength into the action at the decisive point."

Jomini realized that mobile war made it impossible for a nation to adopt a defensive philosophy based upon the false security derived from a fortified frontier. If, during the years after World War I, the policy makers of France had heeded the admonitions of the Swiss general who learned of war in the armies of France, the defeat of the French nation and the early allied reverses of World War II might well have been avoided. When France immobilized her army in the Maginot Line she became a nation incapable of exerting military initiative, a nation that had forgotten that her greatest military glories were gained by an army that had boldly taken the offensive, a nation that had forgotten Jomini's well considered words: "It is bad policy to cover a frontier with fortresses very close together ... To bury an army in entrenchments where it may be outflanked and surrounded, or forced in front even if secure from a flank attack, is manifest folly; and it is hoped that we shall never see another instance of it." How ironic that the nation whose armies were so instrumental in establishing this principle should suffer so disastrously for violating it!

Out of the Napoleonic era came a new and stronger appreciation of the concentration of force upon the decisive point of battle. To Clausewitz this was "the first principle of strategy." Jomini considered the placing of maximum force at the decisive point as "the guiding principle of strategy and tactics." Again, both had interpreted Napoleon correctly. Jomini, discussing the powerful maneuver of columns as developed in the Revolutionary armies, again emphasized the ascendency of concentrated force by deftly explaining that "while the skirmishers made the noise the columns carried the positions."

Jomini accurately perceived the significant developments in the usage of the various arms as they emerged from the Napoleonic school of war. Fire-and-movement was in his opinion the most highly desired type of tactical procedure. His advice in this regard is as valid today as it was when he originally wrote, "an order of battle would be perfect which united the double advantages of the fire of the arms with the impulsion of the attack and the morale effect it produces." The Napoleonic technique of massing artillery did not escape Jomini's attention. He advised that artillery "should concentrate its fire upon the point where a decisive blow is to be struck." In an era that was characterized by mobility and influenced by the legendary exploits of Ney and Marbot, Jomini did not let himself be overimpressed by the role of the cavalry arm. Quite objectively he explained that the "principal value of cavalry is derived from its rapidity and mobility," and that its principal objective is "to open the way for gaining a victory or to render it complete . . ."

In some ways it might be said that Jomini, witnessing the new power of massed artillery and brilliant cavalry operations of Napoleonic battle, was in the same position as military commentators and writers of today who have seen the crushing mobility of armored forces and the devastating might of the air arm.

IX

Unlike some of the more impressionable and less discerning of current writers who acclaim new developments in arms or technique as being the key to total victory, Jomini began his discussion of infantry with the flat assertion that "The infantry is undoubtedly the most important arm . . ." Were Jomini writing such words today he would be as fundamentally accurate as he was when he was in the midst of writing his *Summary* more than a century ago. Napoleonic examples were still influencing his thinking in this regard, for even while crowning infantry as the "Queen of Battle" he carefully explained that infantry without proper support was quite ineffective.

The new emphasis on mobility resulting from the Napoleonic method of making war created a new consciousness of the need for adequate intelligence of the enemy. Efficient espionage coupled with aggressive reconnaissance was Jomini's formula for obtaining the vitally necessary information of the enemy upon which a commander could base his battle plan. Ever the practical soldier, Jomini cautioned that officers especially trained in interrogation technique should be readily available for the questioning of prisoners. Rather than being outmoded by the passing of time, his thoughts on combat intelligence have been reaffirmed on the great battlefields of the twentieth century and are just as valid today as they were when, as Ney's chief of staff, he was directing the search for enemy information before the clash at Bautzen.

In his discussions of combat method he seemed to visualize the ultra-mobile battle of the future, making pointed reference to the necessity of eventually reducing strong positions which have been by-passed. Conservatism had no place in the Napoleonic manner of war of which Jomini wrote with such deep understanding. Then, as now, some commanders were overcautious about their flanks, reluctant to attempt a deep penetration or turning movement for fear of exposing to the enemy a long flank or an extended line of communications. Jomini flatly rejected the theory that a line operation should be free from all enemy forces for a distance to each side equal to the depth of the line.

In advocating audacious but not foolhardy methods he convincingly pointed to the examples of Moreau, Marlborough, Prince Eugene, and Napoleon, and his arguments expressed the boldness of thought destined to be the cornerstone of the blitzkrieg warfare which then lay ahead in the next century.

X

As a product of an age that thought in terms of mass and maneuver, Jomini evidenced an amazing understanding of the use of cover and concealment when he pointed to the necessity for using the irregularities in the terrain to provide shelter for large groups from artillery fire, as well as to gain protection for skirmishers in the assault.

Never hesitant to take issue with the writings of Clausewitz, he differed strongly with the Prussian writer regarding the value of woods, stating rather acidly that "the Skeptic Clausewitz was not afraid to sustain the contrary maxim, and under the singular pretext that he who occupies a wood acts blindly, and discovers nothing of what the enemy is doing, he presents their defense as a fault of tactics."

He continues that Clausewitz, "blinded himself, probably, by the results of the battle of Hohenlinden (1800)" was too prone to confuse "the occupation of a wood in the line of battle with the fault of throwing a whole army in a vast forest without being the master of the issues, to either the front or flanks."

Jomini's topographical knowledge was very profound. There has probably never been a more penetrating observation on the relative virtues of high or low ground than his laconic statement, "It has long been a question whether possession of the mountains controlled the valleys, or whether possession of the valleys controlled the mountains." The discussion of this question is still being continued today in our military magazines.

XI

Supply was a serious problem to Jomini; his writings on this subject indicate that he understood the important place of supply in the scheme of mobile and expansive warfare. His experience in the Peninsular Campaigns and in the Russian invasion convinced him of the difficulty of waging successful war against a nation resorting to what we currently call the "scorched earth" policy. Our modern field commanders are still struggling with the problem that bothered Jomini, that of keeping supplies abreast of rapidly moving troops. All of his writings indicate that he was definitely "supply conscious." In this respect there is reason to believe that he was somewhat more practical in his appreciation of military supply than was Clausewitz, who attempted to separate much of supply from the business of war, stating, "Who would include in the real 'conduct of war' the whole litany of subsistence and administration, because it is admitted to stand in constant reciprocal action with the use of troops, but is something essentially different from it?" Clausewitz was of the further opinion that the subjects which do not belong to fighting itself, but which only belong to maintenance, are "subsistence, care of the sick, and the supply and care of equipment." In Jomini's mind supply was closely woven into the entire pattern of war and constituted a definitely limiting influence on strategical and tactical operations. Instead of considering subsistence as something separate from fighting, he carefully explained how the proper placing of supply installations would facilitate combatant operations and directly influence the success of different tactical formations.

His chapter devoted to the discussion of logistics is particularly significant, not only because of the broad meaning he assigned to the term but also because it contains the bulk of his writing on the status and functions of the military staff. It will be remembered that military staff organization and technique attained its hitherto highest point of development during the Napoleonic wars. Jomini was a part of that staff system, and his description of the staff and its functions comprises one of the more important pieces of staff writing to emerge from the Napoleonic era. True, it was not so detailed as Thiebault's staff manual nor was it so important in establishing staff procedure as was Berthier's *Document on the Staff Organization of the Army of the Alps,* but still the staff doctrine that Jomini enunciated in the *Summary* is a condensation of the staff theory as it was applied in the Napoleonic armies. His writings on the subject are of historic significance for they were widely read and consequently assisted in extending French staff thought throughout the military world.

Jomini wrote not only of definite staff duties; he also probed deeply into the entire question of command and staff relationships. In his *Summary,* as well as in modern doctrine, the staff existed to assist the commander in executing the functions of command, and in so doing to permit the commander to devote his attention to the major problems. Harmonious relations between the commander and the staff, and the unquestioned authority of the commander, were indispensable attributes of a good staff. Warning of a divided authority within the command echelon, he wrote, "Woe to the army when these authorities cease to act in concert." The necessity of having but one prevailing thought within the staff was the subject of one of the elder von Moltke's more famous military dissertations some years later.

XII

Jomini was an efficient and practical staff officer. In the chapter on "Logistics," containing the bulk of his writings on staff functioning, he discussed the manner by which he analyzed enemy causes of action. His analytical processes had much in common with what is known in our modern staff procedure as the "estimate of the enemy situation." In this respect he was perfecting and passing on to coming generations of soldiers the legacy of French staff knowledge that had its roots in the armies of Gustavus Adolphus and its intellectual inception in the staff thinking of Louvois and Bourcet, and which proved its battle effectiveness in the Grand Armeé.

The question of how much information a commander should give a subordinate, as well as the amount of discretion to be allowed in determining the manner of executing an order, has long been a controversial question in military thinking. Jomini disapproved of what he called "the old school" procedure of issuing minutely detailed orders to even the high ranking field commanders who, he observed, "are supposed to be of sufficient experience not to require the same sort of instruction as would be given to junior subalterns just out of school."

While rejecting excessively detailed orders, he also argued against those examples of the other extreme—the type of directives often issued by Napoleon, who, according to Jomini, seldom informed his subordinates of the general concept of the operation in which they were to participate. In Jomini's opinion a proper order would give the subordinate commander the necessary information as to the nature of the entire contemplated operation; instructions pertaining to the execution of his mission would be restricted to the *necessary* directives stipulating what was to be done.

Again, as in so many instances, Jomini's military thinking has been reflected in the contents of our *Field Service Regulations,* which prescribe that "An order should not trespass on the province of a subordinate. It should contain everything that the subordinate must know to carry out his mission, but nothing more." In short, he advocated adherence to the principle by which subordinates are directed "what" to do but not "how" to do it.

XIII

Jomini joined with Frederick the Great and Pierre Bourcet in realizing that intellect would ever be a necessary requisite of a great general. Continuous and expansive war had carried combat far beyond the narrow confines of former feudal and dynastic armed endeavors, with the result that military command and staff duties could only be henceforth properly performed by officers with the necessary military education. To Jomini military education involved more than participation in battle, for it encompassed not only the study of the practical aspects of military method but the theoretical and historical as well. It was in the realm of strategy that Jomini felt that intellectual considerations were of greatest value. In his search for the basic principles of war he became convinced that the fundamentals of war were unchanging, objective, and independent of either weapons or time. The objective study of military history was in Jomini's opinion indispensable to any officer who aspired to high command. "Military history," he said, "accompanied by sound criticism, is indeed the true school of war."

As important as were the intellectual requirements for a great general, Jomini, the veteran of many campaigns, realistically appreciated that mere knowledge, no matter how abundant, could not alone qualify a man for high command. He knew that human nature was and always would be the common denominator of all armed conflict, that control of the human factor in war depended directly upon the qualities of leadership possessed by a commander. Realizing that leadership was a prime requisite of military success Jomini, evidencing a keen appreciation of combat psychology, appraised character as "above all other requisites in a commander in chief." He was aware that just as intellect by itself was valueless as a tool of victory, so a general who had great character but lacked intellectual training would never be a great general. Such reasoning brought him to but one conclusion, that the necessary characteristic of a winning general would be the combination of intellect and natural leadership. His observation that "the union of wise theory with great character will constitute the great captain" is an enduring truism, as ageless as war itself.

With few exceptions the Napoleonic armies were commanded by men who attained high command by virtue of battle experience and a natural ability for war, rather than because of their intellectual training. This was undoubtedly due to the fact that the Napoleonic wars broke too suddenly to permit the deliberate training and culling of potential generals in the Grand Armeé. Yet it was this very army, in which the commanders were products of the school of experience, that produced a new appreciation of the value of intellectual training for the high command. It is one of the curious ironies in the history of the development of military thought that the army commanded largely by generals schooled only by experience should produce military leaders who would give a new importance to the intellectual aspects of generalship.

Out of the Napoleonic army came this new group of officers who realized that a sound military education would be an indispensable part of any great nation's war machine. In the years following Waterloo it was Marshal St. Cyr who labored continuously to raise the intellectual standard of the French Army. General Thiebault focused new attention on the problems of creating and maintaining efficient military staffs; his *Staff Manual*, based upon Berthier's staff directives, strongly influenced European staff development for many years.

Important as were the intellectual contributions of such

broad-visioned military thinkers as St. Cyr and Thiebault, it was Jomini who personified the intellectual developments emanating from the Napoleonic era. It was not that Jomini had a monopoly upon progressive military thinking, but rather that the wide circulation of his books, particularly his *Summary,* carried his opinions throughout the military world. The permanent staff systems and numerous military schools possessed by practically all nations are living evidence of the lasting effect of his writings on the military thinking of the world.

The staff doctrine contained in the *Summary* is of particular interest to United States military readers, for Jomini wrote of French staff thought as it developed under Napoleonic influence, emerging from that era with many of the basic features of modern staff organization and technique. This assumes considerable importance, for in helping to acquaint the military world with the details of French staff thought, Jomini was making staff knowledge available to military thinkers on this side of the Atlantic. In so doing he was helping shape American staff thinking. During this nation's dark years of military retrogression following the Civil War Jomini's writings, more than those of any other military figure, were responsible for keeping alive the dim and flickering light of staff knowledge. The United States staff organization and technique of today traces most of its origin to the command echelons of the Grand Armeé.*

XIV

Past and present military writers have labeled Jomini's concept of war as being restricted in scope. This may be partially true if Jomini is to be judged only on the basis of his discussions of the Base of Operations. But to apply the adjective "restricted" to his entire thinking is indicative that such writers are reading Jomini with a restricted understanding of war. His observation that when

---

* For an elaboration of this, see the Author's *The Military Staff.* The Military Service Publishing Company.

a war involves both terrestrial and naval operations the theater "may embrace both hemispheres," indicates not only that his concept of war was far from being restricted but also that he was thinking in terms of the expansive global wars that even some military philosophers of his time could not envision.

None of Jomini's writings is more suggestive of broad military vision than his chapter on landing operations, which appears under the quaint title of "Descents." For a person who spent his military career fighting the battles of Continental Europe, he displayed an understanding of amphibious theory that is at least remarkable. In the first sentence of his discussion on this subject he drives straight through to the heart of amphibious operations, and sensing that the transition from sea to land is the most delicate of all armed endeavors, stating that such operations are "among the most difficult in war when effected in the presence of a well prepared enemy." His general rules for the conduct of amphibious operations prescribe deception, adequate anchorage, expeditious seizure of necessary points to protect the development of the attack, and the early landing of artillery. These basic rules could well be used today as the summation of a lecture on the general aspects of amphibious operations.

In the discussion of landing operations we find one of the most significant clues to Jomini's scholarly and scientific attitude toward war. While the world was deciding that the failure of Napoleon's plans for an invasion of England assured the survival of Anglo-Saxon culture, Jomini considered it regrettable that Napoleon didn't at least make the attempt, if for no other reason than to see if such a large amphibious operation could be successfully executed. An intellectual product of land warfare, Jomini had an understanding of amphibious problems that is surprisingly profound, for his writings make frequent reference to the hazards of wind and sea to which landing forces are exposed. His practical observation that troops embarked in small boats, battered by rough seas,

and suffering from sea sickness will land with reduced
fighting efficiency, anticipated one of the guiding considerations of all modern amphibious planners. Jomini
knew that the sea was ever the "non-constant factor" in
amphibious planning and execution.

For one whose actual military experience was limited
to land battles, Jomini had a high regard for the strategical status of the seas. It is evident that he had
learned well the great lesson contained in the failure
of Napoleon's Continental Policy, for he says without
equivocation that the nation that is "master of the sea
ought never to want for anything." Again, by thinking
in terms of such broad strategical concepts as mastery of
the ocean area, he showed an understanding of war which
was far from being restricted.

Since he possessed such a sound appreciation of maritime
power it is not particularly strange that Jomini should
occupy the unusual position of making important—
although indirect—contributions to the development of
naval doctrine. Admiral Mahan, author of the
most important book on naval warfare, *The Influence of
Sea Power on History,* studied Jomini's writings and recognized that the basic doctrine enunciated by Ney's former
chief of staff was so universally applicable as to furnish
guiding concepts of naval strategy. The principle of
"interior lines," a basic tenet in Jomini's concept of war,
as well as the theory of the supreme strategical importance
of lines of communication, strongly influenced Mahan's
thinking as he wrote his enduring treatise.

XV

It is not going too far into the field of speculation to
suspect that Adolph Hitler might still be triumphantly
riding the four horses of the Apocalypse if he had read
and heeded what Jomini wrote regarding the possibilities
of a successful all-out invasion of Russia. As Governor of
Smolensk Jomini witnessed the Russian invasion when the
Grand Armee fought its way into the heart of Moscow,

only to see the capital succumb to the torch, after which
Napoleon's army, undefeated in battle, disintegrated as
it staggered in retreat across the endless miles of snow-
covered plains of western Russia. Later, after leaving the
French army and taking a commission under the Czar,
he had an unequaled opportunity to acquaint himself
with the Russian theory and method of war. Long before
the phrase "scorched earth" found its way into our modern
military vocabulary, Russia had learned the efficacy of such
sacrificial procedure. Ever since Ivan the Terrible brought
nationalism to Russia, the military leaders of that nation
have been constantly concerned with maintaining the integrity of the country's far-flung borders that spread across
two continents. As a result of being continuously confronted with the problem of protecting such expansive
territories, the Russian military mind became accustomed
to think in terms of "war in space," realized that territory
could be traded for time, and saw that the endless steppes
of Russia offered a military barrier more effective than
any fortification constructed by man.

Jomini learned the Russian way of war from both sides.
While he says that Napoleon "fully appreciated the
bravery of the Russian Armies," he failed (as did the
would-be Nazi conquerors) because he did not fully
evaluate the military power of "the national spirit and
energy" of the Russian people. Viewing Napoleon's and
Hitler's Russian invasions in retrospect, it appears they
sealed their own doom because they did not possess what
Jomini wisely calls the "moderation in victory to know
how to stop in time."

XVI

Jomini wrote principally as a practitioner rather than
a philosopher of war. Just as at times he displays evidence of possessing a measure of the same philosophic
probity of thought that characterized the thinking of
Clausewitz, he also occasionally shows a trace of the same
kind of practical imagination that permitted Leonardo da

Vinci to catch glimpses of the future world. In the world in which Jomini lived the cavalry horse was still the fastest mode of transportation on the field of battle, and the highest means of observation was a well situated hilltop or a towering church steeple. The bulk of the industrial revolution with most of its technological progress was still beyond the horizon of ordinary men's vision. Yet Jomini, in the midst of such industrially unsuggestive surroundings, objectively discussed the desirability and limitations of aerial observation. He readily averred that it would be decidedly advantageous to an army to be able to have such a means of observing the enemy, for, as he stated, "steeples are not always at hand in the vicinity of battlefields." Among the requisites for successful air observation he included officers capable of judging what was seen from the air and the development of the necessary system of signaling information to the ground. Trained observers and proper air-ground communications are the prime essentials of successful air observation in modern war.

He quite correctly imagined that it would be difficult to distinguish the identity of closely intermingled columns of troops, but that identification would be easier under more open battle conditions. It is very probable that more than a few of our air observers struggling with the problems of orientation and recognition from above the dense troop concentrations of the Remagen bridgehead or bloody Iwo Jima experienced the same difficulties that Jomini attributed to his hypothetical observer who was having trouble distinguishing between Blucher's and Gouchy's columns in the maelstrom of Waterloo. Although Jomini had sufficient imagination to speculate accurately regarding some of the practical aspects of air observation, his vision of the use of the coming air arm was not complete, his thinking on this subject being based entirely on the experimental performance of a few daring balloonists. It is evident that his thoughts pertaining to the potentialities of even free ballons were not projected to a very high level, as he noted that it would be very interest-

ing to know how objects would appear "when seen at
five or six hundred feet of perpendicular elevation."

XVI

Jomini possessed at least a few characteristics which did
not endear him in the hearts of many of his contemporaries. He was ambitious, often vain, and did not hesitate
to assert that he was a foremost military authority of his
age. But coupled with these detracting features it must
be admitted that he had a brilliant intellect and a certain
inner sensitivity. It is probably because of these latter
characteristics that we find in Jomini something that is
paradoxical to a career soldier of his time, and something which it is difficult to discern in all of the philosophic
writings of Clausewitz—a humanitarian resentment against
the devastation of total war, an apprehension of the
destructive power of coming wars, and an almost religious
yearning for international laws to reduce the world's war
potential. Indeed, they are strange thoughts to find in a
mind with such an objective attitude toward the entire
subject of waging efficient war.

There was a larger and more admirable side to Jomini's
character than was indicated by his generous self-esteem
and his transfer from the French to Russian colors. Although deeply disappointed, emotionally embittered, and
completely disgusted as a result of his personal persecution
by Berthier, Jomini did not allow his fiery hatred for Napoleon's chief of staff to alter his personal feeling of allegiance toward Napoleon or the French nation. Jomini
considered the unfortunate incident as a personal affair
between himself and Berthier. Because Jomini sought no
vengeance against the nation or the army, in both of
which Berthier held high position, history has never been
able to label Jomini as either a traitor or a turncoat.

Jomini's conduct after joining the Russian high command seemed to be guided by an unusual sense of pro-
priety. The story is told that once, when attending an
allied council of war, the King of Prussia pointedly ques-

tioned Jomini regarding the location and strength of Napoleon's forces. Jomini declined to divulge the information, and the Czar, also participating in the meeting, approved Jomini's action.

Although he was a general in the Imperial Russian Army, Jomini did not become an enemy of France. His objective attitude was well illustrated by his advice to the Czar as the victorious allied armies neared the Rhine during the latter phase of the campaign of 1813. Jomini advised against invading defeated France, suggesting an equitable treaty of peace. Unsuccessful in his efforts to convince the jubilant allies that an independent France would best serve the cause of European stability, he obtained the Czar's permission to visit Switzerland.

Through the many turbulent years that had passed since leaving his native land, Jomini retained a strong sense of loyalty toward the little country. Jomini's influence with the Czar was an important factor in helping Switzerland avoid the clutches of Austrian ambition and emerge from the post-Napoleonic period of vicious power politics as an independent nation.

Accompanying Czar Alexander to Paris in 1815, Jomini stoutly opposed the execution of his old commander and companion-in-arms, Marshal Ney. It was neither wise nor politic to speak out against the avowed aims of the allied leaders. Yet, so strongly did Jomini defend his former chief that it was proposed to strike Jomini's name from the list of Russian generals. With nothing to gain and much to lose from such activities, Jomini persisted in placing personal loyalty before personal security. Although Jomini did not save him, Ney, in accepting his fate, must have found some consolation in realizing that at least his old chief of staff remained loyal to the end. Indeed, Jomini's actions were far more creditable than those of Napoleon's chief of staff, Berthier, who lost no time in deserting the Emperor after his defeat at Leipzig.

Jomini's refusal to capitalize his former position of trust in the French army, his enduring interest in his native country, and his stalwart loyalty to Ney flowed neither from a soul fired by religious fervor nor from a heart pounding with patriotism. Rather, his courageous adherence to persons and causes stemmed from his own personal sense of morality.

Truly, Antoine Henri Jomini possessed great strength of character. Otherwise, such admirable traits could not have survived a soldier of fortune's constant exposure to the temptations of expediency that inspired the political and military machinations of the Napoleonic era.

XVII

As Ney's chief of staff he personally participated in the great holocaust of death and destruction which engulfed the European continent in the wake of the Napoleonic conquests. By interpreting the Napoleonic era as the beginning of a new method of all-out wars between nations, he recognized that future wars between nations would be total wars in every sense of the word. In the new power of a "nation in arms," exemplified by a reborn France, he saw the great national armies of the coming wars, in which the individual would be readily expendable. The *levee en masse* would provide the multitude of men needed for wars of annihilation. Jomini must have realized that the red fury that engulfed Moscow represented more than a mere disastrous conflagration. He sensed that the towering tongues of fire were evidences of more than the physical destruction of a great city, and that each finger of flame pointed to a new kind of war in which the people of a nation as well as the soldiers were participants, a war in which self-destruction was preferable to capitulation. No longer was war the private affair of a monarch. Napoleon introduced the modern world to total war. Jomini knew that henceforward Europe's wars would be total wars.

He also grasped the profound significance of Napoleon's ability to wage war without heed to national boundaries or great distances, and realized the implications of Napoleonic expansive war in terms of military history yet to be made, stating that "remoteness is not a certain safeguard against invasion."

There is a strong trace of emotionalism in his statement that "a person may desire that wars of extermination might be banished from the code of nations." The wanton death and destruction of modern war seemed to sicken him and make him wish for the return of the days when the issues were decided on limited fields of battle by professional soldiers rather than in the fields, the homes, and the very souls of the entire peoples of nations. There is both revulsion against the new kind of war and a longing for the old in his statement, "I acknowledge that my prejudices are in favor of the good old times when the French and English guards courteously invited each other to fire first as at Fontenoy (1795, War of the Austrian Succession), preferring them to the frightful epoch when priests, women, and children throughout Spain plotted the murder of isolated soldiers." He was able to picture the coming wars in which rockets, shrapnel, and fast breech-loading field guns would be but means of increasing the slaughter, and it was this vision of the impending carnage to be wrought by scientific advancement that caused him to say satirically, "What a beautiful text for preaching universal peace and the exclusive reign of railroads."

It has been said with good reason that "Napoleon was the god of war and Jomini was his prophet." Even more than that, though, Jomini was a prophet of the war to come. It was not until the twentieth century that the war-frightened world seemed to heed Jomini's advice to limit the means of war by "laws of nations."

Only now is the world, shocked by the blasts at Nagasaki, Hiroshima and Bikini, coming to realize the full importance and dreadful implications of Jomini's terse, somber prophesy: "The means of destruction are approaching perfection with frightful rapidity."

Jomini wrote as a practical theorist whose teachings were based upon long battle experience. In presenting his beliefs he wrote as teacher to the world's military thinkers, and he specialized in teaching the Napoleonic manner of war. By so doing he was actually teaching the world the art of modern war. When one realizes that it was largely through his writings that Napoleonic doctrine was first made available to the military world, when it is remembered that our total wars of today are but magnifications of Napoleonic wars, as taught by Jomini, there is considerable justification for concluding that there have been few people in history who have exerted such a strong influence on the development of military thought as did Antoine Henri Jomini.

There is reason to believe that Jomini and Clausewitz looked upon each other much as competitors in the field of military writing. Perhaps it has been an extension of this line of thinking which has resulted in the peculiar fact that the world of military thought has permitted the ascendancy of one only at the expense of the other. True, there are some points of theory and technique on which Jomini and Clausewitz are widely divided. But when their works are compared, not on the basis of individual discussions or opinions, but rather according to the broad concepts on which both based their writing, much military thought is common to both; Jomini's practical teachings tend to complement the philosophic analysis of Clausewitz while the Prussian's emphasis upon the intangible components of war seems to give even greater strength to Jomini's principles. There is no reason why this should be particularly illogical, for both were writing of the same thing—the new way of war born in the Napoleonic era. No one can intelligently contend that Jomini's writings could ever displace the great works of Clausewitz; neither can intelligent opinion hold that the Clausewitzian classics render valueless the historically important writings of Jomini. There is abundant military knowledge in the works of both. There is room for both in military literature.

Probably more than any other book, Jomini's *Précis de*

l'Art de la Guerre assembled, analyzed, standardized, and codified the military method and thought inherent in the Napoleonic concept of war. History must accord Antoine Henri Jomini the distinction of writing one of the first and most enduring text-books on modern war.

J. D. HITTLE

THE PRESENT THEORY OF WAR
AND ITS UTILITY

The art of war has existed in all time, and strategy especially was the same under Caesar as under Napoleon. But the art, confined to the understanding of great captains, existed in no written treatise.

The books all gave but fragments of systems, born of the imagination of their authors, they contained, usually, minute (not to say puerile details) upon the most accessory points of tactics—the only part of war, perhaps, which it is possible to subject to fixed rules.

Writers had not penetrated very far into the mine which they wished to explore. To form a just idea of the state of the art in the middle of the 18th Century, it is necessary to read what Marshal Saxe wrote in the preface to his *Reveries.**

"War," said he, "is a science replete with shadows in whose obscurity one cannot move with assurance. Routine and prejudices, a natural consequence of ignorance are its foundation.

"All sciences have principles, war alone has none. The great captains who have written give us none. One must be profound even to understand them.

"Gustavus Adolphus has created a method, but it was soon deviated from, because it was learned by rote. There are then nothing but usages, the principles of which are unknown to us."

This was written about the time when Frederick the Great preluded the Seven Years War by his victories of Hohenfriedberg, of Soor, etc. And the good Marshal Saxe, instead of piercing those obscurities of which he complained with so much justice, contented himself with writing systems for clothing soldiers in woolen blouses, for forming them upon four ranks, two of which to be armed with pikes; finally for proposing small field pieces

---

* The Military Service Publishing Company, 1944.

which he named "amusettes," and which truly merited
that title on account of the humorous images with which
they were surrounded.

At the end of the Seven Years War, some good works
appeared; Frederick himself, not content with being a
great king, a great captain, a great philosopher and great
historian, made himself also a didactic author by his
Instructions to His Generals.* Guichard, Turpin, Maize-
roy, Menil-Durand, sustained controversies upon the tactics
of the ancients as well as upon that of their own time, and
gave some interesting treatises upon those matters. Turpin
commented on Montecuculi, and Vegetius;* the Marquis
de Silva in Piedmont and Santa Cruz in Spain had also
discussed some parts with success. Finally d'Escremeville
sketched a history of the art, which was not devoid of
merit. But all that by no means dissipated the darkness
of which the conqueror of Fontenoy complained.

Germany produced in the interval between the Seven
Years War and that of the Revolution, a multitude of
writings, more or less extensive, on different secondary
branches of the art, which they illumined with a faint
light. Thielke and Faesch published in Saxony, the one,
fragments upon castrametation, the attack of camps and
positions, the other a collection of maxims upon the accessory parts of the operations of war. Scharnhorst did as
much in Hanover; Warnery published in Prussia a pretty
good work on the cavalry; Baron Holzendorf another on
the tactics of maneuvers. Count Kevenhuller gave maxims
upon field warfare and upon that of sieges. But nothing
of all this gave a satisfactory idea of the elevated branches
of the science.

Finally even Mirabeau who, having returned from
Berlin, published an enormous volume upon the Prussian
tactics, an arid repetition of the regulation for platoon
and line evolutions to which some had the simplicity to
attribute the greater part of the successes of Frederick!

---

* The Military Service Publishing Company, 1944.

If such books have been able to contribute to the propagation of this error, it must be owned however that they contributed also to perfecting the regulations of 1791 on maneuvers, the only result which it was possible to expect from them.

After having left the Helvetic service as chief of battalion, I sought to instruct myself by reading, with avidity, all those controversies which had agitated the military world in the last half of the 18th century; commencing with Puysegur, finishing with Menil-Durand and Guibert, and finding everywhere nothing but systems, more or less complete, of battle tactics, which could give but an imperfect idea of war, because they all contradicted each other in a deplorable manner.

I fell back then, upon works of military history in order to seek, in the combinations of the great captains, a solution which those systems of the writers did not give me. Already had the narratives of Frederick the Great commenced to initiate me in the secret which had caused him to gain the miraculous victory of Leuthen (Lissa). I perceived that this secret consisted in the very simple maneuver of carrying the bulk of his forces upon a single wing of the hostile army; and Lloyd soon came to fortify me in this conviction. I found again, afterwards, the same cause in the first successes of Napoleon in Italy, which gave me the idea that by applying, through strategy, to the whole chess-table of a war this same principle which Frederick had applied to battles, we should have the key to all the science of war.

I could not doubt this truth in reading again, subsequently, the campaigns of Turenne, of Marlborough, of Eugene of Savoy, and in comparing them with those of Frederick, which Tempelhoff had just published with details so full of interest, although somewhat heavy and by far too much repeated. I comprehended then that Marshal de Saxe had been quite right in saying that in 1750 there were no principles laid down upon the art of war, but that many of his readers had also very badly interpreted his preface in concluding therefrom that he had thought that those principles did not exist.

Convinced that I had seized the true point of view under which it was necessary to regard the theory of war in order to discover its veritable rules, and to quit the always so uncertain field of personal systems, I set myself to the work with all the ardor of a neophyte.

In 1831, the Prussian General Clausewitz died, leaving to his widow the care of publishing posthumous works which were presented as unfinished sketches. This work made a great sensation in Germany, and for my part I regret that it was written before the author was acquainted with my *Summary of the Art of War,* persuaded that he would have rendered to it some justice.

One cannot deny to General Clausewitz great learning and a facile pen. But this pen, at times a little vagrant, is above all too pretentious for a didactic discussion, in which simplicity and clearness ought to come first. Besides that, the author shows himself by far too skeptical in point of military science; his first volume is but a declamation against all theory of war, whilst the two succeeding volumes, full of theoretic maxims, prove that the author believes in the efficacy of his own doctrines. if he does not believe in those of others.

Marshal de Saxe, if he were to return among us, would be much surprised at the present wealth of our military literature, and would no longer complain of the darkness which shrouds the science. Henceforth good books will not be wanting to those who shall wish to study, for at this day we have principles, whereas they had in the 18th Century only methods and systems.

In weighing all that has been said for or against, in comparing the immense progress made in the science for the last thirty years with the incredulity of M. Clausewitz, I believe I am correct in concluding that the ensemble of my principles and of the maxims which are derived from them, has been badly comprehended by several writers; that some have made the most erroneous application of them; that others have drawn from them exaggerated consequences which have never been able to enter my head, for a general officer, after having assisted in a dozen campaigns, ought to know that war is a great drama, in which a thousand physical or moral causes operate more or less powerfully, and which cannot be reduced to mathematical calculations.

But, I ought equally to avow without circumlocution, that twenty years of experience have but fortified me in the following convictions:

"There exists a small number of fundamental principles of war, which could not be deviated from without danger, and the application of which, on the contrary, has been in almost all time crowned with success.

"The maxims of application which are derived from those principles are also small in number, and if they are found sometimes modified according to circumstances, they can nevertheless serve in general as a compass to the chief of an army to guide him in the task, always difficult and complicated, of conducting grand operations in the midst of the noise and tumult of combats.

"Natural genius will doubtless know how, by happy inspirations, to apply principles as well as the best studied theory could do it; but a simple theory, disengaged from all pedantry, ascending to causes without giving absolute systems, based, in a word, upon a few fundamental maxims, will often supply genius, and will even serve to extend its development by augmenting its confidence in its own inspirations.

"Of all theories on the art of war, the only reasonable one is that which, founded upon the study of military history, admits a certain number of regulating principles, but leaves to natural genius the greatest part in the general conduct of a war without trammeling it with exclusive rules.

"On the contrary, nothing is better calculated to kill natural genius and to cause error to triumph, than those pedantic theories, based upon the false idea that war is a positive science, all the operations of which can be reduced to infallible calculations.

"Finally, the metaphysical and skeptical works of a few writers will not succeed, either, in causing it to be believed that there exists no rule for war, for their writings prove absolutely nothing against maxims supported upon the most brilliant modern feats of arms, and justified by the reasoning even of those who believe they are combatting them."

I hope, that after these avowals, I could not be accused of wishing to make this art a mechanical routine, nor of pretending on the contrary that the reading of a single chapter of principles is able to give, all at once, the talent of conducting an army. In all the arts, as in all the situations of life, knowledge and skill are two altogether different things, and if one often succeed through skill alone, it is never but the union of the two that constitutes a superior man and assures complete success. Meanwhile, in order not to be accused of pedantry, I hasten to avow that, by knowledge, I do not mean a vast erudition; it is not the question to know a great deal but to know well; to know especially what relates to the mission appointed us.

I pray that my readers, well penetrated with these truths, may receive with kindness this new summary, which may now, I believe, be offered as the book most suitable for the instruction of a prince or a statesman.

It must not be concluded that the art of war has arrived at that point that it cannot make another step towards perfection. There is nothing perfect under the sun! And if a committee were assembled under the presidency of the Arch Duke Charles or Wellington, composed of all the strategic and tactical notabilities of the age, together with the most skillful generals of engineers and artillery, this committee could not yet succeed in making a perfect, absolute and immutable theory on all branches of war, especially on tactics!

I. STATESMANSHIP IN RELATION TO WAR

Under this head are included those considerations from which a statesman concludes whether a war is proper, opportune, or indispensable, and determines the various operations necessary to attain the object of the war.

A government goes to war:

1. To reclaim certain rights or to defend them;

2. To protect and maintain the great interests of the state (as commerce, manufactures, or agriculture);

3. To maintain the balance of power;

4. To propagate political or religious theories, to crush them, or to defend them;

5. To increase the influence and power of the state by acquisitions of territory;

6. To gratify a mania for conquest.

These different kinds of war influence in some degree the nature and extent of the efforts and operations necessary to wage them.

Offensive Wars to Reclaim Rights

When a state has claims upon another, it may not always be best to enforce them by arms. The public interest must be consulted before action is taken.

The most just war is one which is founded upon undoubted rights and which, in addition, promises to the state advantages commensurate with the sacrifices required and the hazards incurred.

Frederick II of Prussia, while Austria and France were at war, brought forward an old claim, in 1744 entered Bohemia in force, and seized this province, thus doubling the power of Prussia. This was a stroke of genius.

In wars of this nature no rules can be laid down. "Watch and profit by every circumstance" covers all that can be said. The most natural step would be to occupy the disputed territory; then offensive operations may be carried on according to circumstances and to the respective strengths of the parties, the object of course being to secure the cession of the territory by the enemy. Everything depends upon the alliances the parties may be able to secure with other states, and upon their own military resources. In an offensive movement, scrupulous care must be exercised not to arouse the jealousy of any other state which might come to the aid of the enemy; it is part of the duty of a statesman to foresee this chance, and to obviate it by making proper explanations and giving proper guarantees to other states.

In a war an ally is to be desired, all other things being equal. Although a great state will more probably succeed than two weaker states in alliance against it, still the alliance is stronger than either would be separately. All history teaches that no enemy is so insignificant as to be despised and neglected by any power, however formidable.

Wars Defensive Politically But Offensive Militarily

There are often advantages in a war of invasion; there are also advantages in awaiting the enemy upon one's own soil. The first course will spare a country's territory from devastation, carry on the war at the expense of the enemy, excite the ardor of its soldiers, and depress the spirits of the adversary. Nevertheless, in a purely military sense, it is certain that an army operating in its own territory, upon a theater of which all the natural and artificial features are well known, and where all movements are aided by an intimate knowledge of the country, the favor of the citizens, and the aid of the constituted authorities, possesses great advantages.

Wars of Intervention

To interfere in a contest already begun promises more advantages to a state than war under any other circumstances. The reason is plain; the power which interferes throws upon one side of the scale its whole weight and influence, and it interferes at the most opportune moment, when it can make decisive use of its resources.

There are two kinds of intervention: 1. Intervention in the internal affairs of neighboring states. 2. Intervention in external relations.

Whatever may be said as to the moral character of interventions of the first class, instances are frequent. The Romans acquired power by these interferences, and the empire of the English India Company was assured in a similar manner. These interventions are not always successful. While Russia added to her power by interference with Poland in 1654-1667, Austria, on the contrary, was almost ruined by her attempt to interfere in the internal affairs of France during the Revolution.

Intervention in the external relations of states is more legitimate and perhaps more advantageous. It may be doubtful whether a nation has the right to interfere in the internal affairs of another people, but it certainly has a right to oppose it when it propagates disorder which may reach the adjoining states.

History is filled with examples of powers which have fallen by neglect of these principles. "A state begins to decline when it permits the immoderate aggrandizement of a rival, and a secondary power may become the arbiter of nations if it throws its weight into the balance at the proper time."

In wars of intervention the essentials are to secure a general who is both a statesman and a soldier; to have clear stipulations with the allies as to the part to be taken by each in the principal operations; finally, to agree upon an objective point which shall be in harmony with the common interests. Because of neglect of these precautions the greater number of coalitions have failed, or have maintained a difficult struggle with a power more united but weaker than the allies.

Wars of Opinion

Wars of opinion between two states rather belong to the class of wars of intervention, for they result either from doctrines which one party desires to propagate among its neighbors or from dogmas which it desires to crush. Although originating in religious or political beliefs, these wars are most deplorable for, like national wars, they enlist the worst passions and become vindictive, cruel, and terrible.

The wars of Islamism,[1] the Crusades,[2] The Thirty Years' War,[3] and the wars of the Holy League[4] present nearly the same characteristics. Often religion is the pretext to obtain political power, and the war is not really one of dogmas. The successors of Mohammed cared more to extend their empire than to preach the Koran, and Philip II, bigot as he was, did not sustain the League in France for the purpose of advancing the Roman Church. We agree with M. Ancelot that Louis IX, when he went on a crusade in Egypt (1249, The Seventh Crusade), thought more of the commerce of the Indies than of gaining possession of the Holy Sepulcher.

Sometimes the dogma is not only a pretext, but also a powerful ally—for it excites the ardor of the people, and often creates a closely-knit party.

In wars of political opinions the chances of support and resistance are about equal. It may be recollected how in the French Revolution associations of fanatics thought it possible to propagate throughout Europe the famous Declaration of The Rights of Man, and how in 1792 governments became justly alarmed and rushed to arms, probably only with the intention of forcing the lava of this volcano back into its crater and there extinguishing it. The means were not fortunate, for war and aggression are inappropriate measures for arresting an evil which lies wholly in the human passions, excited in a temporary paroxysm, of less duration as it is the most violent. Time is the true remedy for all bad passions and for all anarchical doctrines. To attempt to restrain such a mob by force is to attempt to restrain the explosion of a mine when the powder has already been ignited: it is far better to await the explosion and afterward fill up the crater than to try to prevent it and perish in the attempt.

History contains but a single example of a struggle like that of the French Revolution. It appears to demonstrate clearly the danger of attacking an intensely excited nation.

Religious wars are above all the most deplorable. We can understand how a government may find it necessary to use force against its own subjects in order to crush factions which would weaken the authority of the throne and the national strength, but it is difficult to conceive that it should murder its citizens to compel them to say their prayers in French or Latin, or to recognize the supremacy of a foreign pontiff. Never was a king more to be pitied than Louis XIV (King of France 1643-1715), who persecuted a million industrious Protestants who had put upon the throne his own Protestant ancestor. Wars of fanaticism are horrible when mingled with exterior wars, and they are also frightful when they are family quarrels.

Wars of Conquest

There are two very different kinds of invasion: one attacks an adjoining state, the other attacks a distant point over intervening territory of great extent whose inhabitants may be neutral, doubtful, or hostile.

Wars of conquest, unhappily, are often prosperous—as Alexander, Caesar, and Napoleon (during a portion of his career) have fully proved. But in these wars there are natural limits which cannot be passed without incurring great disaster. Cambyses II[5] in Nubia, Darius[6] in Scythia, Crassus[7] and the Emperor Julian[8] among the Parthians, and Napoleon in Russia[9] furnish bloody proofs of these truths. The love of conquest, however, was not the only motive with Napoleon: his personal position and his contest with England urged him to enterprises calculated to make him supreme. One might say his victories teach what may be accomplished by activity, boldness, and skill; his disasters, what might have been avoided by prudence.

A war of invasion without good reason—like that of Genghis Khan[10]—is a crime against humanity; but it may be excused, if not approved, when induced by great interests or when conducted with good motives.

The spectacle of a spontaneous uprising of a nation is rarely seen. Though there be in it something grand and noble which commands our admiration, the consequences are so terrible that, for the sake of humanity, we ought to hope never to see it. This uprising must not be confounded with a national defense in accordance with the institutions of the state and directed by the government.

Control of the sea is of much importance in determining the results of a national invasion. If the people possess a long stretch of coast and are masters of the sea, or in alliance with a power which controls it, their power of resistance is quintupled, not only on account of the facility of feeding the insurrection and of alarming the enemy on all the points he may occupy but still more by the difficulties which will be thrown in the way of his procuring supplies by sea.

The nature of the country may facilitate a national defense. In mountainous countries the people are always most formidable; next to these are countries covered with extensive forests.

When the people are supported by a considerable nucleus of disciplined troops, the difficulties are particularly great. The invader has only an army, whereas his adversaries have both an army and a people in arms, making means of resistance out of everything and with each individual conspiring against the common enemy.

These obstacles become almost insurmountable when the country is difficult. Each armed inhabitant knows the smallest paths and their connections; he finds everywhere a relative or friend who aids him. The commanders also know the country and, learning immediately the slightest movement on the part of the invader, can adopt the best measures to defeat his projects. The enemy, without information of their movements and not in a condition to reconnoiter, having no resource but in his bayonets and certain of safety only in the concentration of his columns, is like a blind man. His combinations are failures. When, after the most carefully concerted movements and the most rapid and fatiguing marches he thinks he is about to accomplish his aim and deal a terrible blow, he finds no signs of the enemy but his campfires. So while, like Don Quixote, he is attacking windmills, his adversary is on his line of communications, destroys the detachments left to guard it, surprises his convoys and his depots, and carries on a war so disastrous for the invader that he must inevitably yield after a time.

No army, however disciplined, can contend successfully against such national resistance unless it be strong enough to hold all the essential points of the country, cover its communications, and at the same time furnish an active force sufficient to beat the enemy wherever he may present himself. If this enemy has a regular army of respectable size to be a nucleus around which to rally the people, what force will be sufficient to be superior everywhere and to assure the safety of the long lines of communication against numerous bodies?

The Peninsular War (1808-1814, British *vs*. French in Spain and Portugal) should be carefully studied to learn all the obstacles which a general and his brave troops may encounter in the occupation or conquest of a country whose people are all in arms.

If success be possible in such a war, the following general course will be most likely to insure it. Make a display of a mass of troops proportioned to the obstacles and resistance likely to be encountered, calm the popular passions in every possible way, exhaust them by time and patience, display courtesy, gentleness, and severity united, and (particularly) deal justly.

I sum up this discussion by asserting that, without being a utopian philanthropist or a professional soldier, a person may desire that wars of extermination may be banished from the code of nations, and that the defenses of nations by disciplined militia, with the aid of good political alliances, may be sufficient to insure their independence.

As a soldier, preferring loyal and chivalrous warfare to organized assassination if it be necessary to make a choice, I acknowledge that my prejudices are in favor of the good old times when the French and English Guards courteously invited each other to fire first—as at Fontenoy —preferring them to the frightful epoch when priests, women, and children throughout Spain plotted the murder of isolated soldiers.

NOTES

[1] 8th to 11th centuries.

[2] 11th to 13th centuries.

[3] 1618-1648.

[4] Formed 1576.

[5] King of Persia 529-522 B.C.

[6] King of Persia 521-486 B.C.

[7] 115 (?)-53 B.C. While governor of Syria undertook campaign against the Parthians; was disastrously defeated at Carrhae (Haran), captured, and executed.

[8] 331-363 A.D. Created Caesar in 355, proclaimed emperor by his troops in 361. Slain in battle against the Persians in the desert beyond Ctesiphon.

[9] 1812.

[10] 1167-1227. Invaded the west 1218-1222.

II. MILITARY POLICY

Military policy embraces the political considerations relating to the operations of armies which belong to neither diplomacy, strategy, nor tactics.

Under military policy we may include the passions of the people to be fought, their military system, their immediate means and reserves, their financial resources, the attachment they bear to their government or their institutions, the character of the executive, the characters and military abilities of the commanders of their armies, the influence of cabinet councils or councils of war at the capital upon their operations, the system of war favored by their staff, the established force of the state and its armament, the military geography and statistics of the state which is to be invaded, and, finally, the resources and obstacles of every kind likely to be met.

There are no fixed rules on such subjects, except that the government should neglect nothing in obtaining a knowledge of these details, and that it is indispensable to take them into consideration in the arrangement of all plans.

Military Statistics and Geography

By the first of these sciences we understand the most thorough knowledge possible of the elements of power and military resources of the enemy with whom we are called upon to contend. The second consists of the topographical and strategic descriptions of the theater of war, with all the natural or artificial obstacles to be encountered, and the examination of the permanent decisive points which may be found in the whole length of the frontier or throughout the country. Besides the minister of war, the commanding general and his chief of staff should be afforded this information.

Military statistics is not much better known than geography. We have but vague and superficial statements, from which the strength of armies and navies is conjectured, and also the revenue supposed to be possessed by a state—which is far from being the knowledge necessary to plan operations.

Other Influencing Considerations

As the excited passions of hostile people are of themselves always a powerful enemy, both the general and his government should use their best efforts to allay them.

On the other hand, the general should do everything to electrify his own soldiers and to impart to them the same enthusiasm which he endeavors to repress in his adversaries. All armies are alike susceptible of this spirit: only the springs of action and means vary with the national character. Military eloquence is one means, and has been the subject of many a treatise. The proclamations of Napoleon and of Paskevitch,[1] the addresses of the ancients to their soldiers, and those of Suvorov[2] to men of still greater simplicity, are models of their different kinds.

A cherished cause and a general who inspires confidence by previous success are powerful means of electrifying an army and are conducive to victory. Some dispute the advantages of this enthusiasm and prefer imperturbable coolness in battle. Both have unmistakable advantages and disadvantages. Enthusiasm impels to the performance of great actions, but the difficulty is in maintaining it constantly and when discouragement succeeds it, disorder easily results.

The greater or less activity and boldness of the commanders of the armies are elements of success or failure which cannot be submitted to rules. A cabinet and a commander ought to consider the intrinsic value of their troops, and that resulting from their organization as compared with that of the enemy. A Russian general, commanding the most solidly organized troops in Europe, need not fear to undertake anything against undisciplined and unorganized troops in an open country, however brave may be its individuals.* Concert in action makes strength; order produces this concert, and discipline insures order; and without discipline and order no success is possible. The Russian general would not be so bold before European troops having the same instruction and nearly the same discipline as his own. Finally, a general may attempt with a Mack[3] as his antagonist what it would be madness to do with a Napoleon.

The action of a cabinet in reference to the control of armies influences the boldness of their operations. A general whose genius and hands are tied by an Aulic council five hundred miles distant cannot be a match for one who has liberty of action, other things being equal.

As to superiority in skill, it is one of the most certain pledges of victory, other things being at all equal. It is true that great generals have often been beaten by inferior ones, but an exception does not make a rule. An order misunderstood, a fortuitous event, may throw into the hands of the enemy all the chances of success which a skillful general had prepared for himself by his maneuvers. But these are risks which cannot be foreseen nor avoided. Would it be fair on that account to deny the influence of science and principles in ordinary affairs?

If the skill of a general is one of the surest elements of victory, it will readily be seen that the judicious selection of generals is one of the most delicate points in the science of government and one of the most essential parts of the military policy of a state. Unfortunately, this choice is influenced by so many petty passions that chance, rank, age, favor, party spirit, or jealousy will have as much to do with it as the public interest and justice.

Military Institutions

One of the most important points of the military policy of a state is the nature of its military institutions. A good

---

* Irregular troops supported by disciplined troops may be of the greatest value in destroying convoys, intercepting communications, etc., and may—as in the case of the Russians in 1812—make a retreat very disastrous.

army commanded by a general of ordinary capacity may accomplish great feats; a bad army with a good general my do equally well; but an army will certainly do a great deal more if its own superiority and that of the general be combined.

Twelve essential conditions concur in making a perfect army:

1. To have a good recruiting-system,
2. A good organization,
3. A well-organized system of national reserves,
4. Good combat, staff, and administrative instruction,
5. A strict but not humiliating discipline, and a spirit of subordination and punctuality, based on conviction rather than on the formalities of the service, and
6. A well-established system of rewards, suitable to excite emulation;
7. The special arms of engineering and artillery to be well instructed;
8. To have an armament superior, if possible, to that of the enemy, as to both defensive and offensive arms,
9. A general staff capable of applying these elements and organized to advance the theoretical and practical education of its officers,
10. A good system for the commissariat, hospitals, and of general administration, and
11. A good system of assignment to command and of directing the principal operations of war;
12. To excite and keep alive the military spirit of the people.

None of these twelve conditions can be neglected without grave inconvenience.

We are far from saying that a government should sacrifice everything to the army, for this would be absurd, but it ought to make the army the object of its constant care.

There are, indeed, forms of government which do not always allow the executive the power of adopting the best systems. When the control of the public funds is in the hands of those affected by local interest or party spirit, they may be so over-scrupulous and penurious as to take all power to carry on the war from the executive, whom many people seem to regard as a public enemy rather than as a chief devoted to all the national interests. The abuse of badly understood public liberties may also contribute to this deplorable result.

I am far from advising that states should always have the hand upon the sword and always be established on a war-footing. Such a condition of things would be a scourge for the human race, and would not be possible except under conditions not existing in all countries. I simply mean that civilized governments ought always to be ready to carry on a war in a short time—that they should never be found unprepared.

If in ordinary times, under the restrictions of constitutional forms, governments subjected to all the changes of an elective legislature are less suitable than others for the creation or preparation of a formidable military power, nevertheless in great crises these deliberative bodies have sometimes attained very different results and have concurred in developing the national strength to the fullest extent.

It is particularly necessary to watch over the preservation of armies in the interval of a long peace, when they are most likely to degenerate. It is important to foster the military spirit in the armies and to exercise them in great maneuvers which, though but faintly resembling those of actual war, still are of decided advantage in preparing them for war.

As to rewards and promotion, it is essential to respect long service and at the same time to open a way for merit. Three-fourths of the promotions in each grade should be made according to the roster, with the remaining fourth reserved for those distinguished for merit and zeal. In time of war, however, the regular order of promotion should be suspended, or at least reduced to a third of the promotions, leaving the majority for brilliant conduct and marked services.

Superiority of armament may increase the chances of success in war. It does not of itself gain battles, but it is a great element of success.

The new inventions of the last twenty years seem to threaten a great revolution in army organization, armament, and tactics. Strategy alone will remain unaltered, with its principles the same as under the Scipios and Caesars, Frederick and Napoleon, since they are independent of the nature of the arms and the organization of the troops.

The Congreve rockets, the effect and direction of which it is said the Austrians can now regulate, the shrapnel howitzers, which throw a stream of canister as far as the range of a bullet, the Perkins steam-guns, which vomit forth as many balls as a battalion—all will multiply the chances of destruction, as though the hecatombs of Eylau, Borodino, Leipsig, and Waterloo were not sufficient to decimate the European races.

The means of destruction are approaching perfection with frightful rapidity.*

We will here recapitulate, in a few words, the essential bases of the military policy which ought to be adopted by a wise government.

1. The prince should receive an education both political and military. He will more probably find men of administrative ability in his councils than good statesmen or soldiers, hence he should be both of the latter himself.

2. If the prince in person does not lead his armies, it will be his first duty and his nearest interest to have his place well supplied. He must confide the glory of his reign and the safety of his states to the general most capable of directing his armies.

3. The permanent army should not only always be

---

* And we are saying the same thing today about proximity fuzes, recoilless weapons, guided missiles, jet propulsion, and nuclear weapons. EDITOR.

upon a respectable footing, but it should be capable of being doubled, if necessary, by reserves, which should always be prepared. Its instruction and discipline should be of a high character, as well as its organization; its armament should be at least as good as that of its neighbors, and superior if possible.

4. The materiel of war should also be upon the best footing, and abundant. National jealousy should not be allowed to prevent the adoption of all improvements devised in other countries.

5. It is necessary that the study of the military sciences should be encouraged and rewarded as well as courage and zeal. The military corps should be esteemed and honored; this is the only way of securing for the army men of merit and genius.

6. In times of peace the general staff should plan for all possible contingencies of war. Its archives should contain the historical details of the past, and all statistical, geographical, topographical, and strategic treatises and papers for the present and future. Hence it is essential that the chief of this corps, with a number of its officers, should be permanently stationed at the capital in time of peace; the war-office should be simply that of the general staff.

7. Nothing should be neglected to acquire a knowledge of the geography and the military statistics of other states, so as to know their material and moral capacity for attack and defense as well as the strategic advantages of the two parties. Distinguished officers should be employed in these scientific labors, and should be rewarded when they demonstrate marked ability.

8. When a war is decided upon, it becomes necessary to prepare not an entire plan of operations—which is always impossible—but a system of operations in reference to a prescribed aim; to provide a base, as well as all the material means necessary to guarantee the success of the enterprise.

9. The system of operations ought to be determined by

the object of the war, the kind of forces of the enemy, the nature and resources of the country, and the characters of the nations and of their chiefs whether of the army or of the state. In fine, it should be based upon the moral and material means of attack or defense which the enemy may be able to bring into action, and it ought to take into consideration the probable alliances that may obtain in favor of or against either of the parties during the war.

10. The financial condition of a nation is to be weighed among the chances of a war. Still, it would be dangerous to constantly attribute to this condition the importance attached to it by Frederick the Great in the history of his times. He was probably right at his epoch, when armies were chiefly recruited by voluntary enlistment and the last crown brought the last soldier. But when national levies are well organized money will no longer exercise the same influence, at least not for one or two campaigns. If England has proved that money will procure soldiers and auxiliaries, France has shown that love of country and honor are equally productive and that, when necessary, war may be made to support war.

A power might be overrunning with gold and still defend itself very badly. Indeed, history proves that the richest nation is neither the strongest nor the happiest. Iron weighs at least as much as gold in the scales of military strength. Still, we must admit that a happy combination of wise military institutions, of patriotism, of well-regulated finances, and of internal wealth and public credit imparts to a nation the greatest strength and makes it best capable of sustaining a long war.

The Command of Armies

Is it an advantage to a state to have its armies commanded in person by the monarch? Whatever may be the decision on this point, it is certain that if the prince possess the genius of Frederick, Peter the Great, or Napoleon he will be far from leaving to his generals the honor of performing great actions which he might do himself, for in this he would be untrue to his own glory and to the well-being of the country.

When a prince feels the necessity of taking the field at the head of his armies but lacks the necessary self-confidence to assume the supreme direction of affairs, he should be accompanied by two generals of the best capacity: one of them a man of executive ability, the other a well-instructed staff officer. This, unfortunately, is not always done.

In what respects will this choice of a commander be difficult, even when the executive is most anxious to make it a judicious one? In the first place, to choose a skillful general requires either that the person who makes the selection shall be a military man, able to form an intelligent opinion, or that he should be guided by the opinions of others, which opens the way to the improper influence of cliques. The embarrassment is certainly less when there is at hand a general already illustrious by many victories; but, aside from the fact that every general is not a great leader because he has gained a battle (for instance, Jourdan[4] and Scherer[5]), a victorious general is not always at the disposal of the government. In this case it will be difficult to decide whether one general is better than another. Those who have served long in peace will be at the head of their arms or corps, and will have the rank appropriate for this position—but will they always be the most capable of filling it?

The most essential qualities for a general will always be: *first,* a high moral courage, capable of great resolution; *second,* a physical courage which takes no account of danger. His scientific or military acquirements are secondary to these. It is not necessary that he should be a man of vast erudition; his knowledge may be limited but it should be thorough, and he should be perfectly grounded in the principles at the base of the art of war.

Next in importance come the qualities of his personal character. A man who is gallant, just, firm, upright, capable of esteeming merit in others instead of being jealous of it, and skillful in making this merit add to his own glory, will always be a good general and may even pass for a great man. Unfortunately, the disposition to do justice to merit in others is not the most common quality: mediocre minds are always jealous and inclined to surround themselves with persons of little ability, fearing the reputation of being led and not realizing that the nominal commander of an army always receives almost all the glory of its success, even wher least entitled to it.

Often it is asked, is it preferable to assign to the command a general of long experience in service with troops, or an officer of the staff with little experience in the management of troops? Beyond question war is a distinct science, and it is quite possible to be able to combine operations skillfully without ever having led a regiment against an enemy: Peter the Great, Condé, Frederick, and Napoleon furnish examples. It cannot be denied, then, that an officer from the staff may as well as any other prove to be a great general—but he will be capable of the supreme command not because he has grown gray in the duties of a quartermaster, but rather because he has a natural genius for war and possesses the requisite characteristics. So, also, a general from the ranks of the infantry or cavalry may be as capable of conducting a campaign as the most profound tactician. Hence this question does not admit of a definite answer, since almost all will depend upon the personal qualities of the individuals. The following remarks will be useful, however, in leading to a rational conclusion:

1. A general selected from the general staff, engineers, or artillery and who has commanded a division or a corps d'armée will, with equal chances, be superior to one who is familiar with the service of but one arm or special corps.

2. A general from the line who has made a study of the science of war will be equally fitted for the command.

3. The character of the man is above all other requisites in a commander-in-chief.

Finally, the union of wise theory with great character will constitute the great general.

The difficulty of always selecting a good general has led to the formation of a good general staff, which being near the general may advise him and thus exercise a beneficial influence over the operations. A well-instructed general staff is one of the most useful of organizations, but care must be observed to prevent the introduction into it of false principles.

Accordingly, I think it is safe to conclude that the best means of organizing the command of an army, in default of a general approved by experience, is to:

1st. Give the command to a man of tried bravery, bold in the fight and of unshaken firmness in danger.

2d. Assign as his chief of staff a man of high ability, of open and faithful character, between whom and the commander there may be perfect harmony. The victor will gain so much glory that he can spare some to the friend who has contributed to his success. In this way Blücher,[6] aided by Gneisenau[7] and Muffling,[8] gained glory which probably he would not have been able to have earned himself.

Military Spirit and Morale

Adoption of the best regulations for the organization of an army would be in vain if the government did not at the same time cultivate a military spirit in its citizens. It was to the union of the civic virtues and military spirit fostered by their institutions that the Romans were indebted for their grandeur. When they lost these virtues and when, no longer regarding the military service as an honor as well as a duty, they relinquished it to mercenary Goths and Gauls, the fall of the empire became inevitable.

It is doubtless true that whatever increases the prosperity of the country should be neither neglected nor despised. It is also necessary to honor the branches of industry which are the first instruments of this prosperity, but they should always be secondary to the great institutions which make

up the strength of states in encouraging the cultivation
of the manly and heroic virtues. Policy and justice both
agree on this point for, whatever Boileau[9] may say, it is
certainly more glorious to confront death in the footsteps
of the Caesars than to fatten upon the public miseries.

The first means of encouraging the military spirit is to
invest the army with all possible social and public consideration. The second is to give to those who have
rendered services to the state a preference in filling any
vacancies in the administrative departments of the government, or even to require a certain length of military service
as a qualification for certain offices. If these administrative
offices were conferred upon officers retired from the army
in a grade not lower than that of captain, would it not be
a stimulant for officers to attain that rank and would it
not lead them, when in garrisons, to find their recreations
elsewhere than in the theaters and public clubs?

The enthusiasm of an army and its military spirit are
two quite different things, and should not be confounded
even though they produce the same effects. The first is
the effect of more or less temporary passions—of a political
or religious nature, for instance, or of a great love of
country; while the latter, depending upon the skill of the
commander and resulting from military institutions, is
more permanent, depends less upon circumstances, and
should be the object of the attention of every far-seeing
government.* Courage should be recompensed and honored, the different grades of rank respected, and discipline
should exist in the sentiments and convictions rather than
in external forms only.

The officers should feel the conviction that resignation,
bravery, and faithful attention to duty are virtues without
which no glory is possible and no army is respectable, and
that firmness amid reverses is more honorable than enthusiasm in success—since courage alone is necessary to storm a

---

* It is particularly important that this spirit should pervade the
officers and non-commissioned officers: if they be capable and the
nation brave, there need be no fear for the men.

position whereas it requires heroism to make a difficult retreat before a victorious and enterprising enemy, always opposing to him a firm and unbroken front.

By inuring armies to labor and fatigue, by keeping them from stagnation in garrison in times of peace, by inculcating their superiority over their enemies (without depreciating the latter too much), by inspiring a love for great exploits—in a word, by exciting their enthusiasm by every means in harmony with their tone of mind, by honoring courage, punishing weakness, and disgracing cowardice—we may expect to maintain a high military spirit.

Both officers and troops must be warned against those sudden panics which often seize the bravest armies when they are not well controlled by discipline, and when they do not recognize that the surest hope of safety lies in order. An army seized with panic is in a state of demoralization because when disorder is once introduced all concerted action on the part of individuals becomes impossible, the voice of the officers can no longer be heard. no maneuver for resuming the battle can be executed, and there is no course except ignominious flight.

NOTES

[1]1782-1856. Russian field marshal from 1828.

[2]1729-1800. Russian field marshal 1794. Born in Finland of Swedish descent.

[3]1752-1828. Austrian general.

[4]1762-1833. Marshal of France 1804.

[5]1747-1804. French Revolutionary general.

[6]1742-1819. Prussian field marshal.

[7]1760-1831. Prussian field marshal.

[8]1775-1851. Prussian field marshal.

[9]1636-1711. French critic.

III. STRATEGY

Strategy is the art of making war upon the map, and comprehends the whole theater of operations. Grand tactics is the art of posting troops upon the battlefield according to the characteristics of the ground, of bringing them into action, and of fighting upon the ground, in contradistinction to planning upon a map. Logistics comprises the means and arrangements which work out the plans of strategy and tactics. Strategy decides where to act; logistics brings the troops to this point; grand tactics decides the manner of execution and the employment of the troops.

It is true that many battles have been decided by strategic movements and have been, indeed, but a succession of them, but this only occurs in the exceptional case of a dispersed army. For the general case of pitched battles the above definition holds good.

Strategy embraces:

1. Selection of the theater of war, and the discussion of the different combinations which it allows.

2. Determination of the decisive points in these combinations and the most favorable direction for operations.

3. Selection and establishment of the fixed base and of the zone of operations.

4. Selection of the objective point, whether offensive or defensive.

5. The strategic fronts, lines of defense, and fronts of operations.

6. Choice of lines of operations leading to the objective point or strategic front.

7. For a given operation, the best strategic line and the different maneuvers necessary to embrace all possible cases.

8. The eventual bases of operations and the strategic reserves.

9. The marches of armies, considered as maneuvers.

10. The relations between the positions of depots and the marches of the army.

11. Fortresses regarded as strategical means, as a refuge for an army, as an obstacle to its progress; the sieges to be made and to be covered.

12. Points for intrenched camps, *tetes de ponts,* etc.

13. Diversions to be made and the large detachments necessary.

The Fundamental Principle of War

One great principle underlies all the operations of war —a principle which must be followed in all good combinations. It is embraced in the following maxims:

1. To throw by strategic movements the mass of an army, successively, upon the decisive points of a theater of war, and also upon the communications of the enemy as much as possible without compromising one's own.

2. To maneuver to engage fractions of the hostile army with the bulk of one's forces.

3. On the battlefield, to throw the mass of the forces upon the decisive point, or upon that portion of the hostile line which it is of the first importance to overthrow.

4. To so arrange that these masses shall not only be thrown upon the decisive point, but that they shall engage at the proper times and with ample energy.

This principle has too much simplicity to escape criticism. One objection is that while it is easy to recommend throwing the mass of the forces upon the decisive points, the difficulty lies in recognizing those points.

The general theater of operations seldom contains more than three zones—the right, the left, and the center. Each zone, front of operations, strategic position, and line of defense, as well as each line of battle, has the same subdivisions of two extremities and a center. A blow upon one of these three will always be suitable for the attainment of the desired end. A blow upon one of the two remaining will be less advantageous, while upon the third it will be wholly inapplicable. The proper selection of one of these three simple alternatives cannot, surely, be considered an enigma.

The art of giving the proper direction to the masses is certainly the basis of strategy, although it is not the whole of the art of war. Executive talent, skill, energy, and a quick comprehension of events are necessary to carry out any combinations previously arranged.

Systems of Operations

War having been determined upon, the first point to be decided is whether it shall be offensive or defensive. There are several phases of the offensive: if against a great state the whole or a large portion of whose territory is attacked, it is an *invasion;* if only a province or a line of defense of moderate extent be assailed, it is the ordinary *offensive;* finally, if the offensive is but an attack upon the enemy's position, and is confined to a single operation, it is called taking the *initiative.* In a moral and political view the offensive is nearly always advantageous: it carries the war upon foreign soil, saves the assailant's country from devastation, increases his resources and diminishes those of his enemy, elevates the morale of his army, and generally depresses the adversary. But it sometimes happens that invasion excites the ardor and energy of the adversary, particularly when he feels that the independence of his country is threatened.

From a military point of view the offensive has its good and its bad sides. Strategically, an invasion leads to deep lines of operations, which are always dangerous in a hostile country. All the obstacles in the enemy's country—the mountains, rivers, defiles, and forts—are favorable for defense; the inhabitants and authorities of the country are generally hostile. If success be obtained, however, the enemy is struck in a vital point; he is deprived of his resources and compelled to seek a speedy termination of the contest.

For a single operation (which we have called taking the

initiative) the offensive is almost always advantageous, particularly in strategy.

Indeed, if the art of war consists in throwing the masses upon the decisive points, it is necessary to take the initiative. The attacking party knows what he is doing and what he desires to do; he leads his masses to the point where he desires to strike. He who awaits the attack is everywhere anticipated; the enemy fall with large force upon fractions of his force; he neither knows where his adversaries propose to attack him nor in what manner to repel them.

Tactically the offensive also possesses advantages, but they are less positive. Since the operations are limited, the party taking the initiative cannot conceal them from the enemy, who may detect his designs and by the aid of good reserves cause them to fail.

A defensive war is not without its advantages, when wisely conducted. It may be passive or active, taking the offensive at times. The passive defense is always pernicious, but the active may accomplish great successes. The object of a defensive war being to protect as long as possible the country threatened by the enemy, all operations should be designed to retard his progress and to annoy him by multiplying obstacles and difficulties, without, however, compromising one's own army. He who invades does so by reason of some superiority; he will then seek to make the issue as promptly as possible. The defender, on the contrary, desires delay till his adversary is weakened by sending off detachments, by marches, and by privation and fatigue.

An army is reduced to the defensive only by reverses or by a positive inferiority. If what may be called the defensive-offensive is used, it may have strategical as well as tactical advantages. It combines the advantages of both systems, for one who awaits his adversary upon a prepared field, with all his own resources in hand, surrounded by all the advantages of being on his own ground, can take the initiative with hope of success.

During the first three campaigns of the Seven **Years'**
War[1] Frederick the Great was the assailant; in the remaining four his conduct was a perfect model of the defensive-offensive. Wellington's course was mainly the same
in Portugal, Spain, and Belgium, and it was the most
suitable in his circumstances. It seems plain that one of
the greatest talents of a general is to know how to use
these two systems, perhaps alternately, and particularly to
be able to take the initiative during the progress of a
defensive war.

The Theater of Operations

The theater of war comprises all the territory (ground
and sea) upon which the parties may assail each other,
whether it belongs to themselves, their allies, or to weaker
states who may be drawn into the war through fear or
interest. When the war is also maritime, the theater may
embrace both hemispheres.

Independently of its topographical features, each theater
upon which one or more armies operate is composed, for
both parties, of:

1. A fixed based of operations.
2. A principal objective point.
3. Fronts of operations, strategic fronts, and lines of
defense.
4. Zones and lines of operations.
5. Temporary strategic lines and lines of communications.
6. Natural or artificial obstacles to be overcome or to
oppose to the enemy.
7. Geographical strategic points whose occupation is
important for either the offensive or the defensive.
8. Accidental intermediate bases of operations between
the objective point and the primary base.
9. Points of refuge in case of reverse.

It has been taught that rivers are lines of operations
par excellence. Since such a line must possess two or three
roads to move the army within the range of its operations

and at least one line of retreat, rivers have been called lines of retreat and even lines of maneuver. It would be much more accurate to say that rivers are excellent lines of supply and powerful auxiliaries in the establishment of a good line of operations, but never the line itself.

Some authors have affirmed that mountainous countries abound in strategic positions. Others have maintained that, on the contrary, these points are more rare among the Alps than in the plains, and also that because more rare they are more important and more decisive. Some authors have represented that high ranges of mountains are, in war, inaccessible barriers. Napoleon, on the contrary, in speaking of the Rhetian Alps, said that "an army could pass wherever a man could put his foot."

The most important topographical or artificial features which make up the theater of a war will shortly be examined as to their strategic value, but here it is proper to remark that this value will depend much upon the spirit and skill of the general. The great leader who crossed the Saint Bernard and ordered the passage of the Splugen was far from believing in the impregnability of these chains, but he was also far from thinking that a muddy rivulet and a walled inclosure could change his destiny at Waterloo.

Bases of Operations

A base of operations is the portion of country from which the army obtains its reinforcements and resources, from which it starts when it takes the offensive, to which it retreats when necessary, and by which it is supported when it takes position to cover the country defensively.

An army may have in succession a number of bases. For instance, a French army in Germany will have the Rhine for its first base. It may have others beyond this, wherever it has allies or permanent lines of defense, but if it is driven back across the Rhine it will have for a base either the Meuse or the Moselle. It might have a third upon the Seine, and a fourth upon the Loire.

These successive bases may not be entirely or nearly parallel to the first. On the contrary, a total change of direction may become necessary. A French army repulsed beyond the Rhine might find a good base on Béfort or Besancon, on Mézières or Sedan, as the Russian army after the evacuation of Moscow (1812) left the base on the north and east and established itself upon the line of the Oka and the southern provinces. These lateral bases perpendicular to the front of defense are often decisive in preventing the enemy from penetrating to the heart of the country, or at least in making it impossible for him to maintain himself there. A base upon a broad and rapid river, both banks being held by strong works, would be as favorable as could be desired.

The more extended the base, the more difficulty will there be in covering it—but it will also be more difficult to cut the army off from it. A state whose capital is too near the frontier cannot have so favorable a base in a defensive war as one whose capital is more retired.

Strategic, Decisive, and Objective Points

Every point of the theater of war which is of military importance, whether from its position as a center of communication or from the presence of military establishments or fortifications, is a *geographical strategic point.* For example, take the case of the French in Belgium: whoever is master of the line of the Meuse will have the greatest advantages in taking possession of the country, for his adversary, being outflanked and inclosed between the Meuse and the North Sea, will be exposed to the danger of total ruin if he give battle parallel to that sea.* Similarly, the valley of the Danube presents a series of important points which have caused it to be looked upon as the key of southern Germany.

Those points the possession of which would give the

---

* This only applies to continental armies and not to the English, who, having their base on Antwerp or Ostend, would have nothing to fear from an occupation of the line of the Meuse.

control of the junction of several valleys and of the center of the chief lines of communication in a country are also *decisive geographic points*. Leipsig is most certainly a strategic point, inasmuch as it is at the junction of all the communications of northern Germany.

All capitals are strategic points, for the double reason that they are not only centers of communications but also the seats of power and government.

In mountainous countries defiles, the only routes of exit practicable for an army, may be decisive in reference to an enterprise.

Others have a value from the relations they bear to the positions of the masses of the hostile troops and to the enterprises likely to be directed against them; such are *strategic points of maneuver*. Finally, there are points which have only a secondary importance and others whose importance is constant and immense; the latter are called *decisive strategic points*.

I think the name of *decisive strategic point* should be given to all those which are capable of exercising a marked influence either upon the result of the campaign or upon a single enterprise.

It may be laid down as a general principle that the decisive points of maneuver are on that flank of the enemy upon which, if his opponent operates, he can more easily cut him off from his base and supporting forces without being exposed to the same danger. The flank opposite to the sea is always to be preferred because it gives an opportunity of forcing the enemy upon the sea. The only exception to this is in the case of an insular and inferior army, in which case the attempt, although dangerous, might be made to cut it off from the fleet.

If the enemy's forces are in detachments or are too much extended the decisive point is his center, for by piercing that his forces will be more divided, their weakness increased, and the fractions crushed separately.

The decisive point of a battlefield is determined by:

1. Features of the ground.
2. Relation of the local features to the ultimate strategic aim.
3. Positions occupied by the respective forces.

There are two classes of objective points—objective *points of maneuver* and *geographical objective points*. A geographical objective point may be an important fortress, the line of a river, or a front of operations which affords good lines of defense or good points of support for ulterior enterprises. Objective points of maneuver, in contradistinction, derive their importance from (and their positions depend upon) the situation of the hostile masses.

In strategy, the object of the campaign determines the objective point. If this aim be offensive, the point will be the possession of the hostile capital or that of a province whose loss would compel the enemy to make peace. In a war of invasion the capital is, ordinarily, the objective point. In the defensive the objective point, instead of being that which it is desirable to gain possession of, is that which must be defended.

As to the objective points of maneuvers—that is, those which relate particularly to the destruction or decomposition of the hostile forces—their importance may be seen by what has already been said. The greatest talent of a general and the surest hope of success lie in some degree in the good choice of these points. This was the most conspicuous merit of Napoleon. Rejecting old systems, which were satisfied by the capture of one or two points or with the occupation of an adjoining province, he was convinced that the best means of accomplishing great results was to dislodge and destroy the hostile army, since states and provinces fall of themselves when there is no organized force to protect them. To detect at a glance the relative advantages presented by the different zones of operations, to concentrate the mass of the forces upon that one which gave the best promise of success, to be indefatigable in ascertaining the approximate position of the enemy, to fall like lightning upon his center if his front was too much extended or upon that flank by which he could more readily seize his communications, to outflank him, to cut his line, to pursue him to the last, to disperse and destroy his forces—such was the system followed by Napoleon in his first campaigns. These proved this system to be one of the very best.

When in later years these maneuvers were applied to the great distances and the inhospitable regions of Russia, they were not so successful as in Germany. It must be remembered, however, that even if this kind of war is not suitable to all capacities, regions, or circumstances, its chances of success are still very great, and it is based upon principle. Napoleon abused the system—but this does not disprove its real advantages when a proper limit is assigned to its enterprises and they are made in harmony with the respective conditions of the armies and of the adjoining states.

Fronts of Operations and Strategic Fronts

When the masses of an army are posted in a zone of operations, they generally occupy strategic positions. The extent of the front occupied toward the enemy is called the *strategic front*. The portion of the theater of war from which an enemy can probably reach this front in two or three marches is called the *front of operations*.

When a campaign is about to open, usually one of the armies will decide to await the attack of the other and will undertake to prepare a line of defense, which may be either that of the strategic front or more to the rear. Hence the strategic front and line of defense may coincide, as was the case in 1795 and 1796 upon the Rhine, which was then a line of defense for both Austrians and French and at the same time their strategic front and front of operations. This occasional coincidence of these lines doubtless leads persons to confound them, though they are really very different. An army has not necessarily a line of defense, as, for example, when it invades; when its masses are concentrated in a single position, it has no strategic front; but it is never without a front of operations.

The front of operations, being the space which separates the two armies and upon which they may fight, is ordinarily parallel to the base of operations. It will have the same direction and ought to be perpendicular to the principal line of operations, and to extend far enough on either flank to cover this line well. This direction may vary, however, either on account of projects that are formed or on account of the attacks of the enemy. And quite frequently it is necessary to have a front perpendicular to the base and parallel to the original line of operations. Such a change of strategic front is one of the most important of all grand maneuvers for by this means the control of two faces of the strategic field may be obtained, thus giving the army a position almost as favorable as if it possessed a base with two faces.

Lines of Defense

Lines of defense are classified as strategical and tactical. The former are subdivided into: 1. permanent lines of defense, which are a part of the defensive system of a state, such as the line of a fortified frontier, and 2. eventual lines of defense, which relate only to the temporary position of an army.

Every river of any considerable width, every range of mountains, and every defile, having their weak points covered by temporary fortifications, may be regarded as eventual lines of defense, both strategic and tactical, since they may arrest for some time the progress of the enemy or may compel him to deviate in search of a weaker point— in which case the advantage is evidently strategic. If the enemy attack in front, the lines present an evident tactical advantage, since it is always more difficult to drive an army from its position behind a river or from a point naturally and artificially strong than to attack it on an open plain. On the other hand this advantage must not be considered to be unqualified lest we should fall into the system of positions which has been the ruin of so many armies, for, whatever may be the facilities of a position for defense, it is quite certain that the party which remains in it passive and receiving all the attacks of his adversary will finally yield.*

Strategic Positions

Strategic positions are those occupied for some time and which are intended to cover a much greater portion of the front of operations than would be covered in an actual battle. Napoleon's positions at Rivoli (1797), Verona (1796), and Legnano (1797) to overlook the Adige River, and in 1813 in Saxony and Silesia in advance of his line of defense, were strategic. Those of the Anglo-Prussian armies on the frontier of Belgium before the battle of Ligny (1815) and of Massena on the Limmat and Aar in 1799, were also strategic.

Maxims on this subject are few, since fronts, lines of defense, and strategic positions generally depend upon a multitude of circumstances giving rise to infinite variety. But in every case the first general rule is that the communications with the different points of the line of operations be thoroughly assured.

In the defense it is desirable that the strategic fronts and lines of defense should present upon both the flanks and the front formidable natural or artificial obstacles to serve as points of support. Points of support on the strategic front are called pivots of operations; they are practically temporary bases, but quite different from pivots of maneuver. For example, in 1796 Verona was an excellent pivot of operations for all Napoleon's enterprises about Mantua for eight months. In 1813 Dresden was his pivot.

Pivots of maneuver are detachments of troops left to guard points which it is essential to hold while the bulk

* This does not refer to intrenched camps, which make a great difference.

of the army proceeds to the fulfillment of some important
end; when this is accomplished the pivot of maneuver
ceases to exist. Thus, Ney's corps was the pivot of Napoleon's maneuver via Donauwerth and Augsburg to cut
Mack from his line of retreat. A pivot of operations, on
the contrary, is a material point of support and endures
throughout a campaign.

The most desirable quality of a line of defense is that
it should be as short as possible, in order to be readily
covered by the army if it is compelled to take the defensive. It is also important that the extent of the strategic
front should not be so great as to prevent prompt concentration of the fractions of the army upon an advantageous point.

For an army entering a country with the purpose either
of subjugation or of temporary occupation it would always
be prudent, however brilliant may have been its earlier
successes, to prepare a line of defense as a refuge in case
of reverse.

Zones and Lines of Operations

A zone of operations is a certain fraction of the whole
theater of war which may be traversed by an army in
the attainment of its object, whether it act singly or in
concert with other and secondary armies.

The term *zone of operations* is applied to a large fraction of the general theater of war, *lines of operations* to
the part of this fraction embraced by the enterprises of
the army. Whether it follow a single or several routes,
the term *strategic lines* applies to those important lines
which connect the decisive points of the theater of operations either with each other or with the front of operations.
For the same reason, we give this name to those lines
which the army would follow to reach one of these
decisive points or to accomplish an important maneuver
which requires a temporary deviation from the principal
line of operations. *Lines of communications* designate the
practicable routes between the different portions of the

army occupying different positions throughout the zone of operations.

The choice of a zone of operations involves no extensive combinations since there can never be more than two or three zones in each theater and the advantages generally result from the locations. It is somewhat different with lines of operations, as they are divided into different classes according to their relations to the different positions of the enemy, to the communications upon the strategic field, and to the operations planned by the commander.

Simple lines of operations are those of an army acting from a frontier when it is not subdivided into large independent bodies.

Double lines of operations are those of two armies, independent or not, proceeding from the same frontier, or those of two nearly equal armies commanded by the same general but widely separated in distance and for long intervals of time.*

Interior lines of operations are those adopted by one or two armies to oppose several hostile bodies. Their direction allows the general to concentrate the masses and maneuver with his whole force in a shorter time than the enemy would require to oppose to them a greater force.

---

* This definition has been criticized. As it has given rise to misapprehension, it should be explained.

In the first place, it must be borne in mind that it is a question of *maneuver-lines* (that is, of strategic combinations) and not of great routes. It must also be admitted that an army marching upon two or three routes, near enough to each other to permit the concentration of the different masses within forty-eigh hours, would not have two or three lines of operations. When Moreau[2] and Jourdan[3] entered Germany with two independent armies of 70,000 men each, there was a double line of operations, but a French army of which only a detachment starts from the Lower Rhine to march on the Main while the five or six other corps set out from the Upper Rhine to march on Ulm would not have a double line of operations in the sense in which I use the term to designate a maneuver. Napoleon, when he concentrated seven corps and set them in motion by Bamberg to march on Gera while Mortier with a single corps marched on Cassel to occupy Hesse and flank the principal enterprise, had but a single general line of operations with an accessory detachment. The territorial line was composed of two arms or radii, but the operation was not double.

Exterior lines lead to the opposite result. They are formed by an army which operates at the same time on both flanks of the enemy, or against several of his masses.

Concentric lines of operations depart from widely separated points and meet at the same point, either in advance of or behind the base.

Divergent lines are those by which an army would leave a given point to move upon several distinct points. These lines of course require the subdivision of the army.

There are also *deep lines,* which are simply *long lines.*

The term *maneuver lines* I apply to momentary strategic lines, often adopted for a single temporary maneuver. These are by no means to be confounded with the real *lines of operations.*

Secondary lines are those of two armies acting so as to afford each other mutual support—as, in 1796, the army of the Sambre and Meuse was secondary to the army of the Rhine and, in 1812, at Borodino the army of Bagration[4] was secondary to that of Barclay.[5]

Accidental lines are brought about by events which change the original plan and give a new direction to operations. The proper occasions for their use are fully recognized only by a great and active mind.

Comparison of the combinations and results of the most noted campaigns shows that the lines of operations which have led to success have been established in conformity with the fundamental principle already alluded to: that *simple and interior lines enable a general to bring into action, by strategic movements, upon the important point, a stronger force than the enemy.* The student may also satisfy himself that those which have failed contained faults opposed to this principle: an undue number of lines divides the forces and permits fractions to be overwhelmed by the enemy.

From the analysis of many events, the following maxims result:

If the art of war consists in bringing into action upon

the decisive point of the theater of operations the greatest possible force, the choice of the line of operations (as the primary means of attaining this end) may be regarded as fundamental in devising a good plan for a campaign. Napoleon proved this by the direction he gave his armies in 1805 on Donauwerth and in 1806 on Gera—maneuvers that military men cannot study too much.

It may be stated as a general principle that if the enemy divide his forces on an extended front the best direction of the maneuver line will be upon his center, but in every other case when it is possible the best direction will be upon one of the flanks, and then upon the rear of his line of defense or front of operations.

The advantage of this maneuver arises more from the opportunity it affords of taking the line of defense in reverse than from the fact that by using it the assailant has to contend with but a part of the enemy's force. Thus the army of the Rhine in 1800, gaining the extreme left of the line of defense of the Black Forest, caused it to yield almost without an effort. On the right bank of the Danube this army fought two battles which, although not decisive, from the judicious direction of the line of operations brought about the invasion of Swabia and Bavaria. The results of the march of the army of the reserve by way of the Saint Bernard and Milan[6] upon the extreme right of Melas,[7] were still more brilliant. But even when the extremity of the enemy's front of operations is gained it is not always safe to act upon his rear, since by so doing the assailant in many cases will lose his own communications.

Two independent armies should not be formed upon the same frontier. Such an arrangement could be proper only in the case of large coalitions or where the forces are too great to act within the same zone of operations—and even in this case it would be better to have all the forces under the same commander, who accompanies the principal army.

As a consequence of the last-mentioned principle, *with*

equal forces on the same frontier a single line of operations will be more advantageous than a double one.

It may happen, however, that a double line will be necessary, either from the topography of the seat of war, or because a double line has been adopted by the enemy and it will be necessary to oppose a part of the army* to each of his masses. In this case interior or central lines will be preferable to exterior lines, since in the former case the fractions of the army can be concentrated before those of the enemy and thus may decide the fate of the campaign.*

A double line is applicable in the case of a decided superiority of force, when each army will be a match for any strength the enemy can bring against it, since a single line would crowd the forces so much as to prevent them all from acting to advantage. However, it will always be prudent to support well the army which, by reason of the nature of its theater and the respective positions of the parties, has the most important mission.

The principal events of modern wars demonstrate the truth of two other maxims. The first is that *two armies operating on interior lines*, sustaining each other reciprocally, and opposing two armies superior in numbers, should not allow themselves to be crowded into too contracted a space, where the whole might be overwhelmed at once. This happened to Napoleon at Leipsig in 1813. The second is that *interior lines* should not be abused by extending them too far and thus giving the enemy the opportunity of overcoming the corps of observation.

For the same reason, *two converging lines* are more advantageous than two divergent. The first conform better to the principles of strategy and possess the advantage of covering the lines of communication and supply, but to be free from danger they should be so arranged that the

---

* When the fractions of an army are separated from the main body by only a few marches, and particularly when they are not intended to act separately throughout the campaign, these are central strategic positions and not lines of operations.

armies which pass over them shall not be separately exposed to the combined masses of the enemy before being able to effect their junction.

Divergent lines, however, may be preferable when the center of the enemy has been broken and his forces separated either by a battle or by a strategic movement. In this case divergent operations would add to the dispersion of the enemy. Such divergent lines would be interior, since the pursuers could concentrate more readily than the pursued.

Sometimes an army is obliged to change its line of operations in the middle of a campaign. This is a very delicate and important step which may lead to great successes, or to equally great disasters if not applied with sagacity, and is used only to extricate an army from an embarrassing position.

Another point in reference to these lines is much insisted upon by some, but is actually more specious than important. It is that on each side of the line of operations the country should be cleared of all enemies for a distance equal to the depth of this line, otherwise the enemy might threaten the line of retreat. This rule is everywhere belied by the events of war. The nature of the country, the rivers and mountains, the morale of the armies, the spirit of the people, the ability and energy of the commanders—these cannot be estimated by diagrams on paper. It is true that no considerable bodies of the enemy could be permitted on the flanks of the line of retreat, but compliance with this demand would deprive an army of every means of taking a step in a hostile country. There is not a campaign in recent wars, or in those of Marlborough[8] and Eugene[9] (who joined forces 1704-1708), which does not contradict this assertion. Was not General Moreau at the gates of Vienna when Fussen, Scharnitz, and all the Tyrol were in possession of the Austrians? Was not Napoleon at Piacenza when Turin, Genoa, and the Col-di-Tenda were occupied by the army of Mélas? Did not Eugene march by way of Stradella and Asti to the aid of Turin, leaving the French upon the Mincio but a few leagues from his base?

Having been attacked by vain formulas, it is natural that I should defend myself. The only favor which I ask of my critics is to be as equitable toward me as I am toward them. They want war too methodical, too measured; I would make it brisk, bold, impetuous, perhaps sometimes even audacious.

Far from my mind, however, is any thought of ignoring all the precautions which may flow from the principle of even those measured rules, for they could never be neglected entirely. But to reduce war to geometry would be to impose fetters on the genius of the greatest captains and to submit to the yoke of an exaggerated pedantry. For my part, I shall ever protest against such theories, as well as against the apology of ignorance.

Strategic Reserves

Reserves play an important part in modern warfare. From the executive who prepares national reserves down to the platoon leader, every commander now desires a reserve and deserves one.

The reserves of an army are of two kinds—battlefield, and those in training. While organizing, the latter may occupy important points of the theater of war and even serve as strategic reserves. An army on the offensive should always contemplate the possibility of being compelled to act on the defensive; and by posting a reserve between the base and front of operations it gains the advantage of an active reserve on the field of battle. This force can fly to the support of menaced points without weakening the active army.

By organizing central depots for preparing munitions and equipments, making them the rendezvous of all detachments going to and coming from the army, and strengthening them with cadres from a few good regiments, a reserve capable of important service may be formed.

Napoleon never failed to organize these reserves in his campaigns. Even in 1797, in his bold march on the Noric Alps, he had first Joubert[10] on the Adige, afterward Victor[11] (returning from the Roman States) in the neighborhood of Verona. In 1805 Ney[12] and Augereau[13] played the part alternately in the Tyrol and Bavaria, and Mortier[14] and Marmont[15] near Vienna.

The general's talents will be exercised in determining the best use of reserves according to terrain, the length of the line of operations, the nature of the fortified points, the proximity of a hostile state, and the course of the battle.

Old System vs. New—Positions vs. Marches

By the system of positions is understood the old manner of conducting a methodical war: with armies in tents and their supplies at hand, watching each other; one besieging a city, the other covering it; one perhaps trying to acquire a small province, the other counteracting its efforts by occupying strong points. Such was war from the Middle Ages to the era of the French Revolution.

During this revolution great changes occurred. War was commenced in 1792[16] as it had been in 1762:[17] the French encamped near their strong places, the allies besieged them. Not till 1793, when France was assailed from without and within, was this system changed. Thoroughly aroused, she threw upon her enemies a million men in fourteen armies. These armies had neither tents, provisions, nor money. On their marches they bivouacked or were quartered in towns; their mobility was increased and became a means of success. Their tactics changed also. The troops were put in columns, which were more easily handled than deployed lines, and on account of the broken character of the country of Flanders and the Vosges they threw out part of their force as skirmishers to protect and cover the columns. This system, which was thus the result of circumstances, at first met with spectacular success. It disconcerted the methodical Austrian and

Prussian troops as well as their generals. Mack, to whom
was attributed the success of the Prince of Coburg, increased his reputation by directing the troops to extend
their lines to oppose an open order to the fire of skirmishers. It had never occurred to the poor man that
while the skirmishers made the noise the columns carried
the positions.

When Napoleon made his debut in Italy his activity
worsted the Austrians and Piedmontese. Free from useless
incumbrances, his troops surpassed in mobility all modern
armies. He conquered the Italian peninsula by a series of
marches and strategic combats. His march on Vienna in
1797 was rash, but justified by the necessity of overcoming
the Archduke Charles before he could receive reinforcements from the Rhine.

The campaign of 1800, still more characteristic of the
man, marked a new era in the conception of plans of
campaign and lines of operations. He adopted bold objective points which looked to nothing less than the capture or destruction of whole armies.

The system of Napoleon was to march twenty-five miles
a day, to fight, and then to camp in quiet. He told me
that he knew no other method of conducting war than
this. A great truth was demonstrated by Napoleon's wars
—that remoteness is not a certain safeguard against invasion.

Depots, and Their Relation to Marches

The subject most nearly connected with the system of
marches is the commissariat, for to march quickly and for
a long distance food must be supplied and the problem of
supporting a numerous army in an enemy's country is a
very difficult one. A general should be capable of making
all the resources of the invaded country contribute to the
success of his enterprises. Caesar said that war should
support war, and he is generally believed to have lived
at the expense of the countries he overran.

It is hard to imagine how Darius [18] and Xerxes [19] subsisted their immense armies in Thrace,[20] where now it would be a hard task to supply thirty thousand men.

Under Louis XIV (1638-1715) and Frederick II (1712-1786) the armies were larger; they fought on their own frontiers and lived from their store-houses, which were established as they moved. This interfered greatly with operations, restricting the troops within a distance from the depots which depended upon the available transportation, the rations they could carry, and the number of days necessary for wagons to go to the depots and return to camp.

During the French Revolution depots of supply were necessarily abandoned. The large armies which invaded Belgium and Germany lived sometimes in the houses of the people, sometimes by requisitions laid upon the country, and often by plunder and pillage. To subsist an army on the granaries of Belgium, Italy, Swabia, and the rich banks of the Rhine and Danube is easy, but this would be very difficult in some other countries and quite impossible in Russia, Sweden, Poland, and Turkey.

This system gave Napoleon great advantages; but he abused it by applying it on too large a scale and to countries where it was impracticable.

The depots should be echeloned as much as possible upon three different lines of communication in order to supply the wings of the army more readily, to extend as much as possible the area from which successive supplies are to be drawn, and lastly, in order that the depots should be as well covered as possible. To this end it would be well to have the depots on lines converging toward the principal line of operations, which will generally be found in the center. This arrangement has two real advantages: *first,* the depots are less exposed to the attempts of the enemy, as his distance from them is thereby increased; *secondly,* it facilitates the movements of the army in concentrating upon a single point of the line of operations to the rear, with a view of retaking the initiative from an enemy who may have temporarily assumed the offensive and gained some advantage.

In national wars where the inhabitants fly and destroy everything in their path (as was the case in Spain, Portugal, Russia, and Turkey) it is impossible to advance unless attended by trains of provisions and without having a sure base of supply near the front of operations. Under these circumstances a war of invasion becomes very difficult, if not impossible.

Not only is it necessary to collect large quantities of supplies, but it is indispensable to have the means of conveying them with or after the army. This is the greatest difficulty, particularly on rapid expeditions. To facilitate their transportation, the rations should consist of the most portable articles (as biscuit, rice, etc.), and the wagons should be both light and strong, so as to pass over all kinds of roads.

The vicinity of the sea is invaluable for the transportation of supplies. Whoever is master on this element can supply himself at will.

Navigable streams and canals, when parallel to the line of operations of the army, render the transportation of supplies much easier and also free the roads from the numerous vehicles otherwise necessary. For this reason, lines of operations thus situated are the most favorable.

I will end this article by recording a remark of Napoleon which may appear whimsical, but which is still not without reason. He said that in his first campaigns the enemy was so well provided that when his troops were in want of supplies he had only to fall upon the rear of the enemy to procure everything in abundance. This is a remark upon which it would be absurd to found a system, but which perhaps explains the success of many a rash enterprise and proves how much actual war differs from narrow theory.

Frontier Defense by Forts and Intrenched Lines; Sieges

Forts serve *first* to cover the frontiers, *secondly* to aid the operations of the campaign.

The defense of frontiers is a problem generally somewhat indeterminate. It is not so for those countries whose borders are covered with great natural obstacles, offering but few points of entry and those defendable through the art of the engineer. The problem here is simple, despite Napoleon's remark that "an army can go wherever man can set foot," but in open countries defense is more difficult.

When the topography of a frontier is open, there should be no attempt to make a complete line of defense by building too many fortresses. These require armies to garrison them and, after all, might not prevent an enemy from penetrating the country. This system has been wrongly imputed to Vauban,[21] who, on the contrary, had a controversy with Louvois [22] about the great number of points the latter desired to fortify. It is much wiser to build fewer works and to have them properly located, not with the expectation of absolutely preventing the ingress of the enemy but to multiply the impediments to his progress, and at the same time to support the movements of the army which is to repel him.

While a fortified place of itself rarely absolutely prevents the progress of an army, it is nevertheless an embarrassment and compels the army to detach a part of its force or to make detours. Formerly the false system prevailed of encircling a city by a whole army, which buried itself in lines of circumvallation and contravallation. These lines cost as much in labor and expense as the siege itself. The famous case of the lines of Turin, which were fifteen miles in length and (though guarded by seventy-eight thousand French) were forced by Prince Eugene with forty thousand men in 1706, is enough to condemn this ridiculous system. Experience has proved that the best way to cover a siege is to beat and pursue as far as possible the enemy's forces which could interfere.

On the other hand, a fort imparts corresponding advantages to the army which holds it, covers its depots, flanks, and movements, and finally is a place of refuge in case of need.

Formerly the operations of war were directed against towns, camps, and positions. Recently they have been directed only against organized armies, leaving out of consideration all natural or artificial obstacles. Exclusive use of either of these systems is faulty: the true course is a mean between these extremes.

Large fortified places which are not in proper strategic positions are a positive misfortune for both the army and state.

As a fortress or an intrenched camp may be highly advantageous as a temporary refuge for an army, so to the same degree is the system of intrenched lines absurd. I do not now refer to lines of small extent closing a narrow gorge; I speak of extended lines many leagues in length and intended wholly to close a part of the frontiers. For instance, those of Wissembourg, covered by the Lauter flowing in front and supported by the Rhine on the right and the Vosges on the left, seemed to fulfill all the conditions of safety; yet they were forced every time they were assailed.

However well they may be supported by natural obstacles, their great extent paralyzes their defenders and they are almost always susceptible of being turned. To bury an army in intrenchments, where it may be outflanked and surrounded or forced in front even if secure from a flank attack, is manifest folly. May we never see another instance of it.

Strategic Operations in Mountains

A mountainous country may be the whole theater of the war, or but a zone. It may be mountainous throughout its whole extent, or there may be a line of mountains upon emerging from which the army may debouch into large and rich plains.

If Switzerland, the Tyrol, the Noric provinces, some parts of Turkey and Hungary, Catalonia, and Portugal be excepted, in the European countries the mountains are in single ranges. In these cases there is but a difficult defile to cross—a temporary obstacle which, once overcome, is an advantage rather than an objection. In fact, the range once crossed and the war carried into the plains, the chain of mountains may be regarded as an eventual base upon which the army may fall back and find a temporary refuge. The only essential precaution to be observed is, not to allow the enemy to anticipate the army on this line of retreat.

When an extremely mountainous country (such as the Tyrol or Switzerland) is but a zone of operations, the importance of these mountains is secondary. They must be considered like a fortress, the armies deciding the great contests in the valleys. It will, of course, be otherwise if this be the whole theater of war.

It has long been a question whether possession of the mountains controled the valleys, or whether possession of the valleys controled the mountains. The Archduke Charles, a very intelligent and competent judge, has declared for the latter and demonstrated in 1796 that the valley of the Danube is the key to Southern Germany.

When a country whose whole extent is mountainous is the principal theater of operations, the strategic combinations cannot be based entirely upon maxims applicable in an open country.

Maneuvers parallel to the front of operations of the enemy are always very difficult, often impossible. In such a country a considerable army can be maneuvered only in a small number of valleys, where the enemy will take care to post advanced guards of sufficient strength to delay the army long enough to provide means for defeating the enterprise. Since the ridges which separate these valleys will generally be crossed only by paths impracticable for the passage of an army, transversal marches can be made only by small bodies of light troops.

The important natural strategic points will be at the junctions of the larger valleys or of the streams in those valleys, and will be few in number. If the defensive army occupy them with the mass of its forces, the invader will generally be compelled to resort to direct attacks to dislodge it.

However, if great strategic maneuver in these cases be more rare and difficult, it by no means follows that they are less important. On the contrary, if the attacker gains possession of one of these centers of communication between the large valleys upon the line of retreat of the enemy, it will be more serious for the latter than it would be in an open country since the occupation of one or two difficult defiles will often cause the ruin of the whole army.

If the attacking party has difficulties to overcome, it must be admitted that the defense has quite as many. It must cover all the outlets by which an attack in force may be made upon the decisive points, and faces great difficulties in making the marches required to cover the menaced points.

On the other hand, the general on the defensive may in a level country concentrate a large part of his forces, for if the enemy scatter to occupy all the roads by which the defensive army may retire the latter can easily crush these isolated bodies. But in a very mountainous country, where there are ordinarily but one or two principal routes into which other valleys open, even from the direction of the enemy, the concentration of forces becomes more difficult since serious results may follow if even one of these important valleys be not observed.

Nothing can better demonstrate the difficulty of strategic defense in mountainous regions than the perplexity in which we are involved when we attempt simply to give advice in such cases—to say nothing of laying down maxims for them. If it were but a question of the defense of a single definite front of small extent, consisting perhaps of four or five converging valleys the common junction of which is two or three short marches from the summits of the ranges, it would be easier of solution. Then it would be sufficient to recommend the construction of a good fort at the narrowest and least easily turned point of each of these valleys. Protected by these forts, a few brigades of infantry should be stationed to dispute the passage while half the army should be held in reserve at the junction, where it would be in position either to sustain the advanced guards most seriously threatened or to fall upon the assailant with the whole force when he debouches. If to this be added good instructions to the commanders of the advanced guards, whether in assigning them the best point for rendezvous when their line of forts is pierced or in directing them to continue to act in the mountains upon the flank of the enemy, the general on the defensive may regard himself as invincible, thanks to the many difficulties which the country offers to the assailant. But if there be other fronts like this upon the right and left, all of which are to be defended, the problem is changed: the difficulties of the defense increase with the extent of the fronts, and this system of a cordon of forts becomes dangerous—while it is not easy to adopt a better one.

History seems to prove that if a country covered with high mountains be favorable for defense from a tactical point of view, it is different in a strategic sense because it requires a dispersion of the troops. This can be remedied only by giving them greater mobility and by passing often to the offensive.

General Clausewitz, whose logic is frequently defective, maintains on the contrary that since movements are the most difficult part of this kind of war, the defensive party should avoid them as by such a course he might lose the advantages of the local defenses. He, however, ends by demonstrating that a passive defense must yield under an active attack—which goes to show that the initiative is no less favorable in mountains than in plains. If there could be any doubt on this point, it ought to be dispelled by Massena's campaign in Switzerland in 1799, where he sustained himself only by attacking the enemy at every opportunity, even when he was obliged to seek him on the Grimsel and the Saint Gothard. Napoleon's course was similar in 1796 in the Tyrol, when he was opposed to Wurmser[23] and Alvinczy.[24]

Mountain operations teach us the vanity of all theory *in details,* and also that in such a country a strong and heroic will is worth more than all the precepts in the world. After such lessons, need I say that one of the principal rules of this kind of war is, not to risk one's self in the valleys without securing the heights? Shall I say also that in this kind of war, more than in any other, operations should be directed upon the communications of the enemy? And finally, that good temporary bases or lines of defense at the confluence of the great valleys, covered by strategic reserves, and combined with great mobility and frequent offensive movements, will be the best means of defending the country?

I cannot terminate without remarking that mountainous countries are particularly favorable for defense when the war is a national one, in which the whole people rise to defend their homes with the obstinacy which enthusiasm for a holy cause imparts. Every advance is then dearly bought. But to be successful it is always necessary that the people be sustained by a disciplined force, more or less numerous. Without this they must finally yield.

The offensive against a mountainous country also presents a double case: it may either be directed upon a belt of mountains beyond which are extensive plains, or the whole theater may be mountainous.

In the first case there is little more to be done than to feint upon the whole line of the frontier to induce the enemy to extend his defense, and then force a passage at the point which promises the greatest results. The problem in such a case is to break through a cordon which is strong less on account of the numbers of the defenders than from their position; if broken at one point the whole line is forced. The capture of· Leutasch and Scharnitz in 1805 by Ney (who threw fourteen thousand men on Innsbruck in the midst of thirty thousand Austrians, and by seizing this central point compelled them to retreat in all directions) shows that with brave infantry and bold commanders mountain ranges can generally be forced.

The history of the passage of the Alps, where Francis I turned the army which was awaiting him at Suza[25] by passing the steep mountains between Mont Cenis and the valley of Queyras, is an example of those "insurmountable" obstacles which can always be surmounted.

When we consider the tactical difficulties of this kind of war and the immense advantages it affords the defense, we may be inclined to regard the concentration of a considerable force to penetrate by a single valley as an extremely rash maneuver, and to think that it ought to be divided into as many columns as there are practicable passes. In my opinion this is one of the most dangerous of all illusions. To confirm what I say it is only necessary to refer to the fate of the columns of Championnet[26] at the battle of Fossano (1799). If there be five or six roads on the menaced front they should all, of course, be threatened. But the army should cross the chain in not more than two masses and the routes which these follow should not be divergent, for if they were the enemy might be able to defeat them separately. Napoleon's passage of the Saint Bernard was wisely planned; he formed the bulk of his army on the center with a division on each flank by Mont Cenis and the Simplon, to divide the attention of the enemy and flank his march.

*   *   *

Invasion of a country entirely covered with mountains is a much greater and more difficult task than where a *dénouement* may be accomplished by a decisive battle in the open country, for in a mountainous region, fields of battle for the deployment of large masses are rare and the war becomes a succession of partial combats. Here it would be imprudent, perhaps, to penetrate on a single point by a narrow and deep valley, whose outlets might

be closed by the enemy and thus the invading army
endangered. Yet it might penetrate by the wings on two
or three lateral lines whose outlets should not be too
widely separated, the marches being so arranged that the
masses debouch at the junction of the valleys at nearly
the same instant. The enemy should be driven from all
the ridges which separate these valleys.

Of all mountainous countries, the tactical defense of
Switzerland would be the easiest if all her inhabitants
were united in spirit. With their assistance a disciplined
force might hold its own against a triple number.

Grand Invasions and Distant Expeditions

There are several kinds of distant expeditions. The first
are merely auxiliary; they really belong to wars of intervention. The second are great continental invasions,
through extensive tracts of country which may be friendly,
neutral, doubtful, or hostile. The third are of the same
nature, but made partly on land and partly by sea. The
fourth class comprises those beyond the seas, to found,
defend, or attack distant colonies. The fifth includes great
descents, where the distance passed over is not very great
but where a powerful state is attacked.

Apart from the modifications which result from great
distances, all invasions, after the armies arrive upon the
actual theater, present the same operations as all other
wars. The chief difficulty arises from great distances.

Although so ruinous to Napoleon, the campaign of 1812
was a model for a distant invasion. His care in leaving
Prince Schwarzenberg[28] and Reynier[29] on the Bug while
Macdonald,[30] Oudinot,[31] and Wrede[32] guarded the Dwina,
Victor covered Smolensk, and Augereau was between the
Oder and Vistula, proves that he had neglected no hu-
manly possible precaution in order to base himself safely.
But it also proves that the greatest enterprises may fail
simply on account of the magnitude of the preparations
for their success.

If Napoleon erred in this contest, it was in neglecting

diplomatic precautions; in not uniting under one commander the different bodies of troops on the Dwina and
Dnieper; in remaining ten days too long at Wilna; in
giving the command of his right to his brother, who was
unequal to it; and in confiding to Prince Schwarzenberg
a duty which that general could not perform with the
devotedness of a Frenchman. I do not speak now of his
error in remaining in Moscow after the conflagration since
then there was no remedy for the misfortune, although it
would not have been so great if the retreat had taken place
immediately. He has also been accused of having too
much despised distances, difficulties, and men in pushing
on as far as the Kremlin.

Before passing judgment upon him in this matter, however, we ought to know the real motives which induced
him to pass Smolensk instead of wintering there as he had
intended, and whether it would have been possible for him
to remain between that city and Vitebsk without having
previously defeated the Russian army. It is doubtless true
that Napoleon neglected too much the resentment of
Austria, Prussia, and Sweden and counted too surely upon
a *dénouement* between Wilna and the Dwina. Although
he fully appreciated the bravery of the Russian armies, he
did not realize the spirit and energy of the people.

The fate of all such enterprises makes it evident that the
capital point for their success, and in fact the only maxim
to be given, is "never to attempt them without having
secured the hearty and constant alliance of a respectable
power near enough the field of operations to afford a
proper base, where supplies of every kind may be accumulated and which may also in case of reverse serve
as a refuge and afford new means of resuming the offensive." The safety of deep lines of operations and the
establishment of eventual bases give all the military means
of lessening the danger. To these should be added a just
appreciation of distances, obstacles, seasons, and countries—
in short, accuracy in calculation and moderation in success, in order that the enterprise may not be carried too far.

Summary

1. Know how to make the best use of the advantages which the reciprocal directions of the two bases of operations may afford.

2. Choose from the three zones ordinarily found in the strategic field, that one upon which the greatest injury can be done to the enemy with the least risk to one's self.

3. Establish well, and give a good direction to, the lines of operations.

On the offensive we should follow the system which led to the success of Napoleon in 1800, 1805, and 1806, when he directed his line upon the extremity of the strategic front. Or we might adopt his plan which was successful in 1796, 1809, and 1814, of directing the line of operations upon the center of the strategic front. All of this is to be determined by the respective positions of the armies.

4. Select judicious eventual lines of maneuver. Give them such directions as always to be able to act with the greater mass of the forces and to prevent the parts of the enemy from concentrating or from affording each other mutual support.

5. Combine, in the same spirit of centralization, all strategic positions and all large detachments made to cover the most important strategic points of the theater of war.

6. Impart to the troops the greatest possible mobility and activity so as, by their successive employment upon points where it may be important to act, to bring superior force to bear upon fractions of the hostile army.

The system of rapid and continuous marches multiples the effect of an army and at the same time neutralizes a great part of that of the enemy's. It is often sufficient to insure success, but its effect will be quintupled if the marches be skillfully directed upon the decisive strategic points of the zone of operations, where the severest blows to the enemy can be given.

As a general may not, however, always be prepared to adopt this decisive course to the exclusion of every other, he must then be content with attaining part of the object of every enterprise by rapid and successive employment of his forces upon isolated bodies of the enemy, thus insuring their defeat. A general who moves his masses rapidly and continually and gives them proper directions, may be confident both of gaining victories and of securing great results therefrom.

NOTES

[1] 1756-1763, France and Austria against England and Prussia.

[2] 1763-1813. French general 1796-1804, later (1813) in Russian service.

[3] 1762-1833. Marshal of France 1804.

[4] 1765-1812. Russian general, mortally wounded at Borodino.

[5] 1761-1818. Russian field marshal, of Scottish descent.

[6] May, 1800, before the Battle of Marengo.

[7] 1729-1806. Austrian general.

[8] 1650-1722.

[9] 1663-1736. Prince of Savoy, Austrian field marshal.

[10] 1769-1799. General-in-chief of the army in Italy; killed in action.

[11] 1766-1841. Marshal of France 1807.

[12] 1769-1815. Marshal of France 1804; shot for treason after Waterloo.

[13] 1757-1816. Marshal of France.

[14] 1768-1835. Marshal of France 1804; premier 1834-1835.

[15] 1774-1852. Marshal of France 1809.

[16] War of the First Coalition—Prussia and Austria against France.

[17] The Seven Years War.

[18] 558 (?)-486 B.C. King of Persia 521-486 B.C.

[19] 519 (?)-465 B.C. King of Persia 486-465 B.C. Son of Darius.

[20] 492, 490, and 480 B.C.

[21] 1633-1707. French military engineer; marshal 1703.

[22] 1641-1691. French war minister under Louis XIV.

[23] 1724-1797. Austrian field marshal.

[24] 1735-1810. Austrian general; field marshal 1808.

[25] Early 19th century.

[26] 1762-1800. French Revolutionary general.

[27] 742-814. King of the Franks (768-814) and emperor of the West (800-814).

[28] 1771-1820. Austrian field marshal. Served under Napoleon; commanded allied army against him 1813-1814.

[29] 1771-1814. French general.

[30] 1765-1840. Marshal of France, of Scottish descent.

[31] 1767-1847. Marshal of France 1809.

[32] 1767-1838. Bavarian field marshal.

[33] Before the battles of Amberg and Wurzburg.

IV. GRAND TACTICS AND BATTLES

Battles are the actual conflicts of armies contending about great questions of national policy and of strategy. Strategy directs armies to the decisive points of a zone of operations and influences, in advance, the results of battles; but tactics (aided by courage, genius, and fortune) gains victories.

Grand tactics is the art of forming good combinations preliminary to battles as well as during their progress. The guiding principle in tactical combinations, as in those of strategy, is to bring the mass of the force at hand against a part of the opposing army and upon that point the possession of which promises the most important results.

Battles have been stated by some writers to be the chief and deciding features of war. This assertion is not strictly true, as armies have been destroyed by strategic operations without the occurrence of pitched battles, merely by a succession of inconsiderable affairs. It is also true that a complete and decided victory may bring similar results even though there may have been no grand strategic combinations. But it is the morale of armies, as well as of nations, more than anything else, which makes victories and their results decisive. Clausewitz commits a grave error in asserting that a battle not characterized by a maneuver to turn the enemy cannot result in a complete victory.

At the battle of Zama[1] Hannibal,[2] in a few brief hours, saw the fruits of twenty years of glory and success vanish before his eyes, although Scipio[3] never had a thought of turning his position. At Rivoli[4] the turning-party was completely beaten. Nor was the maneuver more successful at Stockach in 1799[5] or at Austerlitz[6] in 1805. I by no means intend to discourage the use of that maneuver— being, on the contrary, a constant advocate of it—but it is very important to know how to use it skillfully and opportunely. Moreover, I am of opinion that if it be a general's design to make himself master of his enemy's communications while at the same time holding his own, he should employ strategic rather than tactical combinations to accomplish it.

There are three kinds of battles: 1st, defensive battles, or those fought by armies in favorable positions taken up to await the enemy's attack; 2d, offensive battles, where one army attacks another in position; 3d, battles fought unexpectedly, as a result of collision of two armies on the march. We will examine in succession the different combinations they present.

Defensive Battles

When an army awaits an attack, it takes up a position and forms its line of battle. Without adhering strictly to what is called the system of a war of positions, an army may often find it proper to await the enemy at a favorable point, strong by nature and selected beforehand for the purpose of there fighting a defensive battle. Such a position may be taken up when the object is to cover an important objective point (such as a capital, large depots, or a decisive strategic point which controls the surrounding country) or to cover a siege.

There are two kinds of positions, the strategic (which has been discussed) and the tactical. The latter, again, is subdivided. In the first place, there are intrenched positions occupied to await the enemy under cover of works more or less connected—in a word, intrenched camps. Secondly, we have positions naturally strong, where armies encamp for the purpose of gaining a few days' time. Last are open positions, chosen in advance to fight on the defensive. The characteristics to be sought in these positions vary according to the object in view. It is, however, important not to be carried away by the mistaken idea, which too often prevails, of giving preference to positions that are very steep and difficult of access—perhaps

quite suitable for temporary camps, but not always the
best for battlegrounds. To be really strong a position
of this kind must not only be steep and difficult of access,
but should be adapted to the purpose for which it was
occupied, should offer as many advantages as possible for
the kind of troops forming the principal strength of the
army, and, finally, should have obstacles more disadvantageous for the enemy than for the assailed. For example,
it is certain that Massena,[7] in taking the strong position
of the Albis in 1810, would have made a great error if his
chief strength had been in cavalry and artillery, while it
was exactly what was wanted for his excellent infantry.
For the same reason Wellington, whose whole dependence
was in the fire of his troops, made a good choice of position
at Waterloo in 1815, where all the avenues of approach
were well swept by his guns. Moreover, the position of
the Albis was rather a strategic position, that of Waterloo
being simply a battleground.

The rules to be generally observed in selecting tactical
positions are to:

1. Have the communications to the front such as to
make it easier to fall upon the enemy at a favorable
moment than for him to approach the line of battle.

2. Give the artillery all its effect in the defense.

3. Choose ground suitable for concealing the movements of troops between the wings, that they can be
massed upon any point deemed the proper one.

4. Have a good view of the enemy's movements.

5. Have an unobstructed line of retreat.

6. Have the flanks well protected by either natural or
artificial obstacles, so as to render impossible an attack
upon their extremities and thus oblige the enemy to attack
the center, or at least some point of the front.

In a defensive position it often happens that there are
obstacles on other points of the front besides the flanks, of
such a character as to compel an attack upon the center.
Such a position will always be most advantageous for
defense, as was shown at Malplaquet[8] and Waterloo. Great

obstacles are not essential for this purpose, as the smallest accident of the ground is sometimes sufficient: thus, the insignificant rivulet of Papelotte forced Ney to attack Wellington's center at Waterloo, instead of the left as he had been ordered. When such a position is defended, one must hold ready for movement portions of the wings thus covered in order that they may take part in the action instead of remaining idle spectators of it.

The fact cannot be concealed, however, that all these means are but palliatives. The best thing for an army on the defensive is to know *how* to take the offensive at a proper time, and *to take it.*

When discussing strategic operations, mention was made of the varying chances which the two systems (the defensive and the offensive) give rise to. It was seen that especially in strategy the army taking the initiative has the great advantage of bringing up its troops and striking a blow where it chooses, while the army which awaits an attack is anticipated in every direction, is often taken unawares, and is always obliged to regulate its movements by those of the enemy. We have also seen that in tactics these advantages are not so marked, because the operations occupy a smaller extent of ground and the party taking the initiative cannot conceal his movements from the enemy, who may at once counteract them by the aid of a good reserve. Moreover, the party advancing upon the enemy has against him all the disadvantages arising from accidents of ground that he must pass before reaching the hostile line—such as small ravines, thickets, hedges, farm-houses, villages, etc., which must either be taken possession of or be passed by. To these natural obstacles may also be added the enemy's batteries to be carried, and the disorder which always prevails to some extent in a body of men exposed to continued fire. Thus in tactical operations the advantages resulting from taking the initiative are balanced by the disadvantages.

However undoubted these truths may be still another has been demonstrated by the greatest events of history.

Every army which maintains a strictly defensive attitude must, if attacked, be at last driven from its position; but if it takes advantage of the benefits of the defensive system and holds itself ready to take the offensive when occasion offers, it may hope for the greatest success.

Offensive Battles

By offensive battles we mean those which an army fights when assaulting another in position. An army reduced to the strategic defensive often takes the offensive by making an attack, and an army receiving an attack may during the course of the battle take the offensive and obtain the advantages incident to it. History furnishes numerous examples of battles of each of these kinds.

It must be admitted that the assailant generally has a moral advantage over the assailed and almost always acts more understandingly than the latter, who must be more or less in a state of uncertainty.

As soon as it is determined to attack the enemy, some order of attack must be adopted. That is what I feel ought to be called *order of battle*. It happens also quite frequently that a battle must be commenced without a detailed plan, because the position of the enemy is not entirely known. In either case it should be well understood that there is in every battlefield a decisive point the possession of which, more than of any other, helps to secure the victory by enabling its holder to make a proper application of the principles of war. Arrangements should therefore be made for striking the decisive blow upon this point.

The decisive point of a battlefield is determined, as has been already stated, by the character of the position, the bearing of different localities upon the strategic object in view, and by the arrangement of the contending forces. For example, suppose an enemy's flank rests upon high ground from which his whole line might be attained, so that the occupation of this height seemed most important, tactically considered; yet it may happen that the height in question is very difficult of access and situated exactly so as to be of the least importance, strategically considered. At the battle of Bautzen in 1813 the left of the allies rested upon the steep mountains of Bohemia, which province was at that time neutral rather than hostile. It seemed that, tactically considered, the slope of these mountains was the decisive point to be held. Actually it was just the reverse because the allies had but one line of retreat upon Reichenbach and Gorlitz and the French, by forcing the right, which was in the plain, would occupy this line of retreat and throw the allies into the mountains, where they might have lost all their materiel and a great part of their personnel.

The determination of the decisive point depends very much upon the arrangement of the contending forces. Thus, in lines of battle too much extended and divided the center will always be the proper point of attack. In lines well closed and connected the center is the strongest point, since, independently of the reserves posted there, it is easy to support it from the flanks; the decisive point in this case is therefore one of the extremeties of the line. When the numerical superiority is considerable an attack may be made simultaneously upon both extremities, but not when the attacking force is numerically equal or inferior to the enemy's. It appears, therefore, that all the combinations of a battle consist in so employing the force in hand as to obtain the most effective action upon that one of the three points mentioned which offers the greatest number of chances of success, a point readily determined by applying the analysis just mentioned.

The object of an offensive battle can only be to dislodge the enemy or to cut his line, unless it is intended by strategic maneuvers to ruin his army completely. An enemy is dislodged either by overthrowing him at some point of his line, or by outflanking him so as to take him in flank and rear, or by using both these methods at once. To accomplish these different objects, it becomes necessary to make choice of the most suitable order of battle for the method to be used.

There are at least twelve orders of battle:* 1, the simple parallel order; 2, the parallel order with a defensive or offensive crotchet; 3, the order reinforced upon one or both wings; 4, the order reinforced in the center; 5, the simple oblique order, or the oblique reinforced on the attacking wing; 6 and 7, the perpendicular order on one or both wings; 8, the concave order; 9, the convex order; 10, the order by echelon on one or both wings; 11, the order by echelon on the center; 12, the order resulting from a strong combined attack upon the center and one extremity simultaneously.

Each of these orders may be used either by itself or in connection with the maneuver of a strong column intended to turn the enemy's line. To appreciate properly the merits of each, it is necessary to test each by applying the general principles which have been laid down. For example, it is manifest that the parallel order is worst of all, for it requires no tactical skill to fight one line against another, battalion against battalion, with equal chances of success on either side.

There is, however, one important case where this is a suitable order: when an army, having taken the initiative in great strategic operations, shall have succeeded in falling upon the enemy's communications and cutting off his line of retreat while covering its own. When the battle takes place between them that army which has reached the rear of the other may use the parallel order for, having effected the decisive maneuver prior to the battle, all its efforts should now be directed toward the frustration of the enemy's effort to open a way through for himself.

The parallel order with a crotchet upon the flank is

---

* The letter A in the accompanying sketch indicates the defensive army; the letter B the offensive army.

N.B. I have placed the armies on a single line in order not to render the figures too complicated; whether the troops are found deployed, formed in columns of attack, in squares, or *en echequier*, is of little importance, it changes in nothing their tactical disposition.

PLATE I.

ORDERS OF BATTLE, OFFENSIVE AND DEFENSIVE.

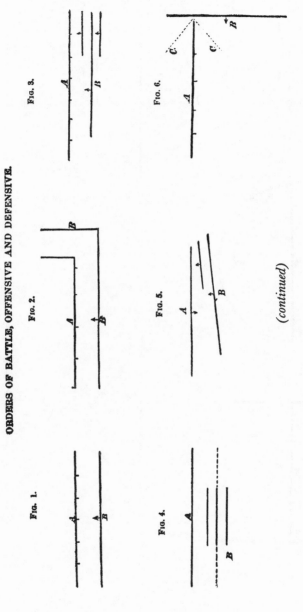

Fig. 1.

Fig. 2.

Fig. 3.

Fig. 4.

Fig. 5.

Fig. 6.

(continued)

Plate I (*continued*)

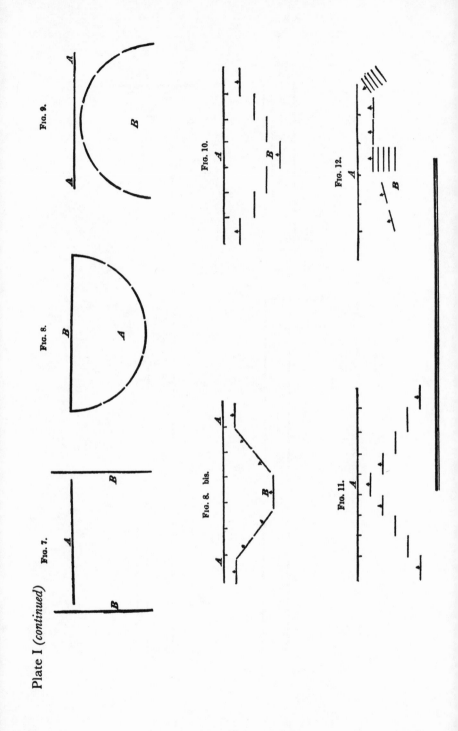

Fig. 7.

Fig. 8.

Fig. 9.

Fig. 8. bis.

Fig. 10.

Fig. 11.

Fig. 12.

most usually adopted in a defensive position. It may be also the result of an offensive combination, but then the crotchet is to the front whereas in the case of defense it is to the rear.

The parallel order reinforced upon one wing or upon the center to pierce that of the enemy, is much more favorable than the two preceding ones and is also much more in accordance with the general principles which have been laid down. On the other hand, when the contending forces are about equal the part of the line which has been weakened to reinforce the other may have its own safety compromised if placed in line parallel to the enemy.

The oblique order is the best for an inferior force attacking a superior. In addition to the advantage of bringing the main strength of the forces against a single point of the enemy's line, it has two others equally important, since the weakened wing is not only kept back from the attack of the enemy but also performs the double duty of holding in position the part of his line not attacked and of being at hand as a reserve for the support, if necessary, of the engaged wing. This order was used by the Theban Epaminondas[9] in his victories over the Spartans at Leuctra in 371 B.C. and at Mantineia in 362 B.C. The most brilliant example of its use was given by Frederick the Great at the Battle of Leuthen in 1757 when he defeated the Austrians.

The perpendicular order on one or both wings can be considered only an arrangement to indicate the direction along which the primary tactical movements might be made in a battle. The inference is that one division of the assailing army would take a position perpendicular to the enemy's wing, while the remainder of the army would approach in front for the purpose of annoying him. This would always bring us back to one of the oblique orders.

An attack on both wings, whatever be the form of attack

adopted, may be very advantageous but it is permissible only when the assailant is very decidedly superior in numbers. If the fundamental principle is to bring the main strength of the forces upon the decisive point, a weaker army would violate it in directing a divided attack against a superior force.

The order concave in the center has found advocates since the day when Hannibal by its use vanquished the Romans at Cannae in 216 B.C. This order may indeed be very good when the progress of the battle itself gives rise to it—that is, when the enemy attacks the center which retires before him and he becomes enveloped by the wings. But if this order is adopted before the battle begins, the enemy instead of falling on the center has only to attack the wings, which present their extremities and are in precisely the same relative situation as if they had been assailed in flank. This order would therefore be scarcely ever used except against an enemy who had taken the convex order to fight a battle.

An army will rarely form a semicircle, preferring rather a broken line with the center retired. If several writers may be believed, such an arrangement gave the victory to the English against the French on the famous days of Crecy (1346) and Agincourt (1415). This order is certainly better than a semicircle since it does not so much present the flank to attack while allowing forward movement by echelon and preserving all the advantages of concentration of fire. These advantages vanish if the enemy, instead of foolishly throwing himself upon the retired center, is content to watch it from a distance and make his greatest effort upon one wing.

The convex order with the center salient is found: (1) in an engagement immediately after the crossing of a river when the wings must be retired and rested on the river to cover the bridges; (2) when a defensive battle is to be fought with a river in rear, which is to be passed and the defile covered, as at Leipsig; and (3) as a natural formation with which to resist an enemy forming a concave line. If an enemy directs his efforts against the center or against a single wing, this order might cause the ruin of the whole army.*

The order by echelon upon the two wings is of the same nature as the perpendicular order. It is better than that, however, because, since the echelons are nearest each other in the direction where the reserve would be placed, the enemy would be less able (as regards both space and time) to throw himself into the interval of the center and at that point make a threatening counterattack.

The order by echelon on the center may be used with special success against an army occupying a position too much cut up and too extended because, its center being then somewhat isolated from the wings and liable to overthrow, the army thus cut in two would probably be destroyed. But, applying the test of the same fundamental principle, this order of attack would appear to be less certain of success against an army having a connected and closed line. Then the reserve is generally near the center, the wings can act either by concentrating their fire or by moving against the foremost echelons, so that either might readily repulse the attacker.

This formation is suitable, as has been said, for penetrating the center of a line too much extended, and might be equally successful against a line unavoidably immovable. If, however, the wings of the attacked line are brought at a proper time against the flanks of the foremost echelons, disagreeable results might follow. A parallel order considerably reinforced on the center might perhaps be a much better arrangement, for the parallel line in this case would have at least the advantage of deceiving

---

* An attack upon the two extremities might succeed also in some cases, when either the force was strong enough to try it or the enemy was unable to weaken his center to support the wings. As a rule, a false attack to engage the center and a strong attack against one extremity would be the best method to use against such a line.

the enemy as to the point of attack and would hinder the
wings from taking the echelons of the center by the flank.

It should be observed that these different orders are by
no means to be understood precisely as the geometrical
figures indicate them. A general who would expect to
arrange his line of battle as regularly as upon paper or on
a drill-ground would be greatly mistaken, and would be
likely to suffer defeat. This is particularly true as battles
are now fought. In the time of Louis XIV (1638-1715) or
of Frederick II (1712-1786) it was possible to form lines
of battle almost as regular as the geometrical figures, because armies camped under tents almost always closely
collected together, and were in the presence of each other
for several days, thus giving ample time for opening
roads and clearing spaces to allow the columns to be at
regular distances from each other. But in our day—when
armies bivouac, when their division into several corps gives
greater mobility, when they take position near each other
in obedience to orders given them while out of reach of
the general's eye and often when there has been no time
for thorough examination of the enemy's position, and
when the different arms of the service are intermingled
in the line of battle—all orders of battle which must be
laid out with great accuracy of detail are impracticable.
These figures have never been of any other use than to
indicate approximate arrangements.

If every army were a solid mass, capable of motion as a
unit under the influence of one man's will and as rapidly
as thought, the art of winning battles would be reduced
to choosing the most favorable order of battle and a
general could reckon with certainty upon the success of
maneuvers arranged beforehand. But the facts are altogether different. The great difficulty of the tactics of
battles will always be to render certain the simultaneous
entering into action of the numerous fractions whose efforts
must combine to make such an attack as will give good
ground to hope for victory. In other words, the chief diffi-

culty is to cause these fractions to unite in the execution of the decisive maneuver which, in accordance with the original plan of the battle, is to result in victory.

Inaccurate transmission of orders, the manner in which they will be understood and executed by the subordinates of the general-in-chief, excess of activity in some, lack of it in others, a defective *coup-d'oeil militaire*—everything of this kind may interfere with the simultaneous entering into action of the different parts, without speaking of the accidental circumstances which may delay or prevent the arrival of a corps at the appointed place. Hence result two undoubted truths: 1. The more simple a decisive maneuver is, the more sure of success will it be; 2. Sudden maneuvers seasonably executed during an engagement are more likely to succeed than those determined upon in advance, unless the latter, relating to previous strategic movements, will bring up the columns which are to decide the day upon those points where their presence will secure the expected result. Waterloo and Bautzen are proofs of the last. From the moment when Blücher and Bulow had reached the heights of Frichermont nothing could have prevented the loss of the battle by the French, and they could then only fight to make the defeat less complete. In like manner at Bautzen, as soon as Ney had reached Klix the retreat of the allies during the night of the 20th of May, 1813, could alone have saved them, for on the 21st it was too late; and if Ney had executed better what he was advised to do, the victory would have been a very great one.

Besides the difficulty of depending upon the exact application of an order of battles arranged in advance, it often happens that battles begin without even the assailant having a well-defined object, although the collision may have been expected. This uncertainty results either from circumstances prior to the battle, from ignorance of the enemy's position and plans, or from the fact that a portion of the army may be still expected to arrive on the field.

From these things many people have concluded that it is impossible to reduce to different systems the formations of orders of battle, or that the adoption of either of them can at all influence the result of an engagement—an erroneous conclusion, in my opinion, even in the cases cited above.   Indeed, in battles begun without any predetermined plan it is probable that at the opening of the engagement the armies will occupy lines nearly parallel and more or less strengthened upon some point.   The party acting on the defensive, not knowing from what quarter the storm will burst upon him, will hold a large part of his forces in reserve to be used as occasion may require.   The assailant must make similar efforts to have his forces well in hand, but as soon as the point of attack shall have been determined the mass of his troops will be directed against the center or upon one wing of the enemy or upon both at once.   Whatever may be the resulting formation, it will always bear a resemblance to one of the figures previously exhibited.   Even in unexpected engagements the same thing would happen—which will, it is hoped, be a sufficient proof of the fact that this classification of the different systems or orders of battle is neither fanciful nor useless.   But I repeat that a line of battle never was a regular geometrical figure, and when such figures are used in discussing the combinations of tactics it can only be for the purpose of giving definite expression to an idea by the use of a known symbol.

Hence we, may conclude that if it seems absurd to desire to mark out upon the ground orders of battle in such regular lines as would be used in tracing them on a sketch, a skillful general may nevertheless bear in mind the orders which have been indicated above and may so combine his troops on the battlefield that the arrangement shall be similar to one of them.   He should endeavor in all his combinations, whether deliberately arranged or adopted on the spur of the moment, to form a sound conclusion as to the important point of the battlefield.   This he can do only by observing well the direction of the enemy's line of battle, and not forgetting the direction in which strategy requires him to operate. He will then give his attention and efforts to this point, using a third of his force to keep the enemy in check or watch his movements while throwing the other two-thirds upon the point the possession of which will insure him the victory.

For the purpose of fighting battles in a truly scientific manner, the following points must be attended to:

1. An offensive order of battle should seek to force the enemy from his position by all reasonable means.

2. The maneuvers indicated by art are those intended to overwhelm one wing only, or the center and one wing at the same time. An enemy may also be dislodged by maneuvers for outflanking and turning his position.

3. These attempts have a much greater likelihood of success if concealed from the enemy until the very moment of the assault.

4. To attack the center and both wings at the same time without having very superior forces, would be entirely in opposition to the rules of the art unless one of these attacks can be made very strongly without weakening the line too much at the other points.

5. The oblique order has no other object than to unite at least half the force of the army in an overwhelming attack upon one wing while the remainder is retired to the rear, out of danger of attack, being arranged either in echelon or in a single oblique line.

6. The different formations (convex, concave, perpendicular, or otherwise) may all be varied by having the lines of uniform strength throughout, or by massing troops at one point.

7. The object of the defense being to defeat the plans of the attacking party, the arrangements of a defensive order should be such as to multiply the difficulties of approaching the position and to keep in hand a strong reserve, well concealed and ready to fall at the decisive moment upon a point where the enemy least expect to meet it.

8. It is impossible to state definitely what is the best method to use in forcing a hostile army to abandon its position. An order of battle would be perfect which united the double advantages of the fire of the arms and of the moral effect produced by an onset. A skillful mixture of deployed lines and columns, acting alternately as circumstances require, will always be a good combination.

9. As it is essential in an offensive battle to drive the enemy from his position and to cut him up as much as possible, the best means of accomplishing this is to use as much material force as can be accumulated against him.

10. The combination of these two methods—that is to say, the attack in front by main force and the turning maneuver—will render victory more certain than the use of either separately, but in all cases too extended movements must be avoided, even in the presence of a contemptible enemy.

11. The manner of driving an enemy from his position by main force is to throw his troops into confusion by a heavy and well directed fire of artillery, increase this confusion by vigorous charges of cavalry, and follow up the advantages thus gained by pushing forward masses of infantry well covered in front by skirmishers and flanked by cavalry. But while we may expect success to follow such an attack upon the first line, the second is still to be overcome and after that the reserve. At this period of the engagement the attacking party would usually be seriously embarrassed did not the moral effect of the defeat of the first line often occasion the retreat of the second and cause the general in command to lose his presence of mind.

12. From the foregoing it may be deduced that the most difficult as well as the most certain of all the means the assailant may use to gain the victory consists in strongly supporting the first line with the troops of the second line, and these with the reserve, and in a proper employment of masses of cavalry and of batteries to assist in striking

the decisive blow at the second line of the enemy; for here is presented the greatest of all the problems of the tactics of battles. Simultaneous employment of the largest number of troops of all arms combined (except the small reserve of each which should be always held in hand) will therefore, at the critical moment of the battle, be the problem which every skillful general will attempt to solve and to which he should give his whole attention.

Turning Maneuvers

It may be laid down as a principle that any movement is dangerous which is so extended as to give the enemy an opportunity, while it is taking place, of beating the remainder of the army in position. It therefore seems difficult to lay down a fixed rule on the subject; the following directions are about all that can be given.

Keep the mass of the force well in hand and ready to act at the proper moment, being careful, however, to avoid the danger of accumulating troops in too large bodies. A commander observing these precautions will be always prepared for anything that may happen. If the opposing general shows little skill and seems inclined to indulge in extended movements, his adversary may be more daring.

By usually adopting an order of battle well closed and well connected, a general will find himself prepared for any emergency and little will be left to chance. It is especially important for him to have a correct estimate of his enemy's character and his usual style of warfare, to enable him to regulate his own actions accordingly. In case of superiority in numbers or discipline, maneuvers may be attempted which would be imprudent were the forces equal or the commanders of the same capacity. A maneuver to outflank and turn a wing should be connected with other attacks and opportunely supported by an attempt of the remainder of the army on the enemy's front, either against the wing turned or against the center. Finally, strategic operations to cut an enemy's line of communications before giving battle and to attack him in rear, the assailing army preserving its own line of retreat, are much more likely to be successful and effectual; moreover, they require no disconnected maneuver during the battle.

Meeting Engagements

The accidental and unexpected meeting of two armies on the march gives rise to one of the most imposing scenes in war.

In the greater number of battles one party awaits his enemy in a position chosen in advance, which is attacked after a reconnaissance as close and accurate as possible. It often happens, however, that two armies approach each other, each intending to make an unexpected attack upon the other. A collision ensues unexpected by both armies, since each finds the other where it does not anticipate a meeting. One army may also be attacked by another which has prepared a surprise for it, as happened to the French at Rossbach in 1757 during the Seven Year's War.

A great occasion of this kind calls into play all the genius of a skillful general and of the warrior able to control events. It is always possible to gain a battle with brave troops, even where the commander may not have great capacity, but victories like those of Lutzen,[10] Luzzara,[11] Eylau,[12] and Abensberg[13] can be gained only by a brilliant genius endowed with great coolness and using the wisest combinations.

There is so much chance in these accidental battles that it is by no means easy to lay down precise rules concerning them. These are the very cases, however, in which it is necessary to keep clearly in mind the fundamental principles of the art and the different methods of applying them, in order that a proper arrangement of maneuvers can be decided upon instantly and in the midst of the noise of battle.

Surprises

Before the invention of fire-arms surprises were more easily effected than at present, for the reports of artillery and musketry firing are heard for so great a distance that the surprise of an army is now next to impossible unless the first duties of field-service are forgotten and the enemy is in the midst of the army before his presence is known because there are no outposts to give the alarm. The Seven Years' War presents a memorable example in the surprise of Hochkirch.[14] It shows that a surprise does not consist simply in falling upon troops that are sleeping or keeping a poor look-out, but that it may result from the combination of a sudden attack upon and a surrounding of one extremity of the army. In fact, to surprise an army it is not necessary to take it so entirely unawares that the troops will not even have emerged from their tents; it is sufficient to attack it in force at the point intended, before preparations can be made to meet the attack.

Advantage should be taken of all opportunities for surprising an adversary, and precautions should be used to prevent such attacks. The regulations for handling any well-organized army should point out the means for doing the last.

NOTES

[1]202 B.C.

[2]247-183 B.C. Carthaginian general.

[3]237-183 B.C. Scipio Africanus, regarded as Rome's greatest general up to Julius Caesar's time.

[4]1797. Napoleon defeated Italians and Austrians.

[5]Archduke Charles defeated Jourdan.

[6]"Battle of the Three Emperors": Napoleon defeated combined Austrian and Russian armies.

[7]1758-1817. Marshal under Napoleon.

[8]Victory by Marlborough and Eugene in 1709; the War of the Spanish Succession.

[9]418 (?)-362 B.C.

[10]1813, the Wars of Liberation, the French beat the Allies.

[11]1702, the War of Spanish Succession.

[12]1807, the War of the Third Coalition.

[13]1809, Napoleon defeated the Austrians.

[14]1758, Jaun of Austria defeated Prussians under Frederick.

V. OPERATIONS BOTH STRATEGICAL AND TACTICAL

The operations of the detachments an army may send out have so important a bearing on the success of a campaign that the determination of their strength and the proper occasions for them is one of the greatest and most delicate responsibilities imposed upon a commander. If nothing is more useful in war than a strong detachment opportunely sent out and having a good *ensemble* of operations with the main body, it is equally certain that no expedient is more dangerous when inconsiderately adopted. Frederick the Great regarded it as one of the essential qualities of a general to know how to make his adversary send out many detachments, with the view of either destroying them in detail or attacking the main body during their absence.

Division of armies into numerous detachments has sometimes been carried to so great an extent, and with such poor results, that many persons now believe it better to have none of them. It is undoubtedly much safer and more agreeable for an army to be kept in a single mass, but sometimes this is impossible or incompatible with gaining a complete or even a considerable success. The essential point in this matter is to send out as few detachments as possible.

There are several kinds of detachments:

1. Large corps may be dispatched to a distance from the zone of operations of the main army in order to make diversions of greater or less importance.

2. Large detachments may be made in the zone of operations to cover important points of this zone, to carry on a siege, to guard a secondary base, or to protect the line of operations if threatened.

3. Sometimes large detachments are made upon the front of operations, in the face of the enemy, to act in concert with the main body in some combined operation.

4. Small detachments may be sent to a distance to try the effect of surprise upon isolated points whose capture may have an important bearing upon the general operations of the campaign.

I understand by diversions those secondary operations carried out at a distance from the principal zone of operations, at the extremities of a theater of war, upon the success of which it is sometimes foolishly supposed the whole campaign depends. Such diversions are useful in but two cases. The first is when the troops thus employed cannot conveniently act elsewhere on account of their distance from the real theater of operations. The second is where such a detachment would receive strong support from the population among which it was sent, this latter case belonging to political rather than military combinations. A few illustrative examples may not be amiss.

In 1805 Napoleon was occupying Naples and Hanover. The allies intended that an Anglo-Russian army should drive him out of Italy, while the combined forces of England, Russia, and Sweden should drive him from Hanover, nearly sixty thousand men being designed for these two widely separated points. But while their troops were collecting at the two extremities of Europe Napoleon ordered the evacuation of Naples and Hanover; Saint Cyr hastened to effect a junction with Massena in the Frioul, and Bernadotte (leaving Hanover) moved up to take part in the operations of Ulm and Austerlitz. After these astonishing successes Napoleon had no difficulty in retaking Naples and Hanover. This is an example of the failure of diversions.

In the civil wars of 1793, if the allies had sent twenty thousand men to La Vendée they would have accomplished much more than by increasing the numbers of those who were fighting fruitlessly at Toulon, upon the Rhine, and in Belgium. Here is a case where a diversion would have been not only very useful, but decisive.

Great movable and temporary detachments are made to:

1. Compel your enemy to retreat to cover his line of operations, or else to cover your own.

2. Intercept a corps and prevent its junction with the main body of the enemy, or facilitate the approach of your own reinforcements.

3. Observe and hold in position a large portion of the opposing army while a blow is struck at the remainder.

4. Carry off a considerable convoy of provisions or munitions on the receipt of which depends the continuance of a siege or the success of any strategic enterprise, or to protect the march of a convoy of your own.

5. Make a demonstration to draw the enemy in a direction where you wish him to go in order to facilitate the execution of an enterprise in another direction.

6. Mask or even invest one or more fortified places for a certain time, with a view either to attack or to keep the garrison shut up within the ramparts.

7. Take possession of an important point upon the communications of an enemy already retreating.

However great may be the temptation to undertake such operations as those enumerated, it must be constantly borne in mind that they are always secondary in importance and that the essential thing is to be successful at the decisive points. A multiplicity of detachments must, therefore, be avoided. Armies have been destroyed for no other reason than that they were not kept together.

River Crossings

Crossing a small stream over which a bridge is already in place or might be easily constructed, presents none of the combinations belonging to grand tactics or strategy. But the passage of a large river—such as the Danube, Rhine, Po, Elbe, Oder, Vistula, Inn, or Ticino—is an operation worthy of the closest study.

The art of building military bridges is a special branch of military science which is committed to *pontoniers* or sappers. It is not from this point of view that I propose to consider the passage of a stream, but as the attack of a military position and as a maneuver.

The passage itself is a tactical operation, but the determination of the point of passage may have an important connection with all the operations taking place within the entire theater of the war. The proper strategic point of passage is easily determined. It is here only necessary to remind the reader that in crossing a river, as in every other operation, there are permanent or geographical decisive points, and others which are relative or eventual, depending on the distribution of the hostile forces.

If the point selected combines strategic advantages with the tactical, no other point can be better. But if the locality presents obstacles exceedingly difficult to pass, another must be chosen, and in making the new selection care should be taken to have the direction of the movement coincide as nearly as possible with the true strategic direction. Independently of the general combinations, which exercise a great influence in fixing the point of passage, there is still another consideration connected with the locality itself. The best position is that where the army after crossing can take its front of operations and line of battle perpendicular to the river, at least for the first marches, without being forced to separate into several corps moving upon different lines. This advantage will also save it the danger of fighting a battle with a river in rear, as happened to Napoleon at Essling.[1]

1. It is essential to deceive the enemy as to the point of passage, that he may not accumulate an opposing force there. In addition to the strategic demonstrations false attacks must be made near the real one, to divide the attention and means of the enemy.

2. The construction of the bridge should be covered as much as possible by troops sent over in boats for the purpose of dislodging any enemy who might interfere with the progress of the work. These troops should at once take possession of any villages, woods, or other obstacles in the vicinity.

3. It is also important to arrange large batteries of heavy caliber not only to sweep the opposite bank but to silence any artillery the enemy might bring up to batter the bridge while building.

4. Presence of a large island near the enemy's bank makes it much easier to pass over troops in boats and to construct the bridge. In like manner, a smaller stream emptying into the larger near the point of passage is a favorable place for collecting and concealing boats and materials for the bridge.

5. It is well to choose a position where the river makes a re-entering bend, as the batteries on the assailant's side can cross their fire in front of the point where the troops are to land from the boats and where the end of the bridge is to rest, thus taking the enemy in front and flank when he attempts to oppose the passage.

6. The locality selected should be near good roads on both banks, so the army may have good communications to the front and rear on both banks of the river. For this reason those points where the banks are high and steep should usually be avoided.

The rules for preventing a passage follow as a matter of course from those for effecting it, as the duty of the defenders is to counteract the efforts of the assailants. The important thing is to have the course of the river watched by bodies of light troops, without attempting to make a defense at every point. Concentrate rapidly at the threatened point in order to overwhelm the enemy while only part of his army shall have passed.

One of the greatest difficulties after a crossing is to cover the bridge against the enemy's efforts to destroy it, without interfering too much with the free movement of the army.

Retreats and Pursuits

Retreats are certainly the most difficult operations in war. This remark is so true that the celebrated Prince de Ligne[2] said, in his usual piquant style, that he could not conceive how an army ever succeeded in retreating.

When we think of the physical and moral condition of an army in full retreat after a lost battle, of the difficulty of preserving order, and of the disasters to which disorder may lead, it is not hard to understand why the most experienced generals have hesitated to attempt such an operation.

What method of retreat shall be recommended? Shall the fight be continued at all hazards until nightfall and the retreat executed under cover of darkness? or is it better not to wait for this last chance, but to abandon the field of battle while a strong opposition can still be made to the pursuing army? Should a forced march be made in the night in order to get as much start on the enemy as possible? or is it better to halt after a half-march and make a show of fighting again? Each of these methods, although entirely proper in certain cases, might in others prove ruinous to the whole army. If the theory of war leaves any points unprovided for, that of retreats is certainly one of them.

If you determine to fight vigorously until night you may expose yourself to a complete defeat before that time arrives; and if a forced retreat must begin when the shades of night are shrouding everything in darkness and obscurity, how can you prevent the disintegration of your army, which does not know what to do and cannot see to do anything properly? If, on the other hand, the field of battle is abandoned in broad daylight and before all possible efforts have ben made to hold it, you may give up the contest at the very moment when the enemy is about to do the same thing; and if this fact comes to the knowledge of the troops you may lose their confidence. Moreover, who can say that a retreat commenced in the daylight in presence of an enterprising enemy may not become a rout?

Retreats are of different kinds, depending upon their causes. A general may retire of his own accord before fighting, in order to draw his adversary to a position which he prefers to his present one. This is a prudent maneuver rather than a retreat. It was thus that Napoleon retired in 1805 from Wischau toward Brunn to draw the allies to a point which suited him as a battlefield. It was thus that Wellington retired from Quatre-Bras to Waterloo ten years later.

A general may retire in order to hasten to the defense of a point threatened by the enemy, either upon the flanks or on the line of retreat. When an army is marching at a distance from its depots, in an exhausted country, it may be obliged to retire in order to get nearer its supplies. Finally, an army retires involuntarily after a lost battle or after an unsuccessful enterprise.

These are not the only causes having an influence in retreats. Their character will vary with that of the country, the distances to be passed over, and the obstacles to be surmounted. They are especially dangerous in an enemy's country—and when the points at which the retreats begin are distant from the friendly country and the base of operations, they become painful and difficult.

There are five methods of arranging a retreat. The first is to march in a single mass and upon one road. The second consists in dividing the army into two or three corps, marching at the distance of a day's march from each other in order to avoid confusion. The third consists in marching upon a single front by several roads nearly parallel and having a common point of arrival. The fourth moves by constantly converging roads. The fifth, on the contrary, moves along diverging roads.

I have nothing to say as to the formation of rear-guards, but take it for granted that a good one should always be prepared and well sustained by a portion of the cavalry reserves. Although this arrangement is common to all kinds of retreats, it has nothing to do with the strategic relations of these operations.

An army falling back in good order, with the intention

of fighting as soon as it shall have received expected reinforcements or reached a certain strategic position, should
prefer the first method. This insures the compactness of
the army and enables it to be in readiness for battle almost
at any moment, since it is simply necessary to halt the
heads of columns and form the remainder of the troops
under their protection as they successively arrived. An
army employing this method must not, however, confine
itself to a single main road, if there are side-roads sufficiently near to be occupied which may render its movements more rapid and secure.

When Napoleon retired from Smolensk in 1812 he used
the second method, having the portions of his army
separated by an entire march. He made therein a great
mistake, because the enemy was not following upon his
rear but moving along a lateral road which brought him
in a nearly perpendicular direction into the midst of the
separated French corps.

Many generals neglect to arrange the manner and times
of halts. Great disorder on the march is the consequence,
as each unit takes the responsibility of halting whenever
the soldiers are a little tired and find it agreeable to
bivouac. The larger the army and the more compactly it
marches, the more important does it become to arrange
carefully the hours of departures and halts, especially if
the army is to move at night. An ill-timed halt of part of
a column may cause as much mischief as a rout.

The third method, of retreating along several parallel
roads, is excellent when the roads are sufficiently near
each other.

Following concentric roads, the fourth method, is undoubtedly the best if the troops are distant from each
other when the retreat is ordered. In such a case nothing
can be better than to unite the forces, and the concentric
retreat is the only method of effecting this.

The fifth method is nothing else than the famous system of eccentric lines, which I have attributed to Bulow[3] and have opposed so warmly in the earlier editions of my works because I thought I could not be mistaken either as to the sense of his remarks on the subject or as to the object of his system. From his definition I gathered that he recommended that a retreating army, moving from any given position, separate into parts and pursue diverging roads with the double object of withdrawing more readily from the enemy in pursuit and of arresting his march by threatening his flanks and his line of communications. I found great fault with the system for the simple reason that a beaten army is already weak enough without absurdly still further dividing its forces and strength in presence of a victorious enemy.

An army in retreat is always in a bad state either physically or morally, because a retreat can only be the result of reverses or of numerical inferiority. Shall such an army be still more weakened by dividing it? I find no fault with retreats executed in several columns, to increase the ease of moving, when these columns can support each other—but I am speaking of those made along diverging lines of operations. Suppose an army of forty thousand men is retreating before another of sixty thousand. If the first forms four isolated divisions of about ten thousand men, the enemy may maneuver with two masses of thirty thousand men each. Can he not turn his adversary and surround, disperse, and ruin all his divisions in succession? How can they escape such a fate? *By concentration.* This being in direct opposition to a divergent system, the latter falls of itself.

I invoke to my support the great lessons of experience. When the leading divisions of the army of Italy were repulsed by Wurmser,[4] Bonaparte collected them all together at Roverbella; although he had only forty thousand men, he fought and beat sixty thousand because he had to contend only with isolated columns. If he had made a divergent retreat, what would have become of his army and his victories? After his first check Wurmser made an eccentric retreat, directing his two wings toward the extremities of the line of defense. What was the result? His right, although supported by the mountains of the Tyrol, was beaten at Trent. Bonaparte then fell upon the rear of his left, and destroyed that at Bassano and Mantua.

When an army retreats, whatever may be the motive of the operation, a pursuit always follows. Even when executed in the most skillful manner and by an army in good condition, a retreat always gives an advantage to the pursuing army. This is particularly the case after a defeat and when the source of supplies and reinforcements is at a great distance, for a retreat then becomes more difficult than any other operation in war and its difficulties increase in proportion to the skill exhibited by the enemy in conducting the pursuit.

The boldness and activity of the pursuit will depend, of course, upon the character of the commanders and upon the physique and morale of the two armies. It is difficult to prescribe fixed rules for all cases of pursuits, but the following points must be remembered:

1. It is generally better to direct the pursuit upon the flank of the retreating columns, especially when it is made where no danger is incurred in moving perpendicularly or diagonally upon the enemy's line of operations (as in one's own country). Care must be taken, however, not to make too large a circuit, for there might then be danger of losing the retreating enemy entirely.

2. A pursuit should generally be executed as boldly and actively as possible, especially when it is subsequent to a battle gained, because the demoralized army may be wholly dispersed if vigorously followed up.

3. There are very few cases where it is wise to make a "bridge of gold" for the enemy, no matter what the old Roman proverb may say, for it can scarcely ever be desirable to pay an enemy to leave a country unless pos-

sibly in the case where an unexpected success is gained
over him by an army much inferior to his.

One of the surest means of making a successful retreat
is to familiarize the officers and soldiers with the ideas
that an enemy may be resisted quite as well when coming
on the rear as on the front, and that the preservation of
order is the only way to save troops who are harassed by
the enemy during a retrograde movement.   Rigid discipline is at all times the best preservative of good order,
but it is of special importance during a retreat.   To
enforce discipline subsistence must be furnished so that
the troops will not have to straggle off to forage for themselves.

Passages of rivers in retreat are also interesting operations. If the stream is narrow and has permanent bridges
the operation is nothing more than the passage of a
defile, but when the river is wide and is to be crossed
upon a temporary military bridge the maneuver is extremely delicate. Among the precautions to be taken, a
very important one is to get the parks well advanced so
they may be out of the way of the army; for this purpose
it is well for the army to halt a half-day's march from
the river. The rear guard should also keep at more than
the usual distance from the main body—as far, in fact, as
the terrain and the respective forces will permit.

If the passage of a large river is difficult when the
enemy is only pressing on the rear of the column, it is
far more so when the army is threatened in both front
and rear and the river is guarded by the enemy in force.
The celebrated passage of the Beresina, by the French in
1812 is one of the most remarkable examples of such an
operation. Never was an army in a more desperate condition, and never was one extricated more gloriously and
skillfully.

The only rules to be laid down are, not to permit your
army to be closely pressed upon, to deceive the enemy as
to the point of passage, and to fall headlong upon the

corps which bars the way before the one which is following the rear of your column can come up. Never place
yourself in a position to be exposed to such danger, for
escape in such a case is rare.

Descents

These operations are rarely found, and may be classed
as among the most difficult in war when effected in presence of a well-prepared enemy.

Before the invention of gunpowder the transports were
also the ships of war. They were moved along at pleasure
by using oars, were light, and could skirt along the coasts.
Their number was in proportion to the number of troops
to be embarked. And, aside from the danger of tempests,
the operations of a fleet could be arranged with almost as
much certainty as those of an army on land.

Since the invention of gunpowder and the changes it
effected in navies, however, transports are so helpless in
presence of the monstrous three-deckers of the present
day, armed as they are with a hundred cannon, that an
army can make a descent only with the assistance of a
numerous fleet of ships of war which can command the
sea at least until the debarkation takes place.

Since the invention of cannon the too-celebrated Armada
(1588) of Philip II was the only such enterprise of any
magnitude until that begun by Napoleon against England
in 1803. All other marine expeditions were of no great
extent. We were, however, on the point of seeing the
solution of the vast problem of the practicability of
descents in great force, if it is true that Napoleon seriously
contemplated the transportation of 160,000 veterans from
Boulogne to the British Isles. Unfortunately, his failure
to execute this gigantic undertaking has left us entirely
in the dark as to this grave question.

Posterity will regret, as the loss of an example to all
future generations, that this immense undertaking was not
carried through or at least attempted. Doubtless many brave
men would have met their deaths, but were not those men

mowed down more uselessly on the plains of Swabia, of
Moravia, and of Castile, in the mountains of Portugal
and the forests of Lithuania? What man would not glory
in taking part in the greatest trial of skill and strength
ever seen between two great nations?

At any rate, posterity will find in the preparations
made for this descent one of the most valuable lessons
the present century has furnished for the study of soldiers
and of statesmen. The labors of every kind performed on
the coasts of France from 1803 to 1805 will be among the
most remarkable monuments of the activity, foresight, and
skill of Napoleon. It is recommended to the careful attention of young officers.

But, while admitting the possibility of success for a great
descent upon a coast so near as the English to Boulogne,
what result should be expected if this armada had had
a long sea-voyage to make? How could so many small
vessels be kept moving, even for two days and nights? To
what chances of ruin would not so many frail boats be
exposed in navigating the open seas! Moreover, the artillery, munitions of war, equipments, provisions, and fresh
water that must be carried with this multitude of men
require immense labor in preparation and vast means of
transportation.

It is difficult to lay down rules for operations of this
character. About the only recommendations I can make
are: deceive the enemy as to the point of landing; choose
a spot where the vessels may anchor in safety and the
troops be landed together; infuse as much activity as possible into the operation; take possession of some strong
point to cover the development of the troops as they
land; and put on shore at once a part of the artillery, to
give confidence and protection to the troops that have
landed.

A great difficulty in such an operation is found in the
fact that the transports can never get near the beach so
the troops must be landed in boats and rafts, which takes
time and gives the enemy great advantages. If the sea

is rough the men to be landed are exposed to great risks—
for what can a body of infantry do, crowded in boats,
tossed about by the waves, and ordinarily rendered unfit
by seasickness for the proper use of their arms?

I can only advise the party on the defensive not to
divide his forces too much by attempting to cover every
point. It is impossible to line the entire coast with batteries and battalions for its defense, but the approaches
to those places where large establishments are to be protected must be closed. Signals should be arranged for
giving prompt notice of the point where the enemy is
landing; all the disposable force should be rapidly concentrated there, to prevent his gaining a firm foothold.

The configuration of coasts has a great influence upon
descents and their prosecution. There are countries where
the coasts are steep and present few points of easy access
for the ships and the troops to be landed. As these few
places may be more readily watched, the descent becomes
more difficult.

Finally, there is a strategical consideration connected
with descents which may be usefully pointed out. The
same principle which forbids a continental army from
interposing the mass of its forces between the enemy and
the sea requires, on the contrary, that an army landing
upon a coast should always keep its principal mass in communication with the shore, which is at once its line of
retreat and its base of supplies. For the same reason its
first care should be to make sure of the possession of one
fortified harbor, or at least of a tongue of land which is
convenient to a good anchorage and may be easily strengthened by fortifications, in order that in case of reverse the
troops may be re-embarked without hurry and loss.

NOTES

[1] 1809. Often called the Battle of Aspern and Essling.

[2] 1735-1814. Austrian soldier and man of letters; created field
marshal by Catherine II of Russia.

[3] 1757-1807. Baron Dietrich Adam Heinrich von Bulow; soldier and
military writer, brother of the Prussian general who was with Blucher
at Waterloo.

[4] 1796. Wurmser was an Austrian field marshal, 1724-1797.

VI. LOGISTICS, OR THE PRACTICAL ART OF MOVING ARMIES

Is logistics simply a science of detail? Or, on the contrary, is it a general science, forming one of the most essential parts of the art of war? Or is it but a term, consecrated by long use, which designates collectively the different branches of staff duty?

The word *logistics* is derived, as we know, from the title of the *major général des logis* (translated in German by *Quartiermeister*), an officer whose duty it formerly was to lodge and camp the troops, give direction to the marches of columns, and locate them upon the ground. Logistics was then quite limited. But when war began to be waged without camps, movements became more complicated and the staff officers had more extended functions. The chief of staff began to transmit the conceptions of the general to the most distant points of the theater of war and to procure for him the necessary documents for arranging plans of operations. The chief of staff was called upon to assist the general in arranging his plans, giving information of them to subordinates in orders and instructions, explaining them, and supervising their execution both in their *ensemble* and in their minute details; his duties were therefore connected with all the operations of a campaign.

To be a good chief of staff it became necessary that a man should be acquainted with all the various branches of the art of war. If the term "logistics" includes all this, the voluminous treatises of the military analysts, all taken together, would hardly give even an incomplete sketch of what logistics is, for it would be nothing more nor less than the science of applying all possible military knowledge.

If it is agreed that the old *logistics* had reference only to details of marches and camps, and, moreover, that the functions of staff officers at the present day are intimately connected with the most important strategical combinations, it must be admitted that "logistics" includes but a small part of the duties of staff officers. If we retain the term we must understand it to be greatly extended and developed in significance so as to embrace not only the duties of ordinary staff officers, but those of generals-in-chief as well. For evidence of this, consider the principal points relating to the movements of armies:

1. Preparation of all the material necessary for setting the army in motion or, in other words, for opening the campaign: drawing up orders, instructions, and itineraries for the assemblage of the army and its subsequent launching upon its theater of operations.

2. Drawing up in a proper manner the orders of the general-in-chief for different enterprises, as well as plans of attack in expected battles.

3. Arranging with the chiefs of engineers and artillery the measures to be taken for the security of the posts which are to be used as depots, as well as those to be fortified in order to facilitate the operations of the army.

4. Ordering and directing reconnaissances of every kind, and procuring in this way (and by using spies) as exact information as possible of the positions and movements of the enemy.

5. Taking every precaution for the proper execution of movements ordered by the general; arranging the march of the different columns so that all may move in an orderly and connected manner; ascertaining that the ease and safety of marches are assured; regulating the manner and time of halts.

6. Giving proper composition to advance guards, rear guards, flankers, and all detached bodies, and preparing both good instructions for their guidance and the means necessary for fulfillment of their mission.

7. Prescribing forms and instructions for subordinate

commanders or their staff officers, relative to the tactical handling of the troops both when encountering the enemy and in battle, according to the nature of the ground and the character of the enemy.*

8. Indicating to advance guards and other detachments well-chosen points of assembly in case of their attack by superior numbers, and informing them what support they may hope to receive in case of need.

9. Arranging and supervising the march of trains of baggage, munitions, provisions, and ambulances, both with the columns and in their rear, in such manner that they will not interfere with the movements of the troops and will still be near at hand; taking precautions for order and security both on the march and when trains are halted and parked.

10. Providing for the successive arrival of convoys of supplies; collecting all the means of transportation of the country and of the army, and regulating their use.

11. Directing the establishment of camps and adopting regulations for their safety, good order, and police.

12. Establishing and organizing lines of operations and supplies, as well as lines of communications with these lines for detached bodies; designating officers capable of organizing and commanding in rear of the army; looking out for the safety of detachments and convoys, furnishing them good instructions; and looking out also for preserving suitable means of communication of the army with its base.

13. Organizing depots of convalescent, wounded, and sickly men, movable hospitals, and workshops for repairs, and providing for their safety.

14. Keeping accurate record of all detachments, either on the flanks or in rear; keeping an eye on their movements and providing for their return to the main column as soon as their service on detachment is no longer nec-

---

* I refer here to general instructions and forms, which are not to be repeated every day; such repetition would be impracticable.

essary; giving them some center of action; and forming strategic reserves.

15. Organizing straggler lines to gather up isolated men or small detachments moving in either direction between the army and its base of operations.

16. In case of sieges, ordering and supervising the employment of the troops in the trenches, and arranging with the chiefs of artillery and engineers as to the work to be done by those troops and their use in sorties and assaults.

17. In retreats, taking precautionary measures for preserving order; posting fresh troops to support and relieve the rear guard; causing intelligent officers to examine and select positions where the rear guard may advantageously halt, engage the enemy, check his pursuit, and thus gain time; making provision in advance for the movement of trains (so that nothing shall be left behind and that they shall proceed in the most perfect order), taking all proper precautions to insure safety.

18. In cantonments, assigning positions to the different corps; indicating to each principal division of the army a place of assembly in case of alarm; taking measures to see that all orders, instructions, and regulations are implicitly observed.

An examination of this long list—which might easily be made much longer by entering into greater detail—will lead every reader to remark that these are the duties rather of the general-in-chief than of staff officers. This truth I announced some time ago—and it is for the very purpose of permitting the general-in-chief to give his whole attention to the supreme direction of the operations that he ought to be provided with staff officers competent to relieve him of details of execution. Their functions are therefore necessarily very intimately connected, and woe to an army where these authorities cease to act in concert! This want of harmony is often seen, first because generals are men and have faults and secondly because in every army there are found individual interests and pretensions which produce rivalry of the chiefs of staff and hinder them in performing their duties.*

Staff Work Detailed

It is not to be expected that this treatise should contain rules for the guidance of staff officers in all the details of their multifarious duties. In the first place, every different nation has staff officers with different names and rounds of duties, so that details for each army would be different; in the second place, these matters are fully entered into in special books pertaining to these subjects. I will therefore merely enlarge a little upon some of the first articles enumerated above.

1. The measures to be taken by the staff officers for preparing the army to enter upon active operations in the field include all those which are likely to facilitate the success of the first plan of operations. Staff officers will prepare all the itineraries that will be necessary for the movement of the several corps of the army to the proper assembly points, making every effort to give such direction to the marches that the enemy shall be unable to learn from them anything concerning the projected enterprise.

2. An essential branch of logistics is certainly that which relates to making arrangements of marches and attacks, which are fixed by the general and notice of which is given to the proper persons by the chiefs of staff. The next most important qualification of a general, after that of knowing how to form good plans, is unquestionably that of facilitating the execution of his orders by their clearness of style. Whatever may be the real business of a chief of staff, the greatness of a commander-in-chief will be always mani-

---

* The chiefs of artillery, of engineers, and of the administrative departments all claim to have direct connection with the general-in-chief and not with the chief of staff. There should, of course, be no hindrance to the freest intercourse between these high officers and the commander, but he should work with them in presence of the chief of staff and send him all their correspondence; otherwise, confusion is inevitable.

fested in his plans—but if the general lacks ability the chief of staff should supply it as far as he can, having a proper understanding with the responsible chief.

I have seen two very different methods employed in this branch of the service. The first, which may be styled the old school, consists in issuing daily, for the regulation of the movements of the army, general instructions filled with minute and somewhat pedantic details, so much the more out of place as they are usually addressed to chiefs of corps, who are supposed to be of sufficient experience not to require the same sort of instruction as would be given to junior subalterns just out of school. The other method is that of the detached orders given by Napoleon to his marshals, prescribing for each one simply what concerned himself and only informing him what corps were to operate with him, on either the right or the left, but never pointing out the connection of the operations of the whole army.* I have good reasons for knowing that he did this designedly, either to surround his operations with an air of mystery or for fear that more specific orders might fall into the hands of the enemy and assist him in thwarting his plans.

It is certainly of great importance for a general to keep his plans secret. Frederick the Great was right when he said that if his night-cap knew what was in his head he would throw it into the fire. That kind of secrecy was practicable in Frederick's time, when his whole army was kept closely about him; but when maneuvers of the vastness of Napoleon's are executed, and war is waged as in our day, what concert of action can be expected from generals who are utterly ignorant of what is going on around them?†

Of the two systems, the latter seems to me preferable. A

* I believe that at the passage of the Danube before Wagram in 1809, and at the opening of the second campaign of 1813, Napoleon deviated from his usual custom by issuing a general order.

. † This seems to be an old debate. Sun Tzu (500 B.C.) advocated keeping subordinates "in total ignorance." Stonewall Jackson, 2300 years later agreed with Sun. EDITOR.

judicious mean may be adopted between the eccentric con-
ciseness of Napoleon and the minute verbosity which laid
down for experienced generals like Barclay de Tolly,[1]
Kleist von Nollendorf,[2] and Wittgenstein [3] precise directions for breaking into companies and reforming again in
line of battle, a piece of nonsense all the more ridiculous
because the execution of such an order in the presence of
the enemy is impracticable. In such cases it would be sufficient, I think, to give the generals special orders relative
to their own corps, and to add a few lines in cipher informing them briefly as to the whole plan of the operations and
the part they are to take individually in executing it.
When a proper cipher is wanting the order may be transmitted verbally by an officer capable of understanding it
and repeating it accurately. Indiscreet revelations need
then be no longer feared, and concert of action would be
secured.

3. In the present manner of marching the calculation
of times and distances becomes more complicated. As the
columns have different distances to pass over, in determining the hour of their departure and giving them instructions the following particulars must be considered:
a. the distances to be passed over, b. the amount of materiel in each train, c. the nature of the country, d. the
obstacles placed in the way by the enemy, e. whether or not
it is important for the march to be concealed or open.

4. An army on the march is often preceded by a general advance guard or, as is more frequent in the modern
system, the center and each wing may have its special
advance guard. Advance guards should be accompanied by
good staff officers capable of forming correct ideas as to the
enemy's movements and of giving an accurate account of
them to the general, thus enabling him to make his plans
understandingly. The commander of the advance guard
should assist the general in the same way.

5. As the army advances and removes farther from its
base, it becomes the more necessary to have a good line of

operations and of depots to link the army with its base. Staff officers will divide the depots into departments, the principal depot being established in the town which can lodge and supply the greatest number of men. If there is a fortress suitably situated, it should be selected as the site of the principal depot. If possible, there should be a transportation pool at each depot, certainly at the principal one in each brigade. The command of all the depots embraced within certain geographical limits should be intrusted to prudent and able general officers, for the security of the communications of the army often depends on their operations.

6. The study of the measures (partly logistical and partly tactical) to be taken by the staff officers in bringing the troops from the order of march to the different orders of battle is very important, but requires going into such minute detail that I must pass it over nearly in silence, contenting myself with referring to a few examples of the great importance of a good system of logistics.

One of these is the wonderful concentration of the French army in the plains of Gera in 1806; another is the entrance of the army upon the campaign of 1815. In each of these cases Napoleon possessed the ability to make such arrangements that his columns, starting from points widely separated, were concentrated with wonderful precision upon the decisive point of the zone of operations. In this way he insured the successful issue of the campaign. The choice of the decisive point was the result of a skillful application of the principles of strategy; the arrangements for moving the troops give us an example of logistics which originated in his own closet. It has been long claimed that Berthier framed those instructions, which were conceived with so much precision and usually transmitted with so much clearness, but I have had frequent opportunities of knowing that such was not the truth. The emperor was his own chief staff officer. Provided with a pair of dividers opened to a distance by the scale of from seventeen to

twenty miles in a straight line (which made from twenty-
two to twenty-five miles, taking into account the windings
of the roads), bending over and sometimes stretched at
full length upon his map where the positions of his corps
and the supposed positions of the enemy were marked by
pins of different colors, he was able to give orders for extensive movements with a certainty and precision which
were astonishing. Turning his dividers about from point
to point on the map, he decided in a moment the number
of marches necessary for each of his columns to arrive at
the desired point by a certain day. Then, placing pins in
the new positions and bearing mind the rate of marching
that he must assign to each column and the hour of its
setting out, he dictated those instructions which are alone
enough to make any man famous.

Ney coming from the shores of Lake Constance, Lannes [4]
from Upper Swabia, Soult and Davout [5] from Bavaria and
the Palatinate, Bernadotte [6] and Augereau [7] from Franconia, and the Imperial Guard from Paris—all were thus
arranged in line on three parallel roads, to debouch simultaneously between Saalfeld, Gera, and Plauen, few persons in the army or in Germany having any conception of
the object of these movements which seemed so very complicated. In the same manner, in 1815—when Blücher had
his army quietly in cantonments between the Sambre and
the Rhine and Wellington was attending fêtes in Brussels,
both waiting a signal for the invasion of France—Napoleon,
who was supposed to be at Paris entirely engrossed with
diplomatic ceremonies, at the head of this guard, which
had been but recently reformed in the capital, fell like a
thunderbolt upon Charleroi and Blücher's quarters. His
columns arrived from all points of the compass on the 14th
of June, in the plains of Beaumont and upon the banks of
the Sambre. (Napoleon did not leave Paris until the 12th.)

Reconnaissances and the Like

One of the surest ways of forming good combinations in
war would be to order movements only after obtaining

perfect information of the enemy's proceedings. In fact, how can any man say what he should do himself if he is ignorant what his adversary is about? Even as it is unquestionably of the highest importance to gain this information, so is it a thing of the utmost difficulty, not to say impossibility. This is one of the chief causes of the great difference between the theory and the practice of war.

From this cause arise the mistakes of those generals who are simply learned men without a natural talent for war, and who have not acquired that practical *coup-d'oeil* which is imparted by long experience in the direction of military operations. It is a very easy matter for a school-man to make a plan for outflanking a wing or threatening a line of communications upon a map, where he can regulate the positions of both parties to suit himself. But when he has opposed to him a skillful, active, and enterprising adversary whose movements are a perfect riddle, then his difficulties begin and we see an exhibition of the incapacity of an ordinary general with none of the resources of genius. I have seen so many proofs of this truth in my long life that, if I had to put a general to the test, I should have a much higher regard for the man who could form sound conclusions as to the movements of the enemy than for him who could make a grand display of theories—things so difficult to put in practice, but so easily understood when once exemplified.

There are four means of obtaining information of the enemy's operations. The first is a well-arranged system of espionage; the second consists in reconnaissances made by skillful officers and light troops; the third, in questioning prisoners of war; the fourth, in forming hypotheses of probabilities. There is also a fifth method—that of signals. Although this is used rather for indicating the presence of the enemy than for forming conclusions as to his designs, it may be classed with the others.

Reports of prisoners are often useful, but it is generally dangerous to credit them. A skillful chief of staff will always be able to select intelligence officers who can so frame their questions as to elicit important information from prisoners and deserters.

Spies, however, may be very useful when the hostile army is commanded by a great captain or a great sovereign who always moves with the mass of his troops or with the reserves. Such, for example, were the Emperors Alexander and Napoleon. If it was known when they moved and what route they followed, it was not difficult to conclude what project was in view; the details of the movements of smaller bodies did not need to be watched particularly.

A skillful general may supply the defects of the other methods by making reasonable and well-founded hypotheses. With great satisfaction I can say that this means hardly ever failed me. Though fortune never placed me at the head of an army, I have been chief of staff to nearly a hundred thousand men and have been many times called into the councils of the greatest sovereigns of the day, when the question under consideration was the proper direction to give to the combined armies of Europe. I was never more than two or three times mistaken in my hypotheses and in my manner of solving the difficulties they offered. A mind fully convinced of these truths and conversant with the principles of war will always be able to form a plan which will provide in advance for the probable contingencies of the future. I will cite a few examples which have come under my own observation.

In 1806, when people in France were still uncertain as to the war with Prussia, I wrote a memoir upon the probabilities of the war and the operations which would take place. I made the three following hypotheses: 1st. The Prussians will await Napoleon's attack behind the Elbe and will fight on the defensive as far as the Oder, in expectation of aid from Russia and Austria; 2d. Or they will advance upon the Saale, resting their left upon the frontier of Bohemia and defending the passes of the mountains of Franconia; 3d Or else, expecting the French by the great Mayence road, they will advance imprudently to Erfurt. I do not believe any other suppositions could be made, unless the Prussians were thought to be so foolish as to divide their forces, already inferior to the French, upon the two directions of Wesel and Mayence—a useless mistake, since there had not been a French soldier on the first of these roads since the Seven Years' War.

These hypotheses having been made, if any one should ask what course Napoleon ought to pursue it was easy to reply "that the mass of the French army being already assembled in Bavaria, it should be thrown upon the left of the Prussians by way of Gera and Hof, for the Gordian knot of the campaign was in that direction no matter what plan they should adopt." If they advanced to Erfurt he could move to Gera, cut their line of retreat, and press them back along the Lower Elbe to the North Sea. If they rested upon the Saale he could attack their left by way of Hof and Gera, defeat them partially, and reach Berlin before them by way of Leipsig. If they stood fast behind the Elbe he must still attack them by way of Gera and Hof.

Since Napoleon's direction of operations was so clearly fixed, what mattered it to him to know the details of their movements? Being certain of the correctness of these principles I did not hesitate to announce *a month before the war* that Napoleon would attempt just what he did, and that if the Prussians passed the Saale battles would take place at Jena and Naumburg! I relate this circumstance not from a feeling of vanity, for if that were my motive I might mention many more of a similar character. I have only been anxious to show that in war a plan of operations may often be arranged, simply based upon the general principles of the art and without much attention necessarily being given to the details of the enemy's movements.

To summarize:

1. A general should neglect no means of gaining information of the enemy's movements. For this purpose he should make use of reconnaissances, spies, bodies of light troops commanded by capable officers, signals, and questioning of deserters and prisoners.

2. Ever multiply the means of obtaining information, for no matter how imperfect and contradictory they may be the truth may often be sifted from them.

3. Perfect reliance should be placed on none of these means.

4. As it is impossible to obtain exact information by the methods mentioned, a general should never move without arranging several courses of action for himself, based upon probable hypotheses that the relative situation of the armies enables him to make and never losing sight of the principles of the art.

I can assure a general that with such precautions nothing very unexpected can befall him and cause his ruin, as has so often happened to others, for unless he is totally unfit to command an army he should at least be able to form reasonable suppositions as to what the enemy is going to do and fix for himself a certain line of conduct to suit each of these hypotheses.* It cannot be too much insisted upon that the real secret of military genius consists in the ability to make these reasonable suppositions in any case; although their number is always small, it is surprising how much this highly useful means of regulating one's conduct is neglected.

To complete this chapter I must state what is to be gained by using a system of signals. Of these there are several kinds. Telegraphic signals (visual) are the most important of all. Napoleon owes his astonishing success at Ratisbon, in 1809, to the fact of his having established a telegraphic communication between the headquarters of the army and France. He was still in Paris when the Austrian army crossed the Inn at Braunau with the intention of invading

---

* I shall be accused, I suppose, of saying that no event in war can ever occur which may not be foreseen and provided for. To prove the falsity of this accusation it is sufficient for me to cite the surprises of Cremona, Berg-op-zoom, and Hochkirch. I am still of the opinion, however, that even such events as these might have been anticipated entirely or in part, as at least within the limits of probability or possibility.

Bavaria and breaking through his line of cantonments. Informed within twenty-four hours of what was happening seven hundred miles away, he threw himself into his traveling-carriage and a week later had gained two victories under the walls of Ratisbon. Without the telegraph the campaign would have been lost. This single fact is sufficient to impress us with an idea of its value.

It has been proposed to use portable telegraphs. Such an arrangement, operated by men on horseback posted on high ground, could communicate the orders of the center to the extremities of a line of battle as well as the reports of the wings to the headquarters. Repeated trials of it were made in Russia but the project was given up—for what reason, however, I have not been able to learn.

An attempt of another kind was made in 1794, at the battle of Fleurus, where General Jourdan made use of the services of a balloonist to observe and give notice of the movements of the Austrians. I am not aware that he found the method very useful, as it was not again used, but it was claimed at the time that it assisted in gaining him the victory. Of this, however, I have great doubts.

It is probable that the difficulty of having a balloonist in readiness to make an ascension at the proper moment, and of his making careful observations upon what is going on below while floating at the mercy of the winds above, has led to the abandonment of this method of gaining information. By giving the balloon no great elevation, sending up with it an officer capable of forming correct opinions as to the enemy's movements, and perfecting a system of signals to be used in connection with the balloon, considerable advantages might be expected from its use. Sometimes the smoke of the battle and the difficulty of distinguishing the columns, that look like liliputians, so as to know to which party they belong, will make the reports of the balloonists very unreliable. For example, a balloonist would have been greatly embarrassed in deciding, at the battle of Waterloo, whether it was Gouchy or Blücher who was seen coming up by the Saint Lambert road—but this uncertainty need not exist where the armies are not so much mixed. I had ocular proof of the advantage to be derived from such observations when I was stationed in the spire of Gautsch, at the battle of Leipsig; and Prince Schwarzenberg's aide-de-camp, whom I had conducted to the same point, could not deny that it was at my solicitation that the prince was prevailed upon to emerge from the marsh between the Pleisse and the Elster. An observer is doubtless more at his ease in a clock-tower than in a frail basket floating in mid-air, but steeples are not always at hand in the vicinity of battle-fields and they cannot be transported at pleasure.

NOTES

[1]1761-1818. Russian field marshal.

[2]1762-1823. Prussian general.

[3]1769-1843. Russian general.

[4]1769-1809. Marshal of France 1804.

[5]1770-1823. Marshal of France 1804.

[6]1763 (?)-1844. General under Napoleon; king of Sweden 1818-1844 as Charles XIV.

[7]1757-1816. Marshal of France.

VII. COMBINED ARMS

Before the French Revolution all the infantry, formed in regiments and brigades, was collected in a single battle-corps drawn up in two lines, each of which had a right and a left wing. The cavalry was usually placed upon the wings and the artillery—which at this period was very unwieldy—was distributed along the front of each line. The army camped together, marching by lines or by wings. As there were two cavalry wings and two infantry wings, if the march was by wings four columns were thus formed. When they marched by lines (which was specially applicable to flank movements) two columns were formed, unless the cavalry or a part of the infantry had camped in a third line on account of unusual local circumstances.

The French Revolution introduced the system of divisions, which broke up the excessive compactness of the old formation and brought upon the field fractions capable of independent movement on any kind of ground. This change was a real improvement, although the formations went from one extreme to the other by returning nearly to the legionary formation of the Romans. These divisions, usually composed of infantry, artillery, and cavalry, maneuvered and fought separately.

Bonaparte in his first Italian campaign remedied this difficulty, partly by the mobility of his army and the rapidity of his maneuvers and partly by concentrating the mass of his divisions upon the point where the decisive blow was to fall. When he became the head of the government and saw the sphere of his means and his plans constantly increasing in magnitude, he readily perceived that a stronger organization was necessary. He avoided the extremes of both the old system and the new, while still retaining the advantages of the divisional system. Beginning with the campaign of 1800 he organized corps of two or three divisions which he placed under the command of lieutenant-

generals, and formed of them the wings, the center, and the
reserve of his army.

This system was finally developed fully at the camp of
Boulogne, where he organized permanent army corps under
the command of marshals who had under their orders three
divisions of infantry, one of light cavalry, from thirty-six
to forty pieces of cannon, and a number of sappers. Each
corps was thus a small army, able at need to act independently. The heavy cavalry was collected in a single strong
reserve composed of two divisions of cuirassiers, four of
dragoons, and one of light cavalry. The grenadiers and the
guard formed an admirable infantry reserve. At a later
period—1812—the cavalry was also organized into corps of
three divisions, to give greater unity of action to the
constantly-increasing masses of this arm.

It is probable that, whatever be the strength and number
of the subdivisions of an army, the organization into corps
will long be retained by all the great powers of Europe and
calculations for the arrangement of the line of battle must
be made upon the basis.

Infantry

Infantry is undoubtedly the most important arm of the
service, since it forms four-fifths of an army and is used in
both the attack and defense of positions. If we must admit
that next to the genius of the general the infantry arm is
the most valuable instrument in gaining a victory, it is no
less true that most important aid is given by the cavalry
and artillery—that without their assistance the infantry
might at times be very seriously compromised and at others
could achieve only partial success.

There are, in fact, only five methods of forming troops
to attack an enemy: 1. as skirmishers; 2. in deployed lines,
either continuous or checkerwise; 3. in lines of battalions
formed in column on the central divisions; 4. in deep
masses; 5. in small squares.

What conclusions shall be drawn from all that has been
said? 1. If the deep order is dangerous, the half-deep is

excellent for the offensive. 2. The column of attack of single battalions is the best formation for carrying a position by assault, but its depth should be diminished as much as possible so that when necessary it can deliver as heavy a column of fire as possible and diminish the effect of the enemy's fire; it ought also to be well covered by skirmishers and supported by cavalry. 3. The formation having the first line deployed and the second in columns is the best suited to the defensive. 4. Either of them may be successful in the hands of a general of talent, who knows how to use his troops properly.

Since this chapter was first written, numerous improvements have been made in the arms of both infantry and artillery, making them much more destructive. The effect of this is to incline men to prefer the shallower formations, even in the attack. We cannot, however, forget the lessons of experience. Notwithstanding the use of rocket-batteries, shrapnel-shot, and the improved musket, I cannot imagine a better method of forming infantry for the attack than in columns of battalions. Some persons may perhaps desire to restore to infantry the helmets and the breastplates of the fifteenth century, before leading them to the attack in deployed lines.

Experience long ago taught me that one of the most difficult tactical problems is that of determining the best formation of troops for battle, but I have also learned that to solve this problem by the use of a single method is impossible.

However discussions like this may terminate, they are useful and should be continued. It would be as absurd to discard as useless the fire of infantry, as it would be to give up entirely the half-deep formation. An army is ruined if forced to adhere to precisely the same style of tactical maneuvers in every country it may enter and against every different nation. It is not so much the mode of formation as the proper combined use of the different arms which

will insure victory. I must except very deep masses, however, as they should be entirely abandoned.

I will conclude by stating that a most vital point to be
attended to in leading infantry to the combat is to protect
the troops as much as possible from the fire of the enemy's
artillery, not by withdrawing them at inopportune moments but by taking advantage of all inequalities and accidents of the ground to hide them from the view of the
enemy. When the assaulting troops have arrived within
musket-range it is useless to calculate upon sheltering them
longer; the assault is then to be made. In such cases cover
is suitable only for skirmishers and troops on the defensive.

It is generally quite important to defend villages on the
front of a position, or to endeavor to take them when held
by an enemy who is assailed—but their importance should
not be overestimated. We must never forget the noted
battle of Blenheim, where Marlborough and Eugene, seeing
the mass of the French infantry shut up in the villages,
broke through the center and captured twenty-four battalions which were sacrificed in defending these posts.

For like reasons, it is useful to occupy clumps of trees or
brushwood which may afford cover to the party holding
them. They shelter the troops, conceal their movements,
cover those of cavalry, and prevent the enemy from
maneuvering in their neighborhood.

The skeptic Clausewitz was not afraid to sustain the contrary maxim. Under the singular pretext that he who
occupies a wood acts blindly and discovers nothing of what
the enemy is doing, he presents their defense as a fault of
tactics. Blinded himself, probably, by the results of the
battle of Hohenlinden, in 1800, the author is too prone to
confound here the occupation of a wood in the line of
battle with the fault of throwing a whole army into a vast
forest without being master of the issues, either of the front
or of the flanks. But he must never have seen a combat
who denies the incontestable importance of the possession
of a wood situated in proximity with a line that he wishes

to defend or attack. The part which the park Hougeumont played in the battle of Waterloo is a great example of the influence that a post well chosen and well defended can have in a combat. In advancing his paradox, Clausewitz had forgotten the importance which woods had in the battles of Kolin in 1757 and Hochkirch in 1758.

Cavalry

The use a general should make of his cavalry depends, of course, somewhat upon its numerical strength as compared with that of the whole army, and upon its quality. Even cavalry of an inferior character may be so handled as to produce very great results, if set in action at proper moments.

The principal value of cavalry is derived from its rapidity and mobility. To these characteristics may be added its impetuosity, but we must be careful lest a false application be made of this last.

Whatever may be its importance in the *ensemble* of the operations of war, cavalry can never defend a position without the support of infantry. Its chief duty is to open the way for gaining a victory, or to render it complete by carrying off prisoners and trophies, pursuing the enemy, rapidly succoring a threatened point, overthrowing disordered infantry, covering retreats of infantry and artillery. An army deficient in cavalry rarely obtains a great victory, and finds its retreats extremely difficult.

All are agreed that a general attack of cavalry against a line in good order cannot be attempted with much hope of success, unless it be supported by infantry and artillery. At Waterloo the French paid dearly for having violated this rule, and the cavalry of Frederick the Great fared no better at Kunersdorf in 1759.

Infantry that has been shaken by a fire of artillery or in any other way may be charged with success. A charge against squares of good infantry in good order cannot succeed.

A general cavalry charge is made to carry batteries of

artillery and enable the infantry to take the position more easily, but the infantry must then be at hand to sustain the cavalry for a charge of this character has only a momentary effect which must be taken advantage of before the enemy can return offensively upon the broken cavalry. The beautiful charge of the French upon Gosa at the battle of Leipsig in 1813 is a fine example of this kind. Those executed at Waterloo with the same object in view were admirable, but failed because unsupported.

General charges are also made against the enemy's cavalry, to drive it from the field of battle and then return more free to act against his infantry.

In the defensive, cavalry may also produce very valuable results by opportune dashes at a body of the enemy which has engaged the opposing line and either broken through it or been on the point of doing so. It may regain the advantages lost, change the situation, and cause the destruction of an enemy flushed and disordered by his own success.

The special cavalry of a corps d'armeé may charge at opportune moments, to cooperate in a combined attack, to take advantage of a false movement of the enemy, or to finish his defeat by pressing him while in retreat.

Whatever method be adopted in charging, one of the best ways of using cavalry is to throw several squadrons opportunely upon the flanks of an enemy's line which is also attacked in front.

Two essential points are regarded as generally settled for all encounters of cavalry against cavalry. One is that the first line must sooner or later be checked: even supposing that the first charge is entirely successful, it is always probable that the enemy will bring fresh squadrons to the contest so that the first line must at length be forced to rally behind the second. The other point is that, with troops and commanders on both sides equally good, the victory will remain with the party having the last squadrons in reserve in readiness to be thrown upon the flank of the enemy's line while his front is also engaged.

Whatever order be adopted, care must be taken to avoid

deploying large cavalry corps in full lines. A mass thus drawn up is very unmanageable: if the first line is checked suddenly in its career the second is also, without having an opportunity to strike a blow. This has been demonstrated many times; for example, in the attack made by Nansouty[1] in columns of regiments upon the Prussian cavalry deployed in front of Chateau Thierry in 1814.

With cavalry even more than with infantry, morale is very important. The quickness of eye and the coolness of the commander and the intelligence and bravery of the soldier, whether in the melee or in the rally, are more apt to ensure a victory than is the adoption of this or that formation.

Whatever system of organization be adopted, it is certain that a numerous cavalry, whether regular or irregular, must have a great influence on the course of a war. It may cause apprehension at distant parts of the enemy's country, it can carry off his convoys, encircle his army, make his communications very perilous, and destroy the ensemble of his operations. In a word, it produces nearly the same results as a rising *en masse* of a population, causing trouble on the front, flanks, and rear of an army and reducing a general to a state of entire uncertainty in his calculations.

Artillery

Artillery is an arm equally formidable in the offensive and defensive. In the offensive a great battery well managed may break an enemy's line, throw it into confusion, and prepare the way for the troops that are to make an assault. As a defensive means it doubles the strength of a position, not only on account of the material injury it inflicts upon the enemy while at a distance and the consequent moral effect upon his troops, but also by greatly increasing the peril of approaching our positions. It is no less important in the attack and defense of fortified places or intrenched camps, for it is one of the main reliances in modern systems of fortification.

I will content myself with laying down a few fundamental rules, observing that they refer to the present state of artillery service (1838). The recent discoveries not yet being fully tested, I shall say little with reference to them.

1. In the offensive, a certain portion of the artillery should concentrate its fire upon the point where a decisive blow is to be struck. Its first use is to shatter the enemy's line, then it assists with its fire the attack of the infantry and cavalry.

2. Several batteries of horse artillery should follow the offensive movements of the columns of attack, besides the foot batteries intended for the same purpose.

3. Half of the horse artillery should be held in reserve, that it may be rapidly moved to any required point.

4. Whatever may be their general distribution along the defensive line, the batteries should give particular attention to those points where the enemy would be most likely to approach.

5. Artillery placed on level ground or ground sloping gently to the front is most favorably situated for either point-blank or ricochet firing. A converging fire is the best.

6. It should be borne in mind that the chief mission of all artillery in battles is to overwhelm the enemy's troops, not to reply to their batteries.

7. If the enemy advance in deployed lines the batteries should endeavor to cross their fire in order to strike the lines obliquely. If guns can be so placed as to enfilade a line of troops, a most powerful effect is produced.

8. When the enemy advance in columns they may be battered in front. It is advantageous also to attack them obliquely, and especially in flank and reverse. The moral effect of such fire upon a body of troops is inconceivable: the best soldiers are generally put to flight by it.

9. Batteries should always have supports of infantry or cavalry, especially on their flanks.

10. It is very important that artillerists, when threatened by cavalry, remain cool. They should fire first solid shot, next shells, and then grape, as long as possible.

11. When infantry threatens artillery the latter should

continue its fire to the last moment, being careful not to commence firing too soon.

12. The proportions of artillery have varied in different wars. Napoleon conquered Italy in 1800 with forty or fifty pieces, while in 1812 he invaded Russia with one thousand pieces thoroughly equipped and yet failed. These facts show that any fixed rule on the subject is inadmissible. Usually three pieces to a thousand combatants are allowed, but this allotment will depend on circumstances.

13. One of the surest means of using the artillery to the best advantage is to place in command of it a general who is at once a good strategist and tactician. This chief should be authorized to dispose not only of the reserve artillery, but also of half the pieces attached to the different corps or divisions of the army. He should also consult with the commanding general as to the moment and place of concentration of the mass of his artillery in order to contribute most to a successful issue of the day; he should never take the responsibility of thus massing his artillery without previous orders from the commanding general.

Use of the Combined Arms

To conclude this summary in a proper manner I ought to treat of the combined use of the three arms, but refrain from so doing after considering the great variety of points necessary to be touched upon if I should attempt to examine all the detailed operations that would arise in applying the general rules laid down for each of the arms. Several authors—chiefly German—have treated this subject very extensively. Their labors are valuable principally because they consist mainly of citations of numerous examples taken from the actual minor engagements of the later wars. These examples must indeed take the place of rules, since experience has shown that fixed rules on the subject cannot be laid down. It seems a waste of breath to say that the commander of a body of troops composed of the three arms should employ them so that they will give mutual support and assistance; but, after all, this is the only fundamental rule that can be established, for an attempt to prescribe for such a commander a special course of conduct in every case that may arise, when these cases may be infinitely varied, would involve him in an inextricable labyrinth of instructions.

I have said all that can properly be said when I advise that the different arms be posted in conformity with the character of the ground and according to the object in view and the supposed designs of the enemy, and that they be used simultaneously in the manner best suited to them, care being taken to enable them to afford mutual support.

NOTE

[1]1768-1815. Napoleon's cavalry commander.

VIII. CONCLUSION

War in its ensemble is not a science, but an art. Strategy, particularly, may be regulated by fixed laws resembling those of the positive sciences, but this is not true of war viewed as a whole. Among other things, combats may often be quite independent of scientific combinations; they may become essentially dramatic; personal qualities and inspirations and a thousand other things frequently are the controlling elements. The passions which agitate the masses that are brought into collision, the warlike qualities of these groups, the energy and talent of their commanders, the more or less martial spirit of nations and epochs*—in a word, everything that can be called the poetry and metaphysics of war—will have a permanent influence on its results.

Shall I be understood as saying that there are no such things as tactical rules, and that no theory of tactics can be useful? What military man of intelligence would be guilty of such an absurdity? Are we to imagine that Eugene and Marlborough triumphed simply by inspiration or by the superior courage and discipline of their battalions? Or do we find in the events of Turin,[5] Blenheim,[6] and Ramillies[7] maneuvers resembling those seen at Talavera,[8] Waterloo, Jena, or Austerlitz,[9] which were the causes of the victory in each case? When the application of a rule and the consequent maneuver have procured victory a hundred times for skillful generals, and always have in their favor the great probability of leading to success, shall their occasional failure be a sufficient reason for entirely denying their value and for distrusting the effect of the study of the art? Shall a theory be pronounced absurd because it has only three-fourths of the whole number of chances of success in its favor?

---

* The well-known Spanish proverb, "He was brave on such a day," may be applied to nations as to individuals. The French at Rossbach[1] were not the same people as at Jena,[2] nor the Prussians at Prenzlau[3] as at Dennewitz.[4]

The morale of an army and its chief officers has an influence upon the fate of a war. This seems to be due to a certain physical effect produced by the moral cause. For example, the impetuous attack upon a hostile line by twenty thousand brave whose feelings are thoroughly enlisted in their cause will produce a much more powerful effect than the attack of forty thousand demoralized or apathetic men upon the same point.

Strategy, as has already been explained, is the art of bringing the greatest part of the forces of an army upon the important point of the theater of war or of the zone of operations.

Tactics is the art of using these masses at the points to which they shall have been conducted by well-arranged marches; that is to say, the art of making them act at the decisive moment and at the decisive point of the field of battle.

A general thoroughly instructed in the theory of war but not possessed of military *coup-d'oeil*, coolness, and skill, may make an excellent strategic plan and be entirely unable to apply the rules of tactics in presence of an enemy. His projects will not be successfully carried out, his defeat will be probable. If he be a man of character he will be able to diminsh the evil results of his failure, but if he lose his wits he will lose his army.

The same general may, on the other hand, be at once a good tactician and strategist, and have made all the arrangements for gaining a victory that his means will permit. In this case, if he be only moderately seconded by his troops and subordinate officers, he will probably gain a decided victory. If, however, his troops have neither discipline nor courage and his subordinate officers envy and deceive him,* he will undoubtedly see his fine hopes

---

* The unskillful conduct of a subordinate who is incapable of understanding the merit of a maneuver which has been ordered, and who will commit grave faults in its execution, may produce the same result of causing the failure of the plans of an excellent commander.

fade away; his admirable combinations can only diminish the disasters of an almost unavoidable defeat.

No system of tactics can lead to victory when the *morale* of an army is bad, and even when it is excellent the victory may depend upon some occurrence like the rupture of the bridges over the Danube at Essling. Nor will victories be necessarily gained or lost by rigid adherence to or rejection of this or that manner of forming troops for battle.

These truths need not lead to the conclusion that there can be in war no sound rules, the observance of which, the chances being equal, will lead to success. It is true that theories cannot teach men with mathematical precision what they should do in every possible case, but it is also certain that they will always point out the errors which should be avoided. This is a highly-important consideration, for in the hands of skillful generals commanding brave troops these rules thus become the means of almost certain success.

The correctness of this statement cannot be denied. It only remains to be able to discriminate between good rules and bad. In this ability consists the whole of a man's genius for war. There are, however, leading principles which assist in gaining this ability. Every maxim relating to war will be good if it indicates the employment of the greatest portion of the means of action at the decisive moment and place.

If a general desires to be a successful actor in the great drama of war, his first duty is to study carefully the theater of operations so that he may see clearly the relative advantages and disadvantages it presents for himself and his enemies. This done, he can understandingly proceed to prepare his base of operations, then to choose the most suitable zone of operations for his main efforts, and, in doing so, keep constantly before his mind the principles of the art of war relative to lines and fronts of operations. The offensive army should particularly endeavor to cut up the opposing army by skillfully selecting objective points of maneuver; it will then assume, as the objects of its subsequent undertakings, geographical points of more or less importance, depending upon its first successes.

On the contrary, the defensive army should seek by all means to neutralize the first forward movement of its adversary, protracting operations as long as possible while not compromising the fate of the war, and deferring a decisive battle until the time when a portion of the enemy's forces are either exhausted by labors or scattered for the purpose of occupying invaded provinces, masking fortified places, covering sieges, protecting the line of operations, etc.

If a few prejudiced military men, after reading this book and carefully studying the detailed and correct history of the campaigns of the great masters of the art of war, still contend that it has neither principles nor rules, I can only pity them and reply, in the famous words of Frederick, that "a mule which had made twenty campaigns under Prince Eugene would not be a better tactician than at the beginning."

Correct theories, founded upon right principles, sustained by actual events of wars, and added to accurate military history, will form a true school of instruction for generals. If these means do not produce great men, they will at least produce generals of sufficient skill to take rank next after the natural masters of the art of war.

The first result of this treatise should be to awaken the attention of men who have the mission of influencing the destinies of armies, that is to say, of governments and generals. The second will be, perhaps, the doubling of the materiel and personnel of the artillery and the adoption of all improvements capable of augmenting its destructive effect. As artillerists will be among the first victims, it will be very necessary to instruct in the infantry men chosen to serve in the ranks of the artillery. Finally, it will be necessary to seek the means of neutralizing the effects of this carnage; the first seem to be modification of the armament and the equipment of troops, then the adoption of a new tactics which will yield results as promptly as possible. This task will be for the rising generation, when we shall have tested by experience all the inventions with which we are occupied in the schools of artillery. Happy will be those who, in the first encounters, shall have a plenty of shrapnel howitzers, many guns charged at the breech, and firing thirty shots a minute; many pieces ricocheting at the height of a man and never failing their mark; finally, the most improved rockets—without counting even the famous steam guns of Perkins, reserved to the defense of ramparts but which (if the written statement of Lord Wellington is to be believed) will yet be able to make cruel ravages. What a beautiful text for preaching universal peace and the exclusive reign of railroads!

But we must take a less somber view of the future with which so many brave men menace us, who by a cruel foresight combine the means of rendering war still more bloody than it is—and that, too, in the hope of assuring the triumph of their banners. A terrible but indispensable emulation, if we would remain on an equality with our neighbors so long as the law of nations shall not have placed limits to those inventions.

NOTES

[1] 1757, French defeated by Frederick the Great.
[2] 1806, French defeated the Prussians.
[3] 1806, Prussians defeated by the French.
[4] 1813, Blucher defeated Ney.
[5] 1706, French defeated by Eugene.
[6] 1704, Marlborough and Eugene defeated the French.
[7] 1706, Marlborough defeated the French.
[8] 1809, French defeated by English and Spanish.
[9] 1805, Napoleon defeated the Russians and Austrians.